The Catholic Church in Haiti

Political and Social Change

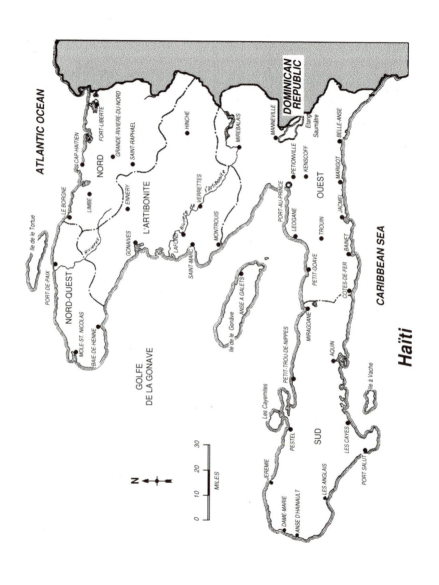

Haïti

The Catholic Church in Haiti

Political and Social Change

Anne Greene

Michigan State University Press
East Lansing
1993

All Michigan State University Press books are produced on paper which meets the requirements of American National Standard of Information Sciences—Permanence of paper for printed materials ANSI Z23.48-1984.

Michigan State University Press
East Lansing, Michigan 48823-5202

Printed in the United States of America

01 00 99 98 97 96 95 94 93 1 2 3 4 5 6 7 8 9 10

Library of Congress Cataloging in Publication Data

Greene, Anne.
    The Catholic Church in Haiti: political and social change / by Anne Greene.
    p.   cm.
    Includes bibliographical references and index.
    ISBN 0-87013-327-6 (alk. paper)
    1. Catholic Church—Haiti—Political Activity. 2. Catholic Church—Haiti—History—20th Century. 3. Church and State—Haiti—History—20th Century. 4. Church and State—Catholic Church—History—20th Century. 5. Haiti—History—1934-1986. 6. Haiti—History—1986-
7. Haiti—Church History. I. Title.
BX1453.2.O74 1993
282' .7294' 09045—dc20   93-2545
                                                          CIP

Acknowledgements

Because of the sensitivity of my topic, I cannot thank by name everyone who has been of help to me. I am, nonetheless, grateful to all of you, Haitian and American scholars, diplomats, members of religious communities, journalists, and librarians, who have so generously shared your time and wisdom with me.

Fortunately, I can acknowledge outright my profound appreciation to two professors, Drs. John Finan and Pope Atkins. I can also say *terima kasish* to the Executive Director of the Centre for Strategic and International Studies in Jakarta, Indonesia; Pak Hadi Soesastro; for his continuing kindness. I can disclose my appreciation to a faithful correspondent on Haiti, Mr. John Bannigan. I can express special gratitude to the Editor in Chief of the Michigan State University Press, Julie L. Loehr. I only wish I could thank the late professor Harold Davis.

How to thank my wonderful husband, Michael, my daughters Diana and Lesley, family and friends for their support, forbearance, and good humor? Impossible.

Contents

Introduction

The principal question raised and addressed in this study is: what was the role of the Catholic Church in Haiti in the downfall of dictator Jean-Claude Duvalier (1971-1986)? This research examines the recent history of the Catholic Church in Haiti in the framework of political events, probes the extent to which a significant sector of the Catholic Church, an institution not usually associated with rebellion, led the citizens of Haiti to revolt against their president, and elucidates the causes of its activism.

Clearly, there were many diverse forces at work in the overthrow of Jean-Claude Duvalier. This book does not intend to minimize them, but seeks to understand the key participation of certain sectors of the Haitian Church.

Although the Church was historically identified with the interests of governments in Haiti, in this instance it took an active role in the overthrow of a president. This work seeks to identify both Church motives and methods, and asks why the Haitian Church abandoned its traditional role of emphasis on baptism and counseling patience and resignation in favor of an active political role. Citing the activist role of Christ in the Bible, many of the clergy and women religious maintained that the Church should be working for social, economic, and political justice. In Haiti, such views appear to have led some members of the Church hierarchy, and many of its priests, nuns, and lay people, to become critical of the government and take a more active part in secular matters. They began to teach the principles of democracy, engage in literacy campaigns, and encourage critical evaluations of disparities between what the government said and did. They began to speak out in parishes and bishoprics, through homilies, encyclicals, letters, messages, and, particularly, the Church radio station, *Radio Soleil*. Discouraged by events and emboldened by the Pope's visit on 9 March 1983 and his pronouncement that things had to change in Haiti, Church leaders increasingly adopted the position that meaningful modifications could not take place with Jean-Claude Duvalier in the presidency. They finally lent their support to overthrow the once deeply-entrenched twenty-nine year dynasty.

1

The Church and State In Latin America

It is important to examine major changes that have taken place in the Church in Latin America, beginning with its establishment in the New World, but concentrating on recent decades in order to assess the role of the Catholic Church [1] in the overthrow of Jean-Claude Duvalier. Developments in the Latin American Church have had an impact on the Haitian Church and on the Church worldwide.

The Church has played a major, if changing, part in Latin America since its arrival in Latin America in 1492.[2] Until the eighteenth century, its goal was the conversion of the indigenous Indians and imported slaves. Beginning in the eighteenth century, its focus shifted. Ideas generated by the Enlightenment prompted many people to become critical of the Church, whose ties were to the Vatican, King, and colonial rulers. Its ambition increasingly became to maintain a presence. Antagonism increased in the nineteenth century as the hierarchy lined up with colonial rulers against the people, who overwhelmingly favored independence. The schism that developed between the Church leadership and the clergy has not completely mended. The focus of the Latin American Church in the twentieth century has shifted again.Popes John XXIII and Paul VI, Liberation Theologians, and many members of the clergy, decided that the Church required reform and updating. John XXIII declared that the Church's mission is to be with the poor.[3] One result of this association with the downtrodden has been to widen the gulf between the increasingly activist clergy and lay workers and the conservative bishops. But even where activist tendencies predominate, the Church has been generally reluctant to confront repressive governments directly.

THE COLONIAL CHURCH IN LATIN AMERICA

In 1492, Jews and Arabs were expelled from Spain.[4] That achievement may account for the zeal of the Churchmen who accompanied the *conquistadores* to Latin America in 1492. Determined to make converts, Jesuit

3

records indicate that they baptized and converted more native Indians and African slaves than they actually encountered. On the other hand, they did not attempt to change the system of slavery. Only a few of the early Churchmen directly criticized the economic system that enriched some through the subjugation of others. Among those who did protest were Bartolomé de las Casas,[5] Antonio de Montesinios, and Juan de Zumárraga. In addition, in the seventeenth and eighteenth centuries, Churchmen, particularly the Jesuits, established settlements called *reducciones* to educate, train, and probably offer the inhabitants some protection.[6]

In time, partially as a consequence of the arrival of less committed orders and secular priests, the Church lost much of its missionary intensity and openly allied itself with the establishment.[7] The relationship between the Church and elite is graphically illustrated in Latin American architecture, where the most elaborate Colonial buildings, the Catholic Church, and the government palace, are located together in the principal plaza of most towns and cities.

The Colonial Church came under intense attack in the eighteenth century from which it has never fully recovered. In the age of Enlightenment, ideas such as the separation of Church and State, anticlericalism, and freemasonry began to take hold in Latin America. Church ties to Spain, the Vatican, and the Colonial elite became increasingly offensive to many inhabitants of Latin America. The Church had some Creole bishops, *mestizo* priests and a few Indian missionaries in the frontier areas, but it was fundamentally a foreign and largely Spanish institution. The Jesuits,[8] so well-regarded in other ways, exacerbated emotions concerning the Church's foreign allegiances by arguing that the pope even had primacy over Kings. Displeased by their tenet of faith, the King of Spain, Carlos III, threw the Jesuits out of Latin America in 1767.

Antagonisms persisted into the nineteenth century, coming to a head over the issue of independence. The pope and Latin American bishops continued to side with colonial rulers against independence up to the Battle of Ayacucho on 9 December 1824, which ended foreign domination of South America.[9] The clergy, on the other hand, which was closer to the people, favored independence. Some priests, such as Father Miguel Hidalgo in Mexico, actually fought on behalf of the revolutionaries and played decisive roles.[10]

THE POST-INDEPENDENCE CHURCH IN LATIN AMERICA

Following independence, the Latin American Church fell into disarray. Its loyalties were split, it was overextended, expensive to maintain, and too wealthy. It needed to reform and redefine its role in society. People outside the Church were determined to move the process along. Two political parties, the Liberals and the Radicals, based their agenda on Church reform.[11] It was their intent to limit the power of the Church by expropriation of its property and curtailment of clerical privileges. The response of the demoralized Church[12] was to retrench, and focus its attention on education of children of the elite.

Despite the legacy of problems with the Church, the new states adopted Catholicism as the official religion, but they sought to control it, as the Spanish king had done, through the *patronato*. The Vatican took exception and refused to reestablish relations with the Latin American Church until 1831, at which time it only agreed to conclude concordats with the most conservative states.

The Latin American Church has undergone tremendous change in the twentieth century. The Great Depression, subsequent recessions and political events have caused the Church to examine its responsibilities and relationships with the state and the people. Vatican II, the regional Latin American Bishops Meetings (CELAM), Liberation Theology, and Christian base communities are signs of this reevaluation.

The Church in Latin America has become more politically and socially minded, but it is not monolithic. There is a conservative sector of the Church found predominantly among the hierarchy.[13] It includes most of the bishops in Argentina, Colombia, and Mexico. Pablo Richard describes this side of the Church as "closed to any social, political or religious change," which helps explain why authoritarian and military governments favor it.[14] There is a part of the Church that is linked historically to the Christian Democratic parties, other social or cultural institutions with a Christian label, and to the middle class. This sector includes most of the region's bishops, but is approaching minority status with the clergy and laity. There are three centrist sectors, which are distinguished politically by their rightist, centrist, and left-wing tendencies. The first is critical of the ideological apparatus of the state. The second has reservations about the state but does not question it. It mediates for those persecuted and thinks of itself as the "voice of the voiceless." The third takes on a political role, questions the government and military, but not the system. It provides political support for democratic opposition. In dictatorships, it is often the only legal institution independent of the state that is tolerated. Finally, there is a sector known as the popular Church. To avoid being connected with the dominant classes, it limits its activities to the poor and marginalized, the inhabitants of the *favelas* and *villas miserias*. It sees society's problems in terms of class struggle, but because it is evangelical, its intent is non-Marxist. Theologically, it identifies with "primitive, apostolic Christianity."[15] It rereads the gospel within the context of oppression, and of struggle against the ruling classes and military or authoritarian regimes.

THE CONTEMPORARY LATIN AMERICAN CHURCH: FORCES FOR CHANGE

Political and Religious Instability

By the time the Second Vatican Conference was called in Rome in 1962, the region and the Church were in a state of flux. A revolution in Cuba in 1959 put a Marxist leader at the head of that Catholic country. By the early 1960s, the Alliance for Progress was fading and the democratic regimes in Latin America were giving way to harsh rightist military dictatorships. The Church was obliged to come to grips with these realities and decide how it was going to deal with governments it did not like, and cope with repression and abuse.

The Church was also facing some troubling structural issues. With half the world's Catholics, the Latin American Church was losing members. Part of the problem was with the rapidly growing population and relative scarcity of priests, the Church was unable to reach everyone, particularly those living in rural areas.[16] In addition, the Protestants were making inroads. Prior to 1800, there were few Protestants in the region; they had been widely scattered and had not attempted to convert others. With anti-clericalism, access to Bibles, and innovative proselytizing, all of this began to change.[17] In some countries, up to ten or fifteen percent of the population is now Protestant. In recent decades, the most successful denominations have been the Baptists, Seventh Day Adventists, Mormons, and Pentecostals.

Papal Inspiration

During World War II, the Church got along with Benito Mussolini; it also signed a concordat with Adolf Hitler. After the war, the Church was obliged to significantly consider its relations with governments, their citizens, and its mission. Two popes were particularly instrumental in guiding the Church in new directions. They were John XXIII (1958–1963) and his successor Paul VI (1963–1978).

Former Jesuit priest and Vaticanologist, Peter Hebblethwaite, describes John XXIII as the pope who "transformed the image of the papacy" more than any other pope in this century. "He did it with goodness . . . he was concerned about things ordinary people cared about, such as peace, justice and living harmoniously together."[18] His sense of history and recognition of need for change within the Church apparently prompted him to call Vatican II.

In anticipation of the Second Vatican Council, John XXIII made a radio address on 11 September 1962, that described a new and committed Church. "With respect to the underdeveloped countries, the Church is as it wants to be—the Church of all the people and, in particular, the poor."[19] The pope's socially oriented encyclicals, such as his 1963 *Pacem in Terris*, with their commitment to democracy, human rights, and religious freedom, were additional testimonies to his convictions.[20] Pope John XXIII and Vatican II fully addressed the issues confronting the Latin American Church.[21] The purpose of Vatican II was *aggiornamento*, renewal or updating of Catholic religious life and doctrine. Pope John XXIII died before Vatican II was over, but his successor, Pope Paul VI, continued the process and even extended some of John's initiatives.[22]

Vatican II

The Latin American Church was well-represented at the Council because of the region's preponderantly Catholic population and the difficulties it was confronting.[23] As a result, the delegates from Latin America were particularly active and open participants.

Vatican II produced sixteen documents. Their purpose was to explain the Church, its doctrines, and its role in the modern world.[24] The documents included some of the following points:

1. According to the Constitution on Sacred Liturgy, local languages, or vernacular, would be permitted in parts of the mass, and congregational participation would be encouraged.

2. The Constitution on Divine Revelation emphasized the importance of the Bible.

3. The Pastoral Constitution in the Church in the Modern World called for loving people regardless of their religious persuasion. It condemned war and enjoined the Community of Nations to end poverty.

4. The Declaration of the Relations of the Church to non-Christians condemned discrimination. The Declaration of Religious Freedom concluded that all men had the right to religious freedom. The Ecumenical Decree pledged the Church to work for the unity of Christianity. The Decree on the Bishops' Pastoral Office in the Church directed them to form national and regional conferences to meet local problems. A synod of bishops would meet with the pope as an advisory board. The Decree of Priestly Formation gave national Church leaders additional power to regulate seminaries

In short, Vatican II emphasized egalitarianism—the Church was all of us, not just the hierarchy; community orientation—the importance of the local Church; and collegiality—"we are witness to the birth of a new humanism, one in which man is defined first of all by his response toward his brothers and toward history."[25]

Christian Base Communities

The American divinity scholar Harvey Cox describes the Catholic Church as "more catholic" as a result of Vatican II, more reflective and aware of the millions of poor, having absorbed new thoughts and new types of political involvement.[26] Not the least important outcome of Vatican II was the endorsement given to Ecclesiastical Base Communities, also known variously as Basic Christian Communities, Ecclesial Base Communities, Christian Base Communities, or Communautés Ecclésiastiques de Base (CEBs).

The date and source of the CEBs are hard to pinpoint, but their structure and purpose are quite uniform. It is generally agreed that they are a Latin American phenomenon, possibly originating in Brazil in the 1950s or 1960s.[27] The CEBs are typically composed of twenty to twenty-five poor and rural families who meet weekly to hear the Word, spread the gospel and discuss daily problems in a Biblical context.[28] Members take turns running the meetings and sharing organizational responsibilities. The CEBs help to compensate for the paucity of clergy, particularly in rural areas, and provide an alternative means of evangelization. In addition, they offer their members a sense of community, the opportunity to discuss problems, and the collective strength to resolve some of them.

By 1984, there were some 200,000 CEBs in Latin America. Although about half were in Brazil,[29] there were CEBs in Chile, Peru, Colombia, Paraguay, Uruguay, Mexico, Ecuador, Nicaragua, and El Salvador.[30] They were organized domestically and internationally. One inter-American CEB meeting took place in Brazil in 1980, followed by one in Ecuador in 1984.

The CEBs have worked well in consciousness-raising, generating confidence, and teaching leadership skills.[31] They have improved the economic lot of the rural farmer through better farming techniques, cooperatives, economies of scale, and by being able to circumvent middlemen. It appears, however, that they have yet to challenge governments to make fundamental changes that would bring the rural poor into the mainstream of national economies, propose a concrete methodology that would create a new international order, or convert large sectors of the poor to this vision.[32]

The future of the CEBs is in question with governments, and it may ultimately be in question with Rome. With their egalitarian and participatory ethos, CEBs have offered new opportunities to laity and nuns. They have become more autonomous than the parish Church, partly because they are generally located in rural areas, but also because they are not as hierarchically structured nor consequently as dependent on priests, bishops, and the Vatican.

Liberation Theology

As we will see, Liberation Theology was influential in Haiti during the Jean-Claude Duvalier era. Its emphasis on the poor and the need for social and economic change led its proponents to confront a repressive government. Uncertainties abound concerning the date, place of origin, causes,[33] and merits of Liberation Theology. Some scholars argue that Liberation Theology dates from the 1940s, while others assert that it is a product of the 1960s.[34] Some claim its origins are European, while others contend they are Latin American.[35] One argument for the Latin American assertion is that several Latin American priests are closely linked to Liberation Theology. Among the most notable are: the Peruvian Gustavo Gutiérrez, the Brazilians Leonardo Boff and Hugo Assmann, and the Uruguayan Juan Luis Segundo.[36]

The theological inspiration for Liberation Theology has been credited to the Bible,[37] in particular to Christ, who struggled on behalf of the downtrodden and confronted corrupt political and religious authorities. Proponents of Liberation Theology believe that the Church should strive to follow the example of Christ and fight for the liberation of all people from all kinds of bondage. They maintain that the motive for creating a just society is that it is what God wants.[38] "The universal love of the Father is inevitably to go against all injustice, privilege, oppression or narrow nationalism. The announcement of the kingdom reveals to society itself the aspiration for a just society." The only way to achieve this just society is to redress the wrongs of the poor.[39] In one of Jesus' parables, a king plans a banquet.[40] When his guests do not arrive, he sends his servants into the street to invite beggars to the meal. This is how the Church should be; "the whole Church, not just the base communities, should be oriented toward the uninvited."[41]

According to the adherents of Liberation Theology, the Church was held together for the first three centuries[42] by the commonalty of faith and by the courage of public martyrs, but after that, it became institutionalized and identified with the authorities and established power. The Church needs to return to its roots. Laypersons, religious, and priests should be making more pastoral decisions in the Church, because the Church is the people of God.[43]

Proponents of Liberation Theology attribute poverty to external political and economic conditions. In Latin America, some of its followers subscribe to "dependency theory," which ascribes poverty to the exploitative economic policies of the United States. They blame capitalism for economic inequalities and call for the implementation of some sort of socialist system as a humane compromise between Marxism and capitalism.[44]

Liberation Theology is a major theological development in Church history. At the CELAM meeting at Medellín, the bishops adopted the liberation theologians' view that the best translation of the Christian doctrine of "salvation" was "liberation." This interpretation appears to have changed the mission of the Church. Rather than continuing to prepare people to participate in a perfect afterlife, in the future the Church would try to perfect this world.[45]

While Liberation Theology has a growing number of followers, it also has its detractors, some of whom hold high Vatican positions. Pope John-Paul II has been critical.[46] At the Bishops' Conference at Puebla, he criticized what he viewed as the politicization of the Gospel message, decried the effort to promote a people's Church in opposition to the institutional Church, and said that "Christ cannot be reduced to the restricted domain of economics, society, and culture." On his March 1983 visit to Nicaragua, he shook his fingers at Ernesto Cardenal, one of four priests who had joined the Nicaraguan government in 1979.

Cardinal Joseph Ratzinger, head of the Congregation for the Doctrine of the Faith (CDF)—formerly the Sacred Congregation of the Universal Inquisition, has been more openly negative. In his view, liberation theologians had become Marxists. In a private memo[47] published by the Italian press in 1984, he called it "a fundamental threat to the faith of the Church." He conducted two investigations of Leonardo Boff, one in 1976 and another in 1980. The CDF sent ten observations on the theology of Gustavo Gutiérrez to the Peruvian Episcopal in March 1983. On 7 September 1984, the Cardinal summoned Leonardo Boff to Rome to explain parts of his book, *The Church, Charism and Power*, and subsequently ordered him not to write, preach, or give interviews for a year.

A high-placed Latin American opponent of Liberation Theology, also on the CDF, is Cardinal Alfonso López Trujillo, formerly archbishop of Medellín. While general secretary of the Latin American Bishops' Conference in 1972,[48] he removed proponents of Liberation Theology from important positions in CELAM.

Liberation Theology, with its emphasis on the poor rural masses and acceptance of conflict as a necessary ingredient for economic and social change, has been a source of some international alarm, provoking studies and assessments in the intelligence community. In 1980, The Council for

Inter-American Security produced *The New Inter-American Policy for the Eighties.*[49] The authors of the "Santa Fe Document," as the paper was informally called, concluded that "United States foreign policy must begin to counter Liberation Theology as it is utilized in Latin America by the 'Liberation Theology' clergy."

In Latin America, Liberation Theology has alienated many traditional Church members, who feel that their values and well-being are being threatened and that they do not fit into this new Church. Others fault Liberation Theology's emphasis on capitalism as the cardinal social sin, claiming worse crimes have been committed in the region with the acquiescence of the Church, such as the destruction of the Aztec and the Mayan civilizations. Black theologians and women point out that Liberation Theology seems to overlook racial and sexual oppression; there is no mention of sexual discrimination in or out of the Church in Gustavo Gutíerrez' book, *A Theology of Liberation.*

Additional issues separate liberation theologians from traditional Catholics. There is the question of Christ's message. Was he really trying to create heaven on earth? How can the hierarchy be expected to voluntarily relinquish power? Some consider Liberation Theology to be somewhat patronizing. It is a movement led by light or white-skinned intellectuals whose adherents are overwhelmingly dark-skinned, poor, and illiterate. The assumption that the poor would behave differently from the rich if they were to gain power and leverage may be fallacious. Dependency as an explanation for underdevelopment sounds naive and overlooks a number of contributing factors, such as limited land and unlimited population growth.

Tensions remain between Liberation Theology and the Vatican, but the Vatican has made some adjustments. Its focus is increasingly directed toward the poor. Some liberation theologians continue to assert that class conflict will inevitably lead to confrontation, but for the time being, most appear to be trying to improve the lot of the poor within the system.

CELAM-Medellín, 1968

The Conference of Latin American Bishops (CELAM) is an organization that began in 1955 in Rio de Janiero, Brazil, inspired by the Brazilian Bishops' Organization (CNBB). To date, it has had a number of distinguished leaders and convened a number pivotal meetings. Some of its notable presidents have included Manuel Larraín, the bishop of Talca, Chile, who was president in 1963, and Avelar Brandão of Brazil, who was president in 1966. The 1968 conference at Medellín, Colombia and the 1979 meeting at Puebla, Mexico were extraordinary events. In the case of Medellín, the

agenda of President (former Franciscan bishop, now Cardinal) Aloisio
Lorscheider and the attendance of Pope Paul VI at the inauguration contributed toward making the meeting unusual.

The demanding conference goal was to reconsider all aspects of religious
life in light of regional events and circumstances. Consequently, it dealt
with poverty, class conflict, sinful behavior of whole social systems, and
state-condoned and perpetrated violence.[50] The text for Medellín was
"Populorum Progressio," and the theme was the need to help the poor
improve their condition.

Medellín has been seen by some to have extended Vatican II and even to
have caused a renewal of Catholicism.[51] The Latin American Church clearly
changed its focus at this conference. Liberation was a major theme. People
needed to participate in improving their own destiny. One phrase encapsu-
lated this new perspective: "preferential option for the poor." The significance of Medellín was to bring home the reforms of Vatican II. A measure
of Church receptiveness to these new ideas can be gauged by the number of
educated and urban-based priests and, especially, nuns who subsequently
left the cities to work with the poor in rural areas.[52]

The conference did not go forward with complete unanimity of spirit.
There was a conservative backlash from some bishops, such as Alfonso
López Trujillo of Bogotá, and from a number of organizations. The Society
for the Defense of Family and Property (TFP) was one of these. A worldwide institution, which began in Brazil and has branches in Chile, Mexico,
and the United States, the TFP supports private landownership, capitalism,
and traditional religious forms. It opposes most post-Medellín changes in
the Church.

CELAM-Puebla, 1979

The Latin American Bishops' Conference was held in Puebla, Mexico, in
1979 in order to commemorate the tenth anniversary of Medellín, take
stock, reevaluate and, certain participants hoped, undo some of what had
been set in motion at the earlier meeting. When Pope John Paul II cautioned against "sociopolitical radicalisms" and "incorrect interpretations of
Medellín,"[53] it appeared that Puebla was going to be a conservative reaction
to the earlier conference. However, that impression was mitigated when he
also spoke positively about liberation and human rights.

Two documents and five themes emerged from the conference.[54] The
themes were: Pastoral Vision, Doctrinal Section, Evangelization, Church
Groups, and Agenda of the Progressives. While no single message dominated, Puebla reiterated some of the themes from Medellín, such as commitment to the poor through a preferential option for the poor and
condemnation of unjust economic and social structures. It announced its

abhorrence of all kinds of violence, its concerns about capitalism and marxism, and its endorsement of CEBs, which it termed a "cause of joy and hope in the Church."[55]

Church Direction and Implications for Haiti

Over the past thirty years, the Catholic Church in Latin America has changed considerably, and it is continuing to reevaluate and redefine its role in the region. Individual theologians, Liberation Theology, Vatican II, the Latin American Bishops' Conferences at Medellín and Puebla, and the CEBs have substantially contributed to the change. Their influence had a profound effect on Haiti, in legitimizing the activities of the progressive elements in the Church. At the 2–6 December 1982 Eucharistic and Marial Congress in Haiti, a delegation of more than one hundred priests, nuns and lay workers identified divisions within the Church. According to them, God wanted the Church to show its solidarity and sense of responsibility for everyone and they concluded that it would require the uprooting of evil in individuals, the Church, and society; involvement; sacrifice; and maybe even lives. That position led the Haitian Church into direct conflict with a despotic government.

The Church has subsequently developed a greater sense of identity with the hemisphere, the individual countries, and the inhabitants of the states, especially their native populations, through increased involvement with social, economic, and political issues. The use of vernacular and inclusion of local customs in religious services have been particularly important in this regard. Understanding and sympathy have grown through contact as increasing numbers of priests, nuns, and lay workers, many now Haitian, have opted to share their lives with the rural poor.[56] The CEB movement became a powerful instrument of consciousness-raising.[57]

The trend over the past thirty years in the Latin American Church has been toward activism, ranging from social and economic to political. Education and literacy programs have multiplied. Catholic political parties and unions have become widespread. CEB leaders routinely teach their members how to organize to protect themselves and improve their situation. Catholics in El Salvador have called on the Catholic Church in the United States to intervene with the government to prevent additional weapons from being sold to the Salvadoran government.[58] Some priests have joined armed resistance movements, such as the FMLN in El Salvador; others have joined revolutionary governments, as Ernesto Cardenal did in Nicaragua.

There have been exceptions to this activist trend in the Catholic Church in Latin America, notably in Cuba and Nicaragua.[59] The Church in Cuba was not revolutionary before 1959,[60] nor has it become so subsequently.

Prior to Fidel Castro, even if the Church was anti-Batista, it was not pro-reform or revolution. Its efforts were directed toward institution building. By the early 1960s, the Catholic hierarchy had become anti-Castro. Since then, it has written pastoral letters questioning the legality of the revolution and the government, opposing land reform and the military draft. As a result, the Church is regarded by the government as the center of counter-revolution.

The Nicaraguan Church initially supported the overthrow of the dictator, Anastasio Somoza.[61] In June 1979, it issued a pastoral letter approving participation in the insurrection. Some in the Church expected a new government to be reformist, but most, including the hierarchy, feared that the government would undertake substantive structural changes. Consequently, since the Revolution, the Nicaraguan Church has been divided with Cardinal Obando y Bravo leading the sector of the Church that believes the government has gone too far.[62]

Clearly, conservative and traditional views are shared by some of the Church hierarchy and members in other parts of Latin America, but even where the Church has initiated reformist programs and taken stands on social, economic, and political matters, it has been wary of confronting governments directly. In some situations where the Church opposed repression because other institutions were unable to do so, it has backed down, as it did in Chile, rather than risk civil war. Lack of funds, international support, political skill, and determination have prevented it from taking revolutionary action.

Summary

In summary, while the Church took an "otherworldly" view of its role until recent decades, beginning in the middle of the twentieth century, it adopted a more socially concerned attitude. This, as we shall see, was reflected in events in the 1970s and 1980s.

NOTES

1. A list of terms can be found in Appendix A.

2. A list of dates can be found in Appendix B.

3. Radio Message of 11 September 1962, in *The Pope Speaks* 8, no. 4 (Spring 1963): 396. Cited by Gustavo Gutiérrez in *A Theology of Liberation, History, Politics and Salvation.* (Maryknoll, NY: Orbis, 1973), 287.

4. In 1453, Muslims took over Constantinople and the rule of the Eastern Christians. Shortly thereafter in 1517, in Germany, Martin Luther issued his Ninety-five Theses attacking Church abuses, prompting many Catholics to leave the Church.

5. Hubert Herring, *A History of Latin America from the Beginnings to the Present*, 3d ed. (New York: Knopf, 1972), 171–75. Bartolomé de las Casas began his career as a soldier of fortune who went to the Dominican Republic, and acquired land and Indians. In 1510, at the age of thirty-six, he became a priest. Several years later, while in Cuba, he changed his mind about slavery and gave up his land and Indians. He spent the rest of his life defending the Indians, even writing a book about them in 1552 entitled *History of the Indies, a Very Brief Recital of the Destruction of the Indies*. Ironically, in the hope of sparing the Indians, de las Casas proposed the importation of African slaves, a recommendation he later regretted.

Antonio de Montesinios, a Dominican, denounced the abuse of Indians from the pulpit in Hispaniola for a couple of Sundays, after which he was recalled to Spain.

The Franciscan Juan de Sumárraga was the first bishop of Mexico. Appalled by the abuse of the natives, he wrote directly to the king, telling him an *iaudiencia* of honorable men was needed to protect the Indians.

6. Pablo Richard, *Death of Christendoms, Birth of the Church: Historical Analysis and Theological Interpretation of the Church in Latin America* (Maryknoll, NY: Orbis, 1987), 30–32. The Inquisition was much milder in Latin America than Spain. However, conditions were unsupportable for many of the Indians and Africans who worked on the *haciendas* and in the mines; there were revolts. Richard counts three slave rebellions: the Arucan rebellion in Chile in 1723, the rebellion lead by Tupac Amaru in Peru from 1780 to 1783, and the slave rebellion near Bahia, Brazil, between 1630 and 1695.

7. Gutiérrez, *A Theology of Liberation*, 265–66. Gutiérrez writes, "the protection that the Church receives from the social class that is the beneficiary and defender of the prevailing capitalist society in Latin America has made the institutional Church into a part of the system and the Christian message into a part of the dominant ideology."

8. Herring, *A History of Latin America*, 181. The Jesuits were the distinguished religious order in Latin America, known for their morality, industriousness, and involvement in education, farming, and business, but they clashed with Spain because they maintained that the pope had primacy over kings. They rejected the regulation known as *Patronato Regio* which, according to Spain, permitted the Spanish kings to regulate religion in Latin America, collect tithes, monitor mail from the Vatican, and send missionaries.

9. Richard, *Death of Christendoms*, 48. Richard writes that Pope Leo XII indirectly called wars of independence illegitimate, saying that they endangered the "integrity of religion" by disturbing the "peace of the country."

10. Ibid., 51.

11. Thomas G. Sanders, "Religion in Latin America," in *Latin America: Perspectives on a Region*, ed. Jack W. Hopkins (New York and London: Holmes & Meier, 1987), 107.

12. Richard, *Death of Christendoms*, 68–71.

13. Ibid., 164–77. This section delineating current sectors of the Latin American Church is drawn from an analysis by Pablo Richard.

14. Ibid., 164.

15. Ibid., 172.

16. Margaret Crahan, *Religion and Revolution: Cuba and Nicaragua* (Washington, DC: Woodrow Wilson Center, 1986). The largely Spanish, Havana-based clergy fled Cuba following Fidel Castro's takeover in 1959, leaving an island where few rural Cubans had ever seen a priest, let alone expected the Church to come to their aid.

17. Sanders, "Religion in Latin America," 113. Over 20 percent of the population in Guatemala is Protestant versus only 6 to 8 percent in Brazil and Chile.

18. Peter Hebblethwaite, *In the Vatican* (Bethesda, MD: Adler and Adler, 1986), 33–34.

19. Harvey Cox, *Religion in the Secular City: Toward a Postmodern Theology* (New York: Simon and Schuster, 1984), 110.

20. Paul E. Sigmund, "Liberation Theology: An Historical Evaluation." Washington, DC: Woodrow Wilson International Center for Scholars, undated (after 1986).

21. The purpose of Vatican I, held 1869–1870, was to establish papal primacy and infallibility.

22. Hebblethwaite, *In the Vatican*, 162. John XXIII established the Secretariat for Promoting Christian Unity (SPUC). Paul VI furthered the outreach to non-Catholics by establishing the Secretariat for Non-Christian Religions (SNCR) in 1964. The charter of the SNCR, *Nostra Aetate*, says, "The Catholic Church rejects nothing which is true and holy in these religion."

23. Sanders, "Religion in Latin America," 109.

24. *The World Book*, s.v. "Vatican Council."

25. Dominic Monte, "Changes in the Catholic Church," Seminar at St. Camillus Church, Silver Spring, MD, 20 October 1986.

26. Cox, *Religion in the Secular City*, 108. Cox argues that the CEBs could ultimately replace the parish structure.

27. Ibid., 113. Cox suggests that the CEBs came about as the result of a mission that Father Lombardi took to Latin America on behalf of Pope Pius XII in the late 1950s to find out how the region could be saved from socialism and Protestantism. Lombardi's verdict: more priests. By the early 1960s, the Church inaugurated a five-year plan called "The First Pastoral Plan for the Brazilian Bishops." To make up for the lack of clergy, the Church would rely on Christian communities and radio courses to renew the faith and spread the Word.

28. Leonardo Boff, *Church: Charism and Power, Liberation Theology and the Institutional Church* (New York: Crossroad, 1985).

29. Cox, *Religion in the Secular City*, 108.

30. Alvarado Oviedo and Stepan Mamontov, "Theology of Liberation: A New Heresy?" *World Marxist Review* 24, no. 3 (March 1986): 86–88.

31. Mary Evelyn Jegen, *Haiti: The Struggle Continues*, Just World Order Series (Erie, PA: Benet Press, 1987), 25–26. According to Sister Jegen, since 1968 the number of CEBs in Haiti has grown to 5,000 and they have spread to all seven dioceses. Organized under a national committee, members typically meet for an hour and a half a week to compare notes, air problems, develop solutions, and receive leadership training. Despite this, even in Cap-Haïtien, where the CEBs are particularly active, Evelyn Jegen writes they have not transformed the diocese, due to continuing "apathy of many and even resistance by some Catholics who prefer the old ways."

32. Edgar Miller, "Hope Sprouts in Haiti," *Catholic Standard*, 12 April 1984. Father Pollux Byas, the Canadian-educated Haitian Holy Cross priest in charge of the CEBs in the diocese of Cap-Haïtien, described the growth, success, and hope generated by the base communities with this caveat: "We are working together; we are praying together, we are doing things together. We are growing in our faith together . . . (however) the communities are not political so far. It is not a revolution. But the people can say 'no' now. And when they say no . . . they are not afraid any more." See Marian McClure, "The Catholic Church and Rural Social Change: Priests, Peasant Organizations, and Politics in Haiti" (Ph.D. diss., Harvard University, 1985), 349. She writes, "the CCD movement creates fairly minimal pressures on the Haitian Government."

33. Gutiérrez, *A Theology of Liberation*, 252. Vatican II gave "an initial impulse" for a revision of what the Church has been. Gutiérrez credits the Latin American Bishops' Meeting at Medellín in 1968 with generating the ideas that produced Liberation Theology (108). Among the ideas that Gustavo Gutiérrez identifies as having emerged from that meeting were: 1. Solidarity of the Church with the Latin American reality. 2. Appreciation by the bishops of misery and exploitation of man by man in Latin America—of "institutional violence." 3. The legitimacy of "just violence of the oppressed" and the right of Christians to oppose injustice. 4. Identification of the Church with the social revolution in progress. 5. Active participation of the poor.

See Alberto M. Piedra, "Some Observations on Liberation Theology," *World Affairs* (Winter 1985–1986): 151–58. Piedra traces some of the theological bases for Liberation Theology to the writings of Pope John XXIII's *Mater et Magistra and Pacem in Terris*, and to Paul VI's encyclical, *Populorum Progressio*, which defends human rights and calls for a balance of rich and poor nations.

34. Paul E. Sigmund and Brady B. Tyson, "Liberation Theology: Its Origins and Evolution" (Seminar at the Woodrow Wilson Center, Washington, DC, November 1986). Tyson credits the "progressive Church" movement of the 1940s with being the catalyst for Liberation Theology.

See Paul Sigmund, *Liberation Theology*, 2–5. Liberation Theology dates from the 1960s. In his opinion, some of the factors that influenced it were: John XXIII's call for *aggiornamento*, Vatican II, the growth of large Christian Democratic parties, increased dialogue with non-Catholics, dissatisfaction with Latin American economic development and political systems in the 1960s, and Gustavo Gutiérrez's conference at Chimbote, Peru, in July 1968. In addition, he cites the Medellín documents that seemed to legitimize radicalization of the Catholic intelligentsia, Gustavo Gutiérrez article in the *Jesuit Journal of Theological Studies* entitled "Notes for a Theology of Liberation," June 1970, argued that the word 'liberation' is more appropriate than 'development' for the poor countries and that violence would be necessary in some cases. He also cites Gustavo Gutiérrez's criticism of the Christian Democrats for "naive reformism," his book that called for building a new man via *conscientization*, CEBs, prohibiting private landownership and capital, and cultivating a "spirituality of liberation. Finally, there was the new way of reading the Gospels that rejected abstract intellectualism in favor of direct social involvement.

Richard, *Death of Christendoms*, 145–46. Richard contends that Liberation Theology predates Medellín. Drawing on Roberto Oliveros's work, *Liberación y Teoligía: Génesis y Creciento de Una reflexíon* (1966–1976) (Lima: CEP, 1977), he argues that Liberation Theology grew out of disillusionment over the failure of ECLA and the Alliance for Progress's "developmentalism," that it was an outgrowth of countries' experiences with, and observations of, revolution—in Mexico, Guatemala, and Cuba.

Some Marxists also believe that Liberation Theology came out of the 1960s, but attribute it to a misunderstanding of underdevelopment and the "congenital effect of capitalist development." Eight hundred Latin American priests produced the *Manifesto of the Bishops of the Third World*, which criticized social and economic practices and favored socialism.

35. Jane Kramer, "Letter from the Elysian Fields," *New Yorker*, 2 March 1987. According to Kramer, the roots of Liberation Theology were European. Latin Americans studying at certain centers in Germany were exposed to the ideas in Jurgen Moltmann's "Theology of Hope" and Johannes Baptist Meltz's "Theology of the World," which they took back to Latin America.

Piedra, "Some Observations of Liberation Theology." Piedra situates the University of Louvan as the cradle of Liberation Theology.

36. The book, *Teologia de la Liberación, Perspectivas*, by Gustavo Gutiérrez in 1971, translated as *A Theology of Liberation*, provided the name for the movement.

Leonardo Boff wrote a book, *Igreja: Carisma e Poder* in 1981, translated into English as *Charism and Power: Liberation Theology and the Institutional Church*, that argued that the Church hierarchy had become too powerful; the Church needed to return to its egalitarian roots through such mechanisms as the CEBs.

Sigmund, *Liberation Theology*, 7. Hugo Assmann wrote *A Theology for a Nomad Church* in 1976, which rejected development as a solution for economic problems. Juan Luis Segundo wrote *Liberation of Theology* the same year. In it he recommended a socialistic system "where the means of production were removed from individuals and handed over to higher institutions whose concern is the common good."

37. Father Charles Finnegan, interview with author, St. Camillus Church, Silver Spring, MD, 2 November 1986. Numerous writers have linked Liberation Theology with the Bible.

See Gutiérrez, *A Theology of Liberation*, 148, 165; Boff, *Church: Charism and Power*, 26; Sanders, "Religion in Latin America," 107–11; and Cox, *Religion in the Secular City*, 152–65.

38. Gutiérrez, *A Theology of Liberation*, 231–32

39. Ibid, 208.

40. Ibid., 165.

41. Gutiérrez, *A Theology of Liberation*, 165.

42. Boff, *Church: Charism and Power*, 51, 58.

43. Gutiérrez, *A Theology of Liberation*, 118.

44. See Oviedo and Mamontov, "Theology of Liberation," 88. The authors discuss Leonardo Boff's economic rationale for favoring a socialist society.

See Piedra, "Some Observations of Liberation Theology," 151–53. Piedra criticizes the proponents of Liberation Theology in part for their association of sin with certain social structures, such as capitalism.

See also Gutiérrez, *A Theology of Liberation*, 134. Gutiérrez anticipates the end of dependency and eventual liberation of all men and speculates that socialism will probably be the vehicle.

See Sigmund's essay, *Liberation Theology*, 5. Sigmund cites Gutiérrez, *A Theology of Liberation*, 276, where he calls for the abolition of private ownership of capital because it leads to the "exploitation of man by man." Also, Sigmund remarks on the strong strain of anticapitalism in writing about Liberation Theology (15).

45. Sigmund, *Liberation Theology*, 3. The subtitle of the Medellín Conference was "Bring Vatican II to Latin America" and it was at this meeting that the bishops agreed to the "preferential option of the poor" (a term implying that the Church was going to look at reality through the eyes of the poor), then asked themselves whether they had been teaching resignation. For Sigmund, the emphasis on Liberation Theology in the Church dates from Medellín.

Alexander Wilde, "Ten years of Change in the Church: What Happened at Puebla," in *Churches and Politics in Latin America*, ed Daniel Levine (London and Beverly Hills: Sage Publications, 1979), 274. The Church has achieved unprecedented national and regional integration since Medellín.

See Kramer, "Letter from the Elysian Fields." Kramer reports that many Catholics say Medellín was a turning point for the Latin American Church.

Oviedo and Mamontov, "Theology of Liberation," 85. These authors also conclude that Medellín contributed to the process of renewal of Catholicism.

46. Sigmund, *Liberation Theology*, 10–11.

47. Ibid., 1.

48. Ibid., 10.

49. L. Francis Bouchey, Roger Fontaine, David C. Jordon, Lt. General Gordon Sumner, and Lewis Tambs (The Committee of Santa Fe). "A New Inter-American Policy for the Eighties." (Washington, DC: The Council for Inter-American Security, May 1980). This document was closely associated with the Reagan Administration since one of its five authors was a member of the National Security Council and another was a special advisor to the Assistant Secretary of State for Inter-American Affairs.

50. John Harrison, "Preface," in *Churches and Politics in Latin,* ed. Daniel Levine (London and Beverly Hills: Sage Publications, 1979), 22–23.

51. Wilde, "Ten years of Change," 269. See also Oviedo and Mamontov, "Theology of Liberation," March 1986.

52. Katherine Anne Gilfeather, "Women Religious, and the Poor, and the Institutional Church in Chile," in Churches, ed. Levine, 201.

53. Phillip Berryman, "What Happened at Puebla," in *Churches*, ed. Levine, 63.

54. Ibid., 73–74.

55. James Timothy Kelly, "Rocks in the Sun: The Roman Catholic Church in Haitian Political Development" (Senior honors thesis, Harvard University, 1988), 45, citing David Nicholls, *Economic Dependence and Political Autonomy: The Haitian Experience*, Center for Developing-Area Studies Occasional Paper Series, no. 9 (Montreal: McGill University, 1974), 10.

56. Yves Voltaire, "Haiti: Terre d'Esperance," *Orient* (March–April 1986): 16. The number of new divinity students has grown annually since 1972. Voltaire reported that there are 210 divinity students in Haiti with an average of fifteen ordinations a year since 1981.

57. See Wilde, "Ten Years of Change." Wilde calls Puebla a "benchmark," saying that there are clear changes ten years later with unprecedented institutional integration both nationally and internationally, and vitality through the base communities.

In Harrison's "Preface" he refers to the growth of the CEBs as "the most remarkable development in Latin American Churches."

See Jegen, *Haiti*, 21–26. After detailing the growth and spread of the CEBs, Jegen discusses some of the practical and psychological benefits members receive through involvement with a Christian community, including the "taste of power, the effectiveness of cooperative activity, to a people accustomed to experiencing themselves as helpless."

Pax Christi International, *Report of the Mission of Pax Christi International to Haiti* (Erie, PA: Pax Christi International, 1986), 61. The mission observed, "a new Church was being born in Haiti in spite of difficulties, a Church that seeks to be part of society through the poor, thanks to CEBs." It concluded that a transformation could be seen in the new generation of priests and religious, and in the base communities animated by them.

McClure, "The Catholic Church and Rural Social Change." The CCDs trained people, raised their consciousness, and created leaders. On page 337, she writes, "The participatory style, small groups base, and strategy of separation from economic elites and state authorities all served to build trust and a sense of efficacy, increase participation, promote equity goals, and enable the movement to address participants' political security needs."

58. Ernest Evans, "The Changing Role of the Catholic Church in Latin America," (Seminar at George Washington University, 21 March 1988).

59. Crahan, *Religion and Revolution*, 5.

60. Ibid., 14.

61. Ibid., 6.

62. Ibid., 14.

2

The State In Haiti

For an understanding of the political collapse of Jean-Claude Duvalier, one must review the history of Haiti from its earliest times. A pattern of political instability becomes apparent that has manifested itself in almost unrelieved dictatorships.

Parallels between the Latin American and Haitian colonial experience are many, from the treatment of native populations and slaves, to the exploitation of the land and other resources and the establishment of a social system based on race, wealth, color, domicile, and language. Haitian history since independence has continued to resemble the colonial experience. Leaders have generally been military men, and occasionally civilians, who have ruled the country by force for personal gain at the expense of the people. François Duvalier held onto power longer than many of his predecessors because of his keen understanding of Haitian history and its dynamics. His son neglected it to his peril.

The United States has played a significant but inglorious role in Haitian history, exacerbating the country's history of political instability. Only after the American Civil War abolished slavery did the United States recognize the country, sixty years after Haitian independence. In 1915, the United States invaded Haiti to protect its assets and continued to occupy it for another nineteen years. Apart from the Carter presidency in the 1970s, U.S. policy toward Haiti has generally been to accept the status quo while pressing quietly for democratic reform.[1] In recent years, human rights organizations and the Congressional Black Caucus have counseled a different tack. As we will see, the role of the Church in the ouster of Jean-Claude Duvalier was also influenced by this history.

THE ISLAND AND ITS EARLY INHABITANTS

Haiti occupies the western third of the island of Hispaniola, which it shares with the Dominican Republic. It is located about 40 miles from

Cuba, 125 miles from Jamaica, and 600 miles from the United States. The second largest island in the Caribbean, its area is about 10,700 square miles, comparable in size to the state of Maryland.[2]

The island's original inhabitants were Indians. The first of four tribes to settle it were the Ciboneys, who are thought to have come from North America around A.D.[sc] 450. The next to arrive were either the Arawaks or Tainos, both agricultural people, who originated in the Orinoco and Amazon basins in the seventh and eighth centuries. The last to arrive were the Caribs, who came from South America just before Columbus landed.[3]

When the Spanish disembarked in Hispaniola in 1492, there were somewhere between 60,000 and 600,000 Indians, but within fifty years, most were gone, killed outright or through overwork in the gold mines.[4] The need for a larger and hardier labor pool ultimately led to the importation of African slaves.[5]

Beginning in the 1620s, English and French buccaneers settled on adjacent Tortuga Island or Ile de la Tortue, which they used as a base to attack English and Spanish ships. In time, the buccaneers began to cross the channel to the western side of Hispaniola to hunt for cattle and wild boar, and some settled.[6]

THE FRENCH COLONY OF ST. DOMINGUE

Haiti today is officially a French-speaking society as a result of the War of the Grand Alliance, which ended with the Treaty of Ryswick in 1697, one of whose conditions was that Spain cede the western third of Hispaniola to France. Contemporary methods of government, class, race, and social structures are a result of patterns that were established in the Colonial era. This new French possession, renamed St. Domingue, was already inhabited by 60,000 whites and mulattos, as well as 50,000 slaves, who were the backbone of its sugar and coffee economy.[7]

Women were in short supply in the colony. Initially, black women were imported from Santo Domingo, the Spanish side of the island, but demand exceeded supply, a situation that was eased in 1665 with the arrival of French women. Frequently billed as "orphan girls,"[8] many were apparently prostitutes and former inmates of the Parisian insane asylum, La Salpetrière.

There was also an increasing labor shortage in the colony. Initially, equal numbers of indentured workers from France and African slaves were brought to the settlement, but when the plantation owners discovered that the slaves had more stamina, demand for them increased.[9]

THE WORK FORCE

The first African slaves were brought from Portugal and Spain,[10] but by 1513, shipping lines had been established exclusively for slaving, and its victims were imported directly from Africa. While most of the slaves came from West Africa,[11] their origins were diverse, representing at least thirty-eight regions in Africa and over one hundred tribes. With time, St. Domingue became the principal slave-importing island in the Caribbean.

The Economy

Frenchmen began to arrive in St. Domingue in the 1720s. They came with the intention of farming indigo, sugar, or coffee, getting rich, and returning to France—many succeeded. St. Domingue was a virtual gold mine, becoming the most prosperous colony in the West Indies and by 1789 responsible for forty percent of French trade.[12] Between 1783 and 1789, agricultural production on the island almost doubled, creating more wealth than the rest of the Caribbean islands combined or the thirteen North American colonies.[13] Sugar was the principal source of its wealth, followed by tobacco.

The profits from these crops permitted planters a luxurious existence. They lived in mansions, dressed elegantly, and owned numbers of slaves.[14] Even so, they did not totally acclimate. The planters continued to regard France as home.[15] They talked about going back "next year," and sent their children to France to be educated.

Slavery

The flourishing economy was based on slavery. According to census figures, there were only 2,312 slaves in St. Domingue in 1681, but by 1789, their number had grown to 620,999.[16] Between 1764 and 1771, 10,000 to 15,000 new slaves arrived in St. Domingue annually, while countless others died at sea en route to the colony.[17]

Many who survived the crossing subsequently perished in St. Domingue, some due to the island's tropical heat, humidity, and diseases, but most as the result of brutal treatment by the plantation owners. Statistics show that there was a complete turnover of slaves every twenty years.[18] Census figures indicate that in 1789, two-thirds of all the slaves in the colony had been born in Africa.

According to French law, when lands became French, their inhabitants were freed, but greed prevented compliance in St. Domingue. King Louis

XIII rationalized that slavery would assure that the slaves became Christians, so he ordered missionaries sent to St. Domingue, "to inspire faith in the true God in the Africans, to take away their old idolatry, and to make them persevering until death in the Christian religion."[19] Perhaps the King's conscience bothered him because in 1685 he devised the *Code Noir* to protect the legal rights of the slaves.

However, the *Code Noir* was largely ignored; slaves were routinely over-worked, underfed, and otherwise abused.[20] Records show that slaves killed themselves in order to escape their plight, and female slaves aborted their fetuses rather than have babies born into bondage. A small number of lucky and audacious slaves managed to escape to the partial security of the mountains.[21]

The plantation owners' response to the religious mandate resembled their response to the *Code*—they ignored it. Many planters were not inter-ested in religion themselves—much less for their slaves. After all, if the sacraments were applied to slaves, they would be encouraged to marry, complicating separations and sales. Fortunately for the planters, few priests were available or interested in the religious education of slaves either.[22]

The Social Structure

The colony was hierarchically structured, based on color and wealth. At the top were the *grands blancs,* which included the white plantation owners, wealthy merchants, and high officials. Beneath them were the *petits blancs,* such as the white shopkeepers. Blacks were on a separate social ladder: at the top were the *gens de couleur,* freedmen who might be black or mulattos, and people with no visible African blood.[23] Beneath them came the mulatto slaves, who often worked in the plantation house and tended to view themselves as superior to the freed black slaves because of their indoor work and lighter color. On the next rung down were the Creole slaves, whose source of pride was that they had been born in the colony. At the very bottom were the slaves who had just arrived and spoke only African languages. As field laborers, they had the hardest work, and were despised by everyone else.[24]

The Struggle for Independence

Racial and social tensions were widespread in St. Domingue in the last years of the colony, extending from planters to the slaves. Plantation owners chafed at the close association with the mother country.[25] Colonial gover-nors were appointed by France, French militia were quartered on the island, and all cargo was required to travel to and from the colony on French ships.[26] On the other hand, the *petits blancs* appreciated French management, probably as a hedge against the planters' authority.

The free blacks, or *affranchis*, and whites were increasingly at odds. As the number of free blacks grew, the whites became anxious. To minimize the their power and presence, the whites passed laws against them.[27] By the 1770s, free blacks were prohibited from entering certain professions, marrying whites, living in France, or being called "*monsieur.*"[28] In addition, they were limited to wearing certain clothing, sitting in special sections of Churches and theaters, and keeping a 9:00 P.M. curfew.[29] The *affranchi* resented these restrictions since many were accustomed to having the same rights as the whites, including the right to own slaves. In 1790, the *affranchi* demanded that they be accorded all the rights of French citizenship; their demands were rejected. The racial and political implications were too threatening. The incensed *affranchi* started a revolt that was quickly crushed.[30]

The slaves were beginning to hear about freedom as a consequence of the French Revolution and from British and French antislavery organizations, such as *Les Amis des Noirs*. The percentage of slaves, *affranchis*, mulattos, and escaped slaves to white colonists was increasing rapidly, and as it did, the potential for a successful insurrection improved.

Slaves were so mistreated in the colony[31] that, had it not been for their masters' vigilance, uprisings would have occurred frequently.[32] As it was, the 14 August 1791 revolt was almost unprecedented. A slave named Boukman, who was also a Voodoo priest, or *houngan* [33] set it up during a Voodoo ceremony at the Turpin plantation in Bois Caiman, near Cap-Haïtien. His revolt was bloody and destructive but not immediately decisive. One thousand whites and ten thousand slaves were killed. Twelve hundred coffee estates and two hundred sugar plantations were ruined.[34] In some places, the planters regained control but in others, they were unable to do so.

The battlefield became a training ground for future leaders. By the end of 1791, Toussaint L'Ouverture had emerged as the preeminent military strategist.[35] Two other military men, Jean-Jacques Dessalines and Henri Christophe, became presidents of Haiti.

Toussaint not only drove all domestic and foreign enemies out of the colony, but also off the island as a result of a convoluted strategy involving a series of alliances with Spain and France.[36] Thereafter, he appointed himself commander-in-chief of St. Domingue and drew up a constitution that designated him president-for-life, established Catholicism as the official religion, and freed the slaves. Subsequently, Toussaint sent the freed slaves back to the plantations as paid laborers and the economy rebounded.[37]

When the revolt began in St. Domingue, Napoleon Bonaparte was distracted by events in France and on the continent. But by 1802, he realized what was happening and was able to spare some troops, so he sent his brother-in-law Admiral Charles-Victor-Emmanuel Le Clerc to retake the island and restore slavery. Le Clerc was initially successful. By playing on Toussaint's fondness for France, Le Clerc was able to convince him that when the French returned, the blacks would retain their freedom. Once Toussaint's defenses were down, he was captured and sent off to prison in the Jura mountains.

But the former slaves did not surrender to Le Clerc. Henri Christophe and Jean-Jacques Dessalines carried on the fight. It lasted another year, cost 55,000 more lives, including most of the remaining whites, and the destruction of many villages and plantations before the French were defeated at Vertières.[38]

On 1 January 1804, Jean-Jacques Dessalines declared that the former French colony of St. Domingue had become an independent nation to be known as Haiti.[39] The new country was an anomaly. It had become the first black republic and only the second free republic in the Western Hemisphere. Equally unprecedented, the former slaves had done it themselves.[40] The new flag, based on the French tricolor, retained the red and blue stripes but not the white ones.

Independence

Jean-Jacques Dessalines ruled the new country from 1804 until his assassination two years later in 1806.[41] Subsequently, the country was divided. From 1807 to 1820, Henri Christophe[42] was the ruler of the Republic of Haiti in the north, and from 1807 to 1818, Alexandre Pétion was the president of the state of Haiti in the south. In 1818, Jean-Pierre Boyer became president in the south and two years later he reunited the country, remaining its president until 1843.

The first Haitian leaders played a large role in the nation's future. Their concerns, policies, and methods of operation established patterns that were followed by succeeding Haitian leaders. Unfortunately, their point of reference was the Colonial system with its hierarchical structure based on color and class, reliance on the military, forced labor, and xenophobia.

Dessalines built up an extensive military and supplemental security apparatus to protect the island from invasion and implement his policies. Convinced that the plantation model was in the best economic interest of the country, Dessalines leased lands to former officers who worked them with indentured former slaves. Subsequently, Christophe used the military to keep reluctant Haitians on the plantations.[43]

Pétion did not rely on force to control his citizens nor insist they work on plantations. Intending to provide restitution to his countrymen for their suffering as slaves, he divided and parceled out land in small increments to individual farmers. The unintended effects of this seemingly charitable act were to destroy the export economy and ultimately undermine subsistence farming.[44] Generations of Haitians have subsequently subdivided their land in order to give some to each offspring, with the result that many of the plots have become too small to support their owners.[45] When Boyer became president, he tried to revive the plantation system, but his attempts failed. Subsequent presidents largely ignored rural Haiti and its problems. Bereft of export earnings needed to cover indemnity payments to France for the loss of its colony, Haiti began to sink into poverty from which it never recovered.[46]

Discrimination based on class and color was another colonial legacy that became entrenched.[47] The upper crust consisted of generally French-speaking, well-educated, Catholic, urban dwelling mulattos.[48] They tended to monopolize the government, economy, and professions. The underclass consisted of the black majority who were exclusively Creole-speaking, illiterate, practiced Voodoo, and lived in the countryside where they worked small plots of land and were outside of the power structure.[49]

Haiti became isolated from the outside world for internal and external reasons. The early presidents legitimately feared renewed invasions. As a result, they devised extensive military, legislative and economic strategies to prevent a takeover. They constructed forts[50] and maintained enormous standing armies.[51] They limited the rights of whites and foreigners to own property in Haiti.[52] A consequence of these actions was to deprive the new nation of valuable foreign economic expertise and entrepreneurship. When Haiti switched to a subsistence economy, its contacts with the outside world were further minimized,[53] reducing its opportunities to acquire foreign credit. Haiti was in turn isolated by the international community,[54] largely for racial reasons. Countries that still had slavery felt threatened by the Haitian experience and kept their distance. The United States withheld recognition until 1862.

The pattern of political instability in Haiti was also set early on. Between 1843 and 1915, leaders came and went with particular rapidity.[55] There were a few exceptions such as Nicholas Geffrard, who stayed in office from 1859 to 1867, Lysius Salomon, who kept his post from 1879 to 1885, and Florvil Hyppolite, who was president from 1889 to 1896.[56]

The U.S. Occupation

Haitians have a strong and pervasive fear of invasion. Dating from the immediate post-independence period, this concern was revived with the U.S. occupation. American Marines landed in Haiti on 27 July 1915, and stayed for nineteen years. They were sent in to stabilize the Haitian government, and consequently protect U.S. economic [57] and security interests.[58]

The occupation force of 2,000 men ran Haiti. It imposed martial law, changed the constitution, selected presidents and lesser officials, dissolved the Chamber of Deputies, and moved Haiti's treasury to New York. It conscripted Haitians into work gangs, hunted down rural resistance forces, and tried to destroy Voodoo.

To make matters worse, the force was racially prejudiced.[59] The U.S. government selected Brigadier General John Russell to head the occupation forces because he was a Georgian and familiar with blacks and it recruited many of the marines because they too were Southerners and were accustomed to blacks. The problem was that they did not like them. As a consequence, the occupation force agitated long-standing racial rivalries through its preferential treatment of mulattos.

During its nineteen year occupation, the force attempted to improve the country's infrastructure. It built roads and bridges, upgraded the sanitation system, dredged the harbors, and automated the phone system. It created an agricultural-technical service, the *Service Technique*. It replaced the constabulary, or *gendarmerie*, with a National Guard and trained and reduced the size of the army.[60] The dollar was linked to the local currency, the *gourde*. Ultimately, the economy improved enough that Haiti was able to pay its indemnity debt to France.

Most of these modifications were temporary. When the occupation force departed, a number of the political changes were immediately reversed and some occurred later. The technical improvements were generally not maintained and, like the paved roads, simply wore down.

Some of the effects of the occupation were unintentional and enduring. The occupation made Haitians culturally introspective. In the past, those with leisure and resources had emulated the French. Following the occupation, some began to explore their African roots and Haitian heritage and reject European values and customs.[61] Others rejected the West altogether; the communist movement in Haiti dates from this time. The occupation resensitized Haitians to the threat of invasion and enhanced their anti-foreign and anti-white bias. It fostered nationalism and generated a *noirist*, or black rights movement, which called for black leadership that led to the presidency of François Duvalier, the father of Jean-Claude Duvalier.

FRANÇOIS DUVALIER

Formative Experiences

Jean-Claude Duvalier inherited a system of government largely constructed by his father, who ruled Haiti from 1957 to 1971. François Duvalier came from a modest but upwardly mobile family with provincial roots. His paternal grandfather was a tailor who came to the capital from Léogâne, a town that is located south of Port-au-Prince. His father, David, was a teacher, who had worked his way up to became a judge; his mother, Uretia Abrahan, was a bakery employee.

François Duvalier attended the Lycée Pétion, a state school with a good academic reputation, with other children of academically ambitious parents who could not afford to enroll them in Catholic schools or send them abroad.[62] After graduation, François Duvalier continued his studies in Haiti, where he became a doctor.[63] Following an internship at Saint-François-de-Salles Hospital, he took a job involving yaws [64] eradication at the Emlie Segineau clinic, located about fifteen miles from Port-au-Prince. The program was successful because penicillin had been discovered to cure the disease. When a second clinic opened, François Duvalier became its director.

In August 1944, François Duvalier went to Michigan State University to obtain a master's degree in public health. However, he left before completing the program, under somewhat obscure circumstances, which seem to have had at least something to do with language. Returning to Haiti, Duvalier resumed his work against yaws.[65]

From François Duvalier's writing and actions, it is clear that he was particularly influenced by history, which is not surprising since he grew up in a politically and economically turbulent time. Dictators came and went, sometimes violently; one of them, Vilbrun Sam, was torn apart by crowds. Foreigners intervened in politics to protect their interests; Germans who owned Haitian utilities hired *cacos* to overthrow unfriendly governments.[66] The U.S. occupation was brutal and racist, and Duvalier's own father was a victim of it.

The Great Depression occurred while Duvalier was still young and it struck Haiti hard. Not only was there less of a demand for Haitian products, but less of a need for its labor force abroad. Foreign workers became targets for racism and violence; 20,000 Haitian cane cutters were slaughtered during this period in the Dominican Republic.

These formative influences on François Duvalier started to become evident about the time he was beginning to launch his medical career. In 1934, Duvalier wrote an article for the nationalist daily, *Action National* [67] that put some of his ideas in print. He was impatient with the mulatto elite and hoped a black Haitian leader would emerge.

Through François Duvalier's interest in literature, ethnography, and politics, he met and came under the influence of Lorimer Denis, in 1929, a black Haitian lawyer who was also a nationalist and mystic [68] with whom he started the Haitian *négritude* movement. In the late 1930s, Duvalier founded a pro-Voodoo, African-focused organization that called itself *Les Griots*, a Guinean term meaning "bards." Thereafter, he helped Dr. Price-Mars form the Bureau of Ethnology, an organization dedicated to the study and propagation of indigenous Haitian customs and values.

François Duvalier's first overtly political act, however, was to join the *Mouvement Ouvrier Paysan*, or Peasant Worker Movement (MOP).[69] MOP was a pro-black party of young professionals founded by Daniel Fignolé, and Duvalier became its general secretary. The MOP candidate did not win the 1946 election, but another black politician who was congenial to the party did—that was Dumarsais Estimé, and Duvalier became his *protegé*.

François Duvalier benefited greatly and suffered briefly from his association with Dumarsais Estimé. As a candidate, Estimé promised to help blacks and include them in his cabinet.[70] On becoming president, he appointed Duvalier minister of work. However, when Estimé was ousted in a bloodless coup in 1950 by members of the mulatto elite and the military, following a scandal and an effort to prolong his presidency, Duvalier was out of a job also.

François Duvalier regarded the ouster of his patron as treason, so he went into hiding and began to plot revenge against the usurper, Paul Magloire, who was brought into office with help from the mulatto elite and the United States.[71] However, when Magloire attempted to extend his stay by resigning as president and appointing himself head of the army, he too was forced out by the military. With national presidential elections scheduled for September 1956, François Duvalier threw his hat in the ring, presenting himself as the heir to Dumarsais Estimé.

His Candidacy

The nine months following the ouster of Magloire were politically unstable.[72] While François Duvalier was not everyone's favorite candidate, many supported him. His proponents saw him as an educated, mild-mannered person who seemed to lack excessive political ambition. Those credentials would enable him to restore peace and honor to the country. Duvalier's international connections would be an asset; he had worked with the U.S. government and studied in Michigan. In addition, he had worked with sick and poor Haitians and was a pro-black nationalist who cared about Voodoo and ethnicity. Finally, one of the most important institutions in Haiti supported him—the army. However, two other important sectors of society did not: the mulatto elite and the Church, which backed the candidacy of Senator Louis Déjoie, a member of a distinguished mulatto family.[73]

Duvalier's cultivated, dull-witted demeanor was only an external manifestation of his political astuteness. Even before the elections, Duvalier had managed to dispose of two of his three major rivals. The elections were historic; everyone over twenty-one was eligible to vote for the first time. When the army counted the ballots, François Duvalier won by a large margin.[74]

The President

The new president made promises to Haitians apparently only to break them. In his first public speech on 22 October 1957, François Duvalier promised a government of unity, reconciliation, and financial redistribution.[75] Yet, within weeks of taking office, he began to crush past and potential political, journalistic, and business opposition. He vowed to support economic development and education in rural Haiti, but this encouragement never materialized, and the gulf between the impoverished, neglected rural sector and the urban areas only widened. Rather than relieve the hardship of the poor, he imposed taxes and levied tariffs that hurt them particularly. He sent Haitians to the Dominican Republic to cut cane and then deducted a $50 finder's fee from each paycheck of the 20,000 workers recruited annually.[76] He collected taxes on products such as flour and sugar, then deposited them in a special account, the *Régie du Tabac*,[77] which he created for personal use.

The image that François Duvalier cultivated of apparent lack of political ambition turned out to be a sham. In 1961, he extended his presidential term for another six years, and in 1964, had himself "elected" president-for-life.[78] He managed by skill, brutality, and determination to do what few other Haitian leaders have managed to do, he not only held office for years but also died in office of natural causes.[79]

The military did not benefit as it might have predicted. Duvalier reshuffled the high command repeatedly over the years in order to prevent anyone from gaining sufficient power to oust him.[80] To the additional consternation of senior officers, he promoted junior black officers to thwart an inside coup and gain the loyalty of the black middle class.

As professionals and members of the business community began to realize that they might not survive this brutal presidency, let alone get along with François Duvalier, they began to leave Haiti. The exodus continued for years. Haitians went to other Caribbean islands, the United States, Canada, France, and Africa—depriving the nation of the expertise it sorely needed.

Some potential enemies who he was unable to completely eliminate, Duvalier outwitted. He managed to keep the United States out of his affairs and even get it to provide him with foreign assistance. Colonel Robert Debs Heinl, Jr., formerly in charge of a contingent of marine, coast guard, and navy personnel deployed to train the Haitian military, tried to warn the administration about Duvalier but the government was in no mood to hear him.[81] Even when Congress finally cut off foreign assistance, the administration continued to dispense it secretly.[82] François Duvalier succeeded with the U.S. government primarily by playing the communist threat card.

François Duvalier could not have been too concerned about communists himself, since his own brother-in-law was one, and he had communists in the cabinet. However, in 1958, when President Duvalier wanted more foreign assistance, he threatened the United States that if it refused to help him, he would turn to Cuba.

The wave of anti-communist fear that overtook the United States in the 1950s increased when Fidel Castro came to power in Cuba in 1959. Duvalier's threat of another communist regime in the region elicited $400,000 in economic development. Two years later, when Duvalier wanted money again he made a speech known as the *Cri de Jacmel* on 25 June accusing the United States of being stingy toward Haiti. In the absence of further U.S. assistance, needy, strategically located Haiti could be forced to turn to communist countries for help. The threat worked again, and the United States additionally offered to train the army and provide equipment to the military.

Subsequently, François Duvalier supported the United States in the diplomatic realm. When a two-thirds majority vote was needed to expel Cuba from the Organization of American States at the OAS meeting in Punta del Este in 1961, Haiti provided the deciding vote—and was in turn able to depend on the United States for additional aid.

Duvalier used U.S. fear of communism for various purposes, repeatedly, and embarrassingly. In 1963, the president expelled the U.S. ambassador from Haiti along with a marine contingent, which had been training the Haitian military, contending that the United States was encouraging an effort by President Juan Bosch of the Dominican Republic to mount an invasion against him.[83] The new ambassador, Benson Timmons III, responded to these diplomatic affronts by attempting to placate the president, congratulating Duvalier on becoming president-for-life and giving him additional economic assistance.[84]

Ill and aging, François Duvalier substantially altered the Haitian Constitution to allow his eighteen year old son to succeed him. When Duvalier died, the current Ambassador, Clinton Knox, pledged to help the grieving family prevent an outside invasion during the transition period. Knox even attended the funeral wearing a button on his lapel that pictured Jean-Claude with his father.[85]

The two most important institutions in Haiti after the government are the military and the Catholic Church.[86] In order to rule unopposed, Duvalier sought to weaken the power of both. While his dealings with the Church were less violent than with the military, his techniques were not entirely dissimilar, as we will see; and, in both cases, he was quite successful.

François Duvalier may have come to the presidency with a social and economic agenda, but staying in power ultimately became his principal preoccupation. Duvalier's longevity in office was due to a combination of immorality, genius, and luck.

If persuasion failed to elicit someone's cooperation, or a person's position appeared to threaten his own, François Duvalier did not hesitate to use force. Clément Barbot was a long-time confidant who had gone into hiding with him during the Magloire years. On becoming president, Duvalier appointed Barbot chief of the secret police. While the president was incapacitated for several months, Barbot ran the country. When François Duvalier recovered, he imprisoned his old friend for over a year in Fort Dimanche, apparently concluding that Barbot had become too powerful and posed a threat to his presidency.[87]

Duvalier exiled former presidential opponents Louis Déjoie and Clément Jumelle. He intimidated the business sector. When businesses tried to protest his decrees by remaining closed, he had them reopened by force. The president destroyed the power of organized labor and reconfigured the army.[88]

Duvalier used his personal special forces, the *cagoulards* or hooded thugs, and their successors, the *tontons macoutes*, to remain in power. Their devotion to this mandate and their macabre imagination verged on the fantastic.[89] On one occasion, François Duvalier had his police and *macoutes* intercept the funeral cortege of his former presidential opponent, Clément Jumelle, and make off with the corpse. In Voodoo-practicing Haiti, the message was that François Duvalier wanted to turn Clément Jumelle into a *zombie*.[90] On another occasion, when bombs exploded during Duvalier's tenth anniversary celebration, he suspected that members of the Presidential Guard were responsible, or simply wanting to get rid of some of them, ordered nineteen top level officers arrested and forced their own colleagues to shoot them under his supervision.[91]

François Duvalier made considerable use of Voodoo as a means of control and support.[92] His legitimization of Voodoo appealed to intellectuals concerned about the preservation of indigenous customs. In addition, it pleased the majority of the population who practice Voodoo and were accustomed to seeing it attacked and denigrated. Duvalier dressed the part of an important Voodoo figure, a tactic that increased subservience by those who concluded their president was an unassailable spirit.

François Duvalier centralized power in himself through a variety of stratagems. One was to identify himself directly with the state. After changing the color of the blue and red Haitian flag to red and black, he dissolved the senate, had himself "elected" to another six years in office, and declared, *"je suis le drapeau haitienne,"* I am the Haitian flag. When elections were held on 14 June 1964 to determine whether citizens wanted Duvalier to be president-for-life, the only selection on the ballots was "yes." When the

U.N. Commission on the Rights of Man wanted to send a team to Haiti, François Duvalier vetoed it. In *Memories of a Third World Leader*, he wrote that he rejected the investigation, demanding

> respect and honor to the national dignity of a small black people of proud origins who had arrived at political independence through the blood and tears of its sons and that more than ever has decided not to tolerate any hindrance to its national sovereignty.[93]

By chance or perhaps design, François Duvalier came to resemble his hero, Jean-Jacques Dessalines. Both men came to power following foreign occupations. Regarded initially as nationalists, they became brutal dictators whose ultimate goals was to stay in power. Both severely damaged the country through their own xenophobia and racism. After their deaths, the nation needed to recuperate.

Assessment

The social and economic liabilities of the François Duvalier government far outweigh its marginal benefits. The attrition of the population through exile and murder was a terrible blow to the country's economic and political development, and its image. It is estimated that between 1957 and 1971, 30,000 to 60,000 people were killed. Religious and racial tensions increased as a result of Duvalier's endorsement of Voodoo and his support for the black urban middle class at the expense of the mulatto elite. Through neglect, the economy generally stagnated despite multilateral and bilateral economic support.[94]

The only positive thing that can be said about his presidency is that François Duvalier provided some new opportunities for the black urban middle class. Before his presidency, the army had been a bastion of the mulatto elite. Duvalier turned it into a medium for black upward mobility, and he offered unprecedented chances for blacks to enter the civil service.

In conclusion, the major foundations of François Duvalier's power that Jean-Claude inherited included a highly centralized government where the authority rested with the president. It was based on a system of checks and balances designed to prevent one elite or another from gaining control. It relied on force and intimidation to keep Haitians cowed and quiet.

JEAN-CLAUDE DUVALIER

Problems for the Succession—The Man Himself

Jean-Claude Duvalier thought he was too young and inexperienced to be president and did not want the responsibility. The heir apparent reportedly begged his parents to appoint his politically ambitious elder sister, Marie Denise, and cried when his pleas were denied.[95] For the next few years, another politically ambitious family member ran the government, Jean-Claude's mother, Simone.[96]

Reports differ on whether Jean-Claude Duvalier was mentally prepared for the job, but there is unanimity about how ill-suited he was for it.[97] Due to a lack of shrewdness and political judgment or ideology, many of his policies appeared contradictory.[98] Duvalier wanted U.S. foreign assistance, so he made appropriate gestures of good faith concerning human rights. In 1977, he signed the Organization of American States' Human Rights Convention, and issued *communiqués* to the security forces that prisoners would henceforth be treated humanely. The president's subsequent actions make mockery of those documents, indicating that he was unable or unwilling to enforce his original policy decision. In 1980, Duvalier fired his ministers and brought in a number of well-regarded young technocrats to clean up the government and impress the United States.[99] Known as the Bayard Group, the new cabinet included Henri Bayard, Pierre Sam, Fritz Pierre Louis, and Guy Noel. Within a short time though, he had dismissed a number of them, some due to his wife's objections, and others because they actually intended to fulfill the assignment.[100]

Jean-Claude Duvalier was indecisive and easily influenced by others. On 9 November 1979, the president called on the police to break up a human rights meeting in Port-au-Prince that he had previously authorized. During the raid, one participant was killed and a number of others were beaten. Members of the Haitian cabinet had prevailed upon Jean-Claude to change his mind about the meeting after an opposition candidate won a seat in the legislative elections, convincing them that liberalization had gone too far.[101] Jean-Robert Estimé, President Dumarsais Estimé's son and a former minister of foreign affairs and religion during the Jean-Claude Duvalier presidency, recalls how the cabinet maneuvered the president. Some minister would tell Jean-Claude that he should act, because, if he did not, "people will say you are not your father's son." Then the police chief would speak up and ask to "handle it." Ultimately, these police actions would be bungled, Ambassador Estimé explained, because "when you give a job to the police, you know it will be handled poorly."

The president often dismissed and replaced cabinet members on the advice of his wife or counsel of some trusted minister. These shake-ups occurred twice a year on average, and the effects were disastrous for the country. The president was left without experienced counsel, citizens had difficulty dealing with the government, and ministers operated in a climate of insecurity and paranoia.

François Duvalier had cultivated blacks. When Jean-Claude became president, he ignored this source of support and upset the racial equilibrium his father had established. As a consequence, he alienated the Duvalierists, the army, the *Volontaires de la Sécurité Nationale* (VSN), the business community, the Voodoo followers, and finally the bulk of the Haitian population.

Clovis Désinor was an old friend and colleague of François Duvalier. Their association dated back to MOP and the ethnography movement. Later, when François became president, Désinor served in several of his cabinets.

Désinor was unequivocally against the appointment of the son to the presidency. In his opinion, the choice of the son was the work of "flatterers" who would tell the ailing father, *"Ou wete trip, ou mete pay?"*—why pull out your intestines and put in a straw—or why select an outsider when you could have your son? When François Duvalier did chose Jean-Claude, a disheartened Désinor gave the boy his best advice, "Don't get involved in cars and women, or you will go from one degradation to another."[102]

Désinor never changed his low opinion of Jean-Claude. He recalled receiving a very flattering phone call from the president in 1973, in which he offered to create the post of first minister just for him and give him the authority to hire all the people he wanted. Désinor turned it down.

François Duvalier created the VSN to enhance his security apparatus and the loyalty of its poor, black, rural recruits. His motivations for filling the ranks of the army with black officers were similar. Jean-Claude neglected the VSN and the military to the point that they had virtually abandoned him by November 1985.

The investment climate improved initially under the son's rule, however, the business sector came to resent the continuing requests from the government and Mrs. Duvalier for donations for various palace charities and the economic advantages that Ernest Bennett, Michèle Duvalier's father, was able to accrue through palace associations.[103] By Fall 1985, the business community was thoroughly demoralized and had abandoned Jean-Claude.

François Duvalier had protected Voodoo leaders and believers against discrimination and violence, but Jean-Claude did not carry on the tradition. He was not interested in religion, ethnography, or African roots. Voodoo was soon neglected and its adherents began to suffer the same fate as other Haitians.

Problems for the Succession—Family and Associates

On 27 May 1980, Jean-Claude Duvalier married Michèle Bennett. Everything about the marriage was contentious—from the celebration to her background, family, race, and character. The wedding itself, a multimillion dollar, two-week extravaganza, made the *Guiness Book of World Records* for lavishness.[104] The televised affair highlighted the disparities between the wealth of the Bennetts and Duvaliers and most Haitians, whose per capita income is the lowest in the Western Hemisphere.

The ceremony itself must have appeared blasphemous to many Catholics. Michèle Bennett was a divorced woman; nevertheless, the couple was married in the Port-au-Prince Cathedral by an archbishop, Wolff Ligondé, the cousin of Michèle's mother.

Michèle Duvalier's family was already well-to-do through its BMW franchise and other business and drug connections at the time of the marriage, but Michèle's father was regarded as an *"un homme dûr"*—a hard man who took full advantage of his new relationship with the president to acquire even more privilege and wealth.[105] His underhanded dealings, unscrupulous business methods, and ostentation made him particularly unpopular, even among his associates.

Not only had Michèle been married previously but her former husband was the son of Captain Alix Pasquet, the man who had launched a coup attempt against François Duvalier in 1958 and was subsequently killed in an attack on the Dessalines barracks. If all of this were not enough of an insult to Duvalierists, Michèle was also a mulatto. Ambassador Estimé confirmed that "by marrying her, Jean-Claude Duvalier showed that he was an ally of the mulatto elite, and this became an important symbol for the Haitian militants and the party of his father, which had stayed strong during the 1970s. The marriage created rivalries."[106]

Once married, Michèle began to take an active interest in politics. She headed charities and approached the diplomatic and business communities for donations.[107] Former Haitian Interior Minister Roger Lafontant blamed Michèle for the downfall of her husband in a television interview for a Canadian program, *"Le Point,"* which was reprinted in *Le Matin* on 14 March 1986. "Because she intervened in all the decisions of state, there was a rupture of the president with his base and a dislocation of the alliance created by the father."

Ambassador Estimé vividly recalled how readily she intervened to influence policy.[108] On one occasion, following some negative television coverage of Haiti, the cabinet was hastily convened to discuss ways to counter it. Ambassador Estimé, as the minister most involved with foreign relations, was charged with finding funds to mount a publicity campaign in the United States. The meeting adjourned and he spent the next couple of weeks preparing a detailed plan of action. When the cabinet reconvened to hear the plan, Michèle Duvalier cut Estimé off before he could speak, saying that his strategy would not be adopted.

Michèle's spending habits were another source of resentment. Her shopping trips to Paris and New York and vast wardrobe of designer clothes, furs, and jewels were a slap in the face of poverty-struck Haitians. In his "Le

Point" remarks, Roger Lafontant seemed to agree, concluding that Jean-Claude "would still be in office if he had not let his wife scorn, or *mépriser* the masses."

Jean-Claude Duvalier's in-laws were a patent problem for the administration. They took up time needed for running the government. Their characters, habits, and politics became a source of scandal and popular resentment. In a memo, the U.S. Embassy described Mrs. Simone Duvalier, Jean-Claude's mother, as a "money-grubbing, corrupt person." It continued: "Jean-Claude's sister, Marie Denise, was the most capable member of the family but tarnished by *'un esprit de putain,'*— by a whore's spirit." Then there was daughter Nicole, who had "the best character." Finally, there was daughter Simone, who was dubbed "a zero."[109]

Mrs. Duvalier Sr. was evidently tough and practical. On one occasion, when four people refused to sell their land to her, she had them arrested and thrown in Fort Dimanche prison.[110] According to the U.S. Embassy, she bribed Auguste Douyon, Jean-Claude's private secretary, to spy on her own son.[111] Even in the tense final months of the Duvalier government, two of Jean-Claude's sisters and the former husband of one and the current lover of the other were quarreling overtly over possession of a chocolate factory.

The family's unsavory activities were an open secret and its blatant corruption concerned the international banking community. In the summer of 1983, the International Monetary Fund reached a new two-year agreement with Haiti, but it was skeptical about the outcome in a country where public finances were, to quote former Ambassador Preeg, "run like a family store" for the benefit of the palace, family, and friends.[112]

Political loyalties were sharply divided within the family. Simone favored the black nationalist cadre, pejoratively known as "dinosaurs" by those who disliked François Duvalier's way of doing business, while Marie Denise preferred the technocrats, pejoratively referred to as "modernizers" by their detractors. Michèle simply disliked any advisor who got too close to her husband.

While press censorship kept some of the first family's legal and marital entanglements out of the news, Jean-Claude's wife and in-laws' economic ostentation was clearly visible. Michèle's shopping jaunts, furs, and real estate acquisitions were public knowledge.[113] Her Christmas trip to Paris in 1985 was a subject of such scandal that it may have been one of the decisive points for the presidency.[114]

It is a measure of how resented the First Family was that the private sector was relieved when the reputable but slow *Société Génerale de Surveillance Suisse* was brought in to manage the ports. While it was anticipated that moving goods through customs in Port-au-Prince would be slower, the delays would be worthwhile if Mr. Bennett were prevented from bringing his merchandise in duty-free.[115] It is significant that Bennett's auto dealership and other property were destroyed the minute Jean-Claude left Haiti.

Drugs were prevalent throughout the administration. Both Michéle's father, Ernest, and her brother, Frantz, were thought to be involved with them; Frantz had even served a prison term in Miami for drug possession and Ernest had attempted to plant a willing agent in a diplomatic post at the Haitian Embassy in Switzerland as a drug connection.[116] In another instance, when one of his drug shipments was on the verge of being discovered, Bennett got Police Chief Albert Pierre to dump 395 kilos of Colombian cocaine in the Port-au-Prince harbor.[117]

Expectations for the Succession

In some ways, Jean Claude's presidency initially seemed like a good thing; he was young, said the right things, and the United States was well-disposed—Ambassador Knox was particularly so.

The succession was accompanied by intriguing promises. The new president announced, "his father had accomplished the political revolution, and his administration would realize the economic revolution."[118] Further, it was his intention to bring democracy to Haiti. On the occasion of the twentieth anniversary of Duvalierism, 22 September 1977, Jean-Claude stated that "the next decade would be one of gradual democratization of institutions," and he punctuated the point by releasing 104 political prisoners from jail.[119] All of this led many people to believe that the quality of life in Haiti was going to improve.

There were signs of political openings. Elections and political parties were promised— at least in part due to pressure from the Carter administration, which tied foreign assistance to democratization. By 1979, Grégoire Eugène and Silvio Claude had formed political parties and a legislative election of sorts had been held, although only one non-Duvalierist had dared run for office.

There were indications of freedom of the press. Certain restrictions on the media were lifted. With this encouragement, radio stations, newspapers, and literary magazines proliferated. Comments along the lines of "the streets need improvement "were tolerated in newspapers such as Le Petit Samedi Soir and Hebdo Jeune Presse.[120] Certain topics, including the First Family and the country's economy remained forbidden topics. When Le Petit Samedi Soir printed more critical material, one of its journalists was murdered. On 16 October 1980, Evans Paul, a writer for Haiti Inter Radio and playwright, was arrested and disappeared. In 1979, the government issued a press law, authorizing censorship of publications, requiring journalists to carry identity cards, and making book sellers responsible for the merchandise on their shelves.[121]

There were indications of respect for human rights. A number of exiles were permitted to return (among them Michèle Bennett) and a human rights team was allowed to visit.[122] Security forces were instructed not to torture persons they arrested; the judicial system was going to be reformed.[123]

Despite Jean Claude Duvalier's lip service in support of human rights, Amnesty International and other international organizations reported that people continued to be arrested without warrant and some of them subsequently disappeared. Prisoners were still held without charge, often *incommunicado* for long periods of time, and tortured. Those charged continued to be denied trials or were given trials that were rigged.

Amnesty International calculated that somewhere between 400 and 3,000 political prisoners were held in Haitian jails between 1975 and 1976. The organization had the names of 255 prisoners but was unable to establish contact with them. It speculated that the regime itself might not know how many there were, or where they were being detained. [124]

When Jean-Claude released 104 persons who had been in jail between two and eight years on 21 September 1977, subsequently announcing that there were no other political prisoners, Haitians panicked. They assumed all the rest were dead. Despite presidential assurances, even as those prisoners were released, others were going to jail, among them three men in Petit Goâve whose crime was refusing to go to Port-au-Prince for the National Ceremonies to applaud the president as he delivered a speech.[125] In its 1978 *Report*, Amnesty International concluded that numerous prisoners remained in jail, based on information from released prisoners who identified cell mates.[126] Arrests and killings continued. Joseph Maxi, a lawyer and founder of the Haitian Human Rights League, was imprisoned the next year and Amnesty reported the deaths of over one hundred prisoners in Fort Dimanche in 1978.[127]

Realities of the Succession

Important sectors of the Church were becoming committed to improving the lot of the poor, to democracy, and to human rights.[128] In order to understand how this affected the overthrow of Jean-Claude Duvalier, it is important to know the distinction between what the young president promised and what he delivered; the difference between peoples' hopes and reality. The heralded economic reform did not begin to address the most needy sector of the economy, rural farmers. The historic gulf between the urban areas, particularly Port-au-Prince, and the rest of the country simply widened. When Jean-Claude Duvalier fired his cabinet in 1982, their places were filled by men who were unassociated with economic reform. Reform, such as it was, ended.

After an initial political relaxation, the administration became increasingly authoritarian and anti-democratic as assertive people were brought into the cabinet and the president began to apply himself to the job of governing the country—in the only way he knew, the way his father had done it. After his ouster, Jean-Claude tried to absolve himself of responsibility by blaming his father. He, Jean-Claude, had wanted "a fraternal regime but his father's reputation had followed him. He was not repressive—the events in the last few months had created victims."[129]

Jean-Claude Duvalier talked about liberalization because it was popular and ingratiating, particularly to the international aid donors on whom he was dependent. Anyone who took liberalization seriously got in trouble. Silvio Claude's Christian Democratic Party was soon repressed and Claude himself spent half the time between 1979 and 1985 in jail.[130] Grégoire Eugène's Social Christian Party met a similar fate in 1979. Eugène was arrested, then exiled until the end of 1984. Only the president's party, the *Conseil National d'Action Jean Claude*, (CONAJEC) was permitted to function. After awhile, the government simply announced a ban on all groups calling themselves political parties pending a law to regulate them. Enacted in June 1985, the law was very restrictive.

The government allowed municipal elections in 1983, legislative elections in 1984, and a referendum in 1985. The administration made much of these events but, in each case, the results were a foregone conclusion.

Liberalization, as previously noted, came to an end in 1980, correlated with the end of Carter presidency and its emphasis on human rights. Police and VSN broke into the offices of *Radio Haiti Inter* on 28 November, 24 days after Ronald Reagan was elected, and arrested the owner's wife. The next day, they invaded a human rights meeting, killing one participant and beating others. Some who attended the function were arrested and expelled from the country. This was only the beginning. International human rights organizations summed up the year: According to the *1980 Amnesty Report*, there had been a "deterioration in human rights since the parliamentary elections in 1979," including arbitrary detentions, torture, and harassment, especially against political leaders, human rights activists, and journalists. It documented prison deaths and illegal deportations. The Inter-American Commission on Human Rights *Report*[131] in 1980 also documented cases of torture and the absence of legal procedures, freedom of expression, and association.

By 1983, the government sorely needed to show some commitment to civil liberties and human rights; it established the National Commission on

Human Rights in May, selecting the members itself. There is no record; however, that it ever did anything.

Some foreigners were still fooled, and they were not only reporters like the journalist with *The New York Times* who wrote that political opposition existed in Haiti.[132] After all, he noted, Hubert De Roncerey, a Haitian sociologist, who had feuded publicly with Jean-Claude Duvalier, was still alive. The president had talked about political parties and said there were no political prisoners. Even after the government shot two persons distributing political pamphlets, and acknowledged it, the writer stuck to his story. The U.S. government also continued to sound encouraging about Haiti's prospects.

Initial liberalizations led to an outspokenness that the government was not able to tolerate, according to Ambassador Estimé, because it was weak.[133] In his opinion, only strong governments can tolerate discord. Consequently, the government relied on repression and violence to elicit cooperation. Prison violence was ongoing. More than one hundred prisoners were killed at Fort Dimanche in 1977 by firing squad.[134] Eleven prisoners waited, tortured and ill in the National Penitentiary from four to nine months without being charged or going to court.[135] In their *1983 Report,* Amnesty International reported on twenty-two people detained in 1980, and found at least nineteen were still being held without charge or trial at the end of 1982. On 29 April 1985, Amnesty reported that of thirty-seven political prisoners in jail in Haiti, all had spent eighteen months *incommunicado* before their trial in September 1984. All but five had been detained from a few weeks to five years without charge. One reported being beaten by a government minister. Being held without due process for long periods and frequent mistreatment was a common story.[136]

The number of *tontons macoutes* more than doubled during the Jean-Claude Duvalier administration, up from 10,000 during his father's rule to over 25,000. According to Jean-Jacques Honorat, a Haitian agronomist, human rights specialist, and subsequent prime minister,[137] they were everywhere and were always busy with their dirty work.[138] He calculated that approximately 50,000 Haitians were killed during the François Duvalier era, but twice that many may have disappeared during the Jean-Claude years.

Jean-Claude Duvalier reorganized the *tontons macoutes* into the VSN in 1978, then presented them as a gentrified force that would no longer be associated with abuses. However, they continued to exploit their authority and tyrannize the population. Ambassador Estimé recalled some of their activities in rural Haiti.[139] He was "forever getting letters from the Church requesting his intercession on behalf of some peasant who had had his land taken away or who had been otherwise mistreated by the VSN."

There is much information on the treatment of Silvio Claude because he was known internationally.[140] That prominence may have saved his life. After being tortured in 1979, he was exiled. When he returned on 28 August 1979 and held a rally, the police invaded, shooting him in the hand. He escaped, but was rearrested shortly afterward and imprisoned in Fort Dimanche. On 6 October 1981, he was still there, suffering from conjunctivitis and the results of medical neglect. He was released only to be rearrested on 9 October 1983; it was his sixth arrest in five years.[140] Silvio Claude's son and daughter, who had been incarcerated with him in October 1980, were brought to trial on 25 August 1981 and given fifteen year terms for arson and plotting against the state's security.

While most of the repression and violence was carried out by security forces, including the police and military, at least one member of the cabinet was directly involved. Pierre Robert Auguste, the editor of *L'Information*, accused Roger Lafontant of having beaten him in jail.[142] Following a *Radio Soleil* broadcast on the shortcomings of an upcoming referendum, the Interior Minister personally warned the station's director, Father Hugo Triest, that he had better stick to evangelizing or "have his balls cut off."[143]

Government legislation and U.S. assistance facilitated repression against communists, and people the government accused of being communists. The 1969 Anti-Communist Law, which was updated and amended in 1980, called for the death penalty for communists. The U.S. Embassy helped by providing names.[144]

The threat of communism has been minimal in Catholic, entrepreneurial Haiti. Even so, the Communist party has frequently been outlawed or harassed, when it was allowed to exist at all, and communist plots were discovered when the government needed a diversion or U.S. assistance.[145] On 7 December 1984, the Minister of the Interior announced the discovery of a Marxist-Leninist plot against state security. On 9 January 1986, a senior Haitian official approached a U.S. political officer in Haiti to recommend that the U.S. government watch communist efforts to exploit the current unrest.[146] One of the people he named as a communist was the future Haitian president, Leslie Manigat, who, he claimed, was amassing forces on the Dominican border.

Clearly the United States has been concerned about communism in the region and in Haiti. Ambassador Jones recalled that there was a communist threat against him during his tenure,[147] "which is one reason [he] did not want to rock the boat in Haiti." He also remembered that the previous envoy, Clinton Knox, had been kidnapped during his tour and later suffered a fatal heart attack.

The economic situation has always been difficult for most Haitians, but, in the 1980s it grew desperate. Shortsighted and selfish political policies, exacerbated by natural disasters, contributed to this situation.[148] By 1986, nearly half of all Haitians were unemployed and many more were under-employed. It was common to see a street vendor whose merchandise con-sisted of three pencils or a few pieces of cake.[149] Most Haitians were not getting enough to eat. The average caloric deficit was 14 percent and mal-nourishment was the second most frequent cause of death.[150] The protein deficit was 32 percent, rising to 40 and even 50 percent in the rural areas.[151] The victims of protein deficiency are conspicuous and omnipresent in rural Haiti; the disease gives its victims' hair a distinctive reddish cast.

The life expectancy in Haiti was only fifty-four years, lower than any-where else in the Caribbean. Many Haitians succumbed to treatable ill-nesses, such as tuberculosis, malaria, and diarrhea. [152] The author visited a home for the dying in Port-au-Prince run by Mother Teresa's order of nuns. Hundreds of young men and women, most between the ages of seventeen and thirty-five, were laid out in long rows of beds with bloody pots on the floors near their heads; they were dying from tuberculosis. Many babies were not going to grow up: the infant mortality rate was 130 to 200 per 1,000, and the crude birth rate was 36 per 1,000. Dehydration and dysen-tery commonly claimed lives. Even when babies survived infancy, they were likely to be sick and nutritionally deprived. Eighty percent of children under six years old had malaria.[153]

The worldwide economic crisis in 1983 hit Haiti and other Third World countries with particular force, causing higher energy prices, inflation, and indebtedness. Haiti was simultaneously impoverished by domestic tragedy. Droughts lasting from 1975 to 1977 and again from 1982 to 1983 dimin-ished production of cash crops. In 1982, Hurricane Allen destroyed its principal agricultural commodity, coffee. An outbreak of swine fever in 1981 led to the slaughter of all pigs on the island by 1984. Pigs provided Haitians with one-half of their meat consumption and a major source of revenue. The pig eradication program remains a source of resentment; many people were neither compensated for the loss of their swine nor given new ones. When the American pink pigs were introduced, they were given only to farmers with sufficient resources to keep them in cement pigsties and feed them the specialized diets they required.[154]

Haiti's few natural resources were disappearing. Its coastal waters were being depleted, and while there are fish further offshore, most Haitians do not have boats sea-worthy enough to get to them. Its mineral deposits have also been exhausted. In 1983, Reynolds Aluminum, which had mined bauxite in Haiti, left. Water is abundant in some places but not in others— water management projects have been particularly corrupt.

When AIDS was first identified, its overseas association was with Haiti. Tourism, a major source of revenue, plummeted,[155] and even foreign-owned assembly plants left. Although it has subsequently been proved that AIDS did not originate in Haiti, and more has been learned about the transmission of the disease, tourism and foreign industry did not return.

In addition to natural disasters, Haiti was faced with ongoing economic problems, which were growing worse. Its population was 6.3 million and its population density overall was 227 per square kilometer. In overwhelmingly rural, agricultural Haiti, the population growth and diminishing availability of land were key problems. The 1.9 percent annual population increase was not extraordinary in worldwide terms, but it was untenable in a country with so little available land and other opportunities for employment.[156]

In many places the land was poor, but farmed anyway because the need was so great. Good land was gone or unavailable.[157] Inheritance laws had forced succeeding generations to subdivide property to pass on to off-spring. As a consequence, the farms had become miniscule, with family plots averaging two acres but often divided into even smaller segments.

Some individuals and the government, the biggest landowner, had a lot of land. Fifteen percent of the population owned 66 percent of it, while two-thirds of the people owned 10 percent, and 300,000 sharecropped on others' property.[158]

Overcultivated and deforested terrain has produced another problem—soil erosion. By the eighteenth century, Moreau de Saint-Méry noted that the felled trees produced winds. Cutting down the trees was greedy and short-sighted, and he predicted that it would cause trouble.[159] In reality, the issue has less to do with greed than simple survival. The trees are used to make charcoal and 85 percent of Haiti's energy comes from wood.[160]

The Haitian farmer's plight is aggravated by antiquated farming methods and insufficient infrastructure. Primitive farming equipment, adherence to traditional techniques, lack of information about technical advances, illiteracy, and shortage of paved roads, railroads, and ports further restrict economic development.

Government agricultural policies increased the problems during the Jean-Claude presidency. Its taxation policies were particularly ill-advised. Individuals and corporations were required to pay very little tax, but indirect taxes were imposed on the agricultural sector, which could least afford them. Coffee producers had to pay taxes of up to 40 percent on prices set by the exporters and middlemen.[161] As a consequence, coffee became too expensive for many farmers to grow.

After a 5 percent growth in productivity from the mid-1970s to the end of the decade, a period of economic decline and stagnation set in, and continued until 1983. From that point, the situation deteriorated. All of the economic and social indicators fell to the bottom of the group of least developed nations.[162]

Haitian industry also declined after 1980,[163] largely as a consequence of protectionism, characterized by stagnant protected import-substitution industries and a growing export assembly subsector. Other policies that created major distortions in the taxation and trade system included the custom of paying producers half the price their goods would get at the border then charging consumers of domestic and imported items twice their value so that the government could pocket the difference. In addition, an array of basic items such as flour, sugar, cooking oil, cigarettes, cement, and matches were taxed, causing additional hardship and discontent.

Some of the government's policies were destined to produce long-term negative effects. It set up expensive and inefficient public enterprises [164] and borrowed money from private banks and suppliers with government guarantees, which added a future debt-servicing hardship on the country.[165]

Skewed priorities and indirection hurt the nation. Employment was a higher priority than economic development, and patronage was more important than skills in selecting employees for government jobs.[166] Despite the fact that the majority of the population continued to live in the rural sector, agriculture was basically ignored,[167] receiving only 10 percent of the budget. Eighty-three percent of the government expenditures went to Port-au-Prince.[168]

With the encouragement of the United States, the newest additions to the Haitian economy were the offshore assembly industries. By 1985, electronic component and textile industries employed 70,000 people.[169] However, these industries produced few other benefits and had some significant disadvantages. Profits from the foreign, mainly American-owned, companies were not reinvested in Haiti but were repatriated. The products were produced exclusively for foreign markets. The prospect of jobs led people to move to the already overcrowded cities. With fewer farms, more food had to be imported, using needed hard currency and raising the cost of living. In order to keep the industrialists happy, laws regulating labor and wages were not liberalized, and unions were prohibited.[170] Working conditions in many industries are very hard. At the Allied Assembly Plant, hundreds of women, hired because "they are more reliable" (and can be paid less than men), sit elbow to elbow in aluminum roofed, nonairconditioned rooms the size of airplane hangers, assembling intricate components for ten hours a day, six days a week. After several years, particularly industrious workers sometimes make the minimum wage of three dollars a day.[171] It is a testimony to the need for employment that people put up with this situation and strive to excel. The manager of the plant praised his workers, saying that Haitian production was higher than Allied's subsidiaries in other parts of the world.

The government initiated a series of three five-year plans in 1972 to address the economic shortcomings. The first two five-year plans would focus on infrastructure, agriculture and industry. The third five-year plan would address three objectives: administrative reform, education and research, and retraining of labor.[172] Because of lack of will and capability, these programs were not carried out.[173]

Soon after Jean-Claude Duvalier took over the presidency in 1971, he received an infusion of multilateral and bilateral assistance.[174] The United States resumed aid to Haiti, which had been cut off officially from 1961 to 1971. USAID increased its loans and grants between 1974 and 1985.[175] But, as other donors discovered, USAID began to have problems with its program due to credit-financed extra budgetary spending and inappropriate government policies.[176] Donors began to drop out or funnel assistance through the private voluntary organizations,[177] such as Cooperating Agencies Responding Everywhere (CARE) or Catholic Charities) CARITAS.

Boat people became a symbol of Haiti's distress. An officer in the U.S. Coast Guard who interviewed refugees trying to leave the country illegally and returned to Haiti, repeatedly heard the same story. They had lost hope that life would improve at home and were willing to risk their lives in boats as often as it took in order to reach the United States.[178] One man had tried to leave five times. He was going to keep trying since he had nothing to lose, there was no future in Haiti. The number of Haitian refugees arriving in Florida during the 1970s doubled by the fall of 1979. They continued to come despite the cool reception and the prospect of being returned to Haiti.[179]

The numbers of boat people led to official callousness and illegal activities that fed on this human misery. One Coast Guard officer worried that providing the returnees with a twenty dollar care package, shovel, and hoe might be breeding dependence.[180] According to Ambassador Estimé,[181] "the real crooks were the people who organized the trips." He was half right. Those who produced policies that drove Haitians to leave in desperation were also responsible, sometimes they were the same people. Government employees were found to be offering trips, green cards, and even promising jobs in the States to the potential refugees. The VSN were also in on the business.[182]

Since legitimate ways of making a living were limited, flagrant corruption existed in both the private and public sector, at the local and national levels in Haiti. The mainstay of political control in the countryside were the *macoutes*, the armed militia trained by, but separate from, the armed forces. They did not receive salaries but made money through extortion.[183] As the economic situation in the country deteriorated and centralized authority diminished under Jean-Claude, the *macoutes* had more freedom to maneuver and their excesses became more pronounced.

The *chefs de section*, or section chiefs, also wielded considerable control in rural Haiti. They were paramilitary figures whose jobs, to some extent, resembled that of rural mayors. Although they controlled the smallest administrative unit, their domain could be extensive, covering some 40 square kilometers and up to 20,000 people. Although not highly paid, the *chefs de section* could add to their income by intimidation.[184]

An incident in Plaisance provides an example of local abuse of power.[185] A man's cow had strayed off his property and the deputy section chief demanded five *gourdes*, or one dollar, to pay for damages incurred by the cow. The owner refused to pay, so the deputy section chief went to the section chief. When the section chief learned that the owner of the cow was a member of a cooperative that he did not like,[186] he instructed his deputy to put the man in jail and incarcerate any visitors the man might have. Ultimately, sixty people were thrown in jail. By the 10th of June, the cow's owner and some of his visitors had been in jail for three days without being brought before a judge.

Abuse of power fueled by greed was not restricted to the countryside. The ministries were also run like rural administrations. Up to 75 percent of the employees had gotten their jobs through nepotism. The budget explicitly provided substantial discretionary funds for presidential use. Under Jean-Claude Duvalier, these funds increased from $400,000 to $4 million a year.[187]

The arrogance of power is exemplified in a conversation between former Interior Minister Luckner Cambrone and an officer at the U.S. Embassy in Haiti. In discussing his new business enterprises—raising agricultural products for export on 7,000 acres of land in the Artibonite and on 34,000 acres in the Plateau Centrale—Luckner Cambrone mentioned that there was a water problem. But that was surmountable, he said, "since [he] had been the Minister of Public Works, you know."[188]

Lower level government employees also used their positions to make money on the side. Even Auguste Douyon, Jean-Claude Duvalier's secretary, took bribes and payoffs for arranging meetings with the president.[189]

The legal system was a travesty. Twenty-six persons arrested in 1980 were denied trial until the end of August 1981, and they were provided lawyers only four hours before their case was to be heard.[190] No witnesses were called and all twenty-six were convicted.

Congress was scheduled to be in session only five months a year. During the other seven months, constitutional rights were lifted and authority reverted to the president. Even when it did sit, the legislature was a rubber stamp for the administration. The one opposition candidate to run for office during the 1979 legislative elections, Alexander Lerouge of Cap-Haïtien, was not allowed to take office despite the fact he had won 90 percent of the votes.[191]

"Kleptocracy" and "*pèzé sucé*," or "squeeze and suck," a reference to a way of eating Haitian popsicles by squeezing the bottom and sucking them from the top, were terms applied to this corruption. In a meeting between a U.S. diplomat and Frantz Merceron, the minister of finance, the American diplomat cautioned him that continuing foreign assistance was unlikely if the United States put money in at the top and the Duvalier family persisted in draining it from below.[192] In 1981, the International Monetary Fund (IMF) struggled over terms of future assistance.[193] Soon afterwards, the Canadians pulled out due to siphoning of funds, and France and Germany showed signs of doing the same. But the U.S. Embassy suggested that they provide the next *tranche* and not penalize the country for falling behind in its debt repayments, even though it suspected that "Haiti fell down in December, probably due to unauthorized transfers of funds from public enterprises straight into the pockets of the Duvaliers."[194]

The first family's corruption was apparent, but the venality of the in-laws, the Bennetts, was excessive and was particularly resented. Ernest Bennett's drug dealing, import practices, and the advantages he reaped from his palace connections have already been mentioned. Michèle Bennett Duvalier drew at least $50,000 a month from the government to meet her own expenses.[195] Following her widely reported Christmas extravaganza in 1985, U.S. Congressman Fauntroy went to see Vice President Bush to urge that something be done. Bush said there was not much interest in the administration in a severe response, but that he would check into it. The national security advisor was also present. Soon thereafter, Secretary of State Shultz said they were moving on it.[196] Corrupt to the end, according to the *Miami Herald*, the Duvaliers managed to abscond with $120 million when they fled Haiti.[197]

According to the *1979 World Bank Report*, in 1977, 40 percent of the government expenses and revenues went through special checking accounts in the National Bank.[198] Money went into these accounts and disappeared so quickly that two-thirds of the 1979 budget had to be covered by external sources. Of the $81 million, 50 percent was paid for by multinational sources, and most of the rest was covered by the United States.[199]

The principal special account continued to be the *Régie du Tabac et des Allumettes*. Used primarily for the president's discretionary expenses, its funds came from the profits of state-owned industries. In a 1977 conversation between Frazier Meade,[200] the deputy chief of mission at the U.S. Embassy, and Guy Noel, a former consultant to Jean-Claude Duvalier, Noel told Meade that the president was going to assign 50 percent of *Régie's* income to a development account in the National Bank. The sum mentioned was $10 to $12 million. Dr. Noel added that the president wanted to put in more, but "the *Régie du Tabac* supports other things."

Relations with the United States

While this book focusses primarily on the role of the Church in the Duvalier regime, it must be made clear that the U.S. government is a major political actor in the dynamics of Haitian power. Since the American occupation of Haiti, the two countries have been closely bound to each other. The United States has become Haiti's principal trading partner and the *gourde* has been tied to the dollar. Haiti has strengthened the alliance by siding with the United States on major issues in the international arena, an important consideration in the aftermath of the communist takeover of Cuba and the establishment of leftist governments in Grenada and Nicaragua.

Background

Tensions developed between the two countries during the Kennedy years as a result of foreign aid irregularities,[201] *macoute* violence, and Duvalier's decision to remain in office for life. Finally, John Kennedy wanted Duvalier removed from office; and, to this end, he allowed anti-Duvalier broadcasts and invasion efforts to emanate from the United States.

Sympathy for ousting François Duvalier ended in 1969 with the advent of the Nixon administration and Vice President Rockefeller's trip to Haiti.[202] After a generally disagreeable tour of Latin America, where he was rudely received and spit on by crowds in Lima, Peru, Rockefeller was warmly received in Haiti on 1 July 1969. Rockefeller and Duvalier waved from the balcony of the palace, as a huge and enthusiastic crowd below cheered. Afterward, the administration sent a well-disposed black diplomat, Clinton Knox, to Haiti as ambassador and relations with Haiti improved. Gérard Gourge, founder of the Haitian Human Rights League,[203] recalls that 1971 to 1974 was a period of good relations between the United States and Haiti, during which there was "a strong dictatorship with lots of people in jail from the François Duvalier years."

The Carter administration focus in Haiti was on human rights, and it put pressure on the government to liberalize politically and to make economic reforms. The proof that this policy had some impact is that many Haitians nostalgically regard the Carter years as the golden era in Haiti. Gourge described the impact by saying, "the new philosophy changed the world view on human rights. Lots of countries with dictators formed organizations"[204]—and it was in 1978 that he founded the Haitian League of Human Rights. The Carter human rights policy captured the country's imagination. Gourge remembers that Jean-Claude Duvalier was apprehensive about receiving a visit from the U.S. ambassador to the United Nations, Andrew Young, in 1977, and that he released 110 prisoners during the visit as a gesture of intent. It was during the Carter years, that the government made an attempt to clean up the *Régie du Tabac* account. However, Ambassador Estimé confirmed what others have suspected: the reform was cosmetic.[205] Following the election of Ronald Reagan, the government reverted to its old ways.

Traditional U.S. Policy Toward Haiti

The Reagan administration was not expected to put such a high priority on human rights. Between his election and inauguration, the Haitian government began the crackdown. A general acceptance of the Haitian government by the Reagan administration became evident. Although the levels of foreign assistance were low, totaling only $6 million between 1981 and 1986, they continued to grow, increasing by 60 percent in a few years.[206]

There were pressures on Haiti to improve human rights and the justice system, to democratize, to promote economic development in order to stem the flow of Haitians to the United States, and to curtail the use of Haiti as a transshipment point for drugs destined for the North American market, but the United States continued to recertify Haiti, and a wide range of bilateral agreements were worked out. Agreements were negotiated to bring the Peace Corps to Haiti, to control illegal immigrants from Haiti to the United States, to combat drug trafficking, and to use PL 480 Title Three funds.[207] Haiti became a participant in the Caribbean Basin Initiative.

U.S. policy toward Haiti has generally been to accept the status quo while quietly encouraging economic, democratic, and human rights improvements. The observable effects of this approach were incongruous and disingenuous to many Haitians. Following the long-awaited announcement of the Law on Political Parties, which dashed remaining hopes for liberalization, Ambassador McManaway announced, "it was an encouraging step forward."[208] Following the sensational expulsion of three Belgian priests and effective closing of *Radio Soleil*, the Department of State merely issued a statement saying that the act undercut the freedom of the press in Haiti. Secretary of State Shultz testified to Congress that Haiti was making great strides during a time of great tension in the country; only a week before violent protests broke out in Gonaïves.[209] Many Haitians concluded that the major U.S. objective was to keep the peace, at their expense.[210]

The Congressional Black Caucus

Several organizations follow events in Haiti, among them Amnesty International, Americas Watch, the Council on Hemispheric Affairs, the National Council on Haitian Refugees, and the Congressional Black Caucus. Like these other institutions, the Congressional Black Caucus has covered affairs closely in Haiti and has differed with administration policy toward Haiti. As a Congressional body, its work and its interaction with the administration concerning Haiti are of particular relevance. The Caucus maintained close contact with members of the Church hierarchy and clergy. As such, its viewpoints shed considerable light on Church thinking during the Jean-Claude Duvalier era.

The Congressional Black Caucus is composed of many of the black members of Congress. Chaired by Congressman Walter F. Fauntroy,[211] the delegate from Washington, D.C., it is directed at the staff level by his legislative assistant, Stephen A. Horblitt.[212] The Congressman's interest in Haiti was piqued in the mid-1970s,[213] when he went to Congresswoman Shirley Chisholm's (D-NY) district to speak about voting rights, only to be asked by Haitians in the audience what was being done about Haiti. Subsequently, Fauntroy and Chisholm turned some of their attention to legal rights of Haitian refugees, the Immigration and Naturalization Service, and court suits.

In 1979, Chisholm and Fauntroy created the Congressional Black Caucus Task Force on Haitian Refugees to address the issues at a policy level, but it was not until Haitian bodies washed up on the shore at Hillsburo Beach, Florida in 1981, that the Caucus expanded its focus to examine conditions giving rise to refugees and began to search for cures to Haitian problems.

Congressman Fauntroy made the first of numerous trips to Haiti.[214] He met the president and proposed a program to be called Partnership for Change that would provide development assistance to Haiti in return for democratic initiatives.[215] He also visited the Dessalines prison, an uncustomary stop for a member of Congress in a country that sees few Congressional delegations.

Increasingly concerned about Haiti, Fauntroy went to the Washington papal nunciature of the former Apostolic Delegate Pio Laghi[216] in 1981 to request that the pope intercede to "encourage democracy and bottom up development in Haiti" and was encouraged to meet with the pope. Congressman Fauntroy and Rev. Jesse Jackson planned to go to Rome, but when Rep. Fauntroy could not make the trip, William Gray (D-PA) and Jesse Jackson went instead.[217] They reportedly told the pope that they were glad that he had been speaking out about Poland, but that there were lots of

Catholics in Haiti and it would be good if he took a stand there also.[218] In March 1983, John-Paul II went to Haiti.

Congressman Fauntroy and his staff saw the end of the Duvalier Regime coming by early 1985 but were unable to convince the administration or get it to change policy appropriately. After an April 1985 trip to Haiti, Congressman Fauntroy concluded that Haitians were fed up and determined to change the situation.[219] Following a December 1985 visit, he predicted the Haitian government had only a couple of months left. On 2 January 1986, he recommended to Congress that the regime be overthrown. This action would have the moral authority of the religious community and general support, given the disaffection in the black middle classes, disgust of the business sector, revulsion of the youth, and alienation of the armed forces.[220]

In a 7 January 1986 letter to Ambassador McManaway, Congressman Fauntroy called for a reevaluation of the assumptions underlying U.S. policy toward Haiti.[221] Given the First Family and army's involvement with drugs and the corruption and continued illegal immigration, the regime was incapable of protecting U.S. strategic interests in the Caribbean. Firing the "Super Cabinet" would not solve the problems. Recertification would only increase U.S. support for the dictatorship.

The administration remained unconvinced and perhaps uninformed. In late January, it told Congress that the best option was to "work for reforms within the regime."[222] After meeting with Vice President Bush and his National Security Advisor on 21 January, Horblitt reported to Congressman Fauntroy that the vice president "did not know anything about the situation,"[223] leading Horblitt to muse about the quality of the Central Intelligence Agency (CIA) station chief in Haiti. Horblitt also met with Ambassador McManaway in Washington, assuring him it was "absolutely over," that the United States would have to shift gears. "The government in Haiti was an economic, political, and military disaster." It had lost the Church, the youth, and the business sector. On 29 January, Horblitt met with the National Security Advisor to the vice president, telling him that the end of the Duvalier reign was coming.

Congress was coming to a similar conclusion. On 30 January, Representative Gus Yatron, the Chairman of the House Foreign Affairs Subcommittee on Human Rights, called on the administration to deny Haitian certification for U.S. assistance. The next day, Congressman Fauntroy issued a news release saying that Jean-Claude Duvalier's departure would be good and necessary. On 6 February, the Congressional Black Caucus issued a memo to the vice president and secretary of state concerning the desirability of a non-violent resolution of the crisis in Haiti. It listed goals that included: keeping communists out of control, curbing the refugee and drug flow, supporting economic development of the agricultural and private sectors, and promoting human rights. It recommended administrative and structural plans, as well as long-term priorities for the new government—along with a timetable. The same day, Fauntroy introduced House Concurrent Resolution 282 that would terminate assistance and Caribbean Basin Initiative (CBI) benefits, lower tariffs on imports, as long as Jean-Claude Duvalier was in power.

One day before Jean-Claude Duvalier actually departed Haiti, Vice President Bush called Congressman Fauntroy to say that the White House and Department of State had developed a plan and they were putting together a task force. "Our thinking is coincidental."[224]

U.S. Ambassadors and Diplomacy

Notwithstanding the continuity of U.S. policy, it is clear that individual ambassadors and their staffs have made a difference. There was considerable variety among the envoys to Haiti during the Jean-Claude administration. For a start, two of the six were black—Clinton Knox, (1969–1973), and William Jones (1977–1980).

Through temperament, personality and intellect, some ambassadors became more involved with Haiti than others. Ambassador Knox was enthusiastic about Haiti and got along fine with François Duvalier and his family. Supporters regarded him as "successful," while his detractors viewed him as "practically a *macoute*."

Ambassador Jones was happy with his tour.[225] He found the staff congenial and competent. He regarded his contacts with human rights activists, the press, and opposition as wide ranging. He viewed presidential access as another mark of success and believed he had it. The ambassador would meet Jean-Claude Duvalier at his secret retreat, where he would "point out to him who in his administration was stealing and corrupt and guide him toward parliamentary government." From Jean-Claude's subsequent behavior, we can only surmise which service the president appreciated most.

Ambassador Jones did not personally share his president's emphasis on human rights.[226] While acknowledging that Jimmy Carter's presidency corresponded to "the most humane period in Haiti," in his view, it tried to do too much and encouraged Haitians to go too far in pursuit of their liberties. When the administration continued to push for human rights, he "would have to go to Pat Derian [the assistant secretary of state for human rights], and explain to her why it was ill-advised, and she understood."

Only one of the six ambassadors was a political appointee, and that was Henry Kimelman (1980–1981), a Virgin Islander in the liquor business who had been a presidential campaign contributor. He served just three months before being replaced, but his appointment was offensive, at least to his predecessor, suggesting that the administration believed "anyone can do it after a black."[227]

Only one ambassador to Haiti had previously had the benefit of holding a high level post at an embassy. Ernest Preeg had been deputy chief of mission in Peru before serving as ambassador to Haiti from 1981 to 1983.[228] In addition to that substantial preparation, Ambassador Preeg and his wife brought a special asset to Haiti. They both liked the country and the people and became immersed in the experience, despite the fact that Mrs. Preeg caught Denge Fever and was sick for a long time.

Clayton E. McManaway Jr. (1984–1987), is remembered for his openness and readiness to listen to the opposition, inviting a wide mix of people to functions at the embassy residence. Unlike his predecessors and many of the embassy staffs, he is credited with learning Creole, the only language of the majority of the population. On the negative side, sensitive Haitians were offended because the ambassador's wife was frequently absent from embassy receptions and dinners. They believed that she did not like Haiti. By mid-1985, many Haitians had grown resentful also of an embassy that would not stop lauding Jean-Claude for progress he had not made.

The ambassadorial system for Haiti is far from optimal. In general, the ambassadors have been drawn from a pool of State Department administrators who are on the verge of retirement. They are usually appointed for one short tour of duty, limiting their opportunity to learn the language, culture, and history of the country. A better preparation for an ambassadorship to Haiti would include service as deputy chief of mission (DCM) to Haiti or a French-speaking African country, fluency in French, and training in Creole.[229]

Conclusion

Haitian history reveals certain patterns that continue to be important today. There is the legacy of exploitation, brutal leadership, social divisiveness, lack of commitment to the country, and fear of invasion. François Duvalier is distinguishable from other Haitian presidents by the extent of his cunning and brutality, and his longevity in office. As we have seen, the son did not maintain the balance of power his father had established, so as disillusionment set in, Duvalierists, tontons macoutes, the Army, the business community, Catholics, Protestants, and many Voodoo adherents turned against him. Thus, there are many actors in addition to the Roman Catholic Church in the political dynamics of Jean-Claude Duvalier's rise and decline. Next we will examine specifically the history of the Catholic Church in Haiti.

NOTES

1. President Jimmy Carter continued his interest in Haiti after leaving office. He led an international delegation to monitor national elections in Haiti on 16 December 1990, which contributed to their honesty and lack of violence.

2. A map of Haiti can be found in Appendix C.

3. Selden Rodman, *Haiti: The Black Republic: The Complete Story and Guide* (New York: Devin-Adiar, 1984), 4.

4. Brian Weinstein and Aaron Segal, *Haiti: Political Failures, Cultural Successes* (Stanford: Praeger, 1984), 11.

5. M.L.E. Moreau de Saint-Méry, *A Civilization that Perished,* ed. and trans. Ivor D. Spencer (Lanham, MD: University Press of America, 1985), 7, 40.

6. Ibid. Saint-Méry refers to them as "sorts of scavengers who lived off the land."

According to Rodman, *Haiti: The Black Republic,* the name "buccaneers" comes from the word boucan, the word for the Indian spits on which they cooked their meat.

7. Robert I. Rotberg and Christopher K. Cague, *Haiti: The Politics of Squalor* (Boston: Houghton Mifflin, 1971), 26.

8. Lorimer Denis and François Duvalier, "L'Evolution Stadiale du Vodou," *Bulletin du Bureau d'Ethnologie* 12 (1944): 1–29.

9. Saint-Méry, *A Civilization that Perished,* 40. The indentured Frenchmen, or *engagés,* were also known as "thirty six months" because they generally served three years.

Denis and Duvalier, "L'Evolution Stadiale du Vodou," 1–29. The plantation owners overturned a 1699 law that required parity of slaves and indentured laborers in order to import more slaves. The new law established the ratio at one indentured laborer per twenty slaves.

10. Michel S. Laguerre, "The Place of Voodoo in the Social Structure of Haiti," *The Caribbean Quarterly* 19, no. 2 (1973): 36.

11. Rotberg and Clague, *Haiti: The Politics of Squalor,* 34. See Denis and Duvalier, "L'Evolution Stadiale du Vodou," 12–14.

Denis and Duvalier wrote that the white men were pirates and rascals from Europe and the white women were no better than they should be, whereas the black slaves from Sudan, Dahomey, and the Congo had been empire builders, cultivators, singers, poets, intellectuals, and warriors.

12. Rotberg and Clague, *Haiti: The Politics of Squalor,* 32.

13. C.L.R. James, *The Back Jacobins, Toussaint L'Ouverture and the San Domingo Revolution,* 2d ed. (New York: Random House, 1963), 25.

See Rod Prince, *Haiti: Family Business* (London: Latin America Bureau Limited, 1985), 11.

14. James Leyburn, *The Haitian People* (New Haven and London: Yale University Press, 1966), 15. "Wealthy as a Creole," was an expression that referred to the planters in Haiti, but came to signify great wealth in general. France profited also. By 1789, Leyburn reports that two-thirds of the French foreign commercial interests were in Santo Domingo.

15. Saint-Méry, *A Civilization that Perished,* 22.

16. Laguerre, "The Place of Voodoo," 37.

There is some disagreement about the numbers of slaves in the colony in 1791. The figures range between 480,000 and 700,000.

Prince, *Haiti: Family Business,* 11. Prince claims there were 480,000 slaves on the island in 1791. Weinstein and Segal, *Political Failures, Cultural Successes,* cites Aaron Lee

Segal's "Haiti" in *Population Policies in the Caribbean* (Lexington, MA: Health, 1975) and Ivan Geghin, W. Fougere, King, *L'Alimentation et la Nutrition en Haïti* (Paris: Presses Universitaires de France, 1971), 29, whose authors estimate that there were 30,000 free mulattos and blacks, 40,000 whites, and 500,000 slaves. Leyburn concurs. Saint-Méry, *A Civilization that Perished*, 45. His editor writes that there were approximately 700,000 slaves in St. Domingue in 1791.

17. Saint-Méry, *A Civilization that Perished*, 95. Saint-Méry, describing the harbor at Cape François (Cap-Haïtien), says "an average of 170 ships were in the harbor at a time [adding], it was a rule that the slave ships were kept at the base of the roadstead so the negroes could have the benefit of the fresh breezes and also that the air from these ships could not do any harm to either these people in the harbor or those in the city."

18. Prince, *Haiti: Family Business*, 11.

19. Laguerre, "The Place of Voodoo," 38. Laguerre cites Father Labat in his book, *Voyage Aux Isles De L'Amérique.*

20. Saint-Méry, *A Civilization that Perished* 162. On a "good plantation the reproductive rate of negroes exceeds their death rate"—a possibility Saint-Méry seemed surprised to discover ever happened.

21. James, *The Black Jacobins*, 21.

22. Laguerre, "The Place of Voodoo," 40. "The priests were notorious for their irreverence and degeneracy in a country where unfrocked monks enjoyed easy money, women, and concubines, charging fees for repeated baptism of the same slaves."

23. Saint-Méry, *A Civilization that Perished* 76–77. On the race-conscious colony, terms identified people by the amount of African blood in their veins. A few of the designations, in order of decreasing percent of it, were *mulattoes, quadroons, métis (métif or octoroons), mamelukes, sacatras,* and *griffes.*

See James Leyburn, *The Haitian People*, 15. Leyburn only mentions four social categories: the *grands blancs, petits blancs, gens de couleur,* and slaves.

Saint Méry, 75, reports that there were no freedmen in the 1681 census and only 500 in the 1703 census. there was a big increase in freedmen after 1770, when the number stood at 6,000, a figure that doubled by 1780 and reached 23,000 in 1789.

24. Saint-Méry, *A Civilization that Perished* 225. Saint-Méry says that the *maroon* villages were located particularly in the mountains along the Spanish border because the Spanish did not try to turn them over to their former owners. The militia would "steadily go into the camps to kill or round them up." Slaves were recruited for this work, and offered freedom as payment.

25. Prince, *Haiti: Family Business*, 14. Prince calls the system "absolutism in power," as administrators turned power to profit through the exaction of tribute and rackets. The French Navy Ministry ran the colony and a standing army of 3,000 men and a militia of all adult white males was stationed in the colony. Military officers ran the towns and districts and its financial administration controlled the taxes.

26. Ibid., 11–12.

27. Laguerre, "The Place of Voodoo," 37. The first census of 1681 counted 4,336 mulattos and free blacks. In 1789, the number of mulattos had grown to 36,000, and by 1791, there were 28,000.

Leyburn reminds us that in 1685, Louis XIV had issued the *Code Noir* to cover colonial dealings with slaves. It stated that slaves who bought their freedom or were released, were entitled to all the rights of the citizens. The number and relative wealth of the freedmen was increasing, so that by 1791, the freedmen may have owned up to one-third of the land and one-fourth of the slaves. This caused the jealousy of the *petits blancs.*

28. Saint-Méry, *A Civilization that Perished* 159.

29. Prince, *Haiti: Family Business*, 13.

See also Saint-Méry, *A Civilization that Perished* 132. At the theater on the Cap there were seven third row boxes that took mulatto women and three negresses in a theater that seated 1,500 people. Free negresses had been allowed entry since 1775; however, when they petitioned to be allowed "to sit next to their daughters," they were given separate boxes.

30. Ibid., 15. The mulattos initially said they wanted civil rights so they could stand on the side of the whites—as upholders of slavery. Thirty-seven delegates from St. Domingue went to Paris to present their grievances and they were successful. The National Assembly granted political rights to four hundred mulattos whose parents had both been free. However, the Colonial Association blocked the legislation, asserting that mulattos were not people, but a "bastard and degenerated race." This decision produced demonstrations in Cap-Haïtien, which were put down, ending with the execution of two popular mulatto leaders, Vincent Ogé and J.B. Chavannes.

31. Ibid., 256. The absentee landlords were not always aware of the amount of food the slaves needed. Saint-Méry observed, "You can always expect too much labor from a man who is not fit enough, it is the duty of the government to remind them of it"—but added that the government never did. His editor inserted a remark to the effect that the overseer would continue to send revenues to the absentee owner even when the land was wearing out, and the situation was so desperate that the slaves were running away, aborting their babies, and killing themselves.

32. The colonists did their best to prevent slave revolts. The *Code Noir* helped in one respect. It forbade gatherings of slaves from different plantations in an attempt to disperse and separate slaves who knew each other.

33. James, *The Black Jacobins*, 21. There was only one known example of an organized plan to free the laves in the 100 years up to 1791. The instigator was a *maroon*, François Macandal, who had been a slave in Limbé, but his attempt failed before it got started.

34. Prince, *Haiti: Family Business*, 15.

35. Toussaint L'Ouverture's background was unusual for a slave. Toussaint was literate and employed as a steward in a northern plantation when the revolution began. In 1793, Toussaint discarded his surname, which was "Bréda," in favor of "L'Ouverture," which means "opening" and was selected to signify the emergence of freedom for the slaves.

36. James, *The Black Jacobins*. Toussaint L'Ouverture's apparently contradictory alliance with the French occurred because he saw himself and the colony as French. He envisioned a colony free of slavery but linked to France for the economic benefit of St. Domingue. Wanting to believe Le Clerc's promises he even had some of his advisors who doubted them, such as Sonthonax, killed. L'Ouverture was not alone in being taken in by Le Clerc; Jean-Jacques Dessalines and Alexandre Pétion were also temporarily duped.

37. Leyburn, *The Haitian People*, 27. Leyburn characterizes the growth and success of the economy between 1799 and 1802 as amazing.

38. Weinstein and Segal, *Haiti: Political Failures, Cultural Successes*, 15.

39. The name "Haiti" was derived from an Arawak word "*hayti*" meaning "mountainous."

40. Half a million black slaves had triumphed over the most powerful nation on earth.

41. Dessalines was making enemies due to his increasingly dictatorial conduct when he was killed on 17 October 1806 near Port-au-Prince. however, his brutal murder by a

group of mulatto officers contributed to the legacy of racial friction between blacks and mulattos and the association of Dessalines with black power, independence, and nationalism.

42. It was Henri Christophe's determination to be king that split the country. The Assembly objected and, when he insisted, selected another president, Pétion. As a result, Henri Christophe became king in the north and Alexandre Pétion president in the south.

43. Rotberg and Clague, *Haiti: The Politics of Squalor*, 59. Henri Christophe augmented his security forces with the Royal Dahomets, an army of 4,000 recruits that he imported from Dahomey.

The first civilian president was Michel Oreste, who held the office from 1913 to 1914.

44. Prince, *Haiti: Family Business*, 17.

45. Weinstein and Segal, *Haiti: Political Failures, Cultural Successes*, 132. Weinstein and Segal calculate the loss of arable land at 1 percent a year.

46. The export economy was destroyed in the south following the Civil War and economic collapse has been common following the independence of the colonies in the twentieth century.

47. Leyburn, *The Haitian People*. The origins of these race, class, and geographical divisions date from the time of Christopher Columbus and the Spanish occupation of the island. The colonial governor general was a military officer, who lived in the city. The loyalty of the whites was to Spain rather than Santo Domingo.

See Rodman, *Haiti: The Black Republic*, 74. Rodman regards Jean-Pierre Boyer as unintentionally responsible for solidifying the class distinctions. Since only mulattos were educated, they were chosen for government jobs. The low level of literacy is reflected by statistics such as; in the 1830s, only 1,000 children attended school in Haiti, and only 300 adults subscribed to periodicals.

See James, *The Black Jacobins*, 74. Color and class have been divisive in Haiti except when the country has faced some exceptional threat. Prior to the revolution, as we have seen, certain mulattos were initially undecided about where their best interests lay, and some, in Port-au-Prince and the south, did link up with the whites. Most ultimately joined forces with the black slaves.

During the U.S. occupation, the mulattos received preferential treatment by the Marines, but they too were ultimately offended by the occupation force's brutal treatment of the mercenaries and adherents of Voodoo. At the end of the Jean-Claude presidency, many mulattos who had benefited from the regime, turned against it.

48. Large estates are the source of wealth in much of Latin America; but not in Haiti, as most of them have been divided into small parcels. Wealth in Haiti has consequently been derived from association with the government.

49 Class and race issues are serious matters in Haiti. Although the divisions noted are generally accurate, they are not absolute; a wealthy black may be regarded as a mulatto.

50. President Dessalines built forts and planned to move the capital and cities inland to more defensible sites. President Christophe built a massive fortress, the Citadel in Cap-Haïtien to thwart a renewed invasion by the French. Years later, President Boyer taxed exports heavily in order to discourage foreign trade to keep foreigners away.

51. Prince, *Haiti: Family Business*, 247. At independence, one-fourth of the population was in the military. Leyburn, *The Haitian People*, concluded, "over militarization [was] the bane of nineteenth century Haiti," 36–37.

52. One of Dessaline's first acts after becoming ruler was to order the massacre of the remaining whites. He subsequently pledged that no colonist or European would be

allowed to become master or landowner in Haiti. This injunction was included in succeeding constitutions until the United States occupied the country and rewrote the constitution.

53. Leyburn, *The Haitian People*, 35–36.

54. Although Simón Bolívar was given refuge in Haiti, the Liberator did not invite
Haiti to participate in the regional defense conference in Panama in 1826.

55. Bernard Diederich and Al Burt, *Papa Doc: The Truth About Haiti Today* (New
York: McGraw-Hill, 1969), 17.

56. Rodman, *Haiti: The Black Republic*, 90, 36, 37. According to Rodman, Geffard
established relations with the Vatican and opened diplomatic relations with the United
States. He tried to establish medical, law, and urban secondary schools, improve the cultivation of cotton, and create a middle class.

Lysius Salomon was dynamic, well-informed, and concerned about education and
public works, but when he tried to overstay his term of office he was overthrown.

Florvil Hypolite was also civic-minded. He established a ministry of public works,
introduced telegraph and telephone systems, and built iron markets and bridges
throughout the country.

57. Ibid., 104. In the late 1800s, it became common to hire mercenaries, known as
cacos, to make coups.

The public attitude in the United States toward Haiti at the time was reflected by
Secretary of State Alvey Ardee, who proclaimed in 1888 that the country is "a pubic nuisance at our own doors."

The period 1900 to 1915 was a violent one in Haiti. President Gillaume Sam massa-
cred some of his opponents and was then brutally murdered. It was his gruesome death
that directly led to the U.S. invasion. There were some minimal financial interests at
stake.

According to Prince, *Haiti: Family Business*, 18, they had to do with the railroad, the
Bank of Haiti, and some outstanding Haitian debts to the United States. The 1904
Roosevelt Corollary justified intervention abroad under such circumstances, when a
country was unable to pay its debts to the United States.

58. Through the writing of Admiral Alfred Mahan, the United States was increas-
ingly concerned about sea power and the need to protect sea lanes of communication.
Opening the Panama Canal in 1914 increased the strategic importance of the
Caribbean.

59. Rodman, *Haiti: The Black Republic*, 133.

60. Ibid., 146. According to Rodman, some of the reforms were not broad enough
and others were undone when the marines departed. One charge leveled against the
occupying force was that it did not attempt to widen the political base.

See Weinstein and Segal, *Haiti: Political Failures, Cultural Successes*, 32. These
authors claim that the occupation did not produce any lasting reforms because it was
too short, involved too little interaction with Haitians, and was not innovative.

61. In 1928, the Haitian ethnographer Jean Price-Mars caused a sensation with his
book, *Ainsi Parla L'Oncle*, which extolled African values and Haitian peasants. Other
influential contemporary writers included A. Holly and J.C. Dorsainvil.

62. Weinstein and Segal, *Haiti: Political Failures, Cultural Successes*, 38.

63. Diederich and Burt, *Papa Doc*, 36. These authors allege that François Duvalier
got into medical school without having taken the required entrance exam.

64. Yaws is a parasitic disease common in tropical countries that is characterized by
eruption of raspberry-colored excrescences on the skin.

65. Rotberg and Clague, *Haiti: The Politics of Squalor*, 163.

66. Diederich and Burt, *Papa Doc,* 29–51. These authors provide an excellent characterization of the period.

67. Ibid., 39.

68. Denis was also reputed to have been a *houngan.*

69. His Excellency Clovis Désinor, interview with author, Port-au-Prince, Haiti, 14 July 1986. Désinor said that François Duvalier had been clandestinely involved with politics as early as 1936, when he tried to get a former army commander into the presidency. Furthermore, Désinor claimed that it was he, not Lorimer Denis, who brought Duvalier into the party, as Diederich and Burt had written.

70. Dumarsais Estimé, who was from a modest black family in Verrettes and had been a minister of education in the 1930s, was brought into office by an electorate who specifically wanted a black president.

71. His Excellency Clovis Désinor, interview with author, Port-au-Prince, Haiti, 14 July 1986. Désinor maintained that François Duvalier wanted to start a revolution against Magloire. Ultimately, it was the black middle class and some of the business community who forced him out of office.

72. In that nine-month interval, there were five governments.

73. Diederich and Burt, *Papa Doc,* 77–78.

74. Ibid., 10. According to the authors, it appeared that the army sabotage of the Pierre Eustache Fignolé and Ducasse Jumelle candidacies were engineered by François Duvalier. Of 900 voters, 679,884 ballots were cast for Duvalier and 266,993 for Déjoie.

His Excellency Clovis Désinor, interview with author, Port-au-Prince, Haiti, 14 July 1986. Désinor confirmed that his friend and associate had "not used just and honest methods to gain the presidency."

75. James Ferguson, *Papa Doc, Baby Doc,* (Oxford: Basil Blackwell, 1987), 38.

76. Ibid., 53–54. Starting in 1966, 3 percent was deducted from salaries to create old age pensions for persons over sixty-five. Ferguson notes that the life expectancy in Haiti at that time was only forty.

77. François Duvalier established the *Régie du Tabac,* or government tobacco monopoly, to receive taxes collected on tobacco, cotton, sugar, and other products. He used it as a personal account, as did his son subsequently.

78. Diederich and Burt, *Papa Doc,* 282. François Duvalier put his name at the top of the 22 October 1961 congressional ballots. Those who voted for legislators discovered they had also approved the president's continuation in office. In June 1964, voters were asked to approve or reject the concept of president-for-life but the ballot was only marked with a "oui" or "yes." To write "non" or "no" would have defaced the ballot, which was a criminal action.

79. As we have seen, personalist governments in Haiti have been the norm. James Timothy Kelly refers to them as "sultanistic" in "Rocks in the Sun: The Roman Catholic Church in Haitian Political Development" (Honors thesis, Harvard University, 1988), 15.

80. Leyburn, *The Haitian People,* xix. François Duvalier reorganized the army five times in seven years in order to prevent anyone from acquiring sufficient power to overthrow him.

Duvalier's gratitude was as short-lived as his military promotions. Army Chief General Antonio Kébreaux, an early Duvalier loyalist, was dismissed, demoted, then murdered.

81. Robert Debs Heinl, Jr., "Haiti: A Case Study in Freedom," *The New Republic* (16 May 1964). Heinl recommended that the United States change its policy toward Haiti.

The United States should cut off foreign aid, withhold funds for the jet airport, highways, and waterworks, encourage the IMF to withdraw support for the *gourde*, and discourage travel to Haiti. Major trading partners, such as the Haitian-American Sugar Company, should be encouraged to withdraw their investments in Haiti. The United States should withdraw its support for the government and give it instead to its opponents. In his estimation, if petroleum were withheld from Haiti, the international oil companies could paralyze the country in a couple of weeks.

82. Apart from the period in the early 1960s when John Kennedy tried to have François Duvalier deposed, U.S. administrations have been generally supportive, or at least tolerant, of Haiti.

Ambassador François Benoît, interview with author, Washington, DC, 21 April 1989. Benoît recalled his participation in the Haitian Coalition, an *emigré* organization composed of former Haitian politicians and members of the military that operated out of New York in the 1960s. The Coalition relied on radio broadcasts in order to harass Francçois Duvalier and create a revolutionary climate in Haiti, but its CIA-derived funding diminished following the assassination of President Kennedy.

83. Diederich and Burt, *Papa Doc,* 238–39. According to the authors, François Duvalier personally complicated the ambassador's departure by stalling the arrival and departure of the plane, obliging him to spend the night at the airport, and prohibiting him from returning to collect his belongings.

U.S. acceptance of the regime grew as a function of its desire for stability following its occupation of the Dominican Republic in 1966. Subsequently, opportunities for border strikes and assaults launched from the United States decreased, helping to assure François Duvalier's tenure.

84. Ferguson, *Papa Doc, Baby Doc,* 50.

85. Diederich and Burt, *Papa Doc,* 401–2.

86. See William Paley, "Haiti's Dynastic Despotism: From Father to Son to . . ." *Caribbean Review* (Fall 1985). Paley discusses the way in which François Duvalier gained control through the reduction of his politically powerful opponents, which included the Army and Church hierarchy, the U.S. Embassy, business elites, intellectuals, and union leaders.

See R.M. Morse, ed. *Haiti's Future: Views of Twelve Haitian Leaders* (Washington, DC: Wilson Center Press, 1988). This book describes how Duvalier consolidated power by banning strikes, killing or jailing rivals, censorship, closing unions, and confronting the Church and army.

See also David Nicholls, *From Dessalines to Duvalier* (Cambridge: Cambridge University Press, 1979), 213–16. Nicholls distinguishes two periods in the François Duvalier government: the first seven years during which Duvalier violently pursued his opposition, and the next eight during which he sought to contain the military and obtain Church neutrality.

87. Barbot harbored his resentment against Duvalier for quite a while after his release. When he did act, it was against the Duvalier children, whom he attempted to sabotage and kill on their way to school.

88. Ferguson, *Papa Doc, Baby Doc,* 39.

89. Diederich and Burt, *Papa Doc,* recount a number of them in Chapter Ten.

90. Rotberg and Clague, *Haiti: The Politics of Squalor,* 218.

91. Ambassador Jean-Robert Estimé, former minister of foreign affairs and religion, interview with author, Wheaton, MD, 5 May 1988.

92. Diederich and Burt, *Papa Doc,* 147. In a chapter entitled "Voudou in his Arm," the authors ascribe part of François Duvalier's power to Voodoo. He notes the connec-

tion between the appearance, dress, and movement of Duvalier and *Papa Guede Nimbo,* a Voodoo figure. He recalls Duvalier's early support of Haitian folklore and the stories which circulated about Voodoo rites being practiced in the palace, Voodoo being used to eliminate enemies, and how he equated himself with the gods. Diederich and Burt point out that Duvalier appointed a well-known *bocor*, Zacharie Delva, to head the militia and invited Voodoo priests to the palace.

See Wade Davis, *The Serpent and The Rainbow* (New York: Simon and Schuster, 19850. Davis analyzes Duvalier's bases of power, one of which was Voodoo. He traces the germs of support from intellectuals and traditional society to *Les Giots*, a magazine which espoused nationalism, African roots, and Voodoo as the legitimate religion of the people. Davis describes how Duvalier sought the endorsement of *houngans* in the 1957 election and used some Voodoo temples as campaign headquarters. Following the election, Duvalier recognized the legitimacy of the Voodoo religion (the first president to do so in 100 years), invited Voodoo leaders to the palace, employed the Bizango secret societies to help maintain control in the countryside, and appointed their leaders to important positions in the *tonton macoute* hierarchy.

93. François Duvalier, *Mémoires d'Un Leader du Tiers Monde* (Paris: Hachette, 1969), 358.

94. Ferguson, *Papa Doc, Baby Doc*, 58–59, quantified the cost of preserving "stability" in Haiti, when he wrote that by 1963 the International Commission of jurists calculated that François Duvalier was taking $10 million annually from the treasury and that 80 percent of the aid was squandered and pilfered.

95. Elizabeth Abbott, *Haiti: The First Inside Account: The Duvaliers and their Legacy* (New York: McGraw-Hill, 1988) 163. Abbott states that Jean-Claude hated being president-elect and that he repeatedly urged his parents to designate his older sister, Marie Denise.

An American diplomat who served in Haiti reported that Jean-Claude had cried when told he was going to be president and that, in the course of his presidency, he threatened to resign several times.

96. Department of State, American Embassy, Port-au-Prince. "Duvalier Family," Memorandum of conversation, 24 May 1976. A memo acquired through the Freedom of Information Act (FIA) from the U.S. Embassy in Haiti stated, "Jean-Claude lets his mother and Henri Didait handle business."

97. His Excellency Clovis Désinor, interview with author, Port-au-Prince, Haiti, 14 July 1986. Désinor dismissed Jean-Claude Duvalier as "a person of no importance, not intellectual, someone who stayed a kid."

Diederich and Burt, *Papa Doc*, 399. The authors wrote that Jean-Claude had a "modest intellect."

In contrast, an American diplomat who served in Haiti from 1980 to 1983 characterized him as "bright." Jean Sosa, telephone interview with author, Washington, DC, 30 June 1986. Comparing Jean-Claude to his father, Sosa described him as "not being strong, decisive, or politically astute."

Jean-Robert Estimé, interview with author, Wheaton, MD, 23 March 1988. Jean-Robert Estimé, Jean-Claude's minister of foreign affairs and religion from 1982 to 1985, limited himself to saying that the president "was not a politician."

98. Ambassador Jean-Robert Estimé, interview with author, Lanham, MD, 19 December 1988. The ambassador faulted the president for his lack of interest in social issues, in particular for his for his neglect of the poor, rural peasants.

99. Ibid. Estimé denied that Jean-Claude Duvalier had selected a new cabinet because he intended to make reforms. That explanation was "pure politics." The

president needed new people as a result of internal conflicts. In addition, it had been a difficult year in which he had been sick and there had been an invasion attempt on the island of La Tortue.

100. A former advisor to Jean-Claude Duvalier, interview by author, Port-au-Prince, Haiti, 7 July 1986. The advisor spoke at some length about Michèle's jealousy of this group and unhappiness over its access to her husband.

Ambassador Jean-Robert Estimé, interview with author, Lanham, MD, 19 December 1988. Estimé commented on the reasons for the ouster of Minister Bayard in 1982. When Michèle's brother was indicted in Miami on drug charges, Bayard suggested that the First Family separate itself from Bennett (her father), to which Michèle reportedly responded that she would sooner pack her bags and leave.

101. Ambassador Jean-Robert Estimé, interview with author, Wheaton, MD, 5 May 1988. Estimé described it as "an obsession of the Duvalier government to stop action before it got out of hand."

102. His Excellency Clovis Désinor, interview with author, Port-au-Prince, Haiti, 14 July 1986. Désinor's contempt for Jean-Claude was, no doubt, exacerbated by his own foiled expectation of being the successor.

103. Raymond Joseph, "Haitian Religious and Business Leaders Stop Pampering Baby Doc," *The Wall Street Journal,* 7 February 1986.

104. Michèle and Jean-Claude were divorced on 2 February 1990 in France, according to an announcement in the *Haïti-Observateur,* 7–14 February 1990. According to the brief article, their wedding had cost $7 million.

105. Yves Germain Joseph, a former counselor to the minister of finance for Jean-Claude Duvalier, interview with author, Port-au-Prince, Haiti, 8 July 1986.

106. Ambassador Jean-Robert Estimé, interview with author, Wheaton, MD, 29 March 1988.

107 Michèle Duvalier reportedly admired and emulated Eva Peron and was said to have watched the movie "Evita" frequently at the palace. There are obvious similarities between the two women. Both were determined, beautiful people who established foundations to demonstrate their generosity.

Ambassador Ernest Preeg, interview with author, Department of State, Washington, DC, 31 March 1988. Preeg described how Michèle financed her foundation. She would ask the ambassadors to contribute, but the United States would decline, since the law prohibited it. In 1981, all of the ambassadors decided to withhold contributions and Michèle was furious. Consequently, Ambassador Preeg was not invited to a single social meeting at the palace for his entire tour.

108. Ambassador Jean-Robert Estimé, interview with author, Lanham, MD, 19 December 1988.

109. U.S. Department of State, American Embassy, Port-au-Prince. Memorandum from the U.S. Embassy in Haiti to the Department of State, "Duvalier Family," 24 May 1976.

110. Ibid.

111. U.S. Department of State, American Embassy, Port-au-Prince. "Auguste Douyon," Biographic file (23 October 1973).

112. Charles R. Foster and Albert Valdman, eds. *Haiti Today and Tomorrow* (Lanham, MD: University Press of America, 1984), 10. See the "Introduction" by Ambassador Ernest Preeg.

Using public office to obtain international loans and embezzle funds has a long history in Haiti. See Kelly, "Rocks in the Sun," 16, 23. Kelly cites an early example of presidential corruption involving a loan floated by President Michel Dominique who ruled from 1874–1876. After commenting that later presidents, among them, Elie Lescot and Dumarsais Estimé, continued the tradition, Kelly describes Paul Magloire as "remarkable in this regard, mostly for embezzling international development and relief funds."

113. *Time*, "Small Stirrings of Change," 13 January 1986.

114. Stephen A. Horblitt, "Report on the Mission to Haiti and Recommendations for Future Action." Memorandum to Congressman Fauntroy, 1 January 1986. In this memo Horblitt mentions the more than $1.7 million Michèle spent on Christmas purchases in Paris and the $7 million she spent on French real estate.

115. U.S. Department of State, American Embassy, Port-au-Prince. Memorandum to the ambassador concerning a conversation regarding illegal imports from Barry Eurnett, Chief DDE. Undated.

116. U.S. Department of State, American Embassy, Port-au-Prince. Narcotics: "The Haitian Ambassador to Geneva Recalled." Cable to secretary of state, confidential. Port-au-Prince, 4 April 1985.

117. Ibid., "Duvalier's Last Days." Cable to secretary of state, 19 February 1986.

118. Carolyn Fowler, "The Emergence of the Independent Press in Haiti," *The Black Collegian* (April-May 1981): 149.

119. Ferguson, *Papa Doc, Baby Doc*, 67.

120. Dominique Levanti, reporter for *Agence France Presse*, interview with author, Port-au-Prince, Haiti, 7 July 1986.

121. Weinstein and Segal, *Haiti: Political Failures, Cultural Successes*, 76.

122. Michael Hooper, "The Politicization of Human Rights in Haiti," in *Haiti Today and Tomorrow*, ed. Charles R. Foster and Albert Valdman (Lanham, MD: University Press of America, 1984).

123. A U.S. diplomat who served in Haiti, interview with author, Washington, DC, July 1986.

124. *Amnesty International Report* (London: Amnesty International, 1977), 101–2.

125. Urgent Action Letter, *Amnesty International* (London: Amnesty International, 1977).

126. *Amnesty International Report*, 1978, 125–26.

127. Urgent Action Letter, *Amnesty International*, November 1979. See also *Amnesty International Report*, 1979, 66–67.

128. Marian McClure, "The Catholic Church and Rural Social Change: Priests, Peasant Organizations, and Politics in Haiti" (Ph.D. diss., Harvard University, 1985), 141–43. McClure cites the sources of Church activism and traces their history in Haiti from the early 1960s through the early 1980s. She describes the birth and growth of the CCDs, IDEA, and the *Ti-Légliz*. She writes about how priests in Haiti wanted to actively fight for the poor, and how their social activism drew in the prelates. For another account of the evolution of Church commitment to improving the lot of the poor beginning in the late 1960s, see Mark Persily, Untitled paper by an intern at the Washington Office on Haiti, on the Church in Haiti, summer 1988, 2–4.

129. Jean-Claude Duvalier, "Je Paye Pour Papa Doc," *Paris Match* (12 February 1988).

130. Americas Watch, *Haiti: Human Rights Under Hereditary Dictatorship* (New York: Americas Watch and National Coalition for Haitian Refugees, October 1985), 9.

131. *Amnesty International Report*, 1980, 146–58.

132. *New York Times*, "Some Signs of Political Relaxation," 16 July 1985, A1.

133. Ambassador Jean-Robert Estimé, interview with author, Wheaton, MD, 5 May 1988.

134. *Amnesty International Report*, 1978, 125–26.

135. Urgent Action Letter, *Amnesty International,* 1977.

136. *Amnesty International Report,* 1983, 145–47.

137. Jean-Jacques Honorat later accepted the position of prime minister in the military regime that ousted democratically elected president Jean-Bertrand Aristide on 30 September 1991.

138. Jean-Jacques Honorat, interview with author, Port-au-Prince, Haiti, 7 July 1986.

139. Ambassador Jean-Robert Estimé, interview with author, Wheaton, MD, 2 May 1988. The tone of this remark would appear to be indicative of government compassion.

140. Council on Hemispheric Affairs, "Haitian Refugees Flee Harsh Political Situation," press release, 5 April 1980.

141. Hooper, "The Politicization of Human Rights in Haiti."

142. Americas Watch, *Haiti: Human Rights Under Hereditary Dictatorship,* 1–9. Lafontant was killed in jail in September 1991, while serving a life sentence for trying to overthrow the interim administration of Ertha Trouillot the previous January, allegedly by the Aristide government on the eve of being overthrown itself.

143. Ibid., 10. See Joseph B. Treaster, "Without Suspense, Haitians Vote Today on President-for-Life," *New York Times,* 22 July 1985, for a discussion of the history of corrupt Haitian referendum.

144. Ambassador Jean-Robert Estimé, interview with author, Wheaton, MD, 5 May 1988.

145. In light of this anti-Communist legacy, it is somewhat ironic to find the Haitian legislature and the U.S. government in 1992 urging ousted Jean-Bertrand Aristide to appoint René Theodore, the formerly reviled and erstwhile Communist leader, as his prime minister in order to make his presidency more respectable and return to power more likely.

146. *Amnesty International Report,* 1977, 165–69. See U.S. Department of State, American Embassy, Port-au-Prince. Cable to the Department of State, "Palace Official Warns Embassy of Threats to Regime," 9 January 1986.

147. Ambassador William B. Jones, interview with author, Washington, DC, 27 April 1988.

148. The 1982 cabinet appeared to have been selected to address the country's economic problems. Marc Bazin, who had had a long and distinguished career with the World Bank, was appointed finance minister. Within a short time, he announced that 36 percent of the government funds were being stolen, and he set out to retrieve them. The government tolerated "Mr. Clean" for five month before firing him and sending him into exile.

149. Maureen Taft-Morales, "Haiti: Political Developments and US Policy Concerns" (Washington, DC: Foreign Affairs and National Defense Division, Congressional Research Service, 11 October 1988).

See *Washington Post,* "Haiti's Misery: Economy Remains Stagnant, Hostage to Political Unrest," 22 December 1986, 1. According to the Post, the per capita urban income in Haiti in 1986 was $377, down 9 percent from 1980. In 1983, the per capita income was reportedly only $315, but probably closer to $50 in rural areas.

150. Ramon A. Rodriguez, *Caribbean Contact* 12, no. 12 (May 1985).

151. William Steiff, "Haitian Hell: A Government Gone Awry," *Multinational Monitor* 6, no. 18 (December 1985): 6.

152. Kathy Graunke, "Gesture in Face of Haiti's Poverty" *National Catholic Reporter,* 22 January 1982. Dr. Graunke is a pediatrician who volunteered with the Missionaries

of Charity in Port-au-Prince from February to June 1981. She emphasizes how the bad economic situation in the country contributes to rampant health problems. "There is a tension between doing simple, direct works of mercy and working to change the structures that fail to meet local needs. This tension increases the more one becomes aware of how directly related the structures (political, economic, and cultural) are to the human suffering."

153. Hooper, "The Politicization of Human Rights in Haiti," 228.

154. The U.S. Agency for International Development (USAID) and experts working on the pig repopulation program expect that the new pigs will ultimately adapt to Haiti, have bigger litters, and become more hardy.

155. Steiff, "Haitian Hell," 8. World Bank figures show 306,500 visitors to Haiti in 1980. That figure dropped to 214,600 in 1984.

156. Sources: *World Bank Atlas,* 1988 and the Haitian Institute of Statistics and Data Processing, 1987. Figures estimated to 1988 using growth rate. Data received from Hassan Fazel, economist, World Bank, 24 May 1989.

157. Prince, *Haiti: Family Business.* There were over 500 people per square mile in Haiti, leaving little land available for cultivation. Forty-three percent of the land was cultivated even though only 29 percent was considered to be of suitable quality.

158. Rodriguez.

159. Saint-Méry, *A Civilization that Perished* 15.

160. Prince, *Haiti: Family Business.*

161. Weinstein and Segal, *Haiti: Political Failures, Cultural Successes,* 90–94. These problems did not disappear with the Jean-Claude Duvalier regime. In interviews with coffee producers in northern Haiti in 1986, I heard repeatedly that the middle men were still there, extorting undue money from the small growers.

162. Hassan Fazel, economist, World Bank, telephone interview with author, Washington, DC, 8 April 1988.

163. Steiff, "Haitian Hell," 6.

164. Hassan Fazel interview, 8 April 1988.

165. Ibid.

166. Derrick W. Brinkerhoff and Jean-Claude Garcia-Zamor, *Politics, Projects and Peasants: Institutional Development in Haiti* (New York: Praeger, 1986), 8.

167. Steiff, "Haitian Hell," 4–5. Agriculture represented one-third of the GDP versus one-half of the GDP in the 1950s.

168. Hooper, "The Politicization of Human Rights in Haiti," 228.

169. David Nicholls, "Past and Present in Haitian Politics, in *Haiti Today and Tomorrow,* ed. Charles R. Foster and Albert Valdman (Lanham, MD: University Press of America, 1984).

170. *Central Latinoamericana de Trabajadores,* New release, "Increases Repression Against Union in Haiti," Caracas, Venezuela, 17 December 1980. This news release details Haitian government repression of trade unions in Haiti.

171. The author visited Allied in Port-au-Prince in April 1986.

172. James Walker, "Foreign Assistance," in *Haiti Today and Tomorrow,* ed. Charles R. Foster and Albert Valdman (Lanham, MD: University Press of America, 1984).

173. Ibid., Walker maintains that the programs had limited success due to the lack of government income, deficient control of revenues and expenditures by the minister of finance, the need for administrative and human rights reform, and a rationalized private sector.

174. USAID, "Position Paper for the UN General Assembly, 40th Session" *Economic Assistance to Haiti,* 31 October 1985. In 1985, the United States provided Haiti with

$53.3 million. That year Haiti received $155.1 million from all external sources—including the IBBR, UNDP, and the IDB.

175. Robert McAlister, Haiti desk officer at USAID, telephone interview with author, Washington, DC, 8 April 1988. McAlister reported that in 1974, Haiti received a total of $11.4 million in aid, of which $6 million were loans and $5.4 million were grants. By 1984, the total aid package was $46.6 million, of which $11 million were loans and $36.6 million were grants. This tilt toward grants, which produced a disparity of more than 3 to 1 ration in favor of grants by 1984, and reflects Haiti's increasing poverty since grants are given to the poorer countries.

176. USAID, "Position Paper," 31 October 1985.

177. Rodriguez.

178. U.S. Department of State, American Embassy, Port-au-Prince. Andrew Parker, "Follow Up Trip to Pastel Region," memorandum of conversation, 21 June 1983.

179. Council on Hemispheric Affairs, *Haitian Refugees Flee Harsh Political Situation* Press release (Washington, DC: Council on Hemispheric Affairs, 4 May 1980). Out of 10,000 Haitians awaiting completion of asylum proceedings and 13,000 who had arrived in Florida in the past eight years, only 200 received immigration visas.

180. U.S. Department of State, American Embassy, Port-au-Prince. Memorandum of conversation regarding emigration from a returnee officer, 13 and 15 October 1983.

181. Ambassador Jean-Robert Estimé, interview with author, Wheaton, MD, 29 March 1988.

See Ferguson, *Papa Doc, Baby Doc,* 61. Ferguson claims that the palace itself made some profit on the boat people.

182. U.S. Department of State, American Embassy, Port-au-Prince. Telegram from the U.S. Embassy in Port-au-Prince to the Department of State, 1 August 1980.

183. Prince, *Haiti: Family Business,* 38.

184. Weinstein and Segal, *Haiti: Political Failures, Cultural Successes,* 56.

185. Joseph Bélizaire, "Rapport Sûr Un Cas D'Injustice Survenu à Plaisance les 6, 7, 8, 9 juin, 1984."

186. The cooperative was named *Paka Pala,* which means "I'll Always Be There," and is an allusion to another situation. When Frank Romain, the former mayor of Port-au-Prince, was fired by Jean-Claude Duvalier because Michèle disliked him, he reportedly demonstrated his loyalty to the chief of state by telling him, *paka pala.*

187. Jean-Claude Garcia-Zamor, "Haiti," *Latin America and Caribbean Contemporary Record* (New York: Holmes and Meier, 1983), 579. Cited in Weinstein and Segal, *Political Failures, Cultural Successes,* 61.

188. U.S. Department of State, American Embassy, Port-au-Prince. "Cambrone Visiting the Economic Section of the United States Embassy in Haiti." Memorandum of Conversation, 20 January 1983.

189. U.S. Department of State, American Embassy, Port-au-Prince. "Refugee Business and corrupt Personal Secretary to Jean-Claude Duvalier." Cable to secretary of state, 1 August 1980.

190. *Amnesty International Report,* 1981, 146–48.

191. Council on Hemispheric Affairs, *Human Rights Report, 1979–1980.*

192. U.S. Department of State, American Embassy, Port-au-Prince. "Meeting with Secretary of Finance Frantz Merceron." Cable to Deputy Assistant Secretary of State Michel, Port-au-Prince, 12 February 1984.

193. Rodriguez.

194. Department of State, American Embassy, Port-au-Prince. "United States Aid to Haiti," Cable to secretary of state, 13 February 1985.

195. Prince, *Haiti: Family Business,* 51–52. Prince assessed Michèle's monthly salary at $100,000.

196. Congressman Walter A. Fauntroy, interview with author, Washington, DC, 10 May 1988.

197. Ferguson, *Papa Doc, Baby Doc,* 150.

198. Hooper, "The Politicization of Human Rights in Haiti," 284.

199. Ferguson, *Papa Doc, Baby Doc,* 69.

200. American Embassy, Port-au-Prince to Department of State, "Régie du Tabac," conversation between Frazier Meade, deputy chief of mission and Guy Noel, 26 February 1977.

201. David Nicholls, "Haiti: The Rise and Fall of Duvalierism," *Third World Quarterly* 8, no. 4 (October 1986).

202. Raymond Joseph, publisher of the *Haïti-Observateur,* telephone interview with author, Brooklyn, NY, 9 April 1988.

203. Gérard George, founder of the Haitian League of Human Rights, member of the CNG, and presidential candidate in 1987, interview with author, Port-au-Prince, 7–9 July 1986.

204. Ibid.

205. Ambassador Jean-Robert Estimé, interview with author, Wheaton, MD, 5 May 1988.

206. Mary Evelyn Jegen, Thomas Gumbleton, Fritz Longchamp, and Beverly Bell, "Haiti, a Country in Crisis." Address at the National Press Club, 12 December 1985.

207. In 1981, Congressman Dan Mica of Florida sponsored an amendment to the Foreign Assistance Act, which limited foreign assistance to countries which cooperated to control illegal migration to the United States. In September 1981, the United States signed an International Agreement to control illegal migration. The Peace Corps came to Haiti in 1982 and the Caribbean Basin Initiative began in 1983, both reflecting U.S. government emphasis on development of the private sector.

208. American Embassy, Port-au-Prince, to the secretary of state, U.S. Department of State, "Elections in Haiti," 15 August 1986. After listing the CNG's proposed election schedule in June 1986, Ambassador McManaway concluded by commenting on the Haitian electoral situation in the past. It is apparent that he was not as convinced that the Haitian government was on the path to democracy as his public statements at the time would indicate. According to McManaway, "during the final years of the Duvalier regime, Haiti did not enjoy a democratic system nor did it select its leaders through open and democratic elections. The few elections the government conducted were flawed; in some cases to a serious degree, by coercion, intimidation, fraud, and a reluctance by voters even to participate in an electoral process designed to yield results amenable to a Duvalier regime."

209. Washington Office on Haiti, "Report to Congress," vol. 1 (Washington, DC: Washington Office on Haiti, February 1985).

210. Charlotte Werleigh, former general secretary of *CARITAS.* Material drawn from her talk given at the Washington Office on Haiti, 11 May 1988. In assessing the role of the United States in Haiti, Werleigh concluded the U.S. policy objective has always been to keep the peace by supplying the army with training and weaponry.

211. Congressman Fauntroy left the Hill following his defeat in the Washington, DC mayoral race in 1990. As of 1992, he was busy with speaking engagements, the African American Action Alert Network, and the New Bethel Baptist Church.

212. Stephen Horblitt subsequently left the Hill to become a senior associate with Creative Associates International.

213. Much of this section on the Congressional Black Caucus is drawn from an inter-view with Congressman Fauntroy by the author, Washington, DC, 10 May 1988 and from an article by Stephen Horblitt entitled, "Needed—a Sharp Break with the Past," in *Authoritarian Regimes in Transition*, ed. Hans Binnendijk (Washington, DC: Center for the Study of Foreign Affairs, Foreign Service Institute, U.S. Department of State, 1987).

214. Congressman Walter Fauntroy, interview with the author, Washington, DC, 10 May 1988. The Congressman's visits typically include talks with the ambassador and the embassy country team, meetings with the Haitian president, members of his cabinet, and leaders from the private sector, such as journalists, development workers, opposi-tion leaders, and rural farmers. He also meets with Catholic Church hierarchy, priests, and lay workers because "the Church is the only organization in the country and has the best network."

215. The plan was not implemented.

216. Achbishop Pio Laghi was the Apostolic Pro-Nuncio to the United States from January 1984 when official relations between the Holy See and the United States were restored (official Vatican relations lapsed with non-Catholic countries between 1870 and 1884, the period corresponding to its loss of the papal states) until June 1990 and the appointment of Archbishop Agostino Cacciavillari.

217. Congressman Walter Fauntroy, interview with the author, Washington, DC, 10 May 1988. See the memorandum from Walter Fauntroy to his Excellency Pio Laghi, Apostolic Pro-Nuncio, 18 February, 1986, which recalls this earlier meeting.

218. Karen Payne, "Pope Has 'Great Interest' in Haitians," *Miami News Reporter*, 25 February 1982.

See also "Black Leaders Meet With Pope," *Miami Times*, 25 February 1982. The del-egation consisted of the Rev. Jesse Jackson, Dr. Mary Berry of the U.S. Civil Rights Commission, Jackson's wife, Jacqueline, William Gray (D-PA) of the Congressional Black Caucus, and Camille Cosby, the wife of entertainer Bill Cosby. Following the audience with the pope, Reverend Jackson told *The Miami News* that he had appealed to the pope for mercy for the Haitians. "The reason I was anxious to meet with the pope on this matter was to put the plight of the Haitian people into the international com-munity and into the human rights context."

219. Stephen Horblitt, interview with author, Washington, DC, 25 March 1986. A priest in Haiti had told him that the government was finished; "*Chwal la pedi pye*," or the horse has lost its footing.

220. Ambassador Jean-Robert Estimé, interview with author, Wheaton, MD, 17 November 1989. Estimé said the army and some key sectors of the Haitian society, including members of the business community and the alliance of Protestant churches, let it be known that they would not try to protect the president in a coup attempt.

221. Letter from Congressman Walter Fauntroy to Ambassador Clayton McManaway, 7 January 1986.

222. Horblitt, "Needed—a Sharp Break with the Past," 290.

223. Stephen Horblitt, memorandum to Fauntroy, 19 January 1986.

224. Congressman Walter Fauntroy, interview with author, Washington, DC, 10 May 1988.

225. Ambassador William Jones, interview with author, Washington, DC, 27 April 1988.

226. Ibid. One of Ambassador Jones' recommendations for the U.S. Department of State was that it encourage more black diplomats. In his view, the Reagan administra-tion had "wiped blacks out of the foreign service." Ambassador Jean-Robert Estimé, interview with author, Wheaton, MD, 19 April 1988. Estimé argued that black

ambassadors should not be sent to Haiti because "the Haitians are terrible racists" who believe that "if they get a black ambassador, they are not getting the best quality."

227. Ambassador William Jones, interview with author, Washington, DC, 27 April 1988.

228. Ambassador Ernest Preeg, interview with author, State Department, Washington, DC, 31 March 1988.

229. Conversation with a high-level American diplomat who formerly served in Haiti.

It could be noted that since 24 November 1989, the U.S. ambassador to Haiti has been Alvin Adams. He is Creole-speaking, direct, and determined to see democracy in Haiti. He has been singularly appreciated by Haitians, who applauded him on 13 March 1990 as his vehicle left the National Palace following the installation ceremony for the provisional president.

See "United States Ambassador Adams Acclaimed by Crowd," Port-au-Prince, *Radio Nationale* in Creole, 1400 GMT, 14 March 1990, 6.

See also Jill Smolowe, " A New Start, A Ray of Hope," *Time*, 26 March 1990, 29. Smolowe concludes that the ambassador "played a crucial role in hastening Avril's departure."

3

The Church In Haiti

While we have examined broadly the history of Church and State in Latin America, the experience of the Church in Haiti is peculiar and merits special attention. The role of the Church in the overthrow of Jean-Claude Duvalier cannot be understood without this background.

Church history in Haiti is long and, until the Jean-Claude Duvalier era, unheroic. Its Colonial background resembles the experience of the Church in the rest of Latin America. It arrived in St. Domingue with Spanish explorers at the end of the fifteenth century, emphasizing baptism and spending little time reflecting on the ethics of slavery. A paucity of capable and committed clergy and an emphasis on perfunctory conversions led to contempt by slaves and landowners alike. Despite the weakness of the clergy, strong anticlerical feeling among the population, and Church tolerance of slavery, the institution was allowed to remain in Haiti after independence, but under close governmental control. Early Haitian leaders placed themselves at the head of the Church, limited its legal power, and encouraged Protestantism as a ballast. Haiti did not establish formal relations with the Vatican until 1860.

In some ways, however, the Church experience in Haiti differs from the Latin American one. The clergy and Colonial landowners in St. Domingue were overwhelmingly French and French-speaking while the majority of the population was of African origin and exclusively Creole-speaking. There was a period of fifty-six years after independence during which there was no official Church presence. This allowed elements of Catholicism and African religions to mix, producing Voodoo—the religion of most Haitians today. Freemasonry came to St. Domingue in the mid-eighteenth century, where it remained fashionable and popular among the upper classes for the next century and a half. The Haitian Church remained a predominantly foreign institution until the mid-twentieth century.[1] Its relations with the State have also set it apart from other Churches in the region. Its property is nationalized. Divorce is absolute, and although the Church is supported by the State, it does not have a monopoly on government subsidies for religious purposes.

The post-Concordat Church in Haiti used its privileged position to draw closer to subsequent Haitian and American governments, isolate the Protestants, combat the Freemasons, and attempt to eliminate Voodoo. In the aftermath of the U.S. occupation and the antisuperstitious campaign, some clergy were led to reconsider the Church mission and methods, while François Duvalier took special precautions to make sure the Church would be under his control. Ironically, the concession he won from the Vatican to appoint his own bishops, unintentionally contributed to the creation of the Church that subsequently forced his son out of office.

RELIGION IN HISPANIOLA

Catholicism has played an important role in the history of Hispaniola from the time of the island's discovery by Christopher Columbus. When Columbus landed at Môle St. Nicolas on 6 December 1492, he planted a cross and when he returned to Spain, he took seven Indians with him to be baptized. In a Papal Bull [2] in 1493, Pope Alexander VI accorded Spain the right to all the lands it discovered west of a line of demarcation between the Azores and Cap Verde, on condition that the inhabitants found there would be instructed in the principles of Catholicism.

In 1498, the fledgling colony on Hispaniola requested that priests be sent to instruct the people.[3] In response, the Order of St. Francis arrived in 1505. The Dominicans established the convent of St. Croix on the island in 1512 and bishoprics by 1527.

Criticism of slavery was sporadic and punished. Individual Churchmen and religious orders opposing government policies were forced to leave the island or were silenced. The Dominicans took exception to the enslavement of the native Indians and to the custom of mass adult baptism without prior religious education. In one sermon, Father Antoino de Montesinios spoke out against illicit work done by the Indians and its contravention of divine and human laws.[4] Starting in 1502, Father Bartolomé de las Casas began the first of what turned out to be twelve transoceanic trips to Europe to negotiate on behalf of the Indians. Following a religious inquest held in 1516 on the conditions of slavery on the island, the Church was cautioned to control its ardor. Ironically, it was de las Casas' effort to spare the Indians and his recommendation that Africans be imported instead that led to the slave trade in Hispaniola.

Until the Edict of Nantes in 1598 provided French Protestants relief from domestic persecution, many left the country in search of more tolerant climes, one of which was Hispaniola. For a decade in the 1600s, the island of La Tortue, or Tortuga, located near the north coast of Hispaniola, even had a Protestant governor. Le Vasseur, a French Huguenot, governed until his assassination.[5] Afterward, the governorship was restored to a Catholic, Monsieur de Fontenay.[6] Hispaniola became a less congenial place for Protestants to live, let alone govern, beginning in 1685 with the promulgation of the *Code Noir*, or Black Code, which outlawed the exercise of any religion other than Catholicism and forbade the employment of Protestants in any French colony.

The initial official establishment of the Catholic Church in Hispaniola has had historic repercussions. As the authorized religion throughout the French colonial period, it has continued to enjoy a preeminent position much of the time since independence. When its hegemony has been threatened, the Church has referred to its original mandate and objected strenuously. Consequently, adherents of Voodoo, Freemasons, and Protestants have been regarded as interlopers and obstacles for the Church in the accomplishment of its designated mission.

THE FRENCH COLONY OF ST. DOMINGUE

Religious Foundations

On 31 October 1626, a royal commission authorized the establishment of the first French colony in the Antilles, and Cardinal Richelieu decreed, "Catholicism would be established and the inhabitants instructed in the Faith."[7] Thereupon, the *Ancien Régime* gave the Church a free hand to govern itself in ecclesiastical matters and provided assurances of financial support from the Colonial administration.[8] Both of these *grands gestes* became sources of friction between the Church and the government. Following the Treaty of Ryswick in 1697, which confirmed French possession of the western third of Hispaniola, land grants were made to Catholic missionaries and areas of operation were delineated. Some territorial disputes caused the Church to complain about government intervention in its operations. Relations between the Vatican, Church, and State in Haiti have undergone numerous changes since the seventeenth century and deeply affected the country's history. As we will see, three centuries later, tensions among them contributed to Church participation in the overthrow of Jean-Claude Duvalier.

With the possible exception of the Jesuits, the Church did not attempt to abolish slavery; its goal was to manage it. This put the Church in opposition to the Colonial government and led to governmental constraints on Church authority.

That the Church wielded some power in the colony is clear.[9] It succeeded in getting laws passed that prohibited work on Sundays, allowed slaves to attend mass, marry, and be baptized, although the laws were often disobeyed, particularly in parts of the country that were less accessible to public scrutiny. In addition, it induced King Louis XIV to expel all Jews from the colony in 1683, curtail proselytism and public worship by Protestants, and impose a religious test on new immigrants.

Around 1704, the Jesuit order undertook responsibility for Church building, education, and the slaves in the colony.[10] By 1725, they were working with approximately half of the slaves, which numbered around fifty thousand, and they were also trying to convert the *marons,* or escaped slaves. This interaction with the slaves was too close for the Colonial rulers. On 24 November 1763, after the government accused the Jesuits of corrupting the slaves, insubordination to the Crown, and distortion of the Catholic faith for their own purposes, it gave them six weeks to leave the island.[11]

The Church and government grew increasingly estranged. With the burgeoning slave population, the missionaries were overworked. The Church could no longer reach all the slaves or keep new converts in the fold. Church expenses mounted, but antagonistic slave owners refused to pay their allotted share per slave to the Church.[12] By the second half of the eighteenth century, anticlericalism, one of the products of the Enlightenment, further diluted Church authority.

THE RELIGIOUS PRESENCE

From the end of the sixteenth century to the beginning of the eighteenth, the buccaneers and the filibusters attacked and looted passing vessels, grew increasingly stronger, and led "a life that was little favorable to religion."[13] While the filibusters reportedly prayed before embarking on their expeditions and on return in gratitude for victory, even these token religious observances were neglected by the buccaneers.[14]

As the population of La Tortue grew, it spread onto the mainland, in time attracting a number of French religious orders. The first to arrive were Capuchins, who settled in 1681, followed by the Jesuits in 1704 and the Congregation de Notre Dame in 1733.

The first parish Church in Cap-Haïtien was constructed in 1681.[15] By 1717, there were ten other parishes with twenty thousand parishioners; and, by 1726, there were twelve parishes in the French colony.[16]

Clerical Involvement with the Slaves

Prospective slave buyers and clergy alike met the slave ships; the latter because Article II of the *Code Noir* required slaves to be baptized within eight days of arrival. Responses to this requirement differed among the orders—the Capuchins baptized everyone immediately, while the Jacobins required them to receive some prior instruction. The Jesuits alone appear to have taken the task of religious instruction seriously—a contributing factor in their forced departure from Haiti in 1764.[18]

References abound concerning one priest's work with the slaves. M.L.E. Moreau de Saint Méry, whose *History of St. Domingue* was completed before 1789, wrote of a Father Bouton who held "negro masses," taught outdoor classes on the stairway of the Church, and tried to learn the African languages.[19] Few other names distinguish themselves.

Church records and historical journals show that the Church did not oppose slavery in Haiti. Some in the Church even justified it on the basis that it gave slaves the opportunity to become Christian. A Father Du Tertre reportedly said, "there is almost no Negro in all of the French West Indies who is not a Christian and to whom the missionaries have not given a new birth in the waters of baptism."[20] Moreau de Saint Méry described the attitude of the Church toward the slaves as "generally indifferent."[21] Clerical failure to oppose slavery cannot be dismissed as Breathett does[22] when he writes, "no concept of the dignity of man existed at the time." Biblical commandments as well as papal injunctions, such as those of Pope Urban VIII (reigned 1623–1644), forbade Catholics to participate in slave trade.

The Jesuits were the most socially conscious order in St. Domingue and came the closest to encouraging insurrection. In 1763, the Procurer General of the King complained to the Counsel Superior at Cap-Haïtien, "The Jesuits haven't failed to teach the slaves their subversive theories through catechism, preaching and example."[23] They were expelled from St. Domingue that year.

The best indication of Church acceptance of slavery is that priests owned slaves. Priests were required to make inventories of their personal possessions and those belonging to their mission. The first property listed under "effects" in the inventories was typically slaves. The inventories would detail the number of slaves and their ages; they were generally under thirty years old, and usually included a number of children. The inventories would also list their nationalities, such as Congo or Mindigo, and their last name if they were Creoles, born in the colony. Finally, the inventories would identify those who were "stamped," or branded.[24] A ledger might read, "young negro boy, Creole, named Leonard, about ten years old, stamped on the right breast and belonging to the mission."

The economic situation of the Church in the colony varied. Certain institutions, such as the mission at Léogâne in La Petite Rivière, appear to have been well-off.[25] According to the inventory of 22 June 1773, its two huts measuring 40 by 16 feet housed fifty slaves. Its four-bedroom house contained a study, drawing room, library and office. Its kitchen included a foundry, henhouse, storeroom, and pigeon house. It had two storage places for pig food. It had a drying room and shops for fermenting and refining. This mission operated a store, infirmary, and chapel. An American visitor to St. Domingue in November 1802, H.P. Sannon,[26] alluded to the wealth of the Church in his description of the Hospital of the Fathers of Charity at the Cap (as Cap-Haïtien is sometimes called) which he termed superb. Its gardens, statues, and fountains were "achieved with all the magnificence of the vast revenues of the proprietors."

The Jesuits settled in the Cap outside the city in 1704.[27] But by 1747, they had acquired an extensive domain inside the city limits—five blocks long and two blocks wide. Their two-story-high church had a panoramic view of the city.

In contrast to these institutions, certain clergy were not so well off. Some were poorly paid and others apparently simply squandered their salaries. Historical documents include numerous letters from priests in St. Domingue beseeching relatives and congregations in France to send them additional funds.[28] Father Gourjan de Romerière wrote to Bishop de Sartine of the Community of St. Roch in Paris on 24 September 1777, saying that he needed more money; his father had almost become a pauper supporting him in St. Domingue.

With the continued influx of slaves and colonists, the Church put an end to free services for the slaves[29] and began to find extra-legal methods to raise money. In the process, the Church came up with some novel fundraising techniques. In one scheme, two citizens would be appointed as assistants to work with the priests; chosen from a pool of non-practitioners and non-Catholics, they could be expected to pay to be relieved of their service.[30]

As the Jesuits departed St. Domingue in 1764, a secular clergy arrived. In 1768, a second mission of Capuchins arrived. The presence of less disciplined and committed clergy led to a decline in the moral tone of the Church.

Clerical Conduct and its Repercussions

The early clergy in St. Domingue consequently left a blemished record. Certain priests simply lacked apostolic passion.[31] Some had been sent to the colony as punishment for misdemeanors at home. A number of priests had been defrocked and others were not clergy at all. Their reasons for coming to St. Domingue varied. For many, the motivations were similar to those of other settlers who came for diversion from the confines of the metropolis, for adventure, and wealth.

The historian C.L.R. James concluded that "instead of being a moderating influence, they [the clergy] were notorious for their irreverence and degeneracy."[32] Bishop Jan cites a letter from a Mr. Pouancey written on 30 January 1681 concerning the Capuchins,[33] which said, "It's frightening to see here priests as debauched as these are. Most are apostates, out of their convents for libertinage, and people here have little respect for them." Father Adolphe Cabon refers to a letter written by the Marquis de Choiseal on 7 April 1794[34] that said that since the expulsion of the Jesuits, most priests in St. Domingue have behaved so indecently that the inhabitants and negroes have lost all of the religious sentiment that the Jesuits gave them. Moreau de Saint Méry's criticism of the Dominicans, the missionaries of Port-au-Prince, was less severe.[35] He writes that they generally won the esteem of their flock, even if they did not always obey the vows. However, they made too much noise and went around armed, without written permission.[36] A review of the contemporary literature[37] indicates that certain orders were more upstanding than others. The Jesuits' reputation had generally been good. On the other hand, the Capuchins and Trinitarians, who split up the Jesuits' realm, were viewed as lacking the same religious zeal and not being of the same caliber.

It is difficult to assess the relative behavior of the priests and their impact on the population. From these above, some surely behaved badly and provided poor examples to their followers. However, had there not been some exemplary priests, it is probable that all of the clergy would have been killed in the course of the revolution and that Catholicism would have perished with them.

As we have seen, anticlericalism, stemming from the French Revolution, had an impact on the Church in Latin America in the eighteenth century, and St. Domingue was not immune. Anticlericalism has continued to play a role in Haiti as a consequence of Church behavior and its responses to Freemasonry, Protestantism, and Voodoo. A strong wave of anticlericalism swept over Haiti following the American occupation in response to Church sympathy with the occupation force and its involvement in the antisuperstition campaign. François Duvalier was able to play on the lingering anticlericalism to maintain control. During the Jean-Claude Duvalier administration, the activist sectors of the Church were motivated to commit themselves to the country's poor partly to overcome this legacy.

Catholicism was a needless nuisance and expense to the plantation owners who regarded their slaves as chattel. Laws allowing slaves to attend weekly mass and prohibiting work on the sabbath usurped their control and deprived them of revenue. Supplemental charges for baptisms, confirmations, and burials were doubly insulting to the planters. The planters were consequently quite susceptible to the anticlericalism that was emanating from Europe, and in particular, from France, in the eighteenth century.

By the mid-eighteenth century, the inhabitants of St. Domingue had begun to feel some of the effects of the Enlightenment. They knew about the *Philosophes* such as Montesquieu, Voltaire, and Rousseau, who championed progress, science, reason, and civilization. They were aware of the ideas concerning religious liberty and separation of Church and State; priests were held in increasing contempt. The French government found it impossible to deal with the spiritual law of Rome[38] and on 30 December 1792, the Legislative Assembly passed an antireligious law suppressing the Apostolic Prefects in the French colonies.

An early slave prayer even called for "throwing away the symbol of the god of the whites (the cross)."[39] When slaves revolted, Churches and Church possessions were often targeted. The Catholic Church in Port-au-Prince was spared when the city was burned in 1791, although its documents were destroyed.[40] The Church in Cap-Haïtien was burned in 1793, but not before its belongings were removed for sale at auction.[41] Theft of Church possessions was widespread.

A number of the revolutionary leaders, such as Rigaud, Plverel, and Sonthonax, also tried to destroy Catholicism. Rigaud, whom Bishop Jan[42] refers to as a "priest-killer," forbade the teaching of any religious dogma in schools, except the existence of God.[43] Sonthonax sold off Church belongings in the Cap in 1796 for a mere thirty dollars.[44]

Toussaint L'Ouverture may have had a lot to do with the Church not being banished altogether from St. Domingue. Regarded as a true believer and a devout, Jesuit-trained Catholic, on 19 November 1796, he wrote to Abbey Gregoire asking him to select twelve priests for the island. Addressing the newly freed slaves, he urged them to thank God for their liberation, saying: "God wanted and ordered a revolution."[45] While stationed in Gonaïves in 1794, Toussaint was known to have retained the services of a priest.[46]

Despite his piety, Toussaint L'Ouverture kept a tight rein on the Church. His Constitution controlled the administration of the clergy and prohibited it from forming an association. He had a law enacted on 5 May 1793 that appropriated Church possessions, limited priests to one dwelling per parish, and prohibited them from wearing a religious habit.[47] The Ordinance of 1794[48] tightened regulations adopted in 1781 allowing the Apostolic Prefect to propose new priests, but permitting the governor to accept or reject them.

The Church sustained some severe blows, but it survived. The National Council's decree[49] on 5 October 1797 required each department to have a bishop. According to Article VI of the 9 May 1801 Constitution, the Catholic religion was to be the only publicly professed religion in the colony. Article VII[50] established that each parish would maintain the religion, and its ministers would be paid from vestry profits. Article VIII decreed that the government would assign priests and determine the length of their service.

Most priests left the island following the 22 November 1791 insurrection, either because they feared for their lives or were unsympathetic to the prospect of a free black nation. Sixteen priests were listed as "lost" in northern St. Domingue.[51] While a few of them may have been killed, nearly all probably returned to France.

The Church in St. Domingue was racist or, at any rate, racially insensitive and, as we will see, that situation has continued until recently. Many Churchmen owned slaves and few protested the system. After independence, periodic recommendations to create a Haitian clergy to supplement the inadequate number and quality of foreign priests were never seriously adopted. Resentment against the white, French clergy is a continuing theme in Haitian history. When François Duvalier Haitianized the hierarchy in 1966, he did more to create a Haitian clergy and address the charges that the Church was irrelevant to Haitian society than the Church had done in the previous century. However, while many of the activist priests who contributed to the overthrow of Jean-Claude Duvalier were Haitian, some were not, such as the Belgian director of *Radio Soleil*, Hugo Triest.

A few priests and Religious did remain, and their fates varied. The Sisters of Notre Dame at Cap-Haïtien were among those who decided to stay.[52] Initially spared during the insurrection, they were tortured and murdered two years later on 20 June 1793. When the British left in 1798, the Apostolic Prefect went with them. Father le Cun later wrote that many of his former colleagues who remained behind had their throats slit, and all but three Churches were burned.[53]

Some of the priests who stayed were opportunists who cast their lot with the apparent victor, so that in places where the whites remained in control, they followed the whites, and elsewhere, they attached themselves to the blacks.[54] There was the curious case of Bishop Mauviel,[55] who appeared initially to be a defender of the slaves. When he arrived in St. Domingue in 1801, six priests signed a protest against him, in part because he suggested having black priests. Taking an active part in politics on behalf of the former slaves, he was an accomplice to the murder of Leclerc at Cap-Haïtien on 1 November 1802. But finally, it was Mauviel who betrayed Jean-Jacques

Dessalines to Napoleon Bonaparte and revealed the location of his fortifications and defense plans.[56]

According to C.L.R. James, some Jesuits joined the slave rebellion in 1791.[57] Michael Laguerre writes that priests of Trou and Dondons joined the slaves in their revolt.[58] In any case, only twelve priests were left on the island by 1797, six in the south and six in the north.[59]

Voodoo: Origins, Practices, and Importance

Voodoo has a long history in Haiti. It arrived with the first slaves and has remained the religion of most Haitians despite repeated efforts to eradicate it. With few exceptions, it was publicly scorned and viewed with suspicion until François Duvalier gave it his protection and encouragement, partly as a ballast against the Church and partly as another source of support. Voodoo was instrumental to the overthrow of Jean-Claude Duvalier. Jean-Claude neglected and alienated black, Voodoo-practicing Haitians; and subsequently, they did not stand behind him when he was under fire.

Voodoo is a composite religion containing a mixture of African and Catholic elements. Its African origins are in the countries along the slave coast of West Africa, and its name is derived from a Dahomean word for spirit. According to believers, Voodoo began, and its connection with Africa occurred, after God had created land, animals, and twelve apostles.[60] The apostles turned out to be an argumentative lot who challenged God and rebelled against him. In punishment, He sent them to Guinea, where their number multiplied. They and their descendents became the *loa* or spirits who continue to help their servitors when they are in trouble. Of the original apostles, one who refused to go to Guinea became involved with sorcery and took the name Lucifer. Later, God created the twelve apostles we know.

A high percentage of the slaves in St. Domingue came from the Congo and Dahomey, so it is the religion and culture of these two countries that were predominant in the colony. In Africa, Voodoo had been a snake cult,[61] but as it evolved in St. Domingue, this aspect lost importance. Voodoo arrived on the island with the first slaves in the mid-1600s and was outlawed immediately.

In Voodoo, there is an impersonal god, known as *Le Bon Dieu*, or The Good God. In addition, there are lesser entities, the *loa*, who are intermediaries from God. A preoccupation of believers is to keep the *loa* satisfied, which is referred to as "serving the *loa*." There are two classes of *loa* and each has its own characteristics. They look different—they wear distinctive clothes and colors. Their culinary tastes also differ—some like chicken, while others prefer pork. The Rada *loa* are from Africa and the Petro *loa* are indigenous. Their personalities differ—some are good, some are pranksters, and some are bad, but any of them can cause problems if not properly served.

Voodoo is an animist religion in which special significance is paid to fire, water, and death. Charms, magic, and sorcery are used to alter luck and fortune—even after death. In the absence of the proper religious preparation, a dead person may rise from the grave to become a *zombie*—a member of the nocturnal work force of the living dead.

During the French Colonial period, only the *marons*, or escaped slaves, were able to practice Voodoo in its entirety. Colonial law forbade it, but slaves were allowed to get together on Saturday evenings to dance, which allowed them to perpetuate certain aspects of their religion. With independence, Voodoo could be practiced more openly. The shift away from plantations to subsistence farming, caused some adaptation in Voodoo. As a consequence, it became more family-oriented. Certain *loa* tended to become associated with particular families. In recent years, as the result of urbanization and tourism, Voodoo has undergone additional changes, taking on a more public presence, at least in the cities. Because of this adaptability, Voodoo specialist Michel Laguerre refers to Voodoo as a living religion.[62]

The Voodoo ceremony begins in a *hounfort*, or temple, with prayers, blessings, songs, and candle lighting. The *houngan*, or priest, draws a *vévé*, or tracery, on the floor representing the *loa* who is being asked to appear. A small animal—a goat or chicken, is offered some food. If it eats, the *loa* will appear, and dancing and possession follow. The *loa* makes its presence known by "mounting" the *serviteur*, or possessed person, who has invoked its presence.

Deprived of their native religion, the speedily baptized and often haphazardly converted slaves adopted the accoutrements of Catholicism for their own purposes. Because there was no official Catholic presence in Haiti from independence until 1860, and very little unofficial presence, the distinctions between the two religions were not reinforced for sixty years.

Voodoo incorporated the Catholic saints; Mary's image stands for the Dahomean *loa*, Erzuli. Erzuli is pictured as a rich, beautiful, long-haired, charming, red-eyed, and hot-tempered *mulatta* who lives in the sea. She has a penchant for lovers, a taste for lotions and perfumes, and an appetite for duck and pork. Other Voodoo borrowings include the Apostles' Creed, Hail Mary, Catholic songs, the Lord's Prayer, genuflections, blessings, holy water, and the cross. The cross became a sign of the *loa* Baron Samedi and a symbol of treacherous crossroads, a particular Voodoo concern.[63] The Voodoo service resembles a mass to the extent that Voodoo participants have to be baptized Catholics.

It was a Voodoo ceremony that triggered the insurrection that led to independence.[64] Revolutionary efforts in 1691 and 1696 were also organized by Voodoo leaders.

Beginning with the 1805 Constitution, the Haitian presidents prohibited Voodoo. The early leaders considered it to be a potential threat. From Pétion's and Boyer's presidencies until the government of Dumarsais Estimé, it was additionally scorned as a lower class phenomenon.

The Church was unwilling to compromise with Voodoo, given its historical mission of "inspiring faith in the true God in the Africans, to take away their idolatry and make them persevere until death in the Christian religion."[65] François Gayot, the archbishop of Cap-Haïtien, writes that the longevity of Voodoo shows that society is not meeting peoples' needs.[66] It also appears to indicate that the Church has not been an entirely satisfactory alternative.

THE CHURCH FROM 1804-1860

Official Protection and Other Problems

Rulers have historically sought to control and limit the role of the Catholic Church in Haiti. In order to understand government resentment toward the Church and Church posture during the Jean-Claude Duvalier administration, it is important to review the legal bases of the Church presence in Haiti.

Jean-Jacques Dessalines appears to have hated whites; his 22 February 1804 decree called for killing all of them.[67] However, Madiou and Ardouin claim that he wanted to spare doctors, pharmacists, and priests. Perhaps he did, because following independence, he exempted some clergy from his law that forbade whites from becoming citizens. He permitted the Church to exist and even granted it some favors, but, like Toussaint L'Ouverture, he limited its jurisdiction and took control of its operation. The president set jurisdictional limits for the clergy and appointed parish priests[68]—an example of the latter was his choice of a former drum major to become the parish priest of St. Marc.

His May 1805 Constitution further circumscribed the limits of the Church and the authority of the State. The Church and State would be separate. Article XV[69] said it succinctly: "The law admits no dominant religion." Article XIV[70] made marriage a civil matter and permitted divorce.

Dessalines reverted to the *Ancien Régime* custom of having his own prayer stool and armchair placed near the altar in Church. When he crowned himself emperor, the service included a *Te Deum*.[71] While the

Church must have been happy at these signs of personal devotion, it resented his appointments of priests, the constitutional clause that allowed divorce, and the amendment that accorded illegitimate children equal inheritance rights.[72]

Henry Christophe's involvement with Catholicism was similar to his predecessors'. He took part in it, used it for ceremonial occasions, and controlled its operations. When he crowned himself King on 2 June 1811, it was in a Church with a mass and considerable religious pomp.[73] It was Christophe who had the massive and monumental Church of San Souci built in Cap-Haïtien.

Like his predecessor, Henry Christophe regarded himself as the head of the Church; and consequently, he ordered priests about, appointing and dismissing them. On 7 April 1811, Christophe chose an archbishop for Cap-Haïtien and bishops for Gonaïves, Port-au-Prince and Cayes, and "welcomed all ecclesiastics with good certificates of morality and conduct."[74] Despite the power he was prepared to exercise, in 1814 there were only three priests in northern Haiti, including Archbishop Corneille Brelle.

His Constitution in 1811 showed some preference for Catholicism; but allowed other religions to exist, if not practiced publicly. Despite the restrictions, there is some evidence that Christophe, who was an Anglophile, might have favored Protestantism. Poisset Roman believes that Henry Christophe hoped to introduce Protestantism into the schools through the use of Bibles as texts for translation.[75] Protestantism had some attractions— it was not associated with the French, and its followers had the reputation for morality.[76]

Alexander Pétion also gave Catholicism preferred treatment on paper; his Constitution made Catholicism the official religion of western Haiti. However, the Church was disturbed by a clause that provided equal inheritance rights to illegitimate children and by Pétion's apparent receptiveness to Protestantism. He invited Protestant missionaries to Haiti and in 1817, John Brown and James Catts from Bristol arrived to establish the country's first Protestant institution, the Methodist Wesleyan Church of England.[77] The president even bent the Constitution, which expressly forbade whites from owning property in Haiti,[78] by allowing the Methodists to establish schools.

During President Boyer's quarter-century rule (1818–1843), he manipulated the Church and flirted with Protestantism. Boyer chose the priests, and he tried to select the archbishops. When the island was reunited in 1822, he wanted Archbishop Valera from Santo Domingo to come to Port-au-Prince, but Valera resisted. In retaliation, Boyer promulgated a law on 24 July 1824 declaring that all ecclesiastical property belonged to the State, and with that, he virtually closed down the Church in Santo Domingo. Following the death of a second vicar who declined the president's invitation to move to Port-au-Prince, Boyer denied him a State funeral. Ultimately, Jean-Pierre Boyer got his archbishop, Father Joseph Salgado.

Bishop England was sent to Haiti by the pope in 1834 to reduce tensions and implement a concordat. Between 1834 and Boyer's ouster from office in 1843, five papal delegations went to Haiti and the concordat became the subject of almost constant negotiations. Like some of his predecessors, President Boyer appeared to welcome the Protestants.[79] The Quaker missionary, Grellet, recalled that after he conducted a service in the cathedral in Port-au-Prince, Boyer and most of his officer corps came up to thank him, and subsequently agreed to pay half the rent on a religious school in the capital.[80] Even so, when Pope Gregory wrote to President Boyer in March 1847 to say that he was sending a religious mission to Haiti, the president sent an encouraging reply.[81] He was "convinced that the people of Haiti are essentially Catholic, that they love religion and feel the need of it as he does."

The Catholic Church received support from the early Haitian presidents, but despite official protection, it faced problems in Haiti. The times, the Vatican, religious competition, and the Church itself all complicated matters. The period was rough for the Church in Haiti. The country did not settle down immediately. Within the first forty years, it successively split in half, captured Santo Domingo, reunited, and then lost its acquisition. To varying degrees, the early leaders[82] feared the French would try to reconquer the former colony, and regarded the French clergy as a mechanism of subversion.

Anticlerical, secular views that arrived in Haiti in the eighteenth century became widespread by the early nineteenth century. They also caused suspicion and closer scrutiny of Church activities as did the introduction of two competing movements in Haiti: Freemasonry and Protestantism.

Freemasonry became very popular in nineteenth-century Haiti while Protestantism took hold more slowly.[83] Freemasonry was an immediate concern for the Church, while Protestantism was not viewed as a serious competitor until the early twentieth century.

The breakdown of the plantation system and the dispersion of the population to rural areas favored the entrenchment of Voodoo. Voodoo became a source of increasing embarrassment to the Church because it did not disappear on contact with Catholicism. Where conversions occurred, they were frequently to Protestantism. Following independence, the Vatican cut its ties to Haiti out of ire at laws that made the Church subservient to the state, and allowed divorce, required civil marriage ceremonies, and gave inheritance benefits to illegitimate children. Bereft of official relations, the Vatican lacked much ability to influence the State, or other countries in their dealings with Haiti.[84]

Lacking a comprehensive plan for the evangelization of the population, the limited number of exclusively French-speaking priests tended to cluster in urban areas, ignoring the needs of the rural majority. To make matters worse, the new nation became a dumping ground for other countries' undesirable clergy, and a place where clerical behavior went unsupervised.

Church-State Relations

Vatican disagreements with the Republic led to an interval of twenty years in which there were no official relations and fifty-six years without a concordat to regulate the affiliation. Relations were finally resumed in 1824 when Leo XII was pope. His successor, Pius VIII, furthered the process of *rapprochement* by sending a mediator to Haiti. The succeeding pope, Gregory XVI, apparently took the situation seriously because he wrote to President Boyer in 1841, saying: "We've learned that the Catholic religion has been leaning little by little toward ruin in the Republic you govern, and does not have the influence to correct bad conduct, reform morals—the eternal health of souls is at great risk." He would not "die happy if God didn't permit him the consolation of seeing this country, so sad and lacking in good priests, become Christian again."[85]

An incident in 1852 pointed to the need for improved Church-State relations. President Faustin Soulouque intended to become Emperor Faustin and wanted a bishop to participate in his crowning, but the Vatican would not oblige.[86] Soulouque countered by sending one of his own priests, Father Cessens, to Rome to become a bishop, but he was turned away. Cessens returned to Haiti pretending to have been ordained, but the subterfuge was discovered and Soulouque was obliged to make do without a bishop at his ceremony. Shortly thereafter, the Vatican relented and sent one, but the Emperor was too angry for negotiations concerning the concordat to continue during his reign.

This period was characterized by strain and resentment as the two institutions sought to stake out claims to their own turf. The Church viewed the naming of priests and handling of marriages and funerals as its business. It opposed divorce and legal recognition of illegitimate children. The State regarded its authority as supreme and demanded subservience whenever evangelical issues were not involved. It claimed the right to approve bulls from Rome and ecclesiastical writing, authorize taxes, start schools and seminaries, and appoint parish priests.[87]

The Catholic Clergy

The formal Haitian clergy played a major role in the overthrow of Jean-Claude Duvalier. A truly Haitian clergy only began in the 1920s and became numerically significant merely in the 1950s. By the 1970s, Haitians were well-integrated into the Church. They contributed to the institution's understanding of the country and its problems and they had a number of advantages: they spoke Creole, the language of all Haitians; were familiar with the country's social and political dynamics; and as a result, were particularly committed to finding solutions to its problems.

There was no regular and authorized clergy in Haiti between 1804 and 1860. Those who were there were mainly French.[88] Some of them had come directly, while others arrived via the French Antilles or the United States. Finally, there were a few South American and Corsican priests.

A serious lack of priests led to circumstances where former slaves,[89] who had had some contact with the Church, ran the religious services. An obvious solution to the shortage of bona fide clergy would have been to train Haitians. The idea was initially broached in 1816 in connection with constitutional reform, but took more than a century to happen[90]—even though the arguments were good. The papal emissary, Bishop England suggested training nationals in the course of his 1833–1834 negotiations and even brought along a black, non-Haitian priest in an attempt "to inspire the Haitians."[91] A Father Etcheverria wrote a letter from Haiti to a French seminary on 3 July 1848 requesting a black priest as soon as one finishes his preparation because, "a black priest would have more effect now than ten colored men," but he concluded by saying, "it was the tactic of the coloreds, or mulattos, to leave the blacks in profound ignorance and not allow them any influence."[92]

An indigenous clergy finally began to develop in the 1920s, but as late as the 1950s, only one-fifth were Haitian.[93] The delay in the development of a Haitian clergy had to do with fashion, prejudice, and Church laws. France and things French have had a *cachet* in Haiti. The Catholic clergy in Haiti had always been white and foreign. Educated Haitians went into professions such as business, law, or diplomacy, not the priesthood. There was no infrastructure for developing an indigenous priesthood. There were no preparatory schools for potential seminarians and no seminaries. Finally, Catholic regulations prohibited theological students who were illegitimate or whose parents had not been good Christians. In a country where legal marriages were the exception and Voodoo the norm, these sanctions were significant.

Consequently, the country continued to get priests from abroad and reports reveal the results. Father A. Cabon describes the clergy, "the more a priest seemed unfaithful to his duties as a man and ecclesiastic, the better he was suited for Haiti."[94] The papal envoy to Haiti in the 1840s, Father Tisserant, wrote a letter to the Office of Propaganda in Rome describing the religious situation in Haiti.[95] Approximately forty priests were spread out over fifty-two parishes. Of these priests, about twelve were good. The majority of the remaining priests did not wear habits, had lewd conduct, and had learned not only not to be embarrassed by their depravity but to exult in it. The official government order for the day for priests planning to attend the crowning of President Soulouque was to refrain from getting drunk.[96]

Poor clerical behavior probably offended and alienated some Catholics. Bishop England's coadjutor, Bishop Clancy, who was in Haiti in the 1830s to negotiate a concordat, wrote:

> The people [in Haiti] did not have any confidence in the clergy, generally speaking. As a result, I had, with my chaplain, Mr. Byrne, and a Corsican priest, to hear each morning and each evening for four weeks three hours a day, confessions of twenty to seventy year old adults. I administered confirmation to seven hundred and fifty men, women and children of all colors from all parts of the country. Five hundred received the Eucharist and I have the firm conviction that if I'd had with me ten more priests in whom they could have confidence for confession, I would have had five to six thousand persons for confirmation and communion rites. I had to turn hundreds away for lack of time.[97]

Church Competitors

Church history in Haiti has been punctuated by rivalries with Freemasonry, Protestantism, and Voodoo and overcoming this embarrassing legacy was relevant to its involvement in the overthrow of Jean-Claude Duvalier.

Church relations with Freemasonry were unremittingly hostile from the arrival of Freemasons in the eighteenth through the nineteenth century. By the mid-twentieth century, Freemasonry in Haiti had become largely ceremonial, although as recently as 1988, Leslie Manigat stirred old Church jealousy when he wore the mason insignia to his inauguration.

Protestantism arrived in Haiti in the early nineteenth century. While some Haitian leaders were partial to it, even those who were not used it as leverage against the Church. Jean-Claude Duvalier's government used this tactic, reviving old rivalries, thus limiting religious cooperation against the regime.

Voodoo arrived in Haiti soon after the Church and has continued to be its most enduring antagonist. Jean-Claude Duvalier lost an important source of support that his father garnered by his failure to cultivate its leaders and followers. Following the ouster of Duvalier, many *houngans*, *mambos*, and other Voodoo figures were *désoukéd*. Some people accused the Church of instigating the attacks, while others only blamed it for complicity.

The Ancient Free and Accepted Masons, Freemasons, or simply Masons, were originally stone workers and cathedral builders in Europe around A.D. 900, where they formed guilds, established organizations called lodges, and developed a philosophy promoting brotherhood and morality. By the time the age of Cathedral building had ended, Masonry had evolved into a fraternal and social organization.[98] Anyone who believed in one God could become a Mason, although some religions still forbid it.

By 1748, there were Freemasons in Cap-Haïtien.[99] Freemasonry became so popular that within fifty years, there were Freemasons in each parish in St. Domingue and it was drawing in almost everyone, including members of the clergy, men, women, and children. Most upper class men were Masons. Women named their children after classical characters rather than saints.

Freemasonry became an annoyance to the Church. Not only did the Freemasons usurp parishioners, they took over Churches. Stories abound of Freemasons who invaded Churches to hold their own services. The Church did its best to block them from its doors and the country. Father Tisserant, the apostolic prefect for Haiti, tried to get a law to prohibit pro-Masonic priests and Templars from coming to Haiti. In 1844, he was able to get a decree saying that Masons could only attend church services as observers.

The Protestant denominations went to Haiti under some unusual circumstances. An English ship captain plying Haitian waters around the turn of the nineteenth century asked whether the government would welcome Methodist missionaries. Following a favorable response, they arrived. In another instance, a box of Pentecostal literature inexplicably ended up in Haiti, making converts of the two Haitians who found it a couple of years before the first Pentecostal missionaries arrived.

Protestants began to come to Haiti during the Christophe and Pétion presidencies. These predominantly British and American missionaries were generally welcomed by the government and people, and even by some members of the Catholic clergy, but not always. In a few cases, they were persecuted and forced to depart. Two Quaker missionaries, Etienne de Grellet, a Frenchman, and John Hancock, an Englishman, landed in Les Cayes in 1816, working their way to Port-au-Prince, overcoming the "*malice*" of some priests and Spanish nuns, and hearing from people along the route how "disgusted (they were) with their Roman priests whose conduct they considered a reproach to morality."[100] They preached in the cathedral of Port-au-Prince without objection from the principal priest "whose preoccupation was spending his annual salary."[101] Encouraged by the president and the military high command, they visited schools where they found "the most vicious and obscene books as well as the works of some deist and French philosophers," and they replaced those books with Bibles.

John Brown and James Catts, two English missionaries, arrived at about the same time,[102] having received assurances of government welcome from Secretary of State Ingenac and an invitation to start schools in Haiti. The two established the first Protestant church in Port-au-Prince in 1817. Everything fell apart for them the second year when a crazed Methodist killed his mother, thereby disgracing the missionaries, who were forced to depart. President Boyer apparently bore them no ill since he sent along a five hundred pound check for their ministry when they left. In 1819, two new Methodist ministers, Mssrs. Harvey and Jones, went to Cap-Haïtien where they were welcomed King Christophe. After some persecution, their congregations grew.

The American Baptists sent Thomas Paul, a black minister from Massachusetts, to Cap-Haïtien in 1823. Welcomed by President Boyer, he established some congregations before departing six months later. With time, the Baptists, Methodists, Pentecostals, Seventh Day Adventists, Episcopalians, and others have established roots in Haiti, settled, spread out, undergone many schisms, and produced numerous new denominations.

Protestants were regarded as ethical, economically astute, and upwardly mobile. The government sought them out because of their reputation for honesty; the Methodist minister, Jean Charles Pressoir, was asked to go to the port each Monday to verify the amount of coffee that was being exported.[103] It became clear to the Church that Protestantism was attractive, not only to the uncommitted and Voodoo practitioners, but to Catholics and was turning into a threat to Church membership and privilege. The Vatican envoy who negotiated the concordat wrote to Rome in 1859, saying the logical consequence of the presence of the bad priests was the spread of Protestantism.[104]

Despite their ethical attractiveness, the Protestants' early success in Haiti was limited by several factors. First, they were demanding and strait-laced. In addition, they faced hostility from the Church and sometimes from governments. Finally, they had to confront an historic Haitian bias for things French. Protestantism required followers to renounce other forms of worship. Converts were required to throw away symbols belonging to the Catholic and Voodoo religions. One minister in Cap-Haïtien lost some of his audience when he asked his congregation to give up jewelry.[105]

A Father Jeremie denounced Methodism from the pulpit for three successive weeks beginning on 16 January 1820.[106] "It's a bad religion. Those who follow it will never see God's face but will be eternally condemned to damnation of Hell." Cardinal Fonana, the prefect for propaganda, wrote on 18 May 1820, "a number of heretical preachers have landed [in Haiti] and are trying to divert the inhabitants from the Catholic faith."[107]

President Soulouque, later Emperor Faustin I, was particularly opposed to Protestantism, possibly concluding that people who could change their minds about religion might change them about emperors. In 1850, some Sunday worshipers were inducted into the military as they exited church.[108] On another occasion, he had a group of Protestants "dance to the sound of the drum."

An endemic problem that had to be faced in Haiti was the elite's cultural attachment to France, and by extension, Catholicism. In 1835, after nineteen years of missionary activity in Haiti, the Methodists had only acquired ninety converts.[109] In 1853, the number was two hundred and forty-one.[110]

The Protestant schools afforded a good opportunity for the missionaries to spread their message but this advantage was significantly reduced in 1860 with the conclusion of the Concordat. Subsequently, the number of Catholic schools increased, public schools decreased, and many of those that remained became entwined with the Church.

Voodoo persisted during the Colonial period largely because neither the planters nor the Church cared enough to genuinely convert the slaves. It became more entrenched in the first half of the nineteenth century due to the ruralization of Haiti, the minimal presence of the Church, and the virtual absence of government services, particularly in rural areas.

After independence, government policy was to break up large plantations. In the north, tracts of land were allotted to the military high command. In the south, estates were widely distributed. Ultimately, land was also parceled out in the north. The isolation of rural Haiti provided a congenial environment for the cultivation and preservation of Voodoo.

The Church in Haiti had reached its nadir by mid-century. It lacked power, authority, personnel, and scope—being almost exclusively urban. The Protestants were focusing their attention on the cities also, so Voodoo went largely unchallenged in the countryside.

The government also neglected rural Haiti, providing few schools, hospitals or clinics to the majority of the population. *Houngans* and *bocors*, or sorcerers, attended to the physical, emotional, educational, and social needs of most Haitians, supplying services in the absence of other institutions.

The Quest for Official Relations

It would be difficult if not impossible to understand the changes in relations between the Church and State in the 1970s without reviewing the extensive negotiations which produced the concordat and the problems which subsequently confronted the Church.

The schism between the Vatican and the Government of Haiti was a source of mutual concern and some embarrassment—the Church was acquiring a bad reputation in Europe, in part due to the behavior of priests in Haiti. Although the Vatican and Haiti opened negotiations in 1834, it took twenty-six years to get a concordat. The effort required three Haitian governments—those of Boyer, Hérard and Geffrard, two popes—Gregory XVI and Pius IX, seven diplomatic missions, and six papal negotiators. Vatican priorities included the development of an indigenous clergy, Church selection of clergy, and revocation of laws permitting divorce and civil marriages.

In 1834, Papal Envoy Bishop England produced a concordat for the pope.[111] Among the provisions: Article I made Catholicism the State religion. Article III allowed the president to name auxiliary envoys. Article IV permitted the bishops to choose clergy with presidential agreement. Article XII allowed bishops the right to raise money for their ministries with presidential approval. Article XV authorized the president to name administrators in the event of a prolonged absence of the principal priest. Once a concordat was in place, the president would allow Rome to choose the new archbishop.

This concordat failed because it did not include some of the provisions the Vatican decided were essential, including the right to name bishops and priests, renunciation of laws permitting divorce and civil marriage, and cessation of preferential treatment to Protestants.

In 1836, Bishop Clancy took over the negotiations but his mission failed on a procedural issue, the manner in which he had been appointed.[112] Negotiations resumed in April 1836 with Bishop England. A concordat was signed but ultimately rejected by the Commission of Cardinals because of its position, among other points, on marriage and divorce. On his third mission in March-April 1837, Bishop England negotiated a concordat that was on the verge of being signed when it was undermined by Boyer's Secretary General, Balthasar Ingenac, who was disgruntled at the Church for rejecting his choice of a parish priest for Port-au-Prince.[113]

In 1842, negotiations resumed with a new pope, Gregory XVI, and a new papal negotiator, Bishop Rosati. Their concordat called for free correspondence between Churchmen and Rome, presidential nomination of bishops with papal right of refusal, Church selection of priests with presidential right of refusal, and Church authority to raise money.[114] This version might have made it except for two events: the 1842 earthquake and the ouster of President Boyer the following year.

Father Tisserant took over the negotiations in 1843–1844 in an effort to conclude a concordat with interim President Charles Hérard. The Secretary of State presented a list of government concerns that were intended to limit Church functions.[115] The Church would not censor magistrates. Vatican bulls would not be made public prior to government approval. The Church would not name priests, start schools or seminaries without government approval, nor would it raise taxes under any circumstances. Nomination of priests turned out to be the insurmountable obstacle with this concordat, and the negotiator departed, only to perish at sea.

Negotiations continued from 1852 to 1859. However, the mission, led by Bishop Spaccapietra, was contentious and ultimately scuttled due to Soulouque's resentment at being denied a bishop for his crowning.[116] When new Haitian President F. N. Geffrard and new papal negotiator Pierre Faubert got together, they were successful. Not only did they complete a concordat, they did it in record time. It was signed within four months, on 28 March 1960 and ratified on 25 September 1860.[117]

In general, the government got more oversight authority than the Church wanted. The State would have the right to nominate bishops and clergy. According to Article IV, the president would select the archbishops and bishops, with papal approval, and the president alone would name the priests. Bishops and clergy would swear allegiance and fidelity to the government. The clergy could start new parishes, after notifying the president. The clergy would receive its support from curial funds. The Church would pray for the president. According to Article I, the Church would be the religion of the majority and Article XVI specified that laws would not be passed to its detriment.[118]

Some amendments, notes, additional agreements and protocols were added subsequently, but this concordat largely defines the relations between the Church and Haitian state. The Convention of 6 February 1861, established the limits of the dioceses and salary the treasury would pay for Haiti's bishops and archbishops. The Agreement on 17 June 1862 dealt with various items, including maintenance of the Petit Seminaire. The Protocols of 12 January and 15 August 1966, ratified the appointment of indigenous people to this hierarchy and reaffirmed the will of the Haitian government to provide the Catholic religion with special protection. The Agreement on 8 August 1984 modified Articles IV and V of the fundamental agreement concerning the nomination of bishops.

Regularizing relations between the Vatican and Rome led to increased interaction between Church and state, particularly in the area of education. It resulted in better quality priests, but not immediately. Anti-concordatory priests remained in the country and continued to object to the document through the presidency of Nord Alexis, which ended in 1908.[119]

THE CHURCH FROM 1860 TO 1915

Institutionalization

In order to understand the Church participation in the overthrow of Jean-Claude Duvalier, it is important to recall the multiple bases for Church identification with Haiti. Catholicism was the official religion during the Colonial period. Since independence, most Haitian constitutions have granted Catholicism a special place among the nation's religions. Since 1860, the concordat has guaranteed Catholicism preeminence and protection.

The period from 1860 to 1915 was important for the Church in Haiti. Having finally regularized its relations with the State in 1860, the Church was able to turn its attention to the problems of institutionalization, expansion, and proselytization. The Church became aware of the magnitude of its task and of the obstacles it faced. Haiti presented environmental and medical hazards. There were emotional and monetary strains. The work was hard and life expectancy short. Relations with the state alternated between tense and cooperative. Religious opposition did not diminish.

Haiti was not a healthy place due to malaria, tetanus, tuberculosis, parasites, and epidemics of yellow fever. In 1890, a tally showed that twenty-five priests, approximately one-fourth of those in Haiti, had died there in the previous five years.[120] Environmental disasters were frequent. They included fires that destroyed whole towns, earthquakes, cyclones, floods, and droughts.[121] A cyclone in 1908 damaged a number of towns including Plaisance, Pilate, Borgue, and Fort Liberté. In 1906, the bishopric in Cap-Haïtien was destroyed as the result of a minor accident—fire caused by a spilled gasoline lamp. In 1865, Haiti suffered a civil war, fire in Port-au-Prince, and drought.

The conditions of life for clergy in Haiti depended on their rank and location. Some bishops and priests living in urban areas enjoyed an economic standard of life surpassing what they experienced in their country of origin. For priests in rural parishes, however, conditions were primitive and lonely. In 1900, there was only one priest in Vallière for a population of four thousand. Thomasique was served by a priest from La Source, twelve hours away by horse.[122] A dirge for a priest who died in Haiti said, "He left his homeland, his family and his friends, he crossed the seas, braved fatigue and endangered his life."[123] Annual religious retreats were held in order to give priests a chance to get together and regroup. The theme for the first retreat in 1869 was "To Renew Ourselves."[124] The theme in 1893 was based on Jesus's instructions to his apostles before sending them to preach the evangel. In 1904, it was religious indifference.[125]

Getting to and from Haiti was risky, and travel even within the country was hazardous. Churchmen typically made their rounds on horseback, which involved fording rivers and riding long distances while exposed to the elements.

A priority of the post-concordat Church was to increase the number of clergy in Haiti. Two modes were indicated: recruiting foreign priests and training Haitians. The clergy increased during this period, albeit slowly. In 1916, some parishes had gone without a priest for two years.[126] Bishop Jan

wrote in 1875 that there were two reasons why the Church had trouble getting and holding priests, "the grueling work and killing climate."[127] One
priest, Father Kerhousse, wrote, while dying of a fever, "the missionary isn't
as the imagination and poetry make one think . . . it's a condemned person
with all the physical and moral privations, a victim who suffers slowly and
dies little by little without radiance (éclat), or glory, and often despised."[128]

To acquire clergy for this difficult place, the bishop from Cap-Haïtien
made annual recruiting trips abroad. His efforts were only modestly
rewarded. In 1865,[129] there were only fifty-six priests in the country.
Fourteen new priests came from France between 1870 and 1871.[130]
However, due to deaths, the total number dropped to fifty-seven by the end
of 1871. By 1874, the number had increased to eighty-six.[131]

Bishop Kersuzan went to France, sometimes Belgium and "even
England," in his quest for priests.[132] In France, he also visited seminaries in
order to encourage these institutions to train priests for Haiti. He successfully worked out arrangements with the Congregation of Jesus at Calvaire
Pantchateau in Nantes and a new seminary at St. Jacques de Guiciar.[133]

Training priests abroad or within the country was not very successful.
Haiti lacked seminarians, in part because of the demanding regulations that
have already been mentioned. By the time St. Martial opened in 1896, these
rules had been changed; seminarians were only required to be children of
Christians—illegitimacy was overlooked.[134] Another problem was that the
country lacked seminaries until 1873. In that year, the Grand Seminaire
opened with an enrollment of twenty-five students.[135] In 1896, a presemi-
nary program began at St Martial.[136]

The Church was in an active construction phase. It built chapels,
Churches, and schools all over Haiti. In 1871, there were only five schools
in the archdiocese. By 1921, the Brothers of Christian Instruction were
operating twenty-eight schools, the Daughters of Wisdom, twenty-five, and
the Daughters of Mary, two.[137] On 24 August 1913, the Church signed an
agreement with the government to provide public education in the countryside. These primary institutions, to be known as "rural presbytery
schools," would be under the direction of parish priests and the control of
school inspectors.[138] The following year, the Church established an education system in the cities, mostly Port-au-Prince and Gonaïves.

By 1917, however, only the urban schools were succeeding. It was hard
to get teachers to move to rural areas. Consequently, the gap between met-
ropolitan and provincial Haiti continued to widen.

The problems of institutionalization are evident in a 19 March 1873 cir-
cular issued by Bishop Guilloux of Port-au-Prince. He wrote that the
Church confronted three problems: lack of piety and an excess of
Protestants and Freemasons. The bishop attributed the lack of piety to the
French Revolution and Church subservice to the State. Throughout this

period, the Church tried to overcome these obstacles by stressing the importance of the sacraments in its sermons, Pastoral Letters, and synods. In 1891, Bishop Kersuzan preached a sermon at Ranquette against concubinage.[139] On 6 January 1896, he issued a pastoral letter against superstition.[140] At a synod session in 1908, he lamented that many children did not continue their religious education after first communion.[141] He pronounced a religious retreat in 1909 a failure because 161 girls attended, but only twenty-four boys. Boys and men were derelict in their religious duties, and Bishop Jan sarcastically concluded that a young father in Haiti who fulfilled his Christian duties caused a scandal.[142] In 1912, a Church publication, Le Bulletin Notre Dame, undertook a campaign against "Protestants, indecent fashions, and Voodoo.[143]

The Church offensive appeared to have some success. By 1890, 15 percent of the births at Cap-Haïtien were legitimate; the highest rate in the country.[144] In 1892 in Petite Anse, there were 211 baptisms, 6 legitimate births, 10 marriages and 83 communions.[145]

Economic Challenges

Despite Church, chapel, and school construction, the economic circumstances of the Church during this period appear to have been tight. On occasion, the Church in Cap-Haïtien levied taxes for various services and encouraged donations and bequeaths.

In 1883, the Church asked for one *piastre* per baptism, fifty *centimes* of which were to go to the bishopric.[146] In 1890, the Church in Cap-Haïtien levied a surtax on baptisms to help defray the costs of home leave for the priests, their medical expenses, and the maintenance of the parish.[147] In 1907, it imposed a two *gourde* tax on all religious services, sung masses, and first class burials in Cap-Haïtien—as a means to raise funds to rebuild the bishopric.[148]

The Church encouraged donations. In 1907, a Haitian family gave the Church land to build a chapel and rectory.[149] In 1893, a retired French nun donated property in Britanny to construct a seminary, St. Jacques de Guiclar, that would train priests for Haiti.[150]

Church-State Relations, 1860-1915

The summary consideration given to the various presidencies and virtual lack of attention devoted to foreign affairs in Church chronicles is remarkable. In 1914, Bishop Jan's observations about a new Haitian president are covered by a single sentence. "On 23 February, *Te Deum* for General Oreste Zamor, elected President of the Republic."[151]

Church-State relations, although initially strained by efforts to undue the concordat, unpleasant episodes, and intimation of Church resentments, were generally cooperative. President Geffrard was ousted from the presidency in 1867 by people who hoped to dismantle the concordat. His successor, General Sylvain Salnave disapproved of the concordat, but he was overthrown. In 1888, two generals, S. Telemarque and F.D. Legitime, were vying for control of the Republic when Bishop Kersuzan issued a pastoral letter saying, "the Church stays outside quarrels and political affairs but cannot be indifferent to your woes or *malheurs*" and called on the two sides to make peace.[152] Some people accused the Church of supporting Legitime, who subsequently became president. The Church denied it:[153] "The (priest) doesn't bring trouble or division. On the contrary, he's a support, a pacifier, as much for the doctrine he preaches as for the legitimacy—*forces*, he gives to the sacraments."

The Church and State cooperated in the field of education to develop what were called national religious schools that received state funding and were taught by Religious. By 1895, some 9,800 students were being taught in these schools.[154] At this time, there were also 26,600 public primary students, half-urban and half-rural; although many of the rural students did not actually attend, plus 6,500 private primary and secondary schools, some of which were religious. The national religious schools generally had French teachers, and a good reputation.[155] By the end of the century, they had taken over an increasing share of the education as President Nord Alexis let the public schools deteriorate.

The role of the Church in education, which was a concern to Freemasons and Protestants in the 1860s as a result of the Concordat, was rekindled. In 1913, the government requested that a Catholic teaching order, the Daughters of Mary, come to Haiti in 1913 to take over *L'Ecole Menagère Elie Dubois*.[156]

The Church urged the Haitian government to take an active stand against "superstition" (the Church term for Voodoo),[157] at least through application of existing laws. The government of Cincinnatus Leconte and his military leaders acquiesced, and the Church waxed eloquent about "the union of religion and power—two powerful means to get the progressive disappearance of superstition." The antisuperstition campaign, which began in 1912, was interrupted at the end of the year amid political confusion, then resumed in 1916. Bishop Jan, whose references to Haitian presidencies were usually cursory, was led to write on the occasion of the election of President Théodore in November 1914, "For the last several years, the Chiefs of State of Haiti only pass by: some tragic accident, illness or civil war obliges them to leave for eternity or exile."[158] Théodore was the third president in 1914, and there were two new ones in 1915.

Religious Competition, 1860-1915

From the concordat to the final decade of the nineteenth century in Haiti, conflict between the Church and Freemasonry became more pronounced. According to Bishop Jan, they (the Freemasons) had a "particularly pernicious influence after the Concordat." Freemasonry was a major vexation for the Church in Haiti in those years during the administrations of Silvain Salnave (1867–1869) and René Salomon (1879–1888), both of whom were sympathetic to it in varying degrees. To the horror of the Church, when he became president, René Salomon stated that he had been a Freemason for thirty-five years and saw no reason why he should not continue to be one or accept the title of Grand Protector of the Order of Freemasonry.

Masonry was more openly hostile to the Church during the Salomon government. Freemasons and Protestants published two anti-Church journals, *L'Oeil* and *L'Avant Garde*. The former launched a campaign against the concordat, the pope, the powers of the archbishop and the bishops, accusing Bishop Guilloux of deceiving the pope about Haitian Freemasons, "the respectable people of Haiti," and of cooperating with the pope to disobey Haitian laws.[159] A Masonic publication, *Vente Suprème*, laid out the Masonic goals. They were to eliminate Catholicism and, ultimately, Christianity. Such hostility led Pope Pius IX to denounce Freemasonry in 1865 in an *Allocution Consistenal*, which was widely circulated in Haiti, and caused Pope Leo XIII to issue an encyclical in 1884 entitled *Humanum Genus*, in which he opposed all secret societies. These publications were no doubt gratefully circulated by the Church that was reluctant to attack Masonry because so much of Haitian society belonged to it.[160]

During the Salnave government, the clergy felt actively persecuted by Freemasonry. Freemasons invaded Churches, interrupted religious services,[161] and demanded their members receive sacraments such as last rites.

The concordat caused an initial setback for Protestantism in Haiti and was consequently a source of resentment. One area of tension was the schools. As religious orders came to Haiti, they established new schools, causing a reduction in importance of public education. The concordat, according to Catts Pressoir, was resisted by all those who loved tolerance and the spirit of liberty.[162] The Legislature must have agreed, opposing it so vehemently that it was not returned until 1863.

Although a hindrance, the Concordat was not fatal for Protestantism. Members of new denominations and branches of already established Protestant churches continued to come to Haiti. Many of them were African Americans. James Theodore Holly, a black American Episcopalian deacon, born of free parents, made an initial exploratory trip to Haiti in 1855, then returned in 1861 with 110 followers.[163] President Geffrard per-

sonally encouraged them to come because of their expertise in cotton production. However, the fate of these first Episcopalians was tragic. Within
eighteen months, forty-three had died, mainly of malaria, including Mrs.
Holly and two of the family's four children. Twenty others departed. James
Holly and his two remaining children remained however, and he succeeded
in establishing the first Episcopal parish in Haiti, the Holy Trinity Church
in Port-au-Prince. Within two years, he had confirmed thirty-six people
and established three missions in Cap-Haïtien and Léogâne. In 1874,
Deacon Holly was consecrated bishop of the Haitian Orthodox Apostolic
Church with its six priests, four deacons, eighteen missions, and one thousand baptized members. By the end of his life, Bishop Holly had a congregation consisting of twelve priests, two deacons, two thousand members,
twenty-six missions, nine primary schools, a teachers' training school, a
school of agriculture, and a seminary. The Episcopalians attribute their success, through a none-too-subtle comparison to the Catholics, whom they
do not mention by name, to teaching the Gospel, non-competitiveness with
other religions, and not requiring members to adopt a western pattern of
life—they need only accept Christ.[164]

A number of Baptist groups came to Haiti during this time. Some individuals also came and subsequently started churches, as did Jemina
Straight, who arrived from the United States in 1880.

Methodism was revitalized in Haiti in the late 1880s due to financial
support from abroad, organizational effort, and one charismatic minister.[165] The Bible Society provided the Methodists with one hundred *gourdes*
a month. This sum allowed them to run a library and distribute free material, including Bibles, to support the Christian Union of Young People that
encouraged social service and exemplary life styles, and pay their popular
minister in Cap-Haïtien, who reportedly had audiences converting in tear-
ful rapture.

The Methodists were dogmatically and sometimes directly opposed to
Voodoo, like many of the other Protestant denominations in Haiti. The
Protestant scholar, Catts Pressoir, relates how a minister named Devieux,
spotting a *humfort*, or Voodoo shrine, would race over to the *houngan*, or
Voodoo priest, and urge him to "renounce your bad practices."[166] Despite
their energy and determination, Methodism grew so slowly that by 1903,
there were only 196 of them in Haiti.[167] The Bible Society began to lose its
enthusiasm for Haiti and turned toward Asia and more successful missions
elsewhere in the Caribbean.

The Catholic Church continued to protest the Protestant presence in
Haiti. In 1880, Bishop Kersuzan[168] of Cap-Haïtien charged the government
with encouraging Protestantism, characterizing that branch of Christianity

as opposed to the nature, taste, and character of the Haitian people, who love solemn religious ceremonies and its liturgy. The bishop added that Protestantism did not speak to the Haitians' intelligence, imagination, or heart. He concluded, "with no altar, pictures of saints, it's monotonous as the desert, sad as the tomb and cold as death."

In 1896, the bishop of Cap-Haïtien founded a newspaper called "*La Croix*," to disseminate his antisuperstitious and anti-Protestant views. Published through 1899,[169] the newspaper objected to what it regarded as disproportionate Protestant strength in the schools and in administrative posts, and what it called its "combative, intolerant attitude and pernicious influence."

Emboldened by the concordat, a stronger presence in Haiti and papal support, the Catholic Church launched an antisuperstition campaign in 1898. In November 1895, Bishop Kersuzan set the wheels in motion with a questionnaire to his clergy, soliciting information on Voodoo.[170] He wanted to know about its beliefs and practices and whether the Catholic faithful were involved with it. The following year, on 6 January 1896, the bishop issued a pastoral letter on Voodoo,[171] which included a story of a Catholic who had reverted to Voodoo and died. *La Croix* also carried *exposés* on secret societies and *bocors*.[172] On 26 February 1897, the bishop held an antifetishism conference and launched an organization called the League Against Voodoo. The League spent the following year building public enthusiasm for an attack on Voodoo. A side effect was recommitment to Catholicism. A mission to Port de Paix in June produced five hundred communions and promises of renewed baptisms.[173]

The antifetish and antisuperstition campaign began on 13 February 1898. The bishop traveled widely, speaking about it even, on occasion, at open air meetings. Conferences were held on the "lamentable moral situation" in the country. The pope gave his blessing to the effort—in 1898, Bishop Kersuzan had had an audience with the pope who encouraged him in the fight against Voodoo and fetishism.[174] The government responded by passing a decree that permitted local authorities to prohibit Voodoo dances. Newspapers picked up the theme, competing with each other in the "zeal of their arguments." They identified *bocors* by name and pinpointed religious sites. Bishop Jan marveled at the "magnificent result [produced] from an alliance of religion and civil authority against fetishism."[175]

Over the next few years, the campaign gradually lost intensity as the Church was obliged to address the religious indifference of its own members. In 1910, Bishop Kersuzan again rekindled hope of renewed Church-State cooperation against Voodoo with a speech in which he concluded that Catholicism could defend itself more efficaciously and practically if its actions were supported by public pressure.[176] "The law against superstition exists, but it's inoperative, like so many others, through weakness and complicity of the governed and governing."

In 1912 and again in 1916, the bishop seemed to have found the kind of support he sought. In 1912, President Leconte and his military leaders tried to apply existing laws against Voodoo.[177] In March 1916, the Secretary of State distributed a circular calling for the "destruction of superstition as quickly as possible." Bishop Jan commented that this act "characterizes the decisive spirit of government and a break with the disgraceful past." Despite the verbal resolve, there was little action until the 1940s.[178]

THE OCCUPATION OF HAITI: 1915-1934

Church Trials and Tribulations

We can see that problems that dogged the Church continued in this period. Clerical life remained difficult and religiously unsatisfactory, yielding more confirmations than conversions. Religious competitiveness and cultural insensitivity actually increased. It took until the late-1950s for some members of the clergy to address these issues and until the 1970s before significant sectors of the Church were ready to come to grips with institutional shortcomings.

The Church continued to experience a number of frustrations in Haiti during this period. Protestantism and Voodoo were particular irritants, which the Church continued to respond with a heavy hand. Travel remained tedious and dangerous both to and from Haiti and within the country, despite the fact that ocean travel was expedited by the invention of the steam engine and land travel by the introduction of the automobile. In January 1920, eighteen priests and a bishop disappeared in a shipwreck off the coast of Africa.[179] However, by 1918, it had become possible to travel overland by car from Port-au-Prince to Cap-Haïtien and President Dartiguenave proved it, accomplishing the feat that year in sixteen hours.[180] By 1921, the priests arrived at their annual retreat in a combination of conveyances including horse, stagecoach, train, and car.[181]

Nevertheless, the continuing isolation of the clergy can be surmised by how little attention was devoted to international events and by their lack of contact with outsiders. In 1922, Pope Benedict XV died and Pope Pius XI was elected. This scant observation is all that is mentioned in Bishop Jan's[182] records of Church history in Haiti. In 1927, the apostolic delegate for Mexico and the Antilles, Bishop Caruana from Puerto Rico, called on Haiti. This visit is unique in the documentation to that time.[183]

The Church was having trouble making ends meet. In 1919, it threatened to close St. Martial[184] due to insufficient teachers and high costs—the government added to Church expenses by allowing its own non-paying students to matriculate. In 1922, priests were asked to leave any inheritance to the Church. Bishop Darricade died in France in 1928, after forty years' service in Haiti. According to his obituary, he had used his own money to build boys' and girls' schools in Grand Rivière.[185] In 1921, Bishop Kersuzan urged the Haitian Church to accept women teachers for the boys' schools,[186] arguing that the precedent had been set in the United States. No harm would come of it, at least not for boys up to the age of twelve— "besides, women are less expensive, better groomed, and have higher moral standards."

The Church kept records of the people it baptized, confirmed, and married. The number of persons confirmed was enormous. In 1924, 5,816 people were confirmed during one of Bishop Kersuzan's pastoral visits. The next year, Bishop Jan made a 1,500 kilometer trip that resulted in 11,866 confirmations.[187] However, as in 1917, seven times more girls were confirmed than boys.[188]

Boys were not growing up in the Church. Then, as adults, they were not prepared or disposed to be married in it. In 1924, Bishop Kersuzan issued a pastoral letter complaining about the small numbers of marriages.[189]

The Church was proud of the number of children and adults it baptized and confirmed and cited current statistics to prove that Haiti was a Catholic nation. On the other hand, the Church was painfully aware that taking the sacraments did not assure a conversion. It was only in the 1970s that activist sectors of the Church sought to thoroughly convert Haitians by making Catholicism relevant and casting their fates with the people. Ultimately, it drove them to oppose Jean-Claude Duvalier and his repressive government.

The shortage of priests and the absence of an indigenous clergy continued to be an important obstacle for the Church throughout this period. In 1874, there was one priest per 11,627 Catholics.[190] Forty-four years later, in 1918, the odds had improved somewhat and there was one priest per 8,333 Catholics.[191] By 1930, there were only 205 priests per 2,652,290 Catholics; the ratio had dropped to one priest per 12,938 Catholics.[192] It became increasingly clear that a solution to the lack of priests was the creation of an indigenous clergy, but efforts continued to be stymied by Church rules and prejudice that favored whites. According to James Leyburn, a common refrain was, "baptism by a black will not stick."[193]

By 1920, Haiti had only produced ten Haitian priests. Motivated by a letter from Pope Benoit XV urging bishops to train indigenous clergy, the Church opened a second apostolic school in Haiti;[194] the first one, established in 1895 in Port-au-Prince, had failed. The government agreed to provide some scholarships, and twenty students were enrolled in 1920. In 1922, another occurrence indirectly encouraged the development of a

Haitian clergy—the first catechism was published in Creole. Suddenly the Bible was accessible to many more Haitians.

The psychological moment for an indigenous clergy had arrived. Haitians were growing more critical of their foreign clergy and disposed toward a native one. On learning that he had been selected to replace Bishop Kersuzan, Bishop Jan wrote to his superior on 15 January 1924,[195] acknowledging the atmosphere, "they've had enough of us, French and foreign priests. They want a national clergy, especially leaders who are Haitian. They want them in the parishes and especially at the head of dioceses."

Once opened, it took the Apostolic School of Notre Dame some time to graduate its first priests. The first class of six completed their studies in 1927.[196] In his 29 January 1928 pastoral,[197] the bishop of Cap-Haïtien appealed to families to orient their children toward the sanctuary and to the clergy to help identify likely candidates for the priesthood.

Rural education was not successful.[198] Finding principals and teachers for rural Haiti was a continuing challenge. The Church was stymied in this regard by the government, whose laws limited the number of religious orders and had defaulted on its own commitment in 1916 to train teachers for work in the countryside.[199] When *L'Ecole Normal* opened and began to produce teachers, the graduates had no place to teach.[200] The school closed in 1927.

The McCormick Commission was convened on 6 December 1921 to investigate the handling of the U.S. occupation. Bishop Kersuzan testified, attributing the growth of Protestantism to preferential treatment by the occupation forces. While the indictment was simplistic, it was nevertheless true that Protestantism grew in absolute and relative terms during this period.[201] Between 1905 and 1910, the country had 54,870 Protestants.[202] In the interval between 1921 and 1929, the number increased to 134,963. Protestantism grew at the rate of one hundred percent per decade in the twentieth century until 1930. Between 1930 and 1950, the rate increased to two hundred percent per decade, or at four percent of the population.[203] Between 1905 and 1938, ten new Protestant churches came to Haiti, two of the fastest growing were the Adventist and Pentecostal.

The growth of the Protestant churches can be traced to economic and social causes, religious frustration, and a nudge from the United States. The secretary of the Marines, Edwin Denby, was sent to inspect the Haitian forces in 1921.[204] Shocked at not finding any American missionaries, he contacted the Church of Christ of America. Protestantism made inroads among the displaced rural farmers because of its association with upward mobility. It also attracted converts from Voodoo, when cures failed to work or were too expensive. Protestantism was different from Voodoo, but familiar with its trances, speaking in tongues, music, and dancing. The Church grew increasingly alarmed. *L'Essoir* summed it up on 19 August 1926,

"Mercy, don't let Protestantism and Adventism possess our sons and servants."[205]

The Church response to the widely unpopular occupation was to publicly support it while privately playing a diplomatic role. At a 17 September 1918 meeting with Secretary of State Lansing in Washington, Bishop Kersuzan outlined the areas of friction, then offered his recommendations. Inequities in the *corvée*, or forced labor program, and the extent of the occupation force's control, were particular irritants. Kersuzan suggested a letter of understanding to clarify the limits of the marines' authority.[206] In addition, he recommended that the chief of the occupation army should be French-speaking, and that the occupation force should not get involved with Church-State matters. On return to Haiti, Bishop Kersuzan issued a pastoral letter concerning his meeting in Washington. The goodwill that might have been engendered by the trip was mitigated by his picayune complaints. The bishop and his pastoral received a lot of criticism in the press and the country at large. An anonymous priest protested the bishop's accommodation with the occupation and with his criticisms. According to the writer, the bishop had not addressed the major areas of friction.[207] On 21 January 1919, Bishop Conan further aggravated the public when he issued a pastoral letter[208] that described the occupation as a "humiliating but a bitter remedy that would take us out of our desperate state and ought to cure us." He tried to reassure Haitians that their rights would be respected and urged them to abandon hatred and violence. He concluded by saying that he had "complete confidence in loyal cooperation."[209] Many Haitians decided that the bishop "was blinded by his confidence in the goodwill of the occupiers."[210]

The bishop's message did not take. An organization called the Patriotic Union formed for the purpose of restoring independence. On 30 December 1920, members of the Union approached Bishop Conan in Port-au-Prince and Bishop Kersuzan in Cap-Haïtien to solicit their endorsement. Both refused. Bishop Conan argued that the Union was a political association and clergy could not become involved in politics.[211] Anyway, the Union had already aroused passions unduly. Resentment toward the two bishops increased during the presidency of Louis Borno, a "fervent Catholic and resolute partisan of Haitian-American collaboration."[212]

When the McCormick Commission came to investigate, Bishop Kersuzan testified that the occupation had been morally beneficial and useful because of the roads that had been built.[213] However, it was spoiled by the *corvées*, the removal of Haitian money, and the arbitrary justice system. People had been pushed to the limits, preferring to die fighting Americans than accept the occupation. He objected to a land tax provision in the constitution that could force Haitians to sell their property to Americans. He complained that the financial counselor was an insolent despot and added that Protestantism was being forced on them. The bishop concluded by recommending the abolition of martial law and reduction of taxes on coffee exports.

Bishop Conan spoke to the subsequent investigatory body, the Forbes Commission on 7 March 1930.[214] The clergy in Haiti was almost all foreign, so it should not be involved with politics, however, that did not mean that they were any less interested in the welfare of the country. The Church wanted the occupation to end and see dignity restored. This pro-Haitian testimony reduced some but not all of the bad feelings toward the Church.[215]

The Church was heartened in 1915 when the Haitian Secretary of State announced the government's intention to "destroy superstition as quickly as possible," and enforce the laws against Voodoo that had been in virtually every constitution since 1805.[216] The government called for executing Articles 405 and 406 of the Penal Code relative to Voodoo because "ignorance and superstition are two evils that have kept Haitians from evolving. Wise and energetic measures must be put in place to combat them and extirpate them from the bosom of the masses." The following year, Etienne Dorneval, the Minister of Justice and Religion, ordered the destruction of all "altars of fetishism."[217]

The occupation forces were not *a priori* opposed to Voodoo. Initially, they had announced there would be freedom of conscience; attacks on Voodoo were forbidden. Their attitude changed, possibly because some of the resistance groups practiced Voodoo or because they liked it less as they learned more about it—or both.[218]

Voodoo persevered despite the animosity. In 1922, at a celebration for Saint Anne in Limonade, the clergy reported that it was "sickened to see a swarming crowd with its immoral bowers and drums that boom night and day."[219] In 1928, on a pastoral visit, the bishop described Grande Source de Jean-Rabel as a "region where the influence of *bocors* is all powerful."[220] The same year, the Church began to require its members to show parish cards in order to receive the sacraments, and to provide proof that they had passed a catechism exam in order to receive confession. These procedures were intended to prevent Voodoo *devotés* from participating in Catholic ceremonies.[221]

There was no organized outcry from Voodoo sympathizers to the persecution. A single Frenchman, Jean Price-Mars, did as much as anyone to protect Voodoo by writing a book in 1928 extolling African values, folklore, and Voodoo. *Ainsi Parla L'Oncle: Essais d'Ethnographie* was later used as rallying point by the *noirists*, or black pride supporters, in the 1930s.[222]

The anti-Voodoo movement continued beyond the occupation and crested between 1941 and 1943 during the Elie Lescot presidency. The catalyst for the campaign was an episode involving a rural peasant.[223] St. Giles

St. Pierre, known as Ti-Jules, threw out his Voodoo accouterments after his three children recovered from an illness. God had saved them. In gratitude, he began to urge others to live *sans mélange*, without mixing the two religions. Denounced by his neighbors for denigrating Voodoo, he was touted and paraded by the Church.

In the midst of this campaign, the Church produced an Anti-Voodoo Oath.[224] Catholics were asked to certify that they had renounced Voodoo, destroyed all their Voodoo paraphernalia, would have nothing to do with Voodoo in the future, and intended to raise their children in the Church.

Next, the Church called on the Lescot government to help destroy Voodoo accoutrements. Lescot mobilized the National Guard and it proceeded to vandalize Voodoo sites and demolish religious objects. While the campaign had generated some conversions, the oath created resistance, and the violence was the *coup de grace*. The campaign ended abruptly with following a shooting in Delmas, a suburb of Port-au-Prince.

THE OCCUPATION LEGACY: HAITI FROM 1934 TO 1971

The American occupation produced significant and long-lasting effects. In addition to altering the orientation toward Protestantism, it led to a more favorable attitude toward Voodoo and generated an appreciation of indigenous customs and African roots. It fostered a sense of nationalism and black pride that made black Haitians yearn for political and economic power.[225] The Dumarsais Estimé and François Duvalier governments can be seen as a consequence of those yearnings. It revived the historic fear of invasion and produced a new wave of xenophobia. Finally, it spurred the Church to undertake some self-criticism and reevaluation.

As we have seen, the Church has had a history of siding with white, foreign occupation forces against the interests of the people. When it happened again, many Haitians were incensed. The opprobrium increased following Church involvement in the 1941–1943 antisuperstitious campaign. These events and François Duvalier's treatment of the Church caused it to rethink its relations with governments and its mission, contributing to its decision to speak out against the Jean-Claude Duvalier regime.

Church Competitors

The absence of close Church-State relations allowed Protestantism to carve some substantial inroads. Ten new Protestant churches came to Haiti between 1940 and 1949 and fourteen more arrived between 1950 and 1965.[226] The Church of God settled in Bourdon, a residential area in

Port-au-Prince, in 1934, and the Salvation Army reached the capital in 1950. The Protestant population increased by 370,187 between 1934 and 1938 and by 50,555 between 1950 and 1958.[227]

The Protestants formed some organizations, including L'Union Baptiste d'Haïti and the Council of Haitian Evangelicals. The Ecumenical Research Group, or Groupe Oecumenique de Recherches (GOR), dating from 1968, includes the Episcopal Church, the Salvation Army, the Baptist, and the Afro-Methodist churches.[228] The Protestants also generally enjoyed a closer relationship with the State during this period. François Duvalier welcomed them because they were traditionally apolitical.[229] However, this did not prevent François Duvalier from expelling Episcopal Bishop Alfred Voegeli from the country or impeaching an Episcopal senator.[230]

The Church was overshadowed during the Estimé presidency by other matters, including Voodoo. Dumarsais Estimé favored a change of attitude toward Voodoo and sought to encourage it culturally—in literature, art, and dance.[231] However, he himself was a Catholic, and he and his wife regularly attended mass in the palace chapel.[232]

A notable incident occurred at this time. Dumarsais Estimé's minister of education invited Father Foisset, a man known for his participation in the antisuperstitious campaign and anti-Voodoo stance, to dinner to discuss Church-Voodoo tensions. The minister died during the meal. Former President Leslie Manigat recalls that it was widely believed that President Estimé had tried to poison the priest.[233] Conspiracy theorists conjectured that the minister had intended to kill Father Foisset with a doctored Haitian cola, only to have Father Foisset exchange the glasses, leaving the minister with the fatal dose.[234]

Following the ouster of Dumarsais Estimé, the Church enjoyed a brief reprieve due to its association with President Magloire that lasted until he lost power in 1956. Subsequently, the Church supported the candidacy of Louis Déjoie, and when he lost, close Church-State relations ended.

Church Introspection

There was a general view that the Church needed to undertake some change, but the controversy arose over what changes were most appropriate. The Church offered its suggestions, a number of priests provided alternative suggestions, and François Duvalier offered his own corrections. As we will see, the fundamental questions about the composition, role, and relations of the Church and State continue to be important and central to subsequent events.

A Church document of the period, *Statuts Diocésains,*[235] or *Diocesan Rules,* attempted to codify Church behavior and provides considerable insight on the contemporary Church. To meet the need for priests, it urged the clergy to identify likely candidates among the young, then nurture and protect them "from the contagion of the world."[236] To protect priests and parishioners from Protestantism, the Church sought to keep them apart. Clergy who participated in ceremonies in non-Catholic churches would risk "suspicion of heresy." They were forbidden to go into churches for weddings, funerals, civil or Masonic services, or meetings and prohibited from reading Protestant publications.[237] Likewise, parishioners were forbidden to attend "temples," listen to their sermons, read or own their books.[238] They were to be discouraged from entering "mixed marriages."[239]

To keep Catholic elements out of Voodoo and prevent aspects of Voodoo from getting into Catholicism,[240] it cautioned the clergy to make sure that statues were not confused with idols, that baptismal water was locked up, and that magicians and "superstitious" did not participate in masses, which they could use as a prelude to a Voodoo ceremony.[241] They were to withhold religious services from Voodoo followers, and refuse to give communion to people who practiced Voodoo or give first communion to their children.[242] Priests should refrain from marrying anyone who had already "contracted marriage with Erzulie," or someone who had been involved with Voodoo until he renounced it.[243] However, anyone could have extreme unction, even a person who had consulted *bocors*.[244]

It advised the clergy[245] to refuse to let people wearing "insignias" into Churches and chapels and to excommunicate Freemasons, whether or not they were practicing.[246] The same went for communists and members of several other societies.

It was concerned about the financial, moral, and political activities of its clergy. To this end, it established a code of personal behavior, fixed prices for burials, sung and low masses, set limitations on clerical involvement in politics and cautioned them to refrain from political battles or immersion in political parties.[247] Moral conduct must be beyond reproach. The priests should only hire older women of "*l'âge vulgairement appelé 'canonique'*" for domestic work.[248] They were not to go to cabarets or dance halls and were urged to avoid even sharing a car seat with a woman.[249] The clergy were to instill a sense of etiquette and proper behavior in their parishioners, by preventing inappropriately dressed girls from going to the *table sainte*. They were to discourage dressing up at masses because it put off those who could not afford it.[250]

It advised the clergy to help parishioners understand their religion, and its symbols and ceremonies, so they would be better able to lead a Christian life,[251] because, "nothing is more painful to Catholics than to feel that they are inferior in this to Protestants."[252] It advised the clergy to properly instruct people wanting to become Catholics because it takes time to prepare children and adults for baptisms and communion.[253] It called on the clergy to proselytize and convert heretics, Protestants and the "superstitious" because the Church wanted converts.[254]

A group of young Spiritan priests from St. Martial advocated Church reform,[255] but their views on what needed to be done were not shared by the Spiritan hierarchy. Some of them, including Meinard Hegba, Gérard Bissainth, Jean Parisot, and Jean-Claude Bajeux, left Haiti for Paris in the 1950s, where they joined a number of African priests who were experiencing similar concerns about the Church in Africa. Together, they wrote *Des Prêtres Noirs S'Interrogent.*[256]

In the opinion of these authors, the Church had not thoroughly converted Haitians or Africans because it had failed to take native values and customs into account; its orientation was too Western.[257] The Church needed to recognize the commonalties between the authors of the Bible—the Semites, and the Haitians: both were agriculturalists, with an oral tradition that valued stories and mystery.[258] They were convinced that God was proud of the varied beauty of the institution; consequently, the Church in Haiti should be a reflection by taking on a more negroid aspect.[259] The Church in Haiti should have an indigenous clergy because a foreign missionary would never be as good as a native priest. The Church in Haiti also needed to rethink its liturgy, dogma, religious music, sacred arts, catechism, and priesthood in accordance with the indigenous culture.[260] Meinard Hegba wrote about the need for keeping local traditions and wondered whether it was too daring to regret the slow extinction of Voodoo, "with its shades of Dahomey."[261]

Another book about the Church written in this period was *Clergé Indigène*, by Father Gérard G. Gayot. Its author accuses the Church in Haiti of being a Colonialist power, of being corrupt and ill-suited to the country's needs. He calls for fundamental changes in the Church and in Church-State relations.[262]

According to Father Gayot, the Church needed to be Haitian, composed of Haitians who knew the people and were ready to mix with them.[263] Haiti had had three wars: the first was against the French colonialists; the second was against the "colonialists in khaki," and the third was against the "colonialists in cassocks."[264] The first Haitian bishop, Rémy Augustin, had only been appointed in 1953. There were few Haitian priests; between 1860 and 1956, only 103 were ordained. Prior to the 1860 Concordat, there had only been one, Father Tisserand.[265] The number of new priests was not encouraging[266] and clergy who showed nationalist tendencies were forced to leave.[267]

The author asserted that the Church needed reform. It was operating like a business; "a store where sacraments are sold at exorbitant prices,"

despite biblical opposition to exploitation.[268] The government was supporting a foreign Church and should redirect its funding from the French
seminary, Saint Jacques de France, to the new Haitian seminary, Haut de
Turgeau.[269]

The Church and François Duvalier

It is useful to see how François Duvalier dealt with the Church and the
Vatican to put Jean-Claude Duvalier's subsequent handling of the Church
into perspective, and to appreciate the desire of the Church to reassert itself.

François Duvalier made mockery of the Church by coopting, arresting,
and exiling bishops, a papal nuncio, and numerous clergy, as well as by
confiscating its property. After all of that, François Duvalier succeeded in
getting Vatican approval to name his own hierarchy—a *tour de force* that
contributed to Jean-Claude's downfall.

François Duvalier wanted to be remembered as a devout Catholic. This
is apparent from his autobiography, *Memories of a Third World Leader*,
which is dedicated to popes Paul VI and John XXIII, his father, "who taught
him the beauty of the French language by means of the Psalms," and
Chanoine Albert Dorelien, who "personifies the high tradition of the
Christian Church in Haiti."[270]

Duvalier also wanted to leave the impression that he had gotten along
well with the Church. In his autobiography, he compiled the proof: he had
held the traditional post-inaugural mass, Churchmen had always received
their pay, he had attended John XXIII's funeral, sent a delegation to the
coronation ceremonies for Pope Paul VI, assisted at the ritual *Te Deums*
(even after he had been excommunicated), and had negotiated a new
concordat. Duvalier barely mentions his many confrontations with the
institution.

Despite this professed devotion to the Church, François Duvalier's
innermost religious convictions and true feelings about Voodoo continue
to be a source of speculation.[271] In one speech, Duvalier declared himself a
"Bible Lover," but his true god was "Africa mater." The African gods made it
possible for him to "ascend and assault." In *Catechism of the Revolution*, he
mocks the Holy Trinity, substituting Haitian heroes for the saints, and por-
traying himself as the embodiment of all of them. The *Catechism* even
includes an adaptation of the Lord's Prayer, which begins, "Our Doc who
art in the National Palace for Life."[272]

François Duvalier's professed fidelity to Catholicism is diminished by his
apparent attachment to Voodoo. Duvalier clearly cultivated the impression
that he was associated with Voodoo by adopting the clothing and manner
of one of the principal *loa*, Baron Samedi, keeper of the graveyard, and by

having the word get around that he entertained Voodoo priests and held animal sacrifices at the palace. The foundation of his presumed relationship with Voodoo was at least partially political since it generated popular support and humiliated the Church.

François Duvalier sought and largely managed to limit the power of the Church, one of the country's few potentially influential institutions.[273] His motives apparently were both rational and personal, a consequence of shrewd political judgment and of old grudges. Many of Duvalier's associations with Catholicism were negative. He was educated at a state-owned public school rather than an upper class private Catholic institution. As a member of the Griots in the 1930s, his proposal to devote a year's commemoration to the past was rejected by some influential priests. His former friend and personal secretary, Clémont Barbot, was vehemently anti-Catholic.[274] His hero, Jean-Jacques Dessalines, had almost been captured through clerical trickery. The Church had attempted to destroy Voodoo.[275] Most recently, it had supported his principal political rival, Louis Déjoie, in the 1956–1957 presidential campaign.

François Duvalier sought to avoid confrontation with the Church as a presidential candidate,[276] and his first gestures as a new president seemed to presage good relations.[277] Duvalier named Jean-Baptiste Georges to be minister of education, the first Catholic priest ever appointed to the Haitian cabinet.[278] In 1958, he invited the Jesuits to return to Haiti. After that, things went downhill.[279]

In 1959, Duvalier clashed with the Church and the students for the first time by refusing to provide a meeting place for the National Union of Haitian students. A priest offered a meeting place, agreeing to retract his offer only if the government provided the space. On 20 August, the government expelled him.[280] In 1962, Father Georges was arrested, then expelled from the country, and in 1964, the Jesuit order was accused of spying and harboring one of Duvalier's enemies, again they were thrown out of the country.

The same month, François Duvalier detained and then deported the French rector of the largest Catholic secondary school and also a popular French, small town priest. The faithful who went to the Cathedral in Port-au-Prince to pray for the two ousted ecclesiastics were forcefully dispersed by Duvalier's police chief and troops. When Archbishop François Poirier denounced this police action, he was charged with "overt hostility to the constitutional Government of Haiti,"[281] a case based in part by an earlier slight that occurred when the archbishop failed to come to the palace to wish the president a happy new year.[282]

In 1960, François Duvalier deported Poirier himself. The bishop was unceremoniously thrown out of the country with only a dollar and a book in his possession, on the pretext that Poirier had provided communist students with $7,000 to overthrow the government.

The same year, Duvalier banned the National Union of Secondary Teachers (UNMES)[283] and expelled two of the priests associated with it for "reasons of national security." When a thousand priests and nuns protested the ouster, sixty of them were arrested.[284] Following the publication of some material in the Catholic newspaper La Phalange, which Duvalier considered sensitive, the president exiled the authors, including four priests and Bishop Rémy Augustin.[285] The Vatican responded by excommunicating François Duvalier.[286]

Duvalier was undeterred by the Holy See. Within weeks of his excommunication, he had arrested some twenty-five priests and twenty nuns, among them, the Spiritan priest, Antoine Adrien, who subsequently coordinated opposition activities during the Jean-Claude era and the departure of General Avril from Haiti later, in March 1990.

Wide-ranging and high-level expulsions continued through 1962. They included priests, an archbishop, a bishop, a papal nuncio, and the Anglican bishop, C.A. Voegeli. After twenty-one years of service in Haiti, Voegli displeased the president and was expelled at gunpoint. The case of Bishop Jean-Marie Paul Robert of Gonaïves is illustrative. François Duvalier charged him with looting archeological treasures, failure to conduct masses, and continuing to belittle the presidency—Duvalier recalled that his presidential party had received poor treatment from the bishop on a trip to Gonaïves.[287] In 1962, his Church and storehouse were ransacked; Robert fled the country.

The same year, seven priests from the Artibonite were expelled for failure to include the excommunicated president in their prayers. The Vatican responded by withdrawing the papal nuncio, Bishop Giovanni Ferrofino.[288]

Undaunted by excommunication, Duvalier arranged to have his friend, Haitian bishop Claudius Angenor of Cayes, celebrate the Church's traditional hymn of praise, the Te Deum, when he named himself president-for-life in 1964. During that ceremony, Angenor included a plea for political prisoners in the sermon and was subsequently put under house arrest. In addition to throwing out the whole Jesuit order in 1964, he closed down three Catholic publications, L'Eglise en Marche, Rond Point, and La Phalange, and dissolved the Catholic unions.[289]

By 1965, Duvalier was confident enough of his control of the Church to allow the Jesuits to return to Haiti. This act evidently mellowed the Vatican because it agreed to enter negotiations for a revision of the concordat the following year. It is hard to understand why the Vatican chose to negotiate with a head of state who had caused the Church so much trouble unless it expected to be able to modify his behavior.[290] Astonishingly, François

Duvalier reaped all the advantages. The negotiations moved smoothly and quickly. A protocol with Rome was prepared on 12 January 1966. The pope publicly announced that the negotiations were underway in June. The document was signed on August 15; and by 25 October 1966, it was complete. Bishop Samoré came from the Vatican to celebrate the occasion.[291]

The most significant change in it was to Article IV. In the future, the president would name archbishops and bishops—with the approval of the Holy See. In *Memoires of a Third World Leader,* Duvalier explained that the idea for a black Haitian hierarchy had come to him in 1949 while he was in the United States and read that the first black bishop had been appointed there.[292]

François Duvalier soon nominated five bishops; four of them, including the archbishop, were black. According to the president,[293] his selections were people who were aware of the new social, economic, and political situation, and would serve as an example to the youth of Haiti. In the speech presenting Archbishop Wolff Ligondé and bishops Angenor, Constant, Cousineau, and auxiliary bishops Augustin, Decoste, Peters, and Choquet, the president told his audience, he had renegotiated the concordat to "promote Haitian unity."[294]

François Duvalier correctly regarded the revised concordat as one of his major achievements. The Church would no longer be a white, largely French, institution with foreign loyalties.[295] The presence of Haitian bishops would encourage the growth of an indigenous clergy,[296] who naturally would be fundamentally better able than the foreign clergy to understand the country and its people.[297] The expulsion of foreign clergy left some vacant parishes, which Duvalier filled with Haitian priests.[298]

The president's problems with the Church were not over.[299] Although the new bishops remained gratefully subservient, not all of the clergy were satisfied. In August 1969, the government charged nine priests at St. Martial with communist activities, threw them out of the country, and confiscated St. Martial.

In summary, François Duvalier resented the Church for historical and personal reasons and his relations with the institution were overwhelmingly confrontational. As we will see, his success in managing the Church was better than that of his son.

The Church in the 1960s

The Church in Haiti had entered an important phase. There were a lot of pressures and influences on it in the late 1960s. Among them were presidential policies, Vatican II, the Medellin Conference, and the growing Protestant presence.

Duvalier's bishops continued to be largely uncritical of the government.[300] Some of the clergy resented the hierarchy for its reluctance to respond to continuing State aggression against the Church,[301] and others were apprehensive about a Church under the control of François Duvalier.[302] The Haitian delegation to the First Meeting of Christians for Socialism in Chile in 1973,[303] asserted that the Haitian Church had become completely identified with the State.

With Vatican II, the Catholic Church was called upon to recognize the historically valuable aspects of indigenous religions. Overt Church hostility to Voodoo in Haiti had faded following the antisuperstition campaign and with François Duvalier's protection. Suddenly the Church was asked to see its historic protagonist in positive terms. Far from rejecting everything connected with it, native elements were incorporated into religious ceremonies. Subsequently, masses began to be said in Creole and sacred music was accompanied by drums. These measures brought the Church and Voodoo closer together.

Vatican II also encouraged ecumenism of all sorts, and in Haiti, this meant another difficult adjustment. In 1967, F. Solages, a priest from Cayes, wrote a book entitled, *In Search of a Haitian Pastoral, "Simple Notes,"*[304] which drew on the Brazilian Church and Protestant experience to suggest some new directions for the Haitian Church in keeping with Vatican II.

Vatican II stressed the importance of the people in the Church. The Church was not simply the hierarchy. According to Solages, more and better use needed to be made of the Haitian male and female Religious and laity; the Brazilian Church had shown the way. In that country, Religious baptized, preached, gave communion, and officiated at funerals. When a priest was unavailable for a Sunday mass in Haiti, the author argued for having a Religious officiate; reading the Evangel, singing the psalms, and offering the homily. The Protestants had their *culte* or service on Sunday in their little chapels. Solages mused, "If the Church doesn't have one, what will be said about our religion?"[305]

According to Father Solages, Catholicism had still not acclimated in Haiti. Consequently, "evangelization should be the first task of the Haitian Church [because] religious ignorance is immense in Haiti and most of our ills, from a religious point of view, come from there."[306] The dioceses should handle religious instruction and diocesan schools should be used for catechism. Solages estimated that 90 percent of the baptized did not know the Evangelical message. A contributing factor was a lack of priests; there was only one priest per ten thousand inhabitants.[307] Solages recommended another Brazilian technique for reaching rural areas that lacked priests—masses could be transmitted from the capital by radio.[308]

Many poor did not attend Church because they had nothing to wear. The clergy should encourage parishioners to dress simply at mass and make the poor feel more welcome. These were just short-term answers. The real issue was poverty, and the solution was to end it through economic development.[309] "The needs, aspirations and possibilities of People of God, in Haiti as elsewhere, should be our major concern . . . [we] can't separate the spiritual from the temporal." Father Solages recommended training *animateurs*, or leaders, in what he called communal Christian development, to work in parishes in order to give them a sense of community, and to make them more dynamic, reminiscent of the first Christian communities.[310] This stratagem would discourage Voodoo and Marxism. In the aftermath of the antisuperstitious campaign and Vatican II, Solages recalled that Voodoo was a vestige of "Mother Africa," but, in his view, the Church should not be involved with it. The Church should refuse to allow godparents who were *bocors* and the Church should build dispensaries to combat ignorance. Rather than trying to delete the symbols of Voodoo, the Church should put confidence in Christ in peoples' heads, as the Protestants do. He concluded that the Haitian Church could be saved with an appropriate pastoral, taking into account the country's social, economic, and demographic needs.[311] In his estimation, this Church would be adaptive and willing to learn from others. Its clergy would set the standard of behavior. It would be concerned about population growth, with "its grave repercussions, including urbanization and disillusionment of the masses."[312] It would address the lack of men in the Church and the need for priests, especially in the rural areas. It would make better use of Church property, recognizing that some of it needed to be distributed to the poor.[313] Haitians were religious, baptized, and well-disposed. The Church was a social and moral force that "must know how to infuse courage and confidence in its children."[314]

As the Church moved into the Jean-Claude Duvalier era, it became increasingly involved with the issues Father Solages had raised: its mission, evangelization, commitment to the poor, and social and economic development.

Conclusion

The history of the Church in Haiti was stained despite the genuine dedication of certain individuals and orders. A process of introspection began throughout the Church worldwide in the 1950s and 1960s and the Haitian Church was not exempt. Members of the Church were pained by the contempt the institution garnered through its identification with despotic governments and its hostility toward other religions. They also smarted at the treatment it had received from François Duvalier who had exiled members of the Church who opposed him. Despite the apparent benefits of having an indigenous hierarchy, some of the clergy resented the soporific effect it had on the bishops' critical powers. Understanding the domestic history of the Church in Haiti and the international influences on the institution leads us to an examination of the Church during the Jean-Claude era.

NOTES

1. J. Lloyd Mecham, *Church and State in Latin America*, 2d ed. (Chapel Hill: The University of North Carolina Press, 1966), 288, 290.

2. J. M. Jan, *Collecta Pour L'Histoire Religieuse du Diocèse du Cap-Haïtien*, vol. 2 (Port-au-Prince: Editions Henri Deschamps, undated [1960]), 4.

3. Ibid., 5.

4. Ibid., 7.

5. Ibid., 11.

6. Catts Pressoir, *Le Protestantisme Haïtien*, vol. 1 (Port-au-Prince: Imprimerie de la Société Biblique et des Livres Religieux d'Haïti, 1945), 11.

7. George Breathett, ed., *The Catholic Church in Haiti 1704–1785: Selected Letters, Memoires and Documents* (Salisbury, NC: Documentary Publications, 1982), 1.

8. Adolphe Cabon, *Notes Sur L'Histoire Religieuse d'Haïti de la Révolution au Concordat, 1789–1860* (Port-au-Prince: Petit Séminaire Collège St. Martial, 1933), 9.

9. Breathett, ed., *The Catholic Church in Haiti*, 4.

10. Ibid., 14.

11. Ibid., 16.

12. Ibid., 8–10.

13. Jan, *Collecta* 2: 11.

14. Ibid.

15. Ibid., 14.

16. Ibid., 13.

17. C.L.R. James, *Black Jacobins, Toussaint L'Ouverture and the San Domingo Revolution*, 2d ed. (New York: Random House, 1963), 9.

18. Adolphe Cabon, *Notes Sur L'Histoire Religieuse d'Haïti*, 38. According to Cabon, Toussaint L'Ouverture had received a solid, Catholic religious education as a student of the Jesuits in Northern Haiti.

19. M.L.E. Moreau de Saint-Méry, *A Civilization that Perished: The Last Years of White Colonial Rule in Haiti* (Lanham, MD: University Press of America, 1985), 116–17.

20 Michel S. Laguerre, *Voodoo Heritage* (Beverly Hills: Sage, 1980), 38.

21. Saint-Méry, *A Civilization that Perished*, 116. It is important to recall that Saint-Méry was a Freemason.

22. Breathett, ed., *The Catholic Church in Haiti*, 6.

23. Jan, *Collecta* 2: 15.

24. Breathett, ed., *The Catholic Church in Haiti*, 160.

25. Ibid., 131–39.

26. Jan, *Collecta* 2: 33.

27. Saint-Méry, *A Civilization that Perished*, 119.

28. Breathett, ed., *The Catholic Church in Haiti*, 77.

29. Ibid., 8.

30. Saint-Méry, *A Civilization that Perished*, 116.

31. Mooney Druneau and L. Gabriel, eds., *The Catholic Church and Religions in Latin America*, Monograph ser. no. 18 (Montreal: Center for Developing Area Studies, McGill University, 1985), 216.

32. James, *Black Jacobins*, 32.

33. Jan, *Collecta* 2: 12.

34. Cabon, *Notes Sur L'Histoire Religieuse d'Haïti*, 25.

35. Saint-Méry, *A Civilization that Perished*, 193.

36. Ibid., 205.

37. Breathett, ed., *The Catholic Church in Haiti*, 17.

38. Cabon, *Notes Sur L'Histoire Religieuse d'Haïti*, 39–40.

39. James, Black Jacobins, 87.

40. Cabon, *Notes Sur L'Histoire Religieuse d'Haïti*, 46–47.

41. Jan, *Collecta* 2: 30.

42. Ibid., 93.

43. Cabon, *Notes Sur L'Histoire Religieuse d'Haïti*, 51.

44. Jan, *Collecta* 2: 30.

45. Cabon, *Notes Sur L'Histoire Religieuse d'Haïti*, 68.

46. Jan, *Collecta* 2: 27.

47. Cabon, *Notes Sur L'Histoire Religieuse d'Haïti*, 48–49.

48. Ibid., 53.

49. Jan, *Collecta* 2: 31.

50. Cabon, *Notes Sur L'Histoire Religieuse d'Haïti*, 79.

51. Ibid., 38.

52. Jan, *Collecta* 2: 27.

53. Ibid., 36. The departure of the apostolic prefect brought an end to the legitimate jurisdiction of the Church in St. Domingue.

54. Cabon, *Notes Sur L'Histoire Religieuse d'Haïti*, 35.

55. Ibid., 31, 33.

56. James, *Black Jacobins*, 374.

57. Ibid., 7.

58. Laguerre, *Voodoo Heritage*, 97.

59. Jan, *Collecta* 2: 30.

60. Alfred Métraux, *Le Vaudou Haïtien* (Paris: Gallimard, 1958), 290.

61. George Eaton Simpson, "The Belief System of Haitian Vodun," *American Anthropologist* 47 (1945): 494. Simpson describes Voodoo, before contact with Catholicism, as more of a dance, consisting of singing, fainting, and nervous behavior.

62. Laguerre, *Voodoo Heritage*, 24. Michel Laguerre made a study of Voodoo songs and found that they related to life in the town in which they were sung. See Simpson, "The Belief System of Haitian Vodun," 495. In a study of Voodoo in the Haitian town of Plaisance in 1937, Simpson found that people had lost track of who the *loa* were. Some thought that saints and *loa* were both intermediaries, but that certain *loa* had nothing to do with saints and God. Others believed that the saints and *loa* were "*la même bagaille*," the same thing, while still others felt that saints and *loa* were bitter enemies.

63. Selden Rodman, *Haiti: The Black Republic: The Complete Story and Guide*, 6th ed. (New York: Devin-Adair, 1984), 92.

64. Simpson, "The Belief System of Haitian Vodun," 492–93. Simpson writes about the "fathers of Freedom" in Haiti and, for him, the most important among them were the Voodoo leaders, three of whom were slaves. There was Macandal from the Limbé

plantation, born in Africa, he was a charismatic clairvoyant who was prone to visions. There was Jean François, a fugitive slave from the north, who surrounded himself with sorcerers, bones, and symbolic items. Finally, there was Boukman, who was born in Jamaica, had escaped from a plantation in Morne-Rouge, and led the ceremony that started the revolution. According to Simpson, who draws on Dorainvil's description: The night of the ceremony there was a big storm, an old woman danced with a cutlass, which she stuck into a black hog, and concluded with a ceremony in which the assembled drank its blood. Six days later, the slave revolt began (518).

65. Laguerre, *Voodoo Heritage*, 38.

66. Toumédia, ed., Haïti-Pape 83 (Port-au-Prince: Imprimerie Henri Deschamps, 1983), 41.

67. Jan, *Collecta* 2: 34. Jan cites the former apostolic prefect from Western Haiti, who fled the colony, saying that the slaughter was carried out by the mulattos.

68. James Leyburn, *The Haitian People* (New Haven and London: Yale University Press, 1966), 119.

69. Ibid.

70. Cabon, *Notes Sur L'Histoire Religieuse d'Haïti*, 94.

71. Jan, *Collecta* 2: 34. Reports on this event differ as to whether the *Te Deum* occurred during or after the ceremony. The question is whether it was a civil ceremony. Jan insists that the *Te Deum* followed the service, making it a civil service. In any case, the service was conducted by a parish priest from Cap-Haïtien.

72. Cabon, *Notes Sur L'Histoire Religieuse d'Haïti*, 94. Cabon states that the Church believed the effect of these clauses would be to ruin the family.

73. Jan, *Collecta* 2: 36.

74. Ibid. 2:37.

75. Charles Poisset Romain, *Le Protestantisme dans la Société Haïtienne* (Port-au-Prince: Imprimerie Henri Deschamps, 1986), 70.

76. Jan, *Collecta* 2: 93.

77. Romain, *Le Protestantisme dans la Société Haïtienne*, 51.

78. Pressoir, *Le Protestantisme Haïtien* 1: 94.

79. Ibid. 1: 62.

80. Ibid. 1: 94.

81. Cabon, *Notes Sur L'Histoire Religieuse d'Haïti*, 301.

82. Jan, *Collecta* 2: 18. See Remy Dastien, "Voodoo and Politics in Haiti," in *Churches and Politics in Latin America*, ed. David Levine (London and Beverly Hills: Sage Publications, 1979), 43.

83. Jan, *Collecta* 2: 17. The Curial Law of 17 July 1816 required council notables to inspect Churches and rectories, name Church wardens, and receive their accounts. As of 13 October 1816, priests were not to officiate at baptisms or marriages until a declaration had been made with the state.

84. Michel-Rolph Trouillot, *Haiti, State Against Nation: The Origins and Legacy of Duvalierism* (New York: Monthly Review Press, 1990), 51–52. In the opinion of Trouillot, the Vatican and the United States did the most to isolate Haiti until the second half of the nineteenth century. "Given the United State's vocal refusal to admit Haiti to the community of American states, only papal support might have encouraged the new governments of Catholic Latin America to challenge the U.S. position."

85. Cabon, *Notes Sur L'Histoire Religieuse d'Haïti*, 94–300

86. Ibid., 415. This story is only intended to show the long-term effects of not having diplomatic relations. The question about whether the Church should crown kings was not in contention.

87. Ibid., 334.
88. Ibid., 359.
89. Laguerre, *Voodoo Heritage*, 44. By 1928, Laguerre puts the number of ordained priests at forty.
90. Cabon, *Notes Sur L'Histoire Religieuse d'Haïti*, 105.
91. Jan, *Collecta* 2: 41. The four recommendations were: to name a bishop, to conclude a concordat, to relocate the archbishop's seat from the Dominican Republic to Port-au-Prince, and to create an indigenous priesthood.
92. Cabon, *Notes Sur L'Histoire Religieuse d'Haïti*, 393.
93. J. Parisot, "Vodou et Christianisme," in A. Abble, J.C. Bajeux, J. Bala, and G. Bissainth, eds., *Des Prêtres Noirs S'Interrogent* (Paris: Editions du Cerf, 1956), 240.
94. Cabon, *Notes Sur L'Histoire Religieuse d'Haïti*, 227.
95. Ibid., 353.
96. Jan, *Collecta* 2: 72.
97. Cabon, *Notes Sur L'Histoire Religieuse d'Haïti*, 243–44.
98. "Masonry" *World Book* 20 (Childcraft International, 1979).
99. Jan, *Collecta* 2: 178–82. This section on the Freemasons is largely drawn from Jan's *Collecta*, in which he refers to Freemasonry as "the born enemy of all religion."
100. Pressoir, *Le Protestantisme Haïtien* 1: 56.
101. Ibid., 1: 61.
102. Romain, *Le Protestantisme dans la Société Haïtienne*, 52.
103. Pressoir, *Le Protestantisme Haïtien* 1: 221–22.
104. Cabon, *Notes Sur L'Histoire Religieuse d'Haïti*, 474.
105. Pressoir, *Le Protestantisme Haïtien* 1: 150.
106. Ibid., 1: 120.
107. Jan, *Collecta* 2: 63.
108. Pressoir, *Le Protestantisme Haïtien* 1: 214.
109. Ibid., 1: 140.
110. Ibid., 1: 218.
111. Cabon, *Notes Sur L'Histoire Religieuse d'Haïti*, 219–34.
112. Ibid., 247.
113. Jan, *Collecta* 2: 68–69.
114. Cabon, *Notes Sur L'Histoire Religieuse d'Haïti*, 304–5.
115. Ibid., 334.
116. Jan, *Collecta*, 2: 72–73.
117. James Timothy Kelly, "Rocks in the Sun: The Roman Catholic Church in Haitian Political Development" (Senior honors thesis, Harvard University, March 1988), 12. Kelly asserts that the mulatto elite became convinced of the need for a concordat when it experienced the protection given to Voodoo by Soulouque.
118. Cabon, *Notes Sur L'Histoire Religieuse d'Haïti*, 478–87.
119. Toumédia, ed., *Haïti-Pape* 83, 12.
120. J. M. Jan, *Collecta Pour L'Histoire Religieuse du Diocèse du Cap-Haïtien*, vol. 3 (Port-au-Prince: Editions Henri Deschamps, undated [1960]), 29.
121. Ibid., 3: 82, 85, 87.
122. Ibid., 3: 67.
123. Ibid., 3: 84.
124. Ibid., 3: 83.
125. Ibid., 3: 71.
126. Ibid., 3: 136.
127. Ibid., 3: 110.

128. Ibid., 3: 10.

129. Jan, *Collecta*, 2: 83

130. Ibid., 2:92.

131. Ibid., 2:110.

132. Jan, *Collecta*, 3: 101.

133. Jan, *Collecta*, 2: 45.

134. Jan, *Collecta*, 3: 48.

135. Jan, *Collecta*, 2: 101.

136. Jan, *Collecta*, 3: 43–47.

137. Ibid., 3: 173–74.

138. Ibid., 3: 120–21.

139. Ibid., 3: 34.

140. Ibid., 3: 50.

141. Ibid., 3: 86.

142. Ibid., 3: 93.

143. Ibid., 3: 113.

144. Ibid., 3: 28. Elsewhere Jan writes that in 1874, the rate of legitimate births was 15 percent. In 1875 it had risen to 15.5 percent, and by 1877 it had reached 17 percent (2: 110).

145. Ibid., 3: 40.

146. Jan, *Collecta*, 2: 153.

147. Jan, *Collecta*, 3: 26.

148. Ibid., 3: 84.

149. Ibid., 3: 86.

150. Ibid., 3: 46. President Leslie Manigat, interview with author, Bethesda, MD, 9 September 1988. President Manigat believes this seminary never produced a single Haitian priest.

151. Ibid., 3: 124.

152. Ibid., 3: 42.

153. Ibid., 3: 16–17.

154. Rotberg, *Haiti: The Politics of Squalor*, 99–100.

155. Jan, *Collecta*, 3: 100.

156. Ibid., 3: 174.

157. Ibid., 3: 113.

158. Ibid., 3: 125.

159. Jan, *Collecta*, 2: 177.

160. Ibid., 2: 172–82.

161. Ibid., 2: 170–71.

162. Pressoir, *Le Protestantisme Haïtien*, 1: 232–33.

163. Romain, *Le Protestantisme dans la Société Haïtienne*, 69.

164. "A History of the Episcopal Church in Haiti," church document, nd. This typed document was given to me by Bishop Luc Garnier in July 1986.

165. Ibid.

166. Pressoir, *Le Protestantisme Haïtien*, 1: 264–65.

167. Ibid., 1: 339.

168. Jan, *Collecta*, 2: 137.

169. Jan, *Collecta*, 3: 60.

170. Ibid., 3: 47.

171. Ibid., 3: 52.

172. Ibid., 3: 59.

173. Ibid., 3: 53–54.
174. Ibid., 3: 58.
175. Ibid., 3: 60.
176. Ibid., 3: 101.
177. Ibid., 3: 113.
178. Ibid., 3: 130.
179. Ibid., 3: 157.
180. Ibid., 3: 142.
181. Ibid., 3: 158.
182. Ibid., 3: 163.
183. Ibid., 3: 213.
184. Ibid., 3: 144.
185. Ibid., 3: 248.
186. Ibid., 3: 159.
187. Ibid., 3: 207.
188. Ibid., 3: 137.
189. Ibid., 3: 195. I was told in 1988 by two foreign priest who have worked for years in Haiti that the Church is currently 80 percent female. They assured me that without women, the Church would fail.
190. Jan, *Collecta,* 2: 110.
191. Jan, *Collecta,* 3: 136.
192. Leyburn, *The Haitian People,* 129.
See also Jan, *Collecta,* 3: 171. Jan provides some additional figures concerning the changing numbers of priest during this period: in 1882 there were 104 priests, in 1905 there were 164, in 1914 there were 197, and by 1922 there were 157.
193. Leyburn, *The Haitian People,* 129.
194. Jan, *Collecta,* 3: 155.
195. Ibid., 3: 190.
196. Max-Abner Etienne, "Interview de L'Archêveque François Wolff Ligondé," *Jeune Haïti* (23 April 1986): 92.
197. Jan, *Collecta* 3: 217.
198. Ibid., 3: 163. A plan was proposed by the Church in 1921 to establish a teachers' training school that would accept 15-year-olds, lodge them in dormitories where they would not have any opportunity to get used to city life, "or they would lose the taste for returning to the countryside," train them intellectually and religiously for three years, and then send them to rural areas to teach.
199. Ibid., 3: 174.
200. Ibid., 3: 214.
201. Pressoir, *Le Protestantisme Haïtien,* 1: 36.
202. Romain, *Le Protestantisme dans la Société Haïtienne,* 346.
203. Ibid., 118.
204. Georges Corvington, Port-au-Prince au Cours des Ans: La Capitale d'Haïti Sous L'Occupation 1915–1922 (Port-au-Prince: Henri Deschamps, 1984), 254.
205. Ibid., 262.
206. Jan, *Collecta* 3: 330–31.
207. Ibid., 3: 339.
208. Ibid., 3: 335.
209. Ibid., 3: 144.
210. Corvington, *La Capitale d'Haïti Sous L'Occupation 1915–1922,* 263.
211. Jan, *Collecta,* 3: 317.
212. Corvington, *La Capitale d'Haïti Sous L'Occupation 1915–1922,* 264.

213. Jan, *Collecta*, 3: 350.

214. Ibid., 3: 355.

215. Georges Corvington, *Port-au-Prince au Cours des Ans: La Capitale d'Haïti Sous L'Occupation 1922–1934* (Port-au-Prince: Henri Deschamps, 1958). Corvington writes that the testimony before the Forbes Commission "washed off all suspicion the Church had aroused." This assessment seems unjustified in light of subsequent resentment toward the Church, efforts to separate the Church and state, and to oblige the institution to become more socially responsive.

216. Jan, *Collecta*, 3: 355.

217. Corvington, *La Capitale d'Haïti Sous L'Occupation 1922–1934*, 259.

218. Jan, *Collecta*, 3: 136. Jan claims that the occupation forces changed their minds when they saw the bad faith of the Voodoo practitioners who went to Church in the morning and then practiced Voodoo in the evening. Consequently, they chased the *bocors* and their followers as far away as possible, in some cases, to the border.
See Corvington, *La Capitale d'Haïti Sous L'Occupation 1922–1934*, 259. Corvington suggests that the occupation forces may have turned against Voodoo after hearing the peasants call for killing whites.

219. Ibid., 3: 182.

220. Ibid., 3: 224.

221. Ibid., 3: 249.

222. Jean Price-Mars, *Ainsi Parla L'Oncle: Essais d'Ethnographie* (Port-au-Prince, 1928).

223. Métraux, *Le Vaudou Haïtiten*, 300–1.

224. Ibid., 302–3.

225. Bernard Diederich and Al Burt, *Papa Doc: The Truth About Haiti Today* (New York: McGraw-Hill, 1969), 47. Perhaps the fear of future antisuperstition campaigns led Alfred Métraux to urge that the history of Voodoo be recorded. Jacques Romain, Dr. Price-Mars, and Alfred Métraux subsequently founded the Bureau of Ethnology.

226. Romain, *Le Protestantisme dans la Société Haïtienne*, 14.

227. Ibid., 79.

228. Ibid., 180.

229. Kelly, "Rocks in the Sun: The Roman Catholic Church," 47. Kelly is citing Laënnec Hurbon in Présence Africaine, 109.

230. The Episcopalians fared worse than the other Protestants with Franççois Duvalier because they were more closely connected to the elite, a sector of the population that Duvalier disliked.

231. Jean-Robert Estimé, interview with the author, Wheaton, MD, 13 October 1988. The ambassador says that his family did not practice Voodoo, adding that Voodoo ceremonies were not held in the palace or on its steps during his father's presidency.

232. Leslie Manigat, interview with author, Bethesda, MD, 16 September 1988. Manigat describes the Estimé presidency as an important time for Church-State relations and for the Church. Estimé wanted to redo the concordat, giving more power to the government. In 1946, for the first time, there was a change in the racial situation in the Church. Before then, black priests had been sent to the countryside and generally treated as second-class citizens.

233. Ibid.

234. Jean-Robert Estimé, interview with the author, Wheaton, MD, 13 October 1988. When asked about this incident, the ambassador did not seem to know about it, saying that he was young at the time. After he had spoken with someone who knew about it, perhaps his mother, he said he doubted the minister tried to kill the priest.

235. *Statuts Diocésains* (Port-au-Prince: Imprimerie La Phalange, 1957).
236. Ibid., 6, 94.
237. Ibid., 119.
238. Ibid., 57–58.
239. Ibid., 105.
240. Ibid., 42–43.
241. Ibid., 47, 66, 75.
242. Ibid., 76–77.
243. Ibid., 90, 100.
244. Ibid., 92.
245. Ibid., 139.
246. Ibid., 120.
247. Ibid., 17, 52, 145.
248. Ibid., 14.
249. Ibid., 16, 34.
250. Ibid., 44, 79.
251. Ibid., 51.
252. Ibid., 119.
253. Ibid., 69–70, 76.
254. Ibid., 171–72.
255. Leslie Manigat, interview with author, Bethesda, MD, 16 September 1988. Manigat maintains that these priests were not part of the ethnology movement; they were from the elite and their interest was in socialism. He describes them as the spiritual predecessors of Jean-Bertrand Aristide. They also formed a political party called the New Catholic Party.
256. A. Abble, et al., eds., *Des Prêtres Noirs S'Interrogent* (Paris: Editions du Cerf, 1956).
Some of the Spiritans went to New York. In 1972, they began publishing a magazine in Creole called *Sel*, which criticized the Duvalier regime.
257. E. Verdieu and P. Onia, "Sacerdoce et Négritude," in *Des Prêtres Noirs S'Interrogent*, eds. Abble, et al. (Paris: Editions du Cerf, 1956), 90.
258. Jean-Claudé Bajeux, "Mentalité Noire et Mentalité Biblique," in *Des Prêtres Noirs S'Interrogent*, eds. Abble, et al. (Paris: Editions du Cerf, 1956), 80.
259. Meinrad Hebga, "Christianisme et Négritude," in *Des Prêtres Noirs S'Interrogent*, eds. Abble, et al. (Paris: Editions du Cerf, 1956), 200.
260. Gérard Bissainte, "Catholicisme et Indigénisme Religieux," in *Des Prêtres Noirs S'Interrogent*, eds. Abble, et al. (Paris: Editions du Cerf, 1956), 128, 133.
261. Hebga, "Christianisme et Négritude," 201.
262. Gérard G. Gayot, *Clergé Indigène*, 2d ed. (Montreal: Comité de *Clergé Indigène*, 1965). Gérard is the brother of Bishop François Gayot.
263. Ibid., 115, 140. Gayot virtually accuses the foreign priests of hating Africa, of suffering from what he terms "*africanophobie*."
264. Ibid., "Preface".
265. Ibid., 104.
266. Ibid., 108–9. Of the new seminarians in 1955–56, there were six in Haiti and twelve abroad (the orders of those abroad included two Montfortain, seven Spiritan, one Oblat, one Salesien, and one Saint Croix).
267. Ibid., 109.
268. Ibid., 117–20. There were charges for every sacrament, and the prices varied according to the quality of the service rendered. For example, there were five classes of marriages, burials, and baptisms.

269. Ibid., 126, 130–31, 142. Gayot looks forward to seeing eighteen thousand *gourdes* annually going to the Haitian seminary, adding, "Let the Bretons come here if they want."

270. François Duvalier, *Mémoires d'un Leader du Tiers Monde*. (Paris: Hachette, 1969).

271. Eric Fouchard, "The Haitian Church and Dictatorship," CIF Reports 5, no. 8 (16 April 1966): 58. Translated from the Mexican daily *Novedades*, 20 February 1966, Mexico, D.F. Fouchard writes that it is difficult to determine how far Duvalier's practice of Voodoo influenced his treatment of the Church, but it is almost certain that some of the expulsions of religious personnel were motivated by its rigid attitude against Voodoo during the antisupersition campaign.

272. Diederich and Burt, *Papa Doc*, 283, 284. Diederich and Burt cite sections of *Le Catéchisme de la Révolution*.

273. Fouchard, "The Haitian Church and Dictatorship," 58. Fouchard writes that Duvalier's political attitude toward the Church had no ideological base whatsoever. "He makes use of the Church only so long as she can serve him. He eliminates all real or potential danger which an independent Church might pose for him—clerical criticism, Christian-sponsored movements, etc."

274. Duvalier, *Mémoires*, 143.

275. Marian McClure, "The Catholic Church and Rural Social Change: Priests, Peasant Organizations and Politics in Haiti" (Ph.D. diss., Harvard University, 1985), 139. McClure speculates that Duvalier may have wanted to reduce the foreign presence in the country and to punish the Church for the anti-Voodoo campaign.

276. His resentment was not immediately evident, but one of Duvalier's motives for destroying the French-dominated Church was that it had supported Déjoie in the 1957 elections. See Arnold Antonin, "Haitian Church Standing Up to Duvalier," *Latinamerico Press* 15, no. 9 (17 March 1983): 2.

277. David Nicholls, *From Dessalines to Duvalier: Race, Colour and National Independence in Haiti* (Cambridge: Cambridge University Press, 1979), 210.

278. Mecham, *Church and State in Latin Americai*, 291. Mecham notes that the Duvalier government appointed two successive Haitian-born priests to that position, but that was not enough for Duvalier, who regarded the priests "as agents of a foreign power . . . [of being] socially and politically subversive."

279. Gregory K. Freeland, Religious Elites and Political Activity in Haiti (prepared for delivery at the 1985 Annual Meeting of the Western Political Science Association, Las Vegas, 28–30 March 1985).

280. Kelly, "Rocks in the Sun: The Roman Catholic Church," 31.

281. Duvalier, *Mémoires*, 69. Duvalier justified the archbishop's ouster in his *Mémoires*, charging him with "overt hostility to the constitutional Government of Haiti."

282. Diederich and Burt, *Papa Doc*, 162.

283. Nicholls, *From Dessalines to Duvalier*, 222.

284. Hubert Herring, *A History of Latin America from the Beginnings to the Present*, 3d. ed. (New York: Knopf, 1972), 437.

285. Duvalier, *Mémoires*, 84. The material consisted of several articles that opposed the charter of the university and some correspondence between a priest and the apostolic administrator.

286. Fouchard, "The Haitian Church and Dictatorship," 57. According to Fouchar, 53 of the 462 priests in Haiti in 1959 were expelled by the government. Three of these were bishops. With the exception of 18 Canadian Jesuits, all were French.

287. Ibid., 91. See Nicholls, *From Dessalines to Duvalier*, 181–82.

288. Duvalier, *Mémoires*, 70.
It is unclear how much this hurt the president. Ferrofino was in poor presidential graces, having taken a trip to the Antilles instead of attending a State function.
289. Nicholls, *From Dessalines to Duvalier*, 225.
290. There was a consensus between the Holy See and François Duvalier on two points: they both favored revision of the concordat and additional autonomy for national churches. The Vatican was responding to reformist movements within the Church suggested at Vatican II. François Duvalier must have been thinking about enhancing his own authority.
291. *Primer Encuentro Latinoamericano de Cristianos por el Socialismo* (Havana: Ediciones Camilo Torres, 1973), 112. This report was drafted by Haitian priests in preparation for a meeting of Priests for Socialism that took place in Santiago, Chile, but it was not included in the final paper report.
292. Duvalier, *Mémoires*, 46, 100–1. By 1960 François Duvalier had ousted two French bishops and a number of priests from Haiti. Their departure appeared to create some vacancies and Duvalier wanted to fill them. In a letter from the secretary of state in the Vatican on 15 March 1961, Duvalier was informed that the posts were not vacant. They were full, *seda plena*, and in response to a further inquiry, he was told there was no retirement age for clergy.
293. Ibid., 229.
294. Toumédia, ed., *Haïti-Pape* 83, 16. See Antonin, "Haitian Church Standing Up to Duvalier," 2. According to Antonin, the government appointment of bishops became known euphemistically as the "harmony between the temporal and spiritual orders." In effect, it meant total submission of the Church to the State.
295. Mecham, *Church and State in Latin America*, 291–92. Quoting a Church source in a *New York Times* article on 24 August 1959, Mecham writes that the native origins of the clerical personnel had changed, "for in 1959, the number of Haitian priests had risen to 110, compared with 180 Frenchmen. In addition there were forty Oblate Fathers from Canada and the United States and twenty Belgian priests who had been recently expelled from Red China. Their presence should have served to dilute Duvalier's resentment against the French priest. This was not the case for the dictator's objective was a native clergy subservient to him."
296. Fouchard, "The Haitian Church and Dictatorship," 59. Fouchard writes, "The moment is approaching when the responsibility for the Church will lie in the hands of the native clergy." In April 1966, there were thirty-two seminarians studying in Port-au-Prince, forty-two in Canada, and twenty priests and seminarians in Europe. Groups of laymen were also being prepared.
See Freeland, *Religious Elites and Political Activity in Haiti*, 16–17 and Appendix I for additional information concerning changes in numbers of bishops, clergy, seminarians, members of men and womens' religious orders, and schools. Freeland notes that nearly two-thirds of the Catholic clergy in Haiti were foreigners during the François Duvalier era and that the number had been reversed by 1985, with approximately two-thirds of the 550 priests in Haiti being Haitians, including all of the bishops. Freeland associates the pronouncements of Vatican II with the growth of a politically aggressive and socially conscious clergy who formed the advance guard for subsequent priests who became more politically active. He points to figures showing that the number of priests and religious participants and institutions rose markedly in the year following Vatican II and Medellín.
John Hogan, "Social Change and Development in Haiti" (Seminar, Johns Hopkins University, SAIS, 31 January 1990). Hogan said the Haitianization of the bishops led a number of young priests—trained abroad in countries such as Chile and Canada—to come back to Haiti and begin work in grassroots development.

297. The new Haitian clergy generally came from rural, middle class families. After being ordained, it was natural for them to return to these rural areas to work for the well-being of people there.

298. Fouchard, "The Haitian Church and Dictatorship," 58. Fouchard comments that when the Haitian government gave vacant parishes to native priests, it applied its own criterion, "which was not that of the Church." The result was a "de facto" compromise with the government by certain members of the Haitian clergy. "Unfortunately, the government favors those elements of the Haitian clergy which will hardly create a sound Church."

See Antonin, "Haitian Church Standing Up to Duvalier," 2. Antonin provides some examples of the kind of clergy the government encouraged and the institution's reaction to them. The Church "even overlooked priests directly affiliated with the *tontons macoutes*. One priest, Father Leon Max Bouilaget, a *tonton macoute* leader and pastor of the parish of Léogâne, hunted down opponents of the Duvalier dictatorship with a rifle on his back. Another celebrated Mass with a gun in his belt while still others used the pulpit to defend the regime's abuses." Antonin explains the easy co-optation of the Haitian clergy by its colonial history and lack of earlier opportunity.

299. *Primer Encuentro Latinoamericano de Cristianos por el Socialismo*, 112–13. In this document, the Haitian delegation to the First Meeting of Christians for Socialism in Chile in 1973 charged that the hierarchy of the Church did nothing but cooperate with the government despite the incidents that took place between 1969 and 1971. When a World Day of Peace was organized by the papal nuncio and the minister of religion, the Church presented a plaque lauding François Duvalier's interest in social justice and peace. Following François Duvalier's death, dominance of the Church by the regime continued, and even accelerated. President Jean-Claude Duvalier was taken around the country and received with "jubilation and adoration" by bishops and priests.

See Fouchard, "The Haitian Church and Dictatorship," 59. Fouchard argues against "the anachronism of the Concordats," maintaining that "the Church would do well to rid herself of State support." The concordat has continued to be an issue.

300. See Nicholls, *From Dessalines to Duvalier*, 227, which provides a description of Duvalier's subsequent treatment of the Church. See also *Primer Encuentro Latinoamericano de Cristianos por el Socialismo*, 112–13.

301. See Fouchard, "The Haitian Church and Dictatorship," 59. Fouchard looks at the human rights violations in Haiti. "Christians living under this arbitrary regime of terror need to feel that the priests are still on their side, whether acting individually or in small groups, to inspire, encourage, and teach society. Prudence does not mean non-action, but intelligent, effective action." The first condition for any collective answer though is "to achieve unity between the hierarchy and the clergy so that they can act as a body with clear-cut principles."

302. "L'Episcopat, Le Clergé et Leur Rôle National," *Haïti-Observateur*, 28 December 1984 - 4 January 1985. A number of priests recall being wary of François Duvalier even though they were glad to see the beginning of a Haitianized Church.

303. *Primer Encuentro Latinoamericano de Cristianos por el Socialismo*, 111.

304. F. Solages, A La Recherche d'Une Pastorale Haïtienne, "Simple Notes" (Port-au-Prince: Imprimerie de l'Etat, 1967). This book was printed under the supervision of Carl E. Peters, SMM, the auxiliary bishop of Des Cayes with the permission of the Church. In light of text and the Appendix containing Pope Paul VI's advice to Latin American bishops on 23 November 1965, it is reasonable to conclude that the author was influenced by ideas produced by Vatican II.

305. Ibid., 185.

306. Ibid., 40.

307. Simpson, "The Belief System of Haitian Vodun," 504. One reason the Church wanted more priests becomes obvious when the number of clergy in 1957 is juxtaposed to the number of *houngans* twenty years earlier in 1937. Simpson wrote that there was one *houngan* per one hundred and fifty people (two hundred per thirty thousand population) in the town of Plaisance in 1937.

308. Solages, *A La Recherche d'Une Pastorale Haïtienne*, 187.

309. Ibid., 201–6.

Vatican II and the CELAM meeting provided attendees with the opportunity to discuss their experiences. A common problem in the Third World was that many governments were not meeting the basic needs of their citizens. The Church moved in to meet the need, as can be seen from the escalation of social and economic development projects dating from the late 1960s.

310. *Primer Encuentro Latinoamericano de Cristianos por el Socialismo*, 113. After the disillusionment of the 1960s and the Alliance for Progress, the Christians for Socialism were critical of development as a solution to regional problems. The authors questioned how the Church could be content to focus on development when basic human rights were being violated in Haiti.

311. Solages, *A La Recherche d'Une Pastorale Haïtienne*, 164.

312. Ibid., 28.

313. Ibid., 30.

314. Ibid., 31.

4

The Church and Jean-Claude Duvalier

In this chapter we see how changes in the Church's concept of its mission contributed to its confrontation with the government and involvement in the ouster of President-for-Life Jean-Claude Duvalier. When some other critical sectors in Haitian society were silenced, the Church gradually took over. Initially focusing on attacks against Church people, it increasingly denounced other cases of repression. The government resented this intervention, condemning the Church for exceeding the conditions of the concordat. The Church vehemently denied this, quoting papal authority to justify its social and political role in society. The Church came under additional attack for pointing out government shortcomings, and urging change and adherence to commitments. Those who objected to government behavior and policy were subject to threats, arrests, or worse. The Church was becoming the authority Haitians trusted; working throughout Haiti, protecting people from abuse, and keeping them informed. In mid-1985, *Radio Soleil* accurately predicted that a pending referendum would result in a government landslide despite the low voter turnout and that a promised political opening would not occur. It was saying that the government was incapable of change, and Haitians got the message. When the government offered some concessions to a disgruntled nation, the Church urged people to reject palliatives. Haitians responded by issuing non-negotiable demands. Catholic youth groups called for the ouster of the president, refusing to return to school until this occurred. By mid-January 1986, all sectors of society were convinced: President Duvalier had to leave.

LEGAL BASES AND GOVERNMENT OVERSIGHT OF THE CHURCH

The presence of the Catholic Church in Haiti is based on a text of international law, the concordat of 28 March 1860.[1] Article I states that the Church enjoys a unique position in Haiti and further, as the religion of the majority, it is to be specially protected along with its ministries. The concordat is an international treaty, and Article XVI, referring to this point, states that it does not have to adhere to Haitian law. Nevertheless, it requires the Haitian government to provide for its economic support.[2]

Ambassador Jean-Robert Estimé, the minister of foreign affairs and religion during the most confrontational period in Church-State relations was a key player in the events.[3] He was a historic choice for the post. His own father, Dumarsais Estimé, had been elected president following the occupation and antisuperstitious campaign with the support of black nationalists and followers of Voodoo.[4]

The cabinet that formed in February 1982 caught the public's attention because of its youth and reformist potential. In addition to Estimé, it included Marc Bazin, who became minister of finance, Frantz Merceron who took over the interior ministry, and Gérard Alert, who became minister of commerce.

Duvalier's cabinets were typically short-lived, so Ambassador Estimé's career was unusual. He held the position until December 1985, when he and other members of the "Super Cabinet" were fired in a last-minute effort by the President to prolong his stay in office. Subsequently, Duvalier appointed Estimé ambassador to the Organization of American States, a position he was unable to fill before the government fell.

Jean-Robert Estimé spent his childhood in Europe, initially because the family was in exile. He attended schools in France and Belgium. After graduating from the Engineering School of Agricultural Sciences in Gembloux, Belgium in 1964, he returned to Haiti to work in the countryside as director of research for the Industrial Development Institute, which lent money to farmers. In 1972, Estimé became a professor of ecology at the University of Port-au-Prince, simultaneously completing a master's degree in economics and sociology in Belgium. In 1976, he was made advisor to the National Council of Development and Planning in the Ministry of Planning, where he served until becoming secretary of state for finance and economic affairs in 1979. In 1981, he was named ambassador to France. The following year, he was appointed secretary of state for foreign affairs and religion. In 1983, he became the minister of foreign affairs and religion. In this post, he was in charge of all programs dealing with all religions in Haiti. He inspected and accredited religious denominations and paid the salaries of the Catholic clergy.[5]

Ambassador Estimé enjoyed being minister of foreign affairs but not minister of religion— he "hated it."[6] The latter was frustrating, "*un coup d'épée dans l'eau*," like cutting water with a sword, and it took up over 10 percent of his time.[7] Estimé recalled that his authority was sometimes usurped and that the government was always the loser.

The same issues recurred.[8] Citizens reported that the Church was belittling the government, and the Church complained to him about people who had been arrested or had had their land stolen. The administration tried to solve these problems. It would send "circulars" to the community officials, the *chefs de section*, urging them to stop [taking advantage of people] but "Haitians love power and the problems continued."

Jean-Robert Estimé dealt principally with the Conference of Haitian Bishops (CHB) but also with the Conference of Haitian Religious (CHR) and with religious and diocesan priests—and "had problems with all of them."[9] His ministry requested that the hierarchy control the clergy. Although the bishops promised to deal with the priests and take sanctions against them, "it never happened." Frustration forced him to make two trips to Rome to tell Cardinal Agostino Casaroli and Archbishop Achille Silvestrini that "something had to be done to prevent a worsening situation from leading to serious conflict." Estimé argued that the government did not instigate problems with the Church; it tried to avoid them. Even after some occurrence, the administration would try to find compromises and solutions, which Ambassador Estimé characterized as "erratic positions;" the government was incapable of being "consistent in taking a strong position" because Jean-Claude wanted to avoid "*les ennuis*," or problems. [10]

As the Church's sphere of interests widened, they intersected those of the State. Rural development and literacy were two of these realms. The Ambassador established a *Commission Mixte*,[11] composed of government officials and bishops, to work on issues of mutual interest, such as literacy and rural development in an attempt to prevent problems.

Government suspicion of the Church and its treatment of people connected with Church rural development did not make cooperation easy. Estimé had had minimal interaction with the Christian Base Communities (CEBs) prior to the Duclerville affair,[12] but after meeting some of the lay workers involved with them, recalls being "impressed."[13] In his view, the CEBs were doing the job that the government should have done. Although he thought that some of the CEBs were infiltrated by the left and "shared some ideas with the communists,"[14] he doubted that Duclerville and other lay workers were actually Marxists. Consequently, he wrote a somewhat conciliatory letter on 21 December 1984 to the *Révérends Pères*, [15] saying that an earlier government press release, which had implied that the Institut d'Education des Adultes (IDEA) was a communist organization, was not aimed at the whole organization but only certain members.

Ultimately, Estimé had a lot of contact with the CEBs because they were in the vanguard of Church activism and became principal government targets for assault and arrest. The Church protested through correspondence and visits to the Ministry. Joseph Serge Milot, secretary of the CHB, wrote to Ambassador Estimé on 7 November 1984, "alerting" him to the apprehension of three IDEA *animateurs*. Milot did not know why they had been detained or why one had been taken to Port-au-Prince while the others had been taken to Cap-Haïtien, but he asked the Minister to intercede so none would receive bad treatment.[16]

Literacy, like rural development, was another area in which the government did little itself but resented Church involvement.[17] In 1985, after years of criticizing Church curricula and pedagogy, it joined the Church in its literacy program by providing books and training materials. Its motives were to prevent the Church from using literacy as a pretext for evangelism and to keep it from taking all of the credit.[18]

THE STRUCTURE OF THE CHURCH IN HAITI

Haiti has five dioceses: Cayes, Jérémie, Gonaïves, Port de Paix, and Hinche, and two archdioceses, Port-au-Prince and Cap-Haïtien. The number of parishes varies, but, as of 1984, there were more than 170.[19] It would be difficult to present an all-inclusive diagram of the organization and bureaucratic structure of the Church in Haiti, in part because of its size but also because of its myriad informal relationships.

An overview of the Church structure might start with the papal nuncio.[20] Haiti has had an apostolic nunciature since 1930. Since 29 March 1984, the nuncio has been Paolo Romeo.[21] There is the CHB, whose president is Bishop Léonard P. Laroche of Hinche.[22] There are also a number of major commissions. Among them are Justice and Peace, headed by Bishop Benjamin Constant of Gonaïves, Youth, headed by Bishop Willy Romélus of Jérémie, and Social Affairs, which runs the Church radio station, *Radio Soleil*, which was, until April 1989, directed in Port-au-Prince by Father Hugo Triest. There is the CHR, whose president is Father Fracilus Petti-Homme. There is the Church itself and the *Ti-Légliz*, or Little Church, which forms its popular base.

THE CHANGING MISSION OF THE CATHOLIC CHURCH IN HAITI

The Church mission in Haiti has changed as a consequence of Vatican II (1962–1965), the indigenization of the Haitian hierarchy in 1966, and the regional conferences of Medellín (1968) and Puebla (1979).[23] One Haitian bishop, who witnessed it all, described the transformation as "spectaculaire." The focus of Church evangelism has shifted from concern about spiritual and educational well-being of the urban elite to the collective well-being of the nation, particularly its poor.[24] Its approach to the faithful has become more egalitarian and somewhat less hierarchical. Since 1966, it has increasingly used Creole, the only language of most Haitians, and sought to incorporate Haitian culture into the liturgy.[25] It has taken its evangelical message and socio-economic expertise to rural areas.[26]

The CEBs, known variously as the *Ti-Légliz* (Little Churches), *l'eglise qui vit la vie du peuple*, (the Church that lives the life of the people), and *Ti Kominote* (Little Communities) are the most wide-ranging and perhaps the most important examples of the new Church and synthesis of religious and secular work.[n27 These progressive and preponderantly female groups[28] have become so extensive that a national committee oversees the activities of the more than five thousand CEBs.[29]

As a result of its accessibility and relevance, the Church has attracted new members.[30] Children in increasing numbers are taking communion, parents are having their babies baptized, and couples are participating in marriage counseling.[31] In addition, more Haitians are becoming priests.

The total number of priests did not change significantly between 1959 and 1983; there was a slight decrease, from 465 to 440. However, the ratio of foreign to Haitian priests changed.[32] Although the number of diocesan priests stayed roughly constant, decreasing from 278 to 251, the percentage of Haitian priests more than doubled, rising from 30 percent in 1959 to 67 percent in 1983. In 1959, there were 187 religious priests in Haiti but none were Haitian. By 1983,[33] although the number of religious priests had scarcely changed, thirty-six, or 19 percent, were Haitian.

The number of religious laity also increased between 1959 and 1983, from 178 to 250. In 1959, none were Haitian—by 1983, thirty-five, or 14 percent were Haitian. During the same years, the number of nuns increased from 701 to 1,118. By 1983, 647, or 58 percent, were Haitian.

From the late 1960s, the Church increasingly focused its efforts on improving conditions in rural Haiti through education and economic development.[34] The CEBs were an important developmental and spiritual tool.[35] On his arrival in 1981, Ambassador Preeg referred to the institution as a "quiet Church,"[36] and his embassy characterized it as "not doing much." Robert Tata went even further, writing that "religion was not an influential institution in Haitian national affairs."[37] In the opinion of this observer, these assessments were shortsighted.[38] The Church was actively spreading its network, developing roots in the country and generating the respect and authority that would later be of assistance in its dealings with the government.[39]

Papal authority indirectly supported the Haitian Church in its new mission.[40] Pope Paul VI legitimized the Church role as an agent of social justice in his encyclical, *Populorum Progresio.* John Paul II cited Puebla document, *Gaudiem et Spes*, at the United Nations on 2 October 1979, to justify Church involvement in secular matters, saying, "It would mutilate the gospel to confine its influence only to the personal and familial dimensions and exclude it from the social and political order." Over the years, the Church has drawn on these doctrinal sources and used them to support its positions.

The ministry of religion was not pleased about the changing mission of the Church.[41] "The similarity between the thesis of Puebla and the new doctrinal orientation of the Haitian Church is striking and has the same bad result." The Haitian Church has aligned itself with the Latin American Churches and "these Churches exert on their governments the same types of pressure and have caused the same type of menace to be leveled on them." All over Latin America, the governments are obliged to avoid coming one day face to face with an active and militant solidarity of particular Churches in the region.

On 4 December 1980, following the seizure and exile of many of the country's leading journalists, the CHR took a political stand for the first time in Haitian history. The Conference issued a statement, calling on the government to "reconsider the cases of deportation and imprisonment" of virtually 90 percent of the Duvalier regime's leading critics.[42] It asserted in accordance with the pope's statement in Brazil, when the fundamental rights of man were threatened, we must raise our voices; it was part of the prophetic mission of the Church.[43] "The Church cannot remain silent, for her duty is to make life more humane and people more conscious so all the values of their lives really correspond to true human dignity."[44] The same day, the CHR wrote to the bishops asking where God is, and why the Church, bishops, and priests were not saying anything.[45] Silence is betraying God, the people, the Church, and their mission. The Church was at a turning point. It had to demonstrate the preferential option of the poor. These events prompted the bishops to issue their second statement ever.[46] Little more than one year later, enough priests were demonstrating their opposition to the government that the conservative archbishop of Port-au-Prince, François Wolff Ligondé, was led to write to Father Pétion Laroche, the rector of the Grand Séminaire Haut de Turgeau in Port-au-Prince[47] and urge him to encourage young priests to celebrate mass on national holidays and sing the *Te Deum*, even if they did not like the government.

When the Church held a symposium in Port-au-Prince between 2 and 6 December 1982 as part of the Eucharistic and Marial Congress, 120 bishops, priests, nuns, and lay people participated in the historic meeting,[48] which has been dubbed "the Vatican II of Haiti."[49] At its conclusion, the delegates released an important statement. In it, they acknowledged divisions in the Church, but concluded that God wanted the Church to come together with the people. This task would require uprooting evil in individuals, the Church, and society. It would call for their involvement, sacrifice, and maybe even lives. But they determined to do it because they wanted to become the Church described at the regional meetings and Vatican II.[50]

Henceforth, they were going to be present with the people, become everyone's Church, show their solidarity with the poor, and announce the reign of God in the present, not the future. The delegates concluded their statement in Creole with a phrase that became a motto, *"Légliz se nou, nou se légliz."* The Church is us, we are the Church.

On 11 April 1983, following the symposium and the papal visit, the bishops issued a historic document, the *Declaration on the Foundation of the Church's Involvement in Social and Political Affairs.* [51] In it, they justified Church participation in social and political matters, based on papal authority and earlier Church documents. While the Church was responsible for announcing the gospel for conversion, it was also responsible for the transformation of social and political life. Its duty was to speak out in defense of moral values and human dignity. Any attack on these values was an offense against the Creator. The bishops argued that the basic principles of the social doctrines of the Church included dignity and primacy of the human being. Dignity was secured when the common good was guaranteed. The common good was the prime rule in society and political society was meant to be at the service of man. In Haiti, politics was seen as the privilege of government, but Puebla proclaimed that the political dimension was an important part of human existence. Pope John Paul II at Puebla and at the United Nations on 2 October 1979, had said, "It would mutilate the gospel to confine its [the Church's] influence only to personal and familial dimensions and exclude it from the social and political order."[52] The bishops pointedly concluded the Declaration by urging the government to avoid anything contrary to human rights, including insulting the dignity of man, illegal dispossession of peasants, exploitation of wage earners, violation of justice, torture, moral oppression, and arbitrary arrests without a warrant.

The Second General Assembly of the CHR was held between 23 and 26 April 1984, and Father Yvon Joseph reminded the audience that the theme was "Literacy, Human Promotion, and the Contemplative Dimension of Religious Life." Joseph made a revolutionary recommendation. "A new model of the Church, of society, and religious life is demanded by the kingdom of God. It is a grace, a gift of God but also a task that situates our communion with God and men."[53] They needed "to bring justice to all the marginalized in our society." He concluded his remarks by recalling the pope's words in Haiti, "It is necessary that the poor begin to hope again. The Church has a prophetic mission in this domain, inseparable from its religious mission."

Following the publication of the "Law on the Organization and Function of Political Parties in Haiti," the bishops issued a pastoral message on 16 July 1985.[54] The government appeared to be planning to exclude political parties with religious affiliations from the political process. The bishops argued that there was a place for the Church in the social and political life of the country. It was affirmed by Vatican II in *Constitution Lumen Gentium* that the Church is, in Christ, the sign of the instrument of unity of all humanity, as is the sacrament.[55] The Code of Canon Law,[56] promulgated by Pope John Paul II on 25 January 1983, spoke of Church duty to intervene in the social and political domain. The Church had the duty to announce the principles of moral and social order and make judgments in human experience to the extent that the fundamental rights of human and the well-being of souls calls for it.

THE PAPAL VISIT

There were many changes in relations between the Haitian Church, the government, and the Vatican during the Jean-Claude Duvalier presidency. Some were expected and some were not; and others were closely held secrets. In late 1982, prospects for a papal visit looked auspicious. Government relations with the Vatican appeared to be good[57] and the pre-visit correspondence was encouraging.[58] In November 1982, President Duvalier sent the pope a letter in which he said he looked forward to the visit and offered to modify the concordat because he wanted to tighten the ties between Rome and Haiti and maintain a healthy collaboration between the Church and State for the spiritual and earthly happiness of the nation. Consequently, he was disposed to accept the recommendation of the Vatican Council Decree, *Christus Dominus,* and renounce his concordatory rights and privileges. He hoped that Articles IV and V of the 1860 Concordat could be revised in a spirit and manner that would assure the indispensable equilibrium between the liberation of the Church and the legitimate preoccupation of the State.[59]

On 23 February 1983, the minister of religion received a letter from the papal nuncio[60] with the news that Cardinal Agostino Casaroli, the Vatican secretary of state, had informed him that the Holy See was grateful that Jean-Claude was proposing to renounce the privilege of Article IV in the concordat. Pope John Paul II had also sent his best wishes to President Duvalier "for what he was doing," which "was in the spirit of his political liberalization," or *"se situe dans la ligue de sa politique de libéralisation."* On 23 February 1983, the minister of religion was able to write to the papal nuncio saying the president was ready to renounce the rights and privileges accorded him in the 1860 Concordat to name bishops and archbishops.[61]

Plans for the papal visit went forward. The papal nuncio and the president met. Port-au-Prince was spruced-up,[62] and measures were taken to assure the comfort of the pope during his one day stopover, all of which cost hundreds of thousands of dollars.

Pope John Paul II had considered a visit to Haiti in 1978. Returning from a CELAM meeting in Mexico, his plane stopped briefly in the Dominican Republic. Archbishop Ligondé and some other bishops traveled to Santo Domingo to urge him to stop in Haiti, but to no avail—the Port-au-Prince airport was too small to accommodate the papal Boeing 747.[63] Some believe that this was merely a pretext, that the pope would only come to Haiti when its president agreed to stop naming bishops, stop intervening in religious issues, and allow the pope to go into a poor neighborhood.

Archbishop François Wolff Ligondé,[64] visiting the Vatican in 1980, reminded Pope John Paul II of his missed stopover, and recalling the historical importance of the country for the Church, urged him to go to Haiti.[65] A North American delegation led by Representative William Gray and the Reverend Jesse Jackson, visiting the Vatican in 1982, also urged the pope to go to Haiti.[66] Haitian bishops, making their three to five year *ad limina* visits to the Vatican, added their encouragement. Members of the Haitian exile community, Haitian associations, Protestant churches, and the papal nuncio[67] reinforced the idea, over the objections of some detractors.[68]

In 1982, Pope John Paul II finally agreed to go to Haiti. It would be the final stop on his 2–9 March 1983 trip to Central America, allowing him to preside at the closure of the Haitian Church's Eucharistic and Marial Congress and to convene a CELAM meeting.[69] John Paul II's long-awaited trip to Haiti took place on 9 March 1983. Within hours he was gone, but its impact and legacy are enduring.

The pope arrived at the Port-au-Prince airport via Air Italia, where he was greeted by the president, his ministers, and a crowd, estimated at two hundred thousand.[70] The president opened the ceremonies, confirming his intention to give up the right to name Church hierarchy.[71] "At this time, in the same spirit, in order to complete the symbiosis between Church and State and following the teachings of Vatican II, I intend from now on to waive my concordatory rights and privileges and allow the Vatican to appoint archbishops and bishops."

Then Pope John Paul II spoke.[72] He was pleased to be with the people in Port-au-Prince, and to be in a black country in Latin America for the first time. Haiti was significantly the first Latin American country to proclaim liberty. He recalled that Polish soldiers, sent to recover St. Domingue for France, changed sides on arrival and fought for liberty with the slaves; this liberty was important and should continue to be obtainable at home. In light of the Eucharistic and Marial Congress in progress in Port-au-Prince, John Paul II was led to recall the meaning of the Eucharist, which is service and love, Jesus' death on the cross and love of humanity. Those taking the Eucharist were called to imitate His love, to serve others. The Haitian Church needed to serve everyone, especially the poorest.

The slogan of the Eucharistic and Marial Congress was "something has to change here," and the pope agreed.

> Christians have attested to division, injustice, excessive inequality, degradation of the quality of life, misery, hunger, fear by many, of peasants unable to live on their own land, crowded conditions, people without work, families cast out and separated in cities, victims of other frustrations. Yet, they are persuaded that the solution is in solidarity. The poor have to regain hope. The Church has a prophetic mission, inseparable from its religious mission, which demands liberty to be accomplished.

The pope continued that there was "a deep need for justice, a better distribution of goods, more equitable organization of society and more participation. There was a legitimate desire for freedom of expression, access to food, care, schools, literacy, honest and dignified work, social security, and the fundamental rights of man." All of this had to be done "without violence . . . out of respect and love of liberty." John Paul II concluded his speech by saying that he was with the people, and that he blessed them with all his heart.

Following his address, John Paul II was driven to the palace where he spent half an hour with the president. His next stop was the cathedral. After that, he was taken to the nunciature for a rest. Departing later in the day, the pope addressed the crowd at the airport again.[73] In a short speech, John Paul II offered his best wishes to the people for the prosperity of the country, and his encouragement to the nation's leaders to make this happen, and he appealed to the international community for its assistance.

Many people were deeply moved by the pope's presence.[74] The government was not. Estimé, who was part of the presidential delegation during the pope's visit, recalled the president's reactions.[75] The speech at the airport made Jean-Claude Duvalier angry, embarrassed, and unhappy. Even so, their meeting at the palace was cordial. The afternoon speech was milder, which he regarded as an attempt by the pope to leave on a more harmonious note.[76]

A selective news blackout followed the stopover so that the papal speeches were not immediately published. In its first reaction to the pope's speeches, the government attacked those who "give lessons" and those who "make accusations." This reaction appeared in the official newspaper, *Le Nouveau Monde.* [77] The paper, which did not publish the homily, stressed that the pontiff had pointed out the "efforts made by the government of President Jean-Claude Duvalier to establish a society based on political liberty, social justice and prosperity."[78] Ernest Bennett, the president's father-in-law, also published an article in *Le Nouveau Monde* entitled "Priesthood and Politics," that condemned "some members of the Haitian clergy" and "speculating priests," whose benefits serve "to pay for costly vehicles, trips abroad every three months, or simply to keep expensive mistresses."[79] Bennett contended that John Paul's tour "will be beneficial if the holy father shakes himself of the disinformation spread by some clergy members. . . ."[80]

The government blamed the bishops for the pope's homilies and Ambassador Estimé was convinced they were its authors. While the pontiff was still in Haiti, several ministers accused Archbishop Ligondé and other members of the Episcopal Conference of having drafted the speech, saying "you can't tell (us) that the pope's homily wasn't made in Port-au-Prince."[81] The next day, the Minister of the Interior, Dr. Roger Lafontant, accused Archbishop Ligondé of having spent the drive to the palace with the pope denigrating the president and his government. Eight days later, the bishops had assembled for a meeting with Estimé [82] when the president called to ask if they shared the Archbishop's unkind words against certain ministers. They responded that they did not know about any words but were solidly with the archbishop. The government also blamed "dissidents" for "misinforming the pontiff."[83]

Although the papal visit to Haiti was based on President Duvalier's pledge to revise the concordat, the matter was not settled for another seventeen months, until 8 August 1984, when Bishop Achille Silvestrini, secretary of the Council for Public Affairs of the Church and Jean-Robert Estimé signed the protocol amending articles IV and V.[84] Ambassador Estimé described the lapse as normal; the business day in Haiti is brief, with offices officially open from 9:00 A.M. to 2:00 P.M. but actually only in operation from 10:00 A.M. to 12:30 P.M. Other diplomats and Churchmen disagree, maintaining that the delay was intentional and they cited Lafontant as the principal obstacle to its conclusion. Ambassador Clayton McManaway claimed that it took the intercession of the president himself to get the agreement completed.[85] But the most convincing proof of ministerial displeasure with the Church was that the Haitian government subsequently entered into secret negotiations with the Vatican to substantially change the conditions of the formal relationship between the Church and State.[86]

After agreeing to update the concordat, the chancellery and the Vatican secretary of state convened a working group in Port-au-Prince on 11 November 1985 to draw up a list of questions for examination and to produce a joint memorandum. At their first meeting, the working group identified themes that would serve as the talking points for negotiators.[87]

The Haitian government took the position that "a more modern vision of relations between Church and State was necessary, as was a renewal of the juridical relationship."[88] The negotiations needed to define the following basic principles:

1. The status of the Church, especially its legal status
2. The pastoral autonomy of the Church
3. Church obedience to Haitian laws and the Constitution
4. Integration of Church socio-economic, educational and humanitarian work with national development efforts
5. Assessment of Church institutions and belongings
6. Revision of regulations covering State material obligations to the Church

A source close to the Haitian government, who was familiar with these negotiations, said the salient points for the administration were first, to assure compliance of the Church pastoral mission with Haitian law, second; to establish a code of behavior obliging the Church to operate within the law; third, to assess Church belongings to make sure they were legally acquired and properly taxed; and fourth, to review the level of government funding of the Church.[89]

The Holy See was willing to discuss the principal themes outlined by the Haitian side.[90] Its positions were:

1. The Haitian Church-State accords originating in the nineteenth century needed to be updated to reflect the teachings of Vatican II and official teaching of the Church
2. All material pertaining to Church-State relations needed to go in one document
3. The concordat needed to ratify the following fundamental principles:
   A. The status of the Church in the country
   B. The free exercise of the ministry and pastoral ministry of the Church
   C. The liberty of the Church in evangelization and in its pastoral mission
   D. The autonomy of the Church and its freedom of organization, appointments of ecclesiastics, public exercise of religion as well as its jurisdiction in ecclesiastical matters
   E. The status of the institutions of the Church, such as the religious congregations and different organizations created by the competent ecclesiastical authorities
   F. The financial contribution of the State to the activities of the Church

Given other preoccupations, negotiations did not progress in the final months of the administration. President Manigat revived the idea of revising the concordat in May 1988, when he told the papal nuncio that he was going to be obliged to change Church-State relations through revision of the concordat because the senate was "aggressive against the Church and wanted to change it."[91]

KEY CHURCH PEOPLE AND ORGANIZATIONS

This section touches briefly on some of the religious organizations and individuals associated with the Church who were particularly caught up in the papal mandate for change. From 1983 on, the Church came under increasing attack. Lay workers, parish priests, and those associated with the Catholic radio station—CEBs or IDEA—were frequently assaulted. While the Church was naturally concerned about its own, some groups and individuals within the institution continued to be disturbed about the wider pattern of abuse. A prefect invaded the cathedral of Cap-Haïtien causing a group of Religious from Hinche to write to the board of the CHR on 10 January 1985,[92] urging that the Church not lose sight of "a more serious problem," that of illegal detentions, nor a deeper cause, the ideology of national security. People who protested violence subsequently became victims themselves.[93] The best-known victim was Gérard Duclerville.

The Conference of Haitian Religious (CHR) was the collective conscience of the Church during the Jean-Claude presidency.[94] This preponderantly female organization (over 80 percent of its 16,000 members are women), repeatedly took issue with the government against injustices and encouraged and pressured the CHB to take a stand.

Several religious orders focused their attention on the country's poorest, working in slums and rural areas with the young, illiterate, and neediest. Among them were the Scheut and Holy Cross Fathers, the Salesians, the Montfortins, and the Dominicans. The human rights rally on 9 November 1979 took place at the Salesian Hall.[95]

Hugo Triest, the Belgian Missionhurst priest who was director of the Catholic radio station, *Radio Soleil,* was of central importance. He continued to produce informative and controversial programs despite threats against his life and attacks on the station.

The most outspoken and anti-Duvalierist bishop was the personally fearless Willy Romélus,[96] a man François Duvalier had expected to be one of his most conservative appointees.

Bishop François Gayot had done his doctoral work in Strasbourg on evangelization and development; his thesis argued that the Church could contribute to development. Returning to Haiti, he helped launch IDEA and stood up to the government when it tried to curtail Church activities. Estimé, who dealt with him frequently, characterized Gayot as "tough." However, on 7 February 1986, the bishop offered a Mass of Reconciliation, urging public patience; his continued conservatism has disappointed former followers.

Archbishop François Wolff-Ligondé of Port-au-Prince was one of the three remaining original bishops appointed by François Duvalier in 1966 (the others are Bishops Constant and Angenor).[97] He was regarded as conservative and sympathetic to the government during much of the Jean-Claude era, explained partly by family ties to the Bennetts. An American diplomat recalled that Ligondé had refused to cooperate with the Embassy at one point on a joint human rights *démarche*. A Churchman recalls that when the government attacked an important Church institution, the bishop was indifferent. In 1982, Ligondé was obliged to confront the government and in 1985 he appears to have done so on his own volition.[98]

Three papal nuncios were in residence in Haiti during the Jean-Claude Duvalier presidency. Louis Barbarito was the nuncio from 1969 to 1975. Luigi Conti held the post from 1975 to December 1983, and Paolo Romeo took over in March 1984. Only the last two have come to public attention, reflecting individual personalities and the increasingly public interactions between the Church and State. Described as a "volatile Sicilian," Luigi Conti is recalled by one former member of the diplomatic corps in Haiti as outspoken and openly negative about the Jean-Claude Duvalier government.[99] Ambassador McManaway believes Conti was instrumental in bringing John Paul II to Haiti and in preparing his speeches.[100]

Paolo Romeo's role is less clear. Ambassador Estimé considered him "a good and very conservative nuncio, who did not want Duvalier to leave Haiti until there was no alternative." Several priests in Haiti recalled that Romeo had infuriated the CHR by creating bureaucratic delays.[101] Others credit him with being in the forefront of change in Haiti, arguing that the pope came and recommended change, and then sent this nuncio to help make it happen.[102]

A Chronology of Church Activism

The Church did not become a major force in Haiti overnight. Its activism was the product of its past. Earlier, the Church had tolerated slavery, supported the status quo when changes were necessary, been overly-sympathetic to the U.S. occupation, deferred introduction of a native clergy, and tried to forcefully eliminate Voodoo. Consequently, the Church became an object of disrepute and retaliation. It had alienated some Haitians to the point that they converted to Protestantism, Freemasonry, and other creeds. In the 1940s, others found comfort in the ethnology and *négritude* movements.

Chastised and also motivated by international changes in the Church, the Haitian Church began to evolve in new directions. It became more Haitian with the introduction of a native hierarchy and the adoption of a mission that emphasized economic development and concern for the poor.[103] These developments contributed to the emergence of a Church that was prepared to take ethical stands and play a leadership role.[104]

In 1964, a French secular priest, Robert Ryo, in conjunction with the Oblate Order, established the Laborde Center in rural Haiti.[105] His goal was to help improve peoples' lives through leadership training, agriculture, and medical care. Funded largely from abroad, the Center was reasonably independent and very successful. By 1981, the prototype of the Christian Community Development Centers (CCDs) had spread to most of the northeast and southwest, and into one-fifth of the rural parishes. In the 1970s, the Centers became involved with producers' cooperatives, which led to the creation of IDEA, and the *Ti-Légliz*, or CEBs.[106] Initially, the CCDs limited themselves to challenging local elites and authorities who threatened their interests (as late as 1980–1981, they did not exert much pressure on the government). However, that changed. The succeeding years are replete with examples of lay workers, religious, and members of the hierarchy who confronted the government on behalf of the people. As we have seen, following the 28 November 1980 round-ups and deportations, the CHR put out its momentous statement[107] and prodded the Haitian bishops into action.[108]

Two days later, on 6 December, Luigi Conti did an uncharacteristic thing for papal nuncios, who generally rely on quiet diplomacy. He wrote directly to the CHR, saying he had read their *Communiqué* to the bishops with "great relief."[109] He commended them for protesting the government's treatment of journalists and development workers. In his view, their *Communiqué* reflected the feelings of the silent majority and evangelical spirit of the faithful to the conciliar *Constitution Gaudiem et Spes*, who cast their lot with the poor, the suffering, and those who thirst for justice. The nuncio concluded by saying, "I entirely adhere to it."

Human rights abuses continued in Haiti.[110] A year after the government quelled Haitian journalists and intellectuals in November 1980, the CHR courageously released a report, or *dossier*, subtitled "A Year After."[111] Taking the government to task, it described the awful conditions in the country, the disparities in wealth, the plight of the Haitian cane pickers in the Dominican Republic, the boat people, and the refugees held in camps in the United States.

The Justice and Peace Commission, an organization of priests, nuns, and lay persons, met in full session on 26 November 1981. Shocked "by the increased suffering of the Haitian people and their diminishing opportunity to escape from a life of misery," they wrote to the bishops.[112] Catholics expect the Church to "openly say what would be too dangerous for them to say aloud." In their view, the Church needed to become totally involved in the daily existence of the people. They were looking forward to the Eucharistic and Marial Congress, providing it addressed the conditions in the country. "If [the Church] lets itself be guided by opportunism and fear, it would fail at its mission. 'The Charity of Christ urges us.' The people are waiting for us.'" Henceforth, they were going to be "the eyes, mouth, of the Church in matters dealing with justice and peace in the country."

Evidence of the increasing power of the Church was becoming apparent.[113] A government plan to construct two hydroelectric dams in the Artibonite Valley, which would have destroyed about three thousand acres of farmland and eliminated sixty thousand jobs, caused a local parish priest to organize a protest campaign in the community.[114] In April 1982, seven thousand farmers sent a letter to the government opposing the plan; it was canceled. On 28 November 1982, the board of the CHR wrote to its members, noting that an increasing number of them were being brought before the minister of religion, and concluded, "an obvious campaign of intimidation was being launched against the Church." Far from urging members to be cautious or retreat, it expressed full support for them.[115]

As we have seen, when a large cross-section of the Church held a symposium in the capital in December 1982, it issued a strong statement. The Church had been weak in the past, but it was ready to become the Church of Vatican II, to dedicate itself to the people and to uproot evil everywhere, regardless of the danger.[116]

When Duclerville was seized on 28 December 1982, the CHB and board of the CHR initiated unprecedented action to gain his release.[117] They produced a powerful pastoral letter on 27 January 1983 that was read in all Churches the following Sunday.[118] The pontiff was due to visit Haiti just as the Church in Haiti was experiencing a challenging situation. However, "rather than dividing us, it should unify us. Today it's Gérard and those whose names we don't know. Tomorrow, it's us, you, me. Everyone's a victim. Wherever a man is humiliated and tortured, the whole of humanity is." After a description of Duclerville's abduction, the archbishop's intercession, and letters received from the Christian community, they asked people to dedicate 9 February 1983 to sacrifice and prayer for his liberation. They would pray for all who suffered, especially those in prison, and they would pray God to free Haiti from torture, servitude, egotism, money, and power.

The same day, Archbishop Ligondé sent "a disapproving letter to the Minister of Religion."[119] Shortly thereafter, Bishop Romélus spoke on *Radio Soleil*, asking the faithful to boycott Carnival because the Church was in mourning since the arrest. The director of the Petit Seminaire Collège Saint Martial also used the station to call the government "assassins."[120] *Radio Soleil* played a song nonstop, which included the words, "The flag of violence has been raised." Duclerville was released two days before the national day of fast and prayer was to begin. This event galvanized and unified all sectors of the Church to a hitherto unprecedented extent.

In March the pope came, and the government and its sympathizers were left angry and demoralized. The mayor of Port-au-Prince, Edgar Day, vowed not to let a bunch of radical priests destabilize the government.[121]

Estimé had previously warned Haiti's bishops "that the government would not tolerate further criticism from members of the Roman Catholic Haitian clergy,"[122] and Ernest Bennett reinforced the message in *Le Nouveau Monde*; the president's patience "has run out."[123]

On 11 April 1983, the bishops issued their *Declaration on the Foundation of the Church's Involvement in Social and Political Affairs*.[124] As we have seen, they cited the pope and Church documents to justify an active Church role in social and political matters. They urged the government to treat its citizens with respect.

A Catholic Creole language monthly journal, *Bon Nouvèl*, was particularly daring in its publications.[125] The goals of its founder, Father Joris Ceuppens, a Scheut missionary, were to promote Creole and the Church, to provide opportunities for people to air their grievances, and create interest in journalism. *Bon Nouvèl* published news and satire, information on exiles and boat people, and letters from its readers. By 1980, the journal had thirty thousand subscribers.[126]

In 1983, the government revised the constitution to legalize political parties and a law was passed to regulate their formation and operation. The government also promised honest elections, but when the legislative elections were held, independent candidates were prevented from campaigning, and there was widespread fraud. Bishop Willy Romélus went on *Radio Soleil* on 16 February 1984 to protest, and to remind Haitians that government exists at the will of the people.[127]

In addition to the prominent people who spoke out against injustices, individuals with little protection also acted bravely, jeopardizing their jobs and even their lives. Jacques Lajoie, the chaplain at the Civil Prison of Cap-Haïtien, wrote to the commissioner of the city, Socrate Pierre, on 2 July 1984 [128] to request that commissioners be required to visit prisoners regularly in order to prevent their neglect. In his letter, Lajoie wrote how one prisoner was beaten and another prisoner, suspected of telling the chaplain about it, was subsequently battered and sent to solitary confinement. The chaplain wrote that he did not have "the privilege" of seeing the prisoners; consequently, the two had suffered needlessly. One went untreated for two weeks with a broken wrist and bashed-in skull, the other was condemned to a dungeon.

In the Artibonite Valley, where the soil is particularly fertile and valuable, land ownership is the source of continuing controversy. On 20 November 1984, Emmanuel Constant, the bishop of the diocese containing the Artibonite, wrote to the minister of religion concerning dispossessions. The bishop pointed out that notwithstanding legal decisions, owners were being kept off their land by illegal claimants and the army. "It was a scandal."[129]

The year 1985 was fortuitously designated the International Year of Youth (IYY) by the United Nations, it was then chosen as a theme by the

CHB. On 6 January 1985, the Haitian bishops took advantage of the occasion to deliver an address to Haiti's youth.[130] Speaking Creole, the bishops urged the young people to make something of the year, get involved, improve society, and accept their support. "We're starting the year, looking at the country, wondering about its and our future. Kids are taking wrong turns. God's with us. We're with you. We count on you and you with us. Stand up. 1985 is your year! What do you want to make of it?"[131]

The Church organized a number of meetings, pastoral committees, and young peoples' "Biblical Marches" in all the parishes between February and April 1985 in context of the IYY. The official support made government repression more difficult than otherwise. On 2 February 1985, there were marches in almost all Haitian parishes. In the capital, between 50,000 and 60,000 young people paraded with banners proclaiming, "we march for peace, participation, justice, democracy." Significantly, even conservative Archbishop Ligondé spoke about the need to liberate people from misery, ignorance, hunger, sickness, and fear. "The lack of respect is the biggest wound, which exists, and it kills us. The beating of the people, torture and disappearances have to stop."[132]

The bishops sponsored a Youth Council in Jérémie from 8 to 14 April 1985. In a strong message to the nation's youth, Church leaders, and citizens that began by thanking the papal nuncio for suggesting the event,[133] the Youth Council deplored the condition of the country. The Council charged Haitian leaders with lack of concern for the people, misuse of the country's wealth and exploitation of its citizens. Haitians were afraid. The Church was also to blame, through lack of commitment and failure to dialogue with Protestants and young people. The Council asked for economic and social justice, financial support for infrastructure, education, teacher training, and literacy programs. It wanted protection for people returning from exile, for unions, and for landowners. It called for an end to government abuse. It wanted Creole pigs brought back. The Council concluded with a call for solidarity.

On 11 April, Willy Romélus addressed 20,000 participants at the Youth Council.[134] In a singularly provocative speech, he called their lives intolerable and accused the government of oppression.[135] They should organize, act, even risk their lives for change and the country. "We can't accept our brothers living in these conditions. Enough! People are enchained and they have to be freed. The people have had enough. It's time to take to the streets. Unify! When one suffers, all do. Be ready to die. You are the youth of Haiti. You are responsible. You have a mission to change things. You have to get involved. You have to work for the country and Church."

The government and Church were increasingly opposed from April to December 1985. It was evident that the Church had become a significant adversary.[136] Some of the events that pitted the government and Church against each other were the Political Parties Law, the referendum, the deportation of the Belgians, the murder of the students at Gonaïves, and the closure of *Radio Soleil.*

By the end of December, the Council of Haitian Youth, the Youth of Jérémie, and the Youth of Les Cayes had all put out strong statements demanding justice, change, and activism. They asked each other rhetorically, "Where are you? Are you ready?" In a message dedicated to the victims of Gonaïves, the Council of Haitian Youth proclaimed, "they have not died, they're here with us."[137] Their lives must serve as an example and how will we respond? They are among us as "we prepare to throw ourselves into a battle of liberty for the country." They are among us when we "do not stop at speech only, but decide that we must take action. When we decide, we must work to dig out the foundations until the whole structure is crushed. They died during our year [IYY]. The leaders don't respect the lives of the young Haitians. We're fed up with lies, treachery." They concluded by asking the youth if they were going to die also. Could they count on each other? Could Haiti count on them? This horrible situation needed to change.

In December 1985, the Council of Haitian Youth put out a pronouncement, *The Root Causes of this Suffering.* In it, the Council spelled out some of the country's problems. It blamed the government and called the citizens to arms. Haiti's problems stemmed from a lack of respect for the fundamental rights to life, health, education, and housing by the nation's leaders. The government was responsible for the disappearances, brutality, violence, corruption, and economic disparities. A small group of bourgeoisie were prospering at the expense of the poor. "All these things are causing people to suffer in this country. We who are believers in Christ must create another model of society... We will fight until we obtain what we need." They concluded by asking, "Haiti, where are you? Where's the liberating blood of our ancestors that flowed to liberate us?"

Following a week-long strike, on 5 December, the Youth of Jérémie produced a Declaration. This group saluted all who were crying out from under the "hawk's talons" crushing them. The Youth of Jérémie called for justice regarding Gonaïves, the reopening of *Radio Soleil,* and an end to the abuse of teachers in Les Cayes. The members of the organization would boycott school until these situations were resolved and they urged others to join them: "We ask all students in the four corners of Haiti to be in solidarity with our decision, because we are going to continue digging out the foundations until the structure is completely crushed."[139]

On 13 December 1985, the Youth of Les Cayes released their own statement. "Speaking in the name of Jesus who is the only true leader for life, we the Youth of Les Cayes, send greetings of solidarity to the youth of Port-au-Prince."[140] The group from Les Cayes expressed its solidarity with those killed in Gonaïves and with youth everywhere. The Youth of Les Cayes protested "gagging our *Radio Soleil*" and denounced "all the criminals who are governing us." The group pointed to the lack of justice in Gonaïves and Les Cayes, where neither the prefect nor the president of the government party was brought to justice following the arrests, beatings, and abuses that took place on 2 and 3 December. The Youth of Les Cayes concluded with a warning, "We are brewing an historic surprise that is ready to strike. . . . Down with abuses for life . . . we are fed up, we must cry out . . . and you, Port-au-Prince, are you about to get involved? . . . We will continue to dig out the foundations until the structure is completely crushed."

Following the statements of the Council of Youth and the Youth of Les Cayes and Jérémie, the Haitian bishops' Christmas message appears tame at first glance.[141] The bishops began by saying, "The year 1986 is dedicated to peace" and concluded by wishing all Haitians "peace, joy, and hope." However, in between, they spoke of dashed hopes, continuing problems, government responsibility and shortcomings. The bishops cryptically added that "the Church does not have the pretension of being able to resolve all the problems of the country. That is a job that is urgently calling all Haitians." The Year of Youth had been "sullied by mourning." They had discovered a "lack of peace, and education, institutionalized lies and fear of liberty." Youth wanted peace but were confronted by landless peasants, poor and elderly people, and abandoned children, and by a lack of civil rights, family planning, education, and work. Limits to peace were set by the lack of education, institutionalized lies, fear of liberty, lack of collective responsibility, hard-heartedness, and one-way vision. "This is the moment to say no to lies, servitude, egotism, torture, violence, injustice and hate and yes to dialogue, liberty, sharing, respect for man, truth and justice."

Radio Soleil was the Church institution that played the most significant role in the events leading to the overthrow of the Duvalier regime. An examination of its history, infrastructure, philosophy, programming and, in particular, of its directors, is intended to illuminate how and why it came to play such an important role.

Radio Soleil was the idea of a charismatic diocesan priest from Wisconsin named Joseph Conyard who came to Haiti from the Dominican Republic.[142] Father Conyard's immediate goal in Haiti was to produce educational programs in Creole. Placed under the administrative control of the Commission of Social Affairs of the Church, headed by Bishop Constant, the station took four hundred dollars in start-up funds from the German foundation, *Miséreor,* and the CEBs. The inspiration for its name from the Protestant radio station, *Radio Lumière.* Inaugurated on 30 April 1978, it began operations in 1979.[143]

Father Conyard was responding to an obvious need when he started a school in Creole and sought to expand his radio program. However, his activism and outspokenness made him unwelcome in some circles, and he was forced to leave the country.[144] Hugo Triest arrived in May 1984 as Conyard's replacement, a position he held until the end of March 1989. Apart from Triest and one Oblat sister, the rest of the staff were lay workers. Ten of its thirty employees worked full-time.[145] About 75 percent of *Radio Soleil's* running expenses were covered by *Miséreor* and the Belgian Catholic Bishops' Conference, *Brocderlyk Delen*. The remainder of its funding came from Church sources and domestic fund raising drives.[146] When the station needed a new transmitter in 1985, Caritas supplied the necessary money. After Jean-Claude's departure, two American organizations provided some support. The U.S. Information Agency (USIA) helped *Radio Soleil* extend its programming and literacy campaign, and the Inter-American Foundation helped finance a production and recording studio. Foreign funding, like foreign directors, has made the station more independent than it might otherwise have been.

Hugo Triest explained that the idea of *Radio Soleil* and the philosophy driving it stemmed from Father Conyard, who was motivated by Vatican II and Puebla. Vatican II advocated the use of native languages in the Church and urged the Church to become the voice of the voiceless, the poor, and the excluded. Puebla recommended that the Church be with Latin Americans in their daily life.[147]

Father Conyard initially intended to offer basic and religious education on *Radio Soleil* but he was obligated to drop those plans and concentrate on popular education and agriculture. Teaching basic education to an illiterate audience by radio was too difficult.

Radio Soleil caught on and its scope and programming both increased.[148] Initially the station broadcast three hours a day, exclusively in Cap-Haïtien, but eventually, it was transmitted throughout the country by relays and was on the air eighteen hours a day, seventy-four hours a week.

Several aspects of *Radio Soleil* were distinctive: its broadcast mode, theme song, and participatory format. The programs were transmitted mainly in Creole in order to generate a sense of cultural pride and reach the vast majority of people who spoke no other language. Its catchy theme song,[149] *Lè M'Pa We Solèy La*, or "When I Don't See The Sun," written by Jean Michel Daudier in 1985,[150] became a symbol of the struggle against the dictator and was played repeatedly during the final year of the Duvalier government, whenever the station was about to be closed or something significant was happening in the country. The station provided Haitians with the opportunity to speak out and be heard.[151] Nuns, priests, the CHR, bishops, individual citizens, and groups accompanied by priests or nuns would often come to the station to protest something. Its programs, intended to inform listeners about Haiti and highlight common problems, were provocative and created a feeling of solidarity. One of them, aired in December 1985, was entitled *Sept Diocèses en Sept Jours,* or "Seven Dioceses in Seven Days."[152] In the course of this segment, the station made a "pilgrimage" across the country. It stopped in parishes along the route and spoke to people about their problems. Each installment was linked with a Biblical text and concluded with a song. This program was especially popular and people would ask one another if they had heard the "pilgrimage." The last two days of the pilgrimage involved a visit to Haiti's other religious denominations. After the pilgrimage ended, *Radio Soleil* hosted joint religious services.

Radio Soleil experienced its first trouble with the government in the late 1970s and early 1980s when it did some pieces on small peasant groups such as the Technical and Education Institute (ITICA), which was identified with Jean-Jacques Honorat, and the Diocesan Institute for Adult Education (IDEA), which was more specifically involved with the Church. With the end of the Carter presidency and its emphasis on human rights, the Haitian government no longer had to feign enthusiasm for civil liberties, and conflicts increased.

Given the mission of *Radio Soleil* to speak the truth, educate its audience and defend the poor, it was inevitable that it would continue to come into conflict with the Duvalier government. The arrests and expulsions of journalists, broadcasters, educators, and unionists on 28 November 1980, left the station in an increasingly exposed and vulnerable position. Protected to some extent by the Church and its international donors,[153] *Radio Soleil* continued with its agenda while the government did its best to curb it.[154]

After the government crackdown of November 1980, *Radio Soleil* read the CHR Communiqué on 5 December that said "the Church cannot be silent." Following Duclerville's abduction, Bishop Romélus went on the radio to urge the faithful to demonstrate that the Church was in mourning, and the director of the Petit Seminaire Collège Saint Martial used the station to blast the government. After the second purge of journalists in 1982, even fewer reporters were left to follow events, but *Radio Soleil* remained on the air. The papal visit in March 1983 provided encouragement,[155] leading Director Conyard to conclude that *Radio Soleil* had to continue to tell the truth and report the news. The themes took a more social bent and dealt increasingly with peoples' lives. They covered topics such as Liberation Theology; one program was specifically called "Puebla." Archbishop Ligondé attempted to tone down Father Conyard's programming, but to no avail, and the station continued to attract new listeners.[156]

By the time Father Triest became director, the government also wanted *Radio Soleil* to pull back. The ministry of foreign affairs and religion charged that *Radio Soleil* had exceeded its mandate and was inciting people by reporting inaccuracies. Triest was repeatedly summoned to appear at the ministry of foreign affairs and religion. As Hugo Triest recalled, generally, the minister himself would not be there but a "group of guys with dark glasses were."[157] On one occasion, after *Radio Soleil* did a report on the abuses suffered by Haitians in the Dominican Republic, Father Triest was called to the ministry. In this instance, the minister was present and "he was very mad." The Haitian minister to the Dominican Republic was also in the room. Both insisted that the supporting documentation for the program was pure communist inspiration. Jean-Robert Estimé complained that the government never got an opportunity to tell its side of the story on the station, so the director invited him to send in a piece on the Dominican Republic and it would be read on the radio. The minister sent in his copy and *Radio Soleil* read it. Then the station aired the testimony of twenty-three people who had been victimized in the Dominican Republic, effectively refuting the government story.[158]

There were food strikes in May 1984, principally in Gonaïves and Cap-Haïtien, as a result of the worsening economic situation. *Radio Soleil,* *L'Information, Petit Samedi Soir,* and *Fraternité* covered them. In June, the editors of all the papers except *Radio Soleil* were arrested, leaving it increasingly isolated, or as *Haiti Demain Hebdo* put it, "the only permanent tie with the population."[159]

Radio Soleil did a program on the constitution and political parties prior to the 22 July 1985 national referendum to prepare Haitians for what was likely to occur.[160] Triest predicted that the elections would be fraudulent. Even if few people showed up to vote, the government would say there had been a massive turnout. This prophecy proved accurate. On 22 July, the government announced that 90 percent of the population had voted and that 99.98 percent had supported the government.[161] The administration subsequently accused the station of encouraging people not to vote but Hugo Triest sees it differently. "The station only helped people do what they had to do, and that was to take the responsibility not to vote."[162]

On election day, the government cut off the power at *Radio Soleil* and detained the director.[163] Although there was no warrant for his arrest, Father Triest was taken away in handcuffs, charged with involvement in a traffic accident, and humiliated and roughed up before being released several hours later.

The next day, a seventy-eight-year-old Belgian priest, Albert Desmet, was found beaten to death with a nail-studded club in the Catholic Orders Residence in Port-au-Prince.[164] The presumption was that someone had either mistaken him for Hugo Triest or wanted to show what could happen to outspoken members of the clergy, particularly Belgians. On 24 July,

Triest discovered that he only had one day to leave the country when he heard the minister of religion announce on national television that the residence permits of three missionaries had been revoked.[165] The director remained in hiding at the nunciature until Interior Minister Lafontant, threatened to attack it with a truck-load of soldiers if he were not at the airport by 3 P.M. the next day.[166] The threat was clear to Hugo Triest.[167] If he did not go, he would be taken hostage, the house would be searched, and its possessions stolen. At that point, Father Triest decided to comply with the edict and leave Haiti for the United States and the Missionhurst Fathers' Provincial Center in Arlington, Virginia.

The government ran editorials on its radio station, *Radio National*, and in its paper, the *Quotidien*, condemning the priests. The deportation of the three caused the bishops to criticize the government and refute the charges.[168] Public opinion mounted against the government and *Radio Soleil* continued to broadcast.

Differing opinions over the legitimate scope of *Radio Soleil*'s reporting led to another major confrontation between the government and the station. *Radio Soleil* covered the events in Gonaïves on 27 and 28 November 1985 along with the subsequent government stonewalling and the belated offer to pay off the families. The government had had enough. On 5 December, it closed the station contending that *Radio Soleil* had no right to continue reporting because it was disturbing the peace.[169]

The closure caused an avalanche of protest. On 5 December 1985, the Youth of Jérémie announced its indignation over the closure of *Radio Soleil*. As we have seen, the group threatened to stay out of school until the situation was corrected and urged other students to do the same.[170] On 13 December 1985, the Youth of Les Cayes "protested the gagging of *Radio Soleil*" and announced that it would not be returning to school.[171] In their 1985 Christmas message, the bishops said that they wanted *Radio Soleil*, "the voice of the Catholic Church in Haiti, to continue its program of evangelism, education, local and international news."

The minister of religion met with the bishops in response to the widespread protests against the closure of *Radio Soleil* and offered to allow the station to reopen provided that Bishop Constant, the president of the Episcopal Conference on Social Communications, reviewed the news before it was aired.[172] *Radio Soleil* objected to this censorship. To the chagrin of the station and others, Bishop Constant acquiesced.

When *Radio Soleil* reopened on 31 December, its format and style remained unchanged. Bishop Willy Romélus used it in early January to accuse the government of permitting security forces to kill Haitians. After 7 February 1986, Haitians showed their gratitude to *Radio Soleil* in a number of ways. They organized a march to its headquarters and decorated the wall in front of the station with laudatory drawings and appreciative verses.[173] "Viv Légliz," "Long live the Church," was a frequently expressed sentiment.

GOVERNMENT REPRESSION, CHURCH REACTION

The pattern of officially perpetrated human rights abuse and government neglect of the population increased after 1979.[174] In November 1981, as we have seen, the CHR marked the anniversary of the largest crackdown to date with the dissemination of its Dossier, "A Year After."

Government repression continued, and by 1982, some of its attacks were against Church people, whom it accused of being revolutionaries.[175] The victims were frequently priests who had delivered sermons that were critical of the government and lay workers dedicated to helping the poor.[176] On 23 November 1982, the CHR lent its moral support to its besieged members through a letter of solidarity and encouragement.[177]

When the police picked up Duclerville,[178] the Church reacted quickly on several fronts, as has been mentioned earlier. Pastoral letters, messages to the government, and heated addresses on *Radio Soleil* encouraged the administration to release Gérard.

The most important and prolonged example of government repression and Church reaction in 1983 concerned the papal visit, which was discussed previously. Chastisements from the Ministry, along with solidarity engendered by the Symposium and psychic encouragement stemming from the Papal visit, led to the bishops to publish their *Declaration on the Foundations of Church Intervention in Social and Political Affairs* on 11 April 1983.[179]

The year 1984 began much as 1983 ended, with arrests, disappearances, and indications that conditions in Haiti were going to continue to deteriorate. In February, legislative elections were held, but independent candidates were prevented from campaigning, the results were rigged, and afterward, the government declared that political parties would be banned until a law could be promulgated to regulate them. On 3 March, Archbishop Ligondé issued a pastoral letter that rejected support for or even toleration of injustice and suggested some methods that could be used to obtain equity.[180]

On 23–26 April 1984, the CHR held its Second General Assembly,[181] selecting as its theme, "Human Promotion and Contemplation— Dimensions of Religious Life." This was a historic meeting and milestone in the evolution of the Haitian Church. The conferees were determined to create "A new model of the Church, of society and religious life." The new model of the Church would be "in the spirit of Vatican Council II, of

Medellín, and of Puebla." It derived its inspiration from the Bible, the 1982 symposium, and the pope, who had confirmed and encouraged a new model of the Church on his 9 March trip, requesting it to work immediately for social change in favor of the most deprived classes." They were determined to meet Haiti's needs and be more a part of the country. As a consequence, they formulated a *Global Plan*, [182] which consisted of a number of initiatives, six of which were particularly important "to bring justice to all the marginalized in our society." The conferees intended to:

1. Create a commission of educators to study structures of internal and external dependency
2. Create a commission of inquiry to identify Haitians' problems and needs, and develop a plan of social and economic action
3. Launch a vast literacy campaign through the CHR commission of education
4. Establish a commission of medical and social affairs that would focus on preventive medicine, and take into account traditional medicine
5. Establish a CHR commission of justice and peace to work with the CHB justice and peace commission
6. Establish a commission of migration within the CHR to study problems related to the migration of people from rural areas and from the country for political and economic reasons

In order to create a new model of the Church, the CHR[183] concluded, it would need to:

1. Introduce new evangelization techniques, "taking roots in the needs of eighty-seven percent of the population." It would use Creole, develop the popular culture, and encourage a new pastoral attitude toward Voodoo and customs such as *plaçage*. It would renew the liturgy to increase popular participation, create solidarity and encourage the CEBs
2. Take common action on national issues
3. Create an ecumenical and national commission to share its preferential option for the poor, and establish its social character by supporting justice and respect for human dignity

On 14 May, following Roger Lafontant's *Communiqués* of 7 and 8 May 1984, which further limited freedom of the press and postponed legalization of political parties, U.S. Secretary of State Shultz released a progress report on Haiti[184] in which he characterized the stalled political parties bill as a "positive development." The dichotomy between the secretary's optimism and conditions in Haiti became even more apparent on 21 May, when the city of Gonaïves erupted into violence. Exasperated, jobless, and hungry residents burned the house of a soldier who had beaten a woman, then two days later, plundered the city's food storage depots.[185] The riots spread to Cap-Haïtien, where twelve people were killed by government forces, six of them for destroying a Jean-Claude Duvalier President-for-Life sign. On 18 June, the editors of the newspapers that covered the riots were beaten-up and thrown in prison. Increasingly isolated, *Radio Soleil* continued to cover the events. A month later, on 26 July, the station was broken into and its transmitter turned off.[186]

In early November 1984, there was a second large-scale repression by the government, this time largely focused on persons involved with the Church and its development programs.[187] On 12 November 1984, a concerned "Group of Christians" wrote to the CHB denouncing the "climate of terror and insecurity" in Haiti, protesting the "arrests without mandate and the prolonged arrests," and urging authorities to respect peoples' rights.[188] The same day, the CHB sent a letter to the minister of religion on behalf of families "alarmed" by the violence. Two days later, on the 14th, the CHR sent a strong pastoral letter to its members[189] denouncing the round-ups, urging the bishops to intervene and assuring them of its support. Subsequently, some of the bishops went on *Radio Soleil* demanding that the government provide evidence of the alleged communist plot that was the pretext for the repression.[190]

The year ended with a series of related incidents in various parts of Haiti in which prefects and *macoutes* interrupted Church services to attack the officiating priest, the Church hierarchy, or the Church in general.[191] These local authorities may have been acting on their own but they clearly had the tacit permission of the government, since none of them was subsequently punished.[192] Father Rosemond Fabian had delivered the sermon at the cathedral in Cap-Haïtien on 18 November and was beginning to read a letter the bishops had written on November 12 to the minister of religion when the prefect, Auguste Robinson, knowing that there had been a meeting between the bishops and the government on 16 November, interrupted the service, and, taking control of the microphone, attacked the bishops for not telling the whole truth about their dealings with the government.[193] The Prefect's invasion of the cathedral provoked a series of incensed responses from various parts of the Church. The next day, people demonstrated in the streets of Cap-Haïtien calling on God's help in these "dark hours." Father Fabian sent a report of the incident to the minister of religion, and the CHR sent letters it received. On the 21st, the CHR sent its sympathy to the priest. On 23 November, the bishop of Cap-Haïtien wrote to Estimé protesting an "event [that] was without precedent in the history of relations between the Church and State." In his view, the intrusion was "all the more humiliating as it was a Protestant prefect who interrupted the service; an affront to the Catholic religion." In answer to Robinson's contention that the bishops were withholding information from the public, Bishop Gayot responded that it was the responsibility of the government to inform priests concerning its meetings. It was not the role of the Church to act for the State.[194] On 24 November, the bishops held a "prayer and cleansing service" at the Cathedral.

Within ten days, there were three other Church invasions. On 2 December one hundred armed *macoutes* interrupted a service at Sainte Claire Church in Port-au-Prince at the order of the prefect. The same day, another prefect led a bunch of *macoutes* into a Church in Gonaïves and harangued the congregation.[195] In this case, the prefect was mad at the parishioners because they had written a letter on behalf of Haitian prisoners that was read on *Radio Soleil.* Another incident occurred at the *fête patronale* in Milot on 8 December. Armed militia posted itself inside the Church on each side of the altar throughout the service.

As a result of these invasions, the religious of Cap-Haïtien wrote to the director of the board of the CHR on 6 December.[196] They were concerned that Haitians were becoming the victims of "political and ideological totalitarianism" and wondered whether the government was trying to cause the collapse and disappearance of religion. The bishop of Cap-Haïtien produced an analysis of the situation, pointing out that the invasions violated the concordat and recommending ways to prevent future problems.[197] The CHB sent a *Mémorandum* to the president because it was concerned about the Church invasions, the "campaign of intimidation and attacks against the CEBs, diocesan synod and Caritas. These events were provoking a "deterioration of relations between the Church and State." They concluded by asking the President to intervene.[198]

The bishops met with the minister of religion on 15 December, and told him bluntly that they would no longer accept government interference in the Church. Reportedly, he promised to rectify the situation.[199] However, on 28 December, the bishops wrote to Ambassador Estimé, noting that the situation was still going downhill, people continued to be abducted, and families were alarmed.[200]

There was no shortage of tough cabinet ministers during the Jean-Claude administration, but Interior Minister Roger Lafontant stood out. He had the confidence of the president, was unethical [201] and brutal.[202] Significantly, in October 1985, when President Duvalier wanted to demonstrate that he was liberalizing the government, he fired Roger Lafontant.[203]

Lafontant intervened liberally in the business of the other ministries, including the ministry of religion and foreign affairs. Sometimes, Estimé would discover that a decision regarding his domains had been made after the fact.[204] Two such cases were when Lafontant closed the Dominican border, and when he expelled the Belgian priest and his compatriots.

The government continued its efforts to control the Church in 1985, and the Church resisted. On 9 March, Roger Lafontant called François Ligondé into the ministry of the interior for what he termed an urgent meeting, but Ligondé refused to go.[205] Instead, he wrote a letter [206] to the minister saying he could not come to the chancellery; that would be like coming before a tribunal because, since 1960, all affairs concerning religion were handled by the minister of religion.

On 22 April, a militiaman named Joseph Larose shot at a priest, Emile Joseph, while the priest was in his room at the archbishop's residence.[207] The Church was infuriated. On 3 May, the CHR Peace and Justice Commission sent a *Communiqué*[208] to the government in which it described "this development as a direct consequence of threats and warnings directed at the Church either in public or in private by government officials." In short order, Radio Nationale charged that the clergy who had signed the letter were "subversives." Undeterred, on 14 May, a group of Haitian priests and religious wrote to the government to protest the shooting and premature release of Larose (he was freed two days later and never charged nor tried). It was not just a "wild ball," as the government claimed, it was some sort of terrorism. They resented the minister of religion's statements (dismissing the event somewhat cavalierly) and behavior, and concluded by citing John Paul II, who said that when human rights are attacked, it is necessary to speak out because the Bible calls for the defense of the poor and oppressed. They demanded an investigation.[209]

Between March and June, the government did its best to curb Church-supported activities. On 15 March, *Macoutes* dispersed a group before it could begin its march. Several hundred armed troops descended on crowds in Jérémie at Easter. Interior Minister Lafontant canceled a rally in Port-au-Prince on 21 June by ruling it unconstitutional.[210] The government clearly recognized the political potential of these gatherings, and its fears were justified.[211] The rallies and marches gave students and young people an opportunity to meet, organize, identify leaders, and vent their feelings. In April and May, the government forcibly attempted to recruit youth associated with the Church for its political party, the *Conseil National d'Action Jean-Claudiste* (CONAJEC). Those who did not join risked further harassment or imprisonment.[212]

On 8 June, the government announced that it would introduce the Law of Political Parties that would allow political parties beginning in 1987. However, numerous conditions were attached to the formation and activities of the parties. Any group wanting to become a party would be required to obtain the signatures of 18,000 perspective members, which was equivalent to 0.3 percent of the population. Political parties would be under the jurisdiction of the interior ministry, which would be empowered to suspend political activities without explanation.[213] They would have to accept the principle of the presidency-for-life and remain unconnected to a religious denomination.

The Church concluded that the proposed law, as presented, would exclude it from participation in the political process, so when the government scheduled the referendum on the Political Parties Law, the Church reacted. On 9 July, the CHB wrote to the president, reminding him that John Paul II himself approved of Church involvement in social and political matters.[214] On 16 July, the bishops issued a *Pastoral Message on the Law of the Organization and Functions of Political Parties in Haiti,* [215] concerning the consequences of the Law of Political Parties and prospects of pluralism. They quoted Vatican II and Pope John Paul II on the right and duty of the Church to be involved in social and political issues. In their opinion, this law represented a "systematic attempt to ignore religion in the political and social life of the country." They were particularly disturbed about two of the articles. Article II would make it illegal for a party to be associated with a religion. While they agreed that priests should not take part in political parties, they saw no reason to exclude lay members, or *laics chrétiens.* Article XVIII would forbid the use of religious symbols for political party emblems. They saw no reason why political parties in Haiti should be different from parties in most Christian societies in this regard. The bishops concluded by saying that they were feeling "nervous and excluded." They had written to the president, and now they were calling on the people for unity. They recalled that Jesus said, "take care not to let yourselves be abused, that you will be hated because of his name but not a hair on your head will be lost. You will save your lives by your constancy."

The government refused to allow any meetings on the referendum provisions prior to the elections and apprehended Hubert De Ronceray on 21 June 1985, when he published some anti-government material and announced his intention to hold a march against the presidency-for-life proposition. On 12 July, the government summoned Hugo Triest to the ministry of religion, charging *Radio Soleil* with "inciting" the people against the government with its critical programs concerning the pending referendum. When broadcasts continued, the lines were cut and some of the station's programs were jammed. On election day, the government held a rally in Port-au-Prince to generate enthusiasm; and after the elections, the government claimed a great victory.[216]

The government further antagonized the Church in a letter that the minister of religion sent to the bishops on 30 July.[217] Jean-Robert Estimé wrote that the State was not attempting to ignore the religious dimension in the political and social life of the country; it recognized its importance but wanted to define the relations, or *rapports.* Only fascism and communism were excluded from the political process. The titles of Social Christian and Christian Democrat were perfectly acceptable for parties when they referred to a philosophy rather than a religion or Church; however, the state would not allow the formation of a party controlled by a religion. In its conclusion, the Puebla document had said that in the economic, social and, particularly, political realm decisions, and leadership should not come from priests.[218] The government wanted to continue the principle of separation of Church and State associated with the concordat and avoid the catastrophes that had happened when politics were dominated by religious parties.

Despite the debatable interpretation of the Puebla document and *raison d'être* of the concordat, the Estimé letter might not have been so unpalatable without its gratuitous opening and closing gibes at the Church. It began by saying the Church had "formulated serious and unjustified criticism of the law on political parties, pretending an intention to reject the Christian community from the politics of the country." It ended by hoping that "this will calm them down, as a calmer, more objective reading would have."

Ambassador Estimé was aware of the changes in the Church's conception of its mission, but continues to maintain that the government was correct in its formulation of the Law of Political Parties. As he saw it, "the problem with the Catholic Church in Haiti was that it wanted all the rights without respect for any of the laws. The Church acted as if it were a political party. If it acted like a political party, it should be ready to be treated like one."[219] The limitations of the Church became evident in the events following Jean-Claude's departure. "[The Church] was perfect for overthrowing a government as holy men or *ayatollahs*, [220] but had neither the formation nor structure of political parties. Churchmen are not politicians, they cannot take, keep or manage power, nor have they studied the problems facing a country, such as deforestation. Ultimately, politics is antithetical to the values of Churchmen."

In the wake of the Referendum on Political Parties, the government deported Father Triest and the two other priests. The Church was livid. On 26 July, the CHB sent a memorandum to the president protesting the deportations and informing him that the Church would be limiting its *te-deums* as a consequence of "*renouveau liturgique*," or liturgical renewal.[221] On 28 July, the CHR sent a letter of solidarity to the Scheut Fathers and *Radio Soleil*. On 29 July, the Church canceled masses that were to have commemorated the anniversary of the formation of Haiti's militia. This was a direct insult to the president, who was to have attended a mass opening the celebrations.[222] On 2 August, the Haitian Church observed a day of prayer and fasting to protest the manner in which it was being treated. On 3 August, Bishop Gayot declared that "terrible things are happening in this country. We are effectively in a situation of official Church persecution."[223]

THE CHURCH TAKES THE OFFENSIVE: THE OVERTHROW OF DUVALIER

By July 1985, a significant sector of the Church had practically reversed its historical relationship with the State and the outside world. Far from being an isolated arm of the government, it opposed it and was closely connected to various international institutions, organizations, and countries.[224] By pinpointing the shortcomings of the referendum and accurately predicting its outcome, the Church caused the international donor community and Haitians alike to reassess their commitment to the government.[225] Activists in the United States urged Congress to halt foreign assistance to Haiti, prompting the Haitian government to offer a number of concessions in order to improve its image. On 23 September, it abolished the death penalty for political matters. On 2 October, it allowed an opposition party, the Partie National Progressiste (PNP), to register with the interior ministry. On 4 October, it fired Lafontant.

The Church made other demands and did not back down. On 9 August 1985, the bishops reportedly met for five hours with the minister of foreign affairs and religion and warned him that they were not going to normalize relations with the government until their demands were met.[226] The government subsequently released a *Communiqué,* declaring that negotiations were in progress. The Church did not confirm this announcement. In fact, the Vatican sent a note to the government asking why the priests had been expelled from Haiti, why Desmet had been murdered, and why the government was impeding the work of *Radio Soleil,* which was operating according to Haitian law.[227]

The Church proved that the government was not in a liberalizing mode, making it clear to the international community and Haitians that any government reform would be the consequence of pressure. Dr. Lionel Lainé and Pollux St-Jean, who had organized the PNP in August 1985 and registered it on 2 October, were incarcerated on 11 October. Lainé, who had been previously arrested in 1984 and accused of involvement in a Marxist-Leninist plot, was later found in Port-au-Prince; he had been murdered. St-Jean never turned up. Hundreds of people in Gonaïves demonstrated against the abductions on 30 October. In November, the residents of Gonaïves again took to the streets.

On 26 November, the citizens of Gonaïves assembled to commemorate the 1980 government crackdown, but they did not disband. The next day, they demonstrated for "an end to misery, the Constitution, and the Duvalier government." The demonstrations continued on 28 November, when troops intervened and chased some of the participants into a nearby Catholic school, then randomly opened fire, killing students, who had been previously uninvolved.[228]

The same day, Bishop Constant of Gonaïves, whose bishopric is only a short walk from Immaculate Conception School, put out a terse message to the people of Gonaïves protesting the murders.[229] He knew they were stunned and anguished. The victims were innocents, who had not taken part in the demonstrations. The affair raised questions concerning the regard for life and use of authority. The bishop concluded by calling for justice and calm. Subsequently, the Church demanded a commission of inquiry, a trial of the perpetrators, and dedicated 3 December as a national day of mourning.[230]

The government announced the formation of a combined civil-military commission to investigate the events at Gonaïves on 3 December, but the next day, it lost whatever goodwill this move might have engendered by closing *Radio Soleil* and shortly thereafter, another Catholic radio station, *Ave Maria*. [231] Interior Minister Chanoine[232] justified the closures by citing Broadcasting Law Article LI,[233] which enjoined the media to "prevent inaccurate information from harming or alarming the population."

The murder of the students in Gonaïves and closure of *Radio Soleil* galvanized the population. The young were particularly outspoken.[234] The Council of Youth called for a battle to liberate the country. "Do not forget the three youths who died in one year. This means leaders do not respect lives of young Haitians."[235] The Youth of Jérémie demanded justice for Gonaïves,[236] a government apology, and arrests. They would not return to school until these matters were resolved. The Youth of Port-au-Prince protested the closure of *Radio Soleil*. The Youth of Les Cayes objected to "the gagging of *Radio Soleil* and the criminals governing us."[237] Dozens of anti-government demonstrators were rounded-up.[238]

On 18 December, the bishops sent a memorandum to the president objecting to the closure of *Radio Soleil*.[239] In it, they asked Duvalier to have the station reopened and the equipment returned to working order. In their subsequent Christmas message,[240] the bishops recalled how hopes for the Year of the Youth had been "sullied by mourning." As we have seen, they reflected on the miserable condition of the country and commented that although they planned to launch a literacy program, they could not do everything; this would require the effort of all Haitians. "This is the moment to say no to lies, servitude, egotism, torture, violence, injustice, and hate. . ."

Nevertheless, the violence continued. A school principal from Gonaïves was detained, only to die in prison, leading young people to protest police violence in Gonaïves and Port-au-Prince on 15 December.[241] They demonstrated near the presidential palace, calling for justice and an end to hunger. That evening, the Youth of Port-au-Prince took to the streets to demand the reopening of *Radio Soleil* following a concert by John Littleton.[242]

Marches and demonstrations came to epitomize 1985. Begun in a religious context in conjunction with the IYY, they became the primary means to vent frustration. Ultimately, government reaction to the demonstrations in Gonaïves may have been the last straw, the event that convinced Haitians that the government was beyond redemption.

Gonaïves was a turning point for the government.[243] Despite unwanted domestic and international attention and criticism following the referendum and deportation of the Belgians, the government had, to an extent, gotten away with these actions. It did not get away with Gonaïves. Closing *Radio Soleil* exacerbated the criticism. Estimé called this period a "critical moment" for the Haitian government.[244] The United States put its foot down. It would not recertify Haiti for foreign aid without a trial of those who had killed the students in Gonaïves; the release of De Ronceray, who had been rearrested in early December; and the reopening of *Radio Soleil*. The reputation of the government had sunk so low that even some Duvalierists began to call for the overthrow of the president.

The relationship between the Church and State was changing rapidly. By December, the shift in balance of power was evident. The government allowed *Radio Soleil* to reopen on 31 December after a three-week hiatus with the hope that the station "would conform to its pastoral vocation with scrupulous respect for Haitian laws," but *Radio Soleil* returned unchanged.[245] When the government offered an insignificant amount of money to the parents of the children murdered in Gonaïves, *Radio Soleil* made a story of it.

Schools were scheduled to open the Monday after New Year's Day, but students called for a boycott. Anti-government protests in Petit Goâve and Gonaïves began on 6 January and continued the next day, coupled with school and university strikes. On 8 January the minister of national education simply authorized what had already occurred, the closure of the schools.[246]

By January, the Church not only defied government authority, it also rejected any concessions it had already offered. On 10 January, the government lowered the cost of cooking oil and prices of several other basic consumer items as a conciliatory gesture to Haiti's poor and hungry people, but the Church encouraged them to keep up the pressure and continue their struggles for "just demands."[247] The government invited the Church to talks on 11 and 12 January only to have them subsequently epitomized by the bishops on *Radio Soleil* as "fruitless." Bishop Romélus went on the air to accuse the government of giving security forces permission to kill Haitians.[248]

On 26 January the government announced the reform of the military, the dissolution of the political police, and the retirement from the military of the person responsible for the death of Dr. Lainé. The next day, it added that it would bring to trial those presumed responsible for killing the children in Gonaïves. The public was not appeased. The residents of Gonaïves showed their contempt by setting fire to the customs and courthouse.[249] Tracts circulated calling for the overthrow of the regime.

The government reacted by resorting to its customary methods of controlling dissension: repression and violence.[250] However, the public was no longer intimidated. On 26 January, Cap-Haïtien held its first political demonstration against the government. A second demonstration followed the next day. Young people occupied the Cathedral overnight, police fired, killing three and wounding twenty.[251] On 28 January, a plot to assassinate Bishop Romélus and Fathers Julien and Samedi in Jérémie was uncovered before it could be carried out. Five to six thousand people turned out to show their support for the Churchmen. On 30 January, the government imposed a state of siege.

In late January 1986, the United States declined to recertify that the Haitian government was complying with human rights, one of the conditions for foreign assistance.[252] Aid was withheld due to the "serious repressive actions taken by the Duvalier government in late 1985 and early 1986." On 31 January, when U.S. presidential spokesman Larry Speakes prematurely announced Duvalier's departure, people took to the streets in a delirium of happiness and relief.[253] Duvalier responded by declaring a state of siege, and dispatching the *macoutes* and army. One hundred civilians caught celebrating in Léogâne were killed. Despite threats, a commercial strike begun in Port-au-Prince on 4 February continued. Mass protests persisted all over Haiti.

In order to maintain stability and prevent bloodshed in Haiti, the U.S. government urged Duvalier to leave Haiti and to appoint an interim government before going. On 7 February 1986, Duvalier departed, in the dark of night, with his family, his entourage, and what was left of the nation's assets aboard a C-141 provided by the United States.

There was widespread joy at the news Duvalier had gone. Revelers chanted, "never, never again," and Bishop Gayot dubbed the day, "our second independence."[254] Soon after, schools reopened, broadcast freedom was restored and *Radio Soleil* returned to the air. Political prisoners were released and *macoutes* disbanded and hid. Makeshift red and blue flags were hung everywhere—-the Haitian banner was flying again after thirty years.

Despite the high spirits, few thought the future would be easy. There were social problems, including scores to settle with *macoutes,* Duvalierists, and *houngans* who had committed crimes during the Duvalier administrations. There were economic issues exacerbated by years of mismanagement and government rapaciousness.[255] Principally, there was the matter of establishing a democracy in a country where so few had any direct experience with one. Resistance could be anticipated from all who stood to lose power.

Those concerns have been justified. Seven years after Haiti's liberation, social wounds have not healed. The economic situation has become even more precarious. Between February 1986 and April 1993, there have been seven governments—four overtly military, one quasi-military, one quasi-democratic, one civilian caretaker, two failed elections, and four coups.[256] Human rights abridgments and violence have characterized the post Jean-Claude era to date. U.S. policy remained unchanged until November 1989 when Alvin Adams was appointed ambassador.[257]

Potential leaders and political theoreticians such as Silvio Claude,[258] Grégoire Eugène, Willy Romélus, and Jean-Bertrand Aristide[259] were initially sidelined. Educated and skilled persons living in the diaspora did not return in large numbers to invigorate and transform the nation. The government did not change. It continued to be run by Duvalier's colleagues and to operate by graft, corruption and repression.

Summary

We can see that the past thirty years have been a period of change for the Church in Haiti. International and domestic influences have caused it to become more concerned about the people and their welfare. In the late 1960s, the Church began to assume many functions normally provided by government, and consequently gained the respect of society and hostility of the administration. As repression increased and less powerful institutions were silenced, the Church took on an additional and unaccustomed role—of governmental critic and moral authority. The government accused the Church of exceeding its mandate and threatened to treat it like a political party (they were illegal) if it continued to act like one. It undertook a number of initiatives to silence the Church. It made overtures to the Protestants. It tried intimidation—bishops and the director of *Radio Soleil* were summoned to the government palace. Prefects, *macoutes* and *chefs de section* shot and incarcerated people and invaded Churches. Initially, the Institution mainly reacted to the persecution of Church people but increasingly it adopted the view that it had the duty to protest all abuse, citing papal authority to justify its involvement in social and political matters. A number of individuals and groups associated with the Church were particularly outspoken despite the danger. Among them were Hugo Triest, Willy Romélus, lay workers with economic development and education projects, the CHR, and the Catholic youth groups.

By 1985, *Radio Soleil* concluded that the government was not going to reform. It predicted that no matter how low the turnout for legislative elections, it would claim a major victory. Promises notwithstanding, the government would not allow political parties to operate. The exasperated government exiled Hugo Triest and closed *Radio Soleil,* provoking a nation-wide uproar. The declining economic situation, food riots, and the murder of school children in Gonaïves finally convinced Haitians that things were not going to improve as long as Jean-Claude Duvalier remained President of Haiti. Catholic youth groups, assembled for the International Year of Youth, resolved to take to the streets and even die, and not to return to school in January until their concerns were addressed. At Christmas 1985, the bishops called on Haitians to resolve their problems, it was time to oppose violence, servitude, torture, lies, and injustice. Reopened in late December, *Radio Soleil* took up where it had left off, calling government reparations to the families of the dead children insufficient and projected price cuts inadequate. Bishop Romélus used the station to accuse the government of permitting security forces to kill Haitians.

On 6 February 1986, in the dead of night, Jean-Claude and his retinue left the country. The Church had come a long way from its traditional stance as a supporter of rulers against the wishes of the people. In the next chapter, we will present our findings.

NOTES

1. The concordat has been modified a number of time, most recently on 8 August 1984. It was previously revised in 1861, 1862, 1940, and 1966.

2. Jean-Robert Estimé, interview with author, Wheaton, MD, 13 October 1988. During the Jean-Claude presidency, the annual budget for the Church was approximately $500,000. This provided a monthly salary of $70 to $100 per priest, and some development funds to supplement the work of Catholic organizations such as the Catholic Relief Services. In addition, the Church asked for funds for specific projects, such as Church restoration. The ambassador described the president as "receptive to such requests."

3. Religion had shared a ministry with education.

4. Jean-Robert Estimé, interview with author, Wheaton, MD, 3 October 1988. Ironically, thirty years later, Estimé experienced the *mulattoization* of the cabinet and was himself discriminated against as a black.

5. See Fred D. Wood III, "The Scourged Christ of Haiti: Politics, Economics and the Church in the Island Republic," diss., Wesley Theological Seminary, March 1985), 113, citing J. Lloyd Mecham, *Church and State in Latin America* (Chapel Hill: The University of North Carolina Press, 1966) and figures supplied by the Haitian embassy, Washington, D.C. Wood outlines the government's financial ties with the Church. It provides the salaries of the archbishop, bishops, and priests. Its budget contains allocations for religious purposes, approximately 10 percent of which goes for the support of Protestant churches. The 1963–64 budget provided 1,337,000 *gourdes* for religion and 1,152,341 *gourdes* for the Catholic Church. Of the amount appropriated to the Catholic Church, 941,681 *gourdes* went for clerical personnel, including the priests, and 194,000 *gourdes* went for upkeep of the buildings. Since all Church property was nationalized,

building repair and maintenance of Church structures and property is responsibility of the government and comes under the jurisdiction of the ministry of foreign affairs.

6. Jean-Robert Estimé, interview with author, Wheaton, MD, 13 October 1988. According to Estimé, the low point of his tenure was the expulsion of the priests in the summer of 1985. He was certain that it would lead to more tension with the Church, that it would not resolve the problem, or do any good. He believed other ministers must have advised the president to do it. Roger Lafontant, in particular, always wanted to take a hard line. The highlights of his tenure were the pope's visit, his trips to Rome, and efforts to produce a new concordat.

7. Jean-Robert Estimé, interview with author, Wheaton, MD, 5 May 1988.

8. Ibid.

9. Ibid.

10. Jean-Robert Estimé, interview with author, Wheaton, MD, 21 May 1988.

11. Jean-Robert Estimé, interview with author, Wheaton, MD, 3 October 1988. The ambassador came to the conclusion that the *Commission* was not useful, that it was unable to reach meaningful conclusions.

12. Gérard Duclerville is a Haitian lay worker who was director of the Catholic Volunteers—young volunteers who teach illiterates and organize lay communities and farmer cooperatives. On 13 December 1982, police interrupted a prayer meeting at a facility of the Salesian Fathers, arrested and tortured Duclerville, probably because he had publicly denounced the government practice of rounding up the homeless and unpresentable during the holidays in order to make the capital more attractive to tourists. He was released, on the eve of the papal visit to Haiti, following considerable pressure from the Church.

For additional background on Duclerville, see the article written in January 1983 for *La Iglesia En Haiti,* Comite Haitiano-Venezolano de Defensa de los Derechos Humanos, no. 5, Caracas, Venezuela, 1983, 13–14.

The habit of rounding up undesirables continued at least until May 1986. I spent a day assisting a dentist who annually provided free dental services to children and mentally and physically ill adults in Haiti who had been picked up on the streets and locked up out of sight.

13. François Duvalier got the support of the rural population without doing anything to better their condition. His self-important blue uniformed VSN helped keep people in line, but VSN loyalty dissipated under Jean-Claude because he ignored them. Due to a less vigilant VSN, it became easier for the CEBs to do their work, to fight for literacy without fear.

14. Jean-Robert Estimé, interview with author, Wheaton, MD, 21 May 1988.

15. Letter from Jean-Robert Estimé to the "Reverend Fathers," 21 December 1984. At this time, the government was looking for a pretext to crack down and found it in alleged national security threats.

The Institut d'Education des Adultes (IDEA) was a creation of the Fathers of St. Croix. Committed to rural development in agriculture, education, and appropriate technology, it inspired the *Ti-légliz* movement.

16. Joseph Serge Milot, "Letter to Ambassador Jean-Robert Estimé, 7 November 1984.

Yvon Joseph, "Impact of the Current Political Reality on Community-Based Development Work in Haiti and Prospects for the Future." Seminar for the Coordination in Development Conference, New York, 21 October 1988), 3. In his presentation, Dr. Robert Maguire of the Inter-American Foundation described the founding of IDEA in 1972 as an attempt to promote development structures. Its founder,

Father Yvon Joseph, had come to believe that only by educating the peasants would Haiti have a future. The principle behind IDEA was to stimulate development through individuals. To create a human grassroots infrastructure, IDEA evolved into an Institute for Leadership Training. Its philosophy was that once people had their own management experience, their success would breed success. Other organizations, such as *CARITAS*, joined in programs with the same ideology. Many *animateurs*, or community leaders, were trained. Maguire observed that "In 1984, IDEA received an indication of its success in the North and Northwest when it was attacked and a number of its workers arrested. Its network was growing and that frightened the dictatorship which sought to destabilize the organization."

17. See Michel Bourdeau, Comité Catholique Contre la Faim et Pour le Développement, *Trip Report to Haiti* (Paris, 22 June-6 July 1984), 11. In an interview, Bishop Gayot told Bourdeau that negations between the Church and State were in progress, but the government "isn't lacking in suspicions of subversion on the part of the Church."

For an appreciation of the evolution of the Church literacy program, see *Présence de l'Église En Haïti: Messages et Documents de l'Épiscopat, 1980–1988* (Paris: Éditions SOS, 1988), 44, 93, 95, 121, 127–32.

For details concerning the operation of the program, see Bourdeau, *Trip Report to Haiti*, 11.

18. Jean-Robert Estimé, interview with author, Wheaton, MD, 19 April 1988.

19. Ministry of Foreign Affairs and Religion, *L'Eglise Catholique et l'Etat: Evolution des Rapports*, 1985.

Father René Poirier, interview by the author, Villa Manrèse, Port-au-Prince, 12 July 1986. The number of parishes varies. Additional parishes were needed and some lacked priests. Port-au-Prince had 58 parishes and required 15 more. In Haiti as a whole, 20 parishes were without priests. As of late 1984, Haiti had 171 parishes and 1,919 chapels, 6 dioceses, and 1 archdiocese.

20. The nunciature was established on 17 October 1930. Beginning in 1874, there was an apostolic delegation comprised of the Dominican Republic, Venezuela, and Haiti. From 1916 to 1930, there was a shared Dominican-Haitian nunciature.

21. A number of the people described in this book moved on to other positions in other places after 1986.

22. Bishop Laroche of Hinche was appointed president of the CHB in 1989. Bishop François Gayot of Cap-Haïtien was president of the CHB throughout the Jean-Claude presidency. Gayot was appointed archbishop subsequent to the departure of Jean-Claude Duvalier. I will refer to him as bishop, the title he held until 1987.

In 1980, there were seven bishops in Haiti. By 1986 the number had increased to eight. Five of the eight (Gayot, Ligondé, Angenor, Constant, and Romélus) had served since at least 1980.

23. John P. Hogan, "Haiti's Brief Hour of Hope," review of *The Rainy Season* by Amy Walentz, *Commonweal* (22 September 1989): 506. John Hogan, who was director of the Catholic Relief Services in Haiti from February 1987 through July 1989, described the genesis and role of the Church in social change. Until the François Duvalier presidency, "the problem of the exploited masses drew a compassionate response out of only a small minority of the clergy and religious." It was only after that, that the prevalence of pastoral action began. Then, "beginning roughly in 1976, the Haitian Church entered into a strong commitment to evangelization, social justice, and defense of the poor. A grassroots but still publicly timid Church inspired by Vatican II, Medellín, and Puebla gained tremendous impetus when John Paul II declared that "things must change."

Bishops, priests, sisters, brothers and lay activists who had defended the poor from hiding places were now able to fight in the open. They could count on cover from the official Church." Hogan concluded, "there is no doubt about it, pastoral action on behalf of the poor and oppressed did become the thrust of a large portion of the Haitian Church, and the bishops, even if at times reluctantly, courageously supported such pastoral action.

24. See Colman McCarthy, "A Sign of Promise," *Washington Post*, 30 September 1984 for a description of the dedication and work of Dr. Carlo Boulos and twelve Catholic Sisters of Charity who care for the poor and sick at Cité Simone (now Cité Soleil), a huge urban slum in Port-au-Prince.

25. There are remnants of French influence in the Church. The bishops still write their documents in French and have them translated to Creole, arguing that they cannot express themselves fully in Creole. Some masses in Pétionville continue to be given in French.

26. Ministry of Foreign Affairs and Religion, *L'Eglise Catholique et l'Etat*. This document lists 229 primary schools, 30 specialized schools, 18 hospitals, 10 dispensaries, 38 school canteens, 29 literacy centers, 19 artisan centers, 4 nursing homes, 12 thrift shops, 3 agricultural farms, 9 community development centers, and more than 100 popular banks and cooperatives.

27. Edgar Miller, "Hope Sprouts in Haiti," *Catholic Standard*, 12 April 1984. In his interview with Father Pollux Byas, a Haitian Holy Cross priest who had been a pastor in Cap-Haïtien for the past twenty-four years, Byas described the base communities as a means of improving all aspects of peasants' lives. He estimated that there were three hundred base communities in the parish with about nine thousand members. He was showing the peasants in all of the dioceses' parishes "how to build the new society." "It is not just converting people. Conversion now means something else. It doesn't mean only to save my soul. It is to save my life and my soul, to save all and not only me. The Community, the society. . ." Asked about "Liberation Theology," Father Byas commented: "Liberation is to free people from every evil, evil in life, evil in everything. We have to be free from politics, from social, from economic, from spiritual [concerns]. All life is involved with our plan. It is liberation."

See Hans Buddingh, "Haitian Catholic Church Cited As Potent Force For Change," *The Catholic Transcript* 31 August 1984 for an analysis of the changing Church and the effects of its social and political agenda. Duclerville described the work of the sixty or so lay groups in the capital and three to four hundred of them in the countryside. According to him, their most important achievement is setting up cooperatives. "We speak in small groups about work and social issues. This causes the people to develop greater self consciousness. Through dialogue, the Church has come closer to the people." A joint lay-clergy survey of Haitians about social problems in 1982 is viewed as speeding up changes already under way in the Church. The symposium in late 1982 endorsed it conclusions and committed the Church to a role in deciding social and political questions. With this encouragement, Haitians are getting more cooperatives, private development, technical and financial assistance, improving the lives of thousands of poor farmers.

28. Mark Persily, intern, Washington Office on Haiti. Untitled paper on the Church, Haiti, summer 1988, 3–4. In an interview, Father Polloux Byas pointed out that two-thirds of those involved with the *Ti-légliz* movement were women.

29. Mary Evelyn Jegen, *Haiti: The Struggle Continues*, Just World Order Series (Erie, PA.: Benet Press, 1987), 23. From their beginnings, circa 1968, the CEBs have experienced remarkable and steady growth, particularly over the past eight years. The national

committee is composed of three members from each of the seven diocese. Leadership training seminars are now held on the national, diocesan, and local levels.

The CEBs provide their members with a variety of benefits, ranging from such intangibles as the feeling of solidarity engendered by being in a group, to such tangible benefits as participating in agricultural associations and neighborhood committees.

See Pax Christi International, *Report of the Mission of the Pax Christi International to Haiti* Erie, PA.: Pax Christi International, 1986), 94–97. The members of this mission repeatedly heard testimony that something was changing where these communities were organized. A solidarity was developing among the members, making individuals less vulnerable to intimidation and the authorities unable to do what they wanted so easily.

30. A priest in Haiti stated that the Church was grateful to the Methodists for translating the Bible into Creole and producing an edition that only cost three U.S. dollars.

31. Max-Abner Etienne, "Interview de l'Archêveque François Wolff Ligondé," *Jeune Haïti* 92 (23 April 1986).

32. Yves Voltaire, "Haïti: Terre d'Espérance," *Orient* (March-April 1986): 16. About fifteen divinity student have entered the seminary annually since 1981. Currently, approximately two hundred and ten are enrolled.

Father Bill Quigley, addressing an audience at Saint Charles Catholic Church on 12 July 1989 described the seminary as full but the number of seminarians was limited, due to a lack of educated Haitian students. The curriculum had recently been amended by the bishops to include a fourth year of theology.

33. Toumédia, ed., *Haïti-Pape 83* (Port-au-Prince: Imprimerie Henri Deschamps, 1983), 139. Drawn from Secrétariat du Congrès Eucharistique et Marial.

34. Church commitment to social and economic development is reflected in the bishops' 6 January 1985 *Message to Young People for the IIY*. See *Présence de l'Église En Haïti*, 114. Young people should fight for "*la promotion humaine.*" They will be proud to have worked for peace, "*developpement étant le nouveau nom de la paix.*"

35. Toumédia, ed., *Haïti-Pape 83*, 91. In an interview with Toumédia, Archbishop Ligondé described the growth of Church concern with human welfare through social-economic development projects after 1966, particularly in the rural areas. Page 94 includes a list of schools and center that the Church operated at that time.

See Bourdeau, *Trip Report to Haiti*, 2–4. Bourdeau provides a chronology of Church work in development in Haiti since the 1960s. He discusses the agendas of IDEA, ITECA, and DCCH. In addition to a description of the evolution of Church-related development work, he provides information on the numbers of people involved, the budgets and the scope of the activities. On page 5, he gives additional information on Church work in Cité Simone and Brookling with people who are "*miséreux*" as opposed to simply poor.

John Hogan, "Social Change and Development in Haiti," Seminar, Johns Hopkins University, SAIS, 31 January 1990. Hogan also traces the development of social action in the Haitian Church to the 1960s, spotlighting the role of the American and Canadian priests in the south of the country. They were a product of the Catholic Action programs and the first priests to "go to the people." Hogan concluded that they "did a good job."

Voltaire, "Haïti: Terre d'Espérance." Voltaire speaks of a surge in development work in the 1970s as a reaction to Pope Paul VI's Encyclical "Development of the People." It resulted in the establishment of community organizations, women's and literacy centers, and dispensaries.

See Thomas Weil, et al., *Area Handbook for Haiti* (Washington, D.C.: The American University Press, 1973), 51. The authors wrote about the increasing numbers of priest who were becoming interested in peasants and moving from the domain of the urban upper class to the countryside, contributing to an increase in Catholic vocational training centers, hospitals and rural schools.

36. Ernest H. Preeg, interview with author, State Department, Washington, D.C., 31 March 1988.

See Buddingh, "Haitian Catholic Church Cited As Potent Force For Change" to appreciate the increasing visibility and activism of the Church. By August 1984 a progressive and influential priest is calling the Haitian Church "the most important force for change," and another diplomat speaks of the Church's "new activism." Not only that, it is regarded as "the only institution with any maneuvering room since the Haitian political opposition has been destroyed [by political crackdowns in 1979 and 1980].

37. Robert J. Tata, *Haiti, Land of Poverty* (Washington, D.C.: University Press of America, 1982), 31.

38. Jean-Robert Estimé, interview with author, Wheaton, MD, 23 March 1988. François Duvalier kept "tight control" over the Church following the revision of the concordat, and Estimé characterized government relations with the "beholden" bishops and some of the priests as "good," but added that "some of the priests were very militant."

See "Mounting Tensions Between Christian Churches and the Duvalier Government." *Le Monde*, 2 March 1983. Translation by the Haitian Refugee Project, Washington, D.C. The Church, described in early 1983 as "the only institution in the country which still benefits from freedom of expression, is becoming increasingly aware of the wrongdoing of Jean-Claude Duvalier's regime. Several recent events have allowed it to make its feelings known." The article goes on to describe Church opposition to dam constructions on the Artibonite and the handling of the pig eradication program.

For additional indications of change in the Church, see "Pope Decries Haiti 'Misery' and 'Fear,' Demands Change," *Miami Herald*, 10 March 1983, 1A, 19A. "Led in recent years by six Haitian bishops and a sometimes restive corps of priests . . . the Haitian Church has been largely quiescent. Gradually, though, under the more benign rule of Jean-Claude (Baby Doc) Duvalier, the Church has begun to be heard again on more than religious matters. The Church is taking a stance at long last," said the Rev. Raymond Conrad, a Wisconsin priest who directs the Church's *Radio Soleil*, Haiti's most popular and most outspoken radio station. Later in the same article, speaking about the Church role in the recent release of Duclerville, a priest was quoted as saying, "We have a new Church which speaks against torture, against corruption."

39. Only two years later, Greg Chamberlain, "Difficult Days for Haiti's R. C. Church," *Caribbean Conact*, March 1983, was writing, "Some of Haiti's clergy, notably the National Conference of Priests and Nuns, have taken a stand against the regime's brutalities and the country's stark poverty in contrast to the immense personal fortune of the Duvaliers."

See Gregory K. Freeland, *Religious Elites and Political Activity in Haiti* (prepared for delivery at the 1985 Annual Meeting of the Western Political Science Association, Las Vegas, 28–30 March 1985), 18. Freeland wrote about the impressive sources of Church influence in Haiti by 1985. They derived from:

1. Its people, the priests, schools, orders, seminarians, and bishops. It is transmitted through the priests, who are in charge of parishes in which Catholic doctrine is carried. "Regime restrictions can hinder what is done in these parishes, but Church influence continues to dominate."

2. The base communities, which establish legitimacy for the priests who coordinate them and the programs that allow the peasant farmers to double their production.

3. Church contact and access to all social strata.

4. The economic strength of the Church and its connection to an international institution that has been solvent for several hundred centuries.

5. The mobilization of Church sub-institutions: community churches, associations, laymen, and communications system.

40. *Présence de l'Église En Haïti*, 19. See *Message de Noël* de la Conférence Épiscopale du 21 December 1980. The bishops are concerned about emigration, the plight of Haitians in the Dominican Republic, and the atmosphere of "insecurity and fear" in Haiti. Citing the pope and earlier Church documents, they express their intention to continue to work on social issues, particularly as they relate to family, education and the CEBs.

41. Ministry of Foreign Affairs and Religion, *L'Eglise Catholique et l'Etat*, 8.

42. "Haitian Catholic Leaders Step into Human Rights Void on Eve of Mass Bahamian Deportations," Washington, D.C.: Haitian Refugee Project, 13 January 1981. The initiative was taken by the CHR, which represented 1,475 men and women Religious who "proclaim[ed] the human rights in our country of our brothers and sisters in exile or in prison."

43. Conference of Haitian Religious, *Letter to Our Dear Fathers and Brothers in Christ the Bishops of Haiti* (Port-au-Prince: Conference of Haitian Religious, 4 December 1980).

44. Conference of Haitian Religious, *Communiqué* from twenty-four heads of orders, Port-au-Prince, 4 December 1980.

45. Conference of Haitian Religious, *Letter*. The CHR began their letter by telling the bishops that they are their leaders and guides. The CHR are clearly urging the bishops to do something because "neutrality is a position."

46. The CHB only issued its first message, *L'Église dans la Cité*, in 1972. While it was not inflammatory, it was critical of human rights abuses and the lack of due process.

47. François Wolff Ligondé, *Letter to Révérend Père Pétion Laroche, Recteur du Grand Séminaire, Haut de Turgeau* (Port-au-Prince: Conférence Épiscopale Haïtienne, 6 May 1981).

48. James Timothy Kelly, "Rocks in the Sun: The Roman Catholic Church in Haitian Political Development" (Senior honors thesis, Harvard University, March 1988), 65. Kelly observed that the symposium was held in a historically important place, the Community of St. Mary in Port-au-Prince, where many of the earliest innovations in introducing Haitian cultural elements into the mass had taken place.

49. Etienne, "Interview de l'Archêveque François Wolff Ligondé," 116. See Voltaire, "Haïti: Terre d'Espérance," 12–14. For background information on the Congress, see *Présence de l'Église En Haïti*, 27, 31. On 15 September 1981, the bishops issued a pastoral letter discussing the upcoming congress. Its purpose, "*à construire une communauté réconcilé plus juste et plus fraternelle*," "to construct a reconciled, more just, and fraternal society".

50. Bourdeau, *Trip Report to Haiti*, 1. Bourdeau wrote, "The message of the Symposium traced the line that the Church wanted to follow: from Medellín and Puebla, 'the preferential option for the poor.'"

51. Conference of Haitian Bishops, *Declaration of the Bishops of Haiti on the Foundations of Church Intervention in Social and Political Affairs* (Port-au-Prince: CHB, 11 April 1983).

52. Ibid.

53. Yvon Joseph, *Inaugural Message at the Second General Assembly of the Conference of Haitian Religious.* (Port-au-Prince: Conference of Haitian Religious, 23–26 April 1984), 5.

54. *Présence de l'Église En Haïti,* 135. The CEH particularly objected to Article VII, which said that any political party linked to a religion was illegal, and Article XVIII, which said that the name, symbol, and emblem of a political party could not contain any religious reference.

55. Vatican II, Constitution Lumen Gentium 1.

56. Conference of Haitian Bishops, *Message Pastoral en la Fête de Notre-Dame du Mont-Carmel,* (Port-au-Prince: CHB, 16 July 1985).

57. Relations between the Church and State had grown worse since at least December 1980. Given its network of communications, it is inconceivable that the Vatican was ignorant of what was taking place in Haiti or was pleased with the Haitian government.

See Irene Garzon Fernandez, "CELAM Inica Asamblea en Haiti," Puerto Principe, Haïti, 9 March 1983. The night before the pope arrived in Haiti, some 100,000 Catholics congregated in the Champs de Mars park near the presidential palace. Bishop Willy Romélus spoke for forty minutes attacking the president. "I'm talking directly to you, the people of the military barracks. Stop torturing Haitians. Stop assassinating them. I am talking to you, government ministers. Stop filling your pockets with the country's money. I am talking to you in the national palace, so you have a better vision of the country. One cannot pretend to be a patriot, when one owns such big houses and beautiful automobiles and the people are dying from hunger. Show compassion for the people."

58. The domestic situation was different. The government was isolated and Jean-Claude Duvalier wanted credibility. He thought he could profit from any visit. These views were expressed by a medical doctor who knows the country and by the papal nuncio in an interview with the author at the nunciature in Port-au-Prince on 11 July 1986.

59. Jean-Claude Duvalier, *Letter to the Pope John Paul II,* 23 November 1982.

60. Luigi Conti, *Letter to Ambassador Jean-Robert Estimé, Minister of Foreign Affairs and Religion,* 23 February 1983.

61. Jean-Robert Estimé, *Letter to Papal Nuncio Luigi Conti,* 23 February 1983.

62. Jean-Robert Estimé, interview with author, Wheaton, MD, 29 March 1988.

63. Etienne, "Interview de l'Archêveque Francçois Wolff Ligondé."

64. François Wolff Ligondé, the archbishop of Port-au-Prince, was one of the original bishops appointed by François Duvalier.

65. Etienne, "Interview de l'Archêveque Francçois Wolff Ligondé."

66. The Honorable Walter Fauntroy, Congressman from the District of Columbia and Chairman of the Congressional Black Caucus, interview with author, Rayburn House Office building, Washington, D.C., 10 May 1988.

See Karen Payne, "Pope Has 'Great Interest" in Haitians," *Miami News Reporter,* 25 February 1982.

See also "Black Leaders Meet With Pope," *Miami Times,* 25 February 1982. The five-person delegation consisted of the Reverend Jesse Jackson, Mrs. Jacqueline Jackson, Dr. Mary Berry of the U.S. Civil Rights Commission, Congressman William Gray (D-PA.) of the Congressional Black Caucus, and Mrs. Camille Cosby, the wife of Bill Cosby.

67. Papal Nuncio Paolo Romeo, interview with author, nunciature, Port-au-Prince, 11 July 1986. The Nuncio confirmed that the pope is well-informed about the conditions in various countries.

Thomas Quigley U.S. Conference of Bishops, telephone interview, U.S. Catholic Conference, Washington, D.C., 3 March 1988. Quigley corroborated that an official review of relations takes place before a papal visit.

68. There was some resistance to the visit by the Haitian opposition, which did not want to see pictures of John-Paul II at Jean-Claude Duvalier's side smiling on the front pages of the international press, or a subsequent rise in protest movements followed by repression.

See *La Iglesia En Haiti*, Comite Haitiano-Venezolano de Defensa de los Derechos Humanos, no. 5, Caracas, Venezuela, 1983, 15. A group of Haitian priests living abroad wrote a letter, dated 18 January 1983, to the Latin American bishops planning to attend the CELAM meeting in Haiti. It warned them about how bad things were in the country and of the increasing persecution against the Haitian Church. In a second document, "An Open Letter for the Church in Haiti," written by a Group of Haitian Christians abroad and dated January 1983, the authors are concerned that the bishops may be taken advantage of by the Haitian government and that the pope's visit is likely to be manipulated.

See also "Mounting Tensions Between Christian Churches and the Duvalier Government," *Le Monde*, 2 March 1983, translation by the Haitian Refugee Project, Washington, D.C. and Chamberlain, "Difficult Days for Haiti's R. C. Church."

69. The pope's eight-day, Latin American and Caribbean tour, which began on 2 March 1983, included visits to Costa Rica, Nicaragua, Panama, El Salvador, Honduras, Guatemala, Belize, and Haiti.

70. See Dan Sewell, "Pope Says 'Things Must Change' in Haiti," *Miami News*, 10 March 1983.

71. Thomas E. Ricks, "Defying Duvalier: The Church Visits Haiti Just as the Church There is Challenging the Regime," *Wall Street Journal*, 9 March 1983.

Ambassador Jean-Robert Estimé, telephone interview, Wheaton, MD, 26 May 1989. Ambassador Estimé characterized the change in Article IV as "cosmetic." The government wanted to please the Vatican without taking any real risk. In addition, the worldwide trend was to allow the Vatican to make the selections. "The results are not very different. In either case, mutual approval is a prerequisite for an appointment."

72. Homily of His Holiness, Pope John-Paul II at the airport in Port-au-Prince, 9 March 1983.

73. Farewell speech by His Holiness, Pope John-Paul II at the airport in Port-au-Prince, 9 March 1983.

74. One bishop still marvels at the memory of the occasion and the joy he experienced that day. Many Haitians, including those living abroad, were delighted, viewing it as "a turning point in the life of Haitians."

See Bonita Jones, "Leaders Hopeful of Change After Pope's Visit to Haiti," *The Miami Times*, 17 March 1983.

75. Jean-Robert Estimé, interview with author, Wheaton, MD, 29 March 1988.

In addition to the irritations mentioned by Ambassador Estimé, the first family was also disappointed in its expectations that the pope would baptize their month-old son.

See Arnold Antonin, "Haitian Church Standing Up to Duvalier," *Latinamerica Press*, 17 March 1983.

76. Views differ considerably concerning the afternoon speech. Some, like Ambassador Estimé and the president thought they detected a milder tone.

Dominque Levanti, a French, long-time resident of Haiti and journalist with *Agence France Presse*, interview with author, Agence France Presse Offices, Port-au-Prince, 7 July 1986, agreed, judging the tone of the second speech to be milder, softened perhaps, following criticisms from the interior minister, Lafontant, and recommendations of official caution.

Yves Germane Joseph, former counselor to the minister of finance and a journalist since 1986, interview with author, Hotel Montana, Port-au-Prince, 8 July 1986, concurred calling it "gentler" and attributed the difference to the interim meeting with the president.

A Church scholar in Haiti described the morning speech as "strong and very hard" and the farewell as a little "pomade" given as a result of a ride the pope took in the car with Archbishop Ligondé, during which he believed the Archbishop had said that Jean-Claude Duvalier was good but that his ministers were bad.

On the other hand, some did not detect a milder tone. Grégoire Eugène, founder of the Social Christian Party in Haiti, interview with author, Party Headquarters, Port-au-Prince, 11 July 1986, detected no difference at all. According to him, the farewell message did not apologize or back away from the morning speech; rather, it reinforced it by saying that the country needed outside help.

77. "Government Newspaper Criticizes Pope, Clergy," Paris *AFP* in Spanish, 2002 GMT, 11 March 1983, FBIS, S 12.

78. Ibid.

79. Ibid.

80. Ibid.

81. Etienne, "Interview de l'Archêveque Françcois Wolff Ligondé."

Papal contact with his bishops is evident in *Présence de l'Église En Haïti* (67–71). On the occasion of the bishops' 'ad Limina' visit to Rome on 11 June 1983, the pontiff remarks that in Rome they have had the opportunity to report what was happening in their dioceses and the problems they were confronting.

82. *Présence de l'Église En Haïti*, 44. The bishops met with the ministers of religion, information, and social affairs at the chancellery. According to *Présence*, the purpose of the visit, following the papal visit was to "dégager les voies du dialogue entre l'Englise et l'État," or open up the lines of communication between the Church and State.

83. "Haiti Says Dissident Misinformed Pontiff," *Miami Herald*, 12 March 1983. The *Miami Herald* quotes government sources as saying, "The Pope had been misinformed by dissident priests. Catholic priests had embezzled Church funds to 'keep expensive mistresses.'"

84. See *Présence de l'Église En Haïti*, 99. According to Article IV of the revised concordat, new bishops and archbishops would be Haitian. The pope would name them. However, the Vatican would confidentially notify the government before making its choices public. The State would have thirty to sixty days to object. Silence would signify acceptance. According to Article V, before bishops and archbishops, vicars, principals of Catholic schools, and other religious institutions undertook their duties, they would confirm their loyalty to the state with a pledge that stated: "I promise and commit myself to maintain respect and fidelity to the Haitian constitution and to pursue the common good of the country and to defend the interests of the nation." See also "Modified Protocol Signed by Vatican and Haiti," *The Catholic Transcript*, 17 August 1984, 3. *The Transcript* commented that the loyalty oath appeared to give the government additional confidence in attacking the Church. On numerous occasions in speaking with me, Ambassador Estimé accused the Church of exceeding its legal authority.

85. Clayton McManaway, interview with author, Department of State, Washington, D.C., 8 April 1988.

86. A source close to the Haitian government who wished to remain anonymous.

87. Mémorandum: "Actualisation Du Concordat," November 1985, Haitian Government Publication, Port-au-Prince.

88. Ibid.

89. A source close to the Haitian government who wished to remain anonymous.

90. Mémorandum: "Actualisation Du Concordat."

91. President Lesile Manigat, interview with author, Woodrow Wilson Center, Washington, D.C., 8 December 1988. Asked about the secret agenda, President Manigat said he was aware that there was a file concerning plans to amend the concordat begun by the previous government, but he never saw it. However, he added, "The Senate was aggressive against the Church and wanted to change the concordat. There was a strong nationalistic feeling that a change was needed."

92. Group of Religious from Hinche, *Letter to the Board of the Conference of Haitian Religious*, Hinche, 10 January 1985.

93. Pax Christi International, *Report of the Mission to Haiti*, 79.

94. Women Religious in the Catholic Church played an important, but little understood role of low visibility during the Jean-Claude Duvalier years. However, few have been singled out and credited for their work. Perhaps, as one bishop said, this is because Church emphasis is on communion rather than individualism. It may also reflect the continuing Vatican determination to maintain a male-dominated Church.

See Bourdeau, *Trip Report to Haiti*, 12–13 for a good description of the CHR that identifies its numbers, nationalities of origin of its members and leaders, and the organizations with which they are involved. According to Bourdeau, Jacques Mesidore (the head of the Salesiens), is the most listened-to theologian in Haiti. He participated at Puebla, and currently represents the CHR at meeting of the Conference of Latin American Religious (CLAR).

95. See Elizabeth Abbott, *Haiti: The First Inside Account: The Duvaliers and their Legacy* (New York: McGraw-Hill, 1988), 214. Gérard Gourge planned a meeting of his Human Rights League at the Belgian Salesian Brothers' compound in the Port-au-Prince slum of La Saline on 9 November 1979. Three thousand people, including a number of distinguished Haitians and foreign diplomats came to hear Gourge address the topic of "The Political Climate and Human Rights." No sooner had the meeting begun than it was interrupted by plain-clothed policemen who killed several people, beat others, and sacked the hall. This event is often referred to as "Black Friday at the Salesians" and seen as the end of the era of liberalization in the Jean-Claude Government. Ronald Reagan had been elected president in the United States and the Haitian government anticipated that the new administration would be less interested in human rights than the Carter administration had been.

Although the connection between this meeting and the Church was that the Salesians provided the hall, the Church became increasingly involved in the political and civil rights arena. See Freeland, *Religious Elites and Political Activity in Haiti*, 22.

96. Bourdeau, *Trip Report to Haiti*, 10. Bourdeau describes his repeated confrontations with the police in the course of a single visits with the bishop. It is clear that Romélus was under police surveillance.

See "Mgr. Willy Romélus Tells Congress to Sever All Relations with the Government," *Haïti-Observateur*, 12–19 July 1985. Irked at the government for arresting one of his priests and hauling him off to Port-au-Prince to apologize for criticizing the regime and Jean-Claude, Romélus announced "it was high time the government cease its constant denunciation of priest, because they open the eyes of people." He took a number of measures against authorities, including forbidding them from sitting anywhere in the Church except in their assigned places, prohibiting authorities from addressing Church gatherings, entering presbyteries, or priests' or bishops' lodging. The article concludes by saying that the priest who was taken to Port-au-Prince, refused to apologize and, on return to his parish, received a hero's welcome.

97. François Gayot, interview with author, Episcopate, Cap-Haïtien, 10 July 1986. The bishop distinguished among his colleagues according to their date of appointment. Those who came in 1966 were "under a cloud." In 1975, there was a new wave of bishops, which included Verrier and Romélus. Others were appointed subsequently. The most recent appointments were the most independent.

98. The Council of Jérémie met 8–14 April 1985, and subsequently sent a message to youth and Church leaders in Haiti that was signed by Archbishop Ligonedé. This message was critical of the government's economic, political, human rights, and social positions. It called on the government to "stop abusing and mistreating the people."

99. The pope's attack on poverty while he was in Haiti renewed the dispute over a villa Msg. Luigi Conti had recently built. The new See, located on an exclusive hillside overlooking the capital, was constructed of imported wood and reportedly cost $500,000. The nuncio dismissed criticism concerning the expense, claiming that it was largely covered by the sale of the old See, which was unsuitable because when it rained, it was inaccessible.

See Marlise Simons, "Haitians Bemoan 'The Pope's Purge on Main Street,'" *New York Times*, 9 April 1983.

100. Ambassador Clayton McManawasy, interview with author, State Department, Washington, D.C., 31 March 1988. The ambassador said he thought the papal nuncio was involved in getting the pope to come to Haiti.

101. Jean-Robert Estimé, interview with author, Wheaton, MD, 19 April 1988.

102. Stephen Horblitt, interview with author, Rayburn House Office Building, Washington, D.C., 5 April 1988.

103. Kelly, "Rocks in the Sun," 53–55. Integral development was embodied in the pastoral formation centers begun in the 1960s. The centers were created to provide an institutional network required by the increasing social involvement of the Church. Most of the centers were founded by the clergy and were, to some extent, under Church control. Their activities included projects for economic development, pastoral renewal, and community formation. Kelly describes the varying activities at Siloé, Damus Mariae, Nazareth, the Centre Pasoral pour Developpement Communautaire Chrétien Haïtien, the Emmaus Center in Payaye, IDEA, and L'Equipe Missionaire at Jean Rabel.

104. The evolution of Church activities can be seen with Scheut-founded center in Hinche at Papaye. Initially, the Mouvement des Paysans de Papaye at Hinche trained people for religious work. Then it became interested in social justice issues and has since evolved into a political-social organization calling itself Cosmica. Cosmica operated a cooperative which buys and sells goods, and it publishes booklets such as "*Jezi Nan Sevis Pep La*," which use biblical stories to depict the Haitian reality of exploitation, poverty, and sickness.

105. Marian McClure, "The Catholic Church and Rural Social Change: Priests, Peasant Organizations, and Politics in Haiti" (Ph.D. diss., Harvard University, 1985), 159–63.

106. Ibid., 349.

107. Conference of Haitian Religious, *Communiqué*, 4 December 1980.

See Freeland, *Religious Elites and Political Activity in Haiti*, 18–21. Freeland asserted, "There is a steady rise of religious elites becoming politicized into direct political action since 1980," then provided examples of priests throughout 1982 delivering increasingly political sermons. He concluded that "The Church and its elites find themselves in the position of being the most organized institution in Haiti, thereby making it the most influential rival agenda setter and most serious challenger to regime autonomy." In his view, the response of the religious elites to the socio-economic performance in Haiti produced some of the most dynamic activities. He offered the examples of the increased lobbying efforts of religious elites on behalf of Haitian peasants facing eviction or further poverty due to government policy of expropriating valuable land and resources, and against government-established tax rates that were being abused by local government authorities. Freeland concluded that in these case, the socio-economic outcome would have been different without the activity of religious elites.

108. Conference of Haitian Religious, *Letter*, 4 December 1980.

109. Luigi Conti, *Letter to Father Jacques Mesidor, President of the Haitian Conference of Religious*, Port-au-Prince, 6 December 1980.

110. Seven months after the November 1980 crackdown, at least eighty persons remained in jail. Silvio Claude, who had been arrested in October 1980, was still incarcerated a year later and although suffering from conjunctivitis, was denied medical visits. In October 1981, the government began an interdiction program to stop the increasing number of desperate people who were trying to leave the country. Arrests were wide-ranging and based on flimsy pretexts. On 12 November, a mechanic was arrested and tortured because he had met with some students.

111. Conference of Haitian Religious, *Dossier, A Year After* (Port-au-Prince: CHR, 18 November 1981).

112. Commission Justice et Paix de L'Archdiocèse de Port-au-Prince, "Lettre de la Commission Justice et Paix d'Haïti à la Conférence Épiscopal d'Haïti sur le Congrès Eucharistique et Marial de Port-au-Prince" (Port-au-Prince: Commission Justice et Paix de L'Archdiocèse de Port-au-Prince, 9 December 1981.

See Pax Christi International, *Report of the Mission to Haiti*, 68, 104.

113. Ricks, "Defying Duvalier," *Wall Street Journal*, 9 March 1983. Ricks interviewed a rural area priest about what he did and was told, "I help them to ask questions." Ricks observed that the traditionally quiescent Church had emerged in the past year as "the first broad-based group to mount a sustained criticism of the regime" and cited an embassy officer who was pretty convinced that "the Church will be the driving force in Haitian politics in the future."

Bourdeau, *Trip Report to Haiti*, 6–7. Bourdeau cited a number of additional examples of priests acting as conciliators or go-betweens for peasants. One case involved an American company, Haïti-Citrus, which had duped the peasants into leaving their land.

114. Jeanie Wylie, "Religion in Haiti: Conquering Souls, Pursuing Justice," *Christianity and Crisis*, 11 July 1983. See "Mounting Tensions Between Christian Churches and the Duvalier Government," *Le Monde*, 2 March 1983. Translation by the Haitian Refugee Project, Washington, D.C.

115. Conference of Haitian Religious, *Letter to All Members of the Religious Orders of Haiti* (Port-au-Prince: CHR, 23 November 1982).

116. Pax Christi International, *Report of the Mission to Haiti*, 69. See Toumédia, ed., *Haïti-Pape 83*, 112–18.

117. Conference of Haitian Bishops and Executive Board of Conference of Haitian Religious, *A Pastoral Letter* (Port-au-Prince: CHR, 27 January 1983).

See Freeland, *Religious Elites and Political Activity in Haiti*, 23. Freeland regarded pastoral letters as the religious elites' favorite method of protest. "Analytically beneficial, the signatures reveal the level of consensus among the religious elite." Some, such as the one demanding the release of Duclerville, were also extremely moving.

See William Montalbano, "John Paul Rebukes Haiti for Injustice, Inequality," *Miami Herald*, 10 March 1983. Montalbano noted that the bishops' pastoral letter neither appeared in the Haitian press, nor was it heard on the radio except on *Radio Soleil* because "if the Church crosses the invisible line from participation to opposition, it is likely to invite fresh repression." Nevertheless, some observers considered the statement the "boldest public criticism of the government in a quarter century of Duvalier family rule."

See Chamberlain, "Difficult Days for Haiti's R. C. Church." Chamberlain maintained that "an important obstacle to any clear stand by the Church against the Church was blocked by François Wolff Ligondé, the archbishop of Port-au-Prince, who had been named by François Duvalier and was a cousin of Michèle Duvalier. His silence or feeble protests about the excesses of the Duvaliers earned him the title of a 'loyal Duvalierist.'" However, "the outcry against the detention and torture of Duclerville eventually forced the Archbishop to take a stand."

118. Conference of Haitian Bishops, *Pastoral Letter*, 30 January 1983. The bishops would pray for all who were suffering, particularly those in prison. They would pray to transform the hard hearts of those who were governing so they would be instilled with respect for life and man as a whole human being and for life in general. They would pray for the return to Haiti's spirit of sacrifice, commitment, responsibility, and solidarity.

119. Etienne, "Interview de l'Archêveque François Wolff Ligondé."

120. Ministry of Religion, *L'Eglise Catholique et l'Etat.*

121. Raymond Alcide Joseph, "The Church Challenges Baby Doc," *Nation* (16 April 1983): 463, 481–82.

122. "Quit Assailing Regime, Haiti Warns Bishops," *Miami Herald*, 26 November 1982.

123. Joseph, "The Church Challenges Baby Doc," 481.

124. Conference of Haitian Bishops, *Declaration of the Bishops of Haiti on the Foundations of Church Intervention in Social and Political Affairs* (Port-au-Prince: CHB, 11 April 1983).

125. Pax Christi International, *Report of the Mission to Haiti*, 106–7. The newspaper dated from 1967.

126. Kelly, "Rocks in the Sun," 51. Kelly called "education for a critical conscience" one of the new pastoral strategies of the 1970s and 1980s. He described a number of educational materials designed toward this end, including *Chemin Lavi, Onè Rèspé*, and *Bon Nouvèl*. Kelly identified three "pastoral strategies" for the era: promotion of education, the CEBs, and pastoral formation.

127. Msg. Willy Romélus, Address on *Radio Soleil*, Jérémie, 16 February 1984.

128. Jacques Lajoie, Chaplain of the Civil Prison at Cap-Haïtien, *Letter to the Commissioner and Prefect of Cap-Haïtien*, Socrate Pierre, 2 July 1984.

129. Ministry of Religion, *L'Eglise Catholique et l'Etat.*

130. A number of activities were connected to the IYY. Among them were meetings, including the Council of Youth Meeting at Jérémie from 8–12 April 1985, the meeting in Rome, and marches.

"The Youth of Haiti as the Vanguard," *Haïti-Observateur*, 6–13 December 1985, 14. This article traced the activism of Haiti's youth to the "Year of Youth," and commented on the repercussions. "The year seems to be ending as it began—with cries of rebellion, it's a little different this time. The regime has been put on the defensive. It's more than a symbol when Christian youth keeps to its previously announced schedule of holding a conference in Gonaïves this week to evaluate the past and plan for the future. It's a call to all to stand up and be responsible during this tragic hour for our country."

131. Conference of Haitian Bishops, *Message from the Bishops to the Young of Haiti in Honor of International Youth Year*, 6 January 1985. Text from the *Bulletin d'Information, 1985*, Année International de la Jeunesse, Imprimerie la Phalange, 1985.

132. Pax Christi International, *Report of the Mission to Haiti*, 83.

133. The Council of Jérémie, message to youth and Church leaders in Haiti. See text in Pax Christi International, *Report of the Mission to Haiti*, 85–88.

134. Willy Romélus, *Homélie de Monseigneur Romélus*, concile des Jeunes, 11 April 1985.

135. Cable from an unnamed source in Jérémie to the ministry of religion concerning Church-State relations, April 1985. Before delivering his speech, Bishop Romélus said he was directing it to everyone, including "the spies he hopes will transmit the message faithfully about what he was going to say." The bishop's conjecture that his speech would be monitored was justified. In fact, the ministry of foreign affairs and religion subsequently received a version of the speech in Creole, accompanied by a translation in French, and a cable marked "*Rush, Etat Priorité*" consisting of a talking point outline of Church-State relations that said:

1. In accordance with the 1860 concordat, the Catholic Church enjoys special rights and privileges that are "scrupulously respected by the State." The clergy and bishops are paid by the State.

2. The State has often expressed its "profound and sincere desire to maintain the best possible relations with the Church." It was with this objective in mind that the president renounced his right to name bishops in 1984 and in March 1984 signed an agreement with the Church to promote literacy.

3. A Church-State *Commission Mixte* composed of two bishops and two ministers was established several months before to resolve problems arising between the two. The government frequently brought cases of flagrant Church violations of the concordat and laws of the country, notably the dispositions of the Penal Code [Article 162 on], to the attention of the bishops. These cases particularly concerned homilies of priest against the government and political broadcasts of *Radio Soleil*, which, since 1977, has only had the authorization to evangelize.

4. Despite repeated warnings, certain priests did not improve their behavior and the government was obliged to proceed, according to Articles VII and XLV of the Law of Immigration and Emigration on 24 July 1985 and withdraw the permission of the three Belgian priest to stay in the country because "they were immersed in the political life of the country and had taken public political positions contrary to the Concordat and Haitian law."

136. "Cache-Misère en Haiti," *Le Monde*, editorial du 25 July 1985. *Le Monde* called the Catholic Church "the only organized force [in Haiti and it has] sharpened its criticism against the government through *Radio Soleil*."

137. The Youth of Jérémie, *Declaration of the Youth of Jérémie* 5 December 1985. Dedicated to Jean Robert Cius, Mackenson Michel, and Daniel Israël.

138. The Council of Haitian Youth, *The Root Causes of this Suffering* (Port-au-Prince: Council of Haitian Youth, December 1985).

139. The Youth of Jérémie, *Déclaration*.

140. The Youth of Les Cayes, *Greeting in Solidarity to the Youth of Port-au-Prince* (Les Cayes: Youth of Les Cayes, 13 December 1985).

Les Cayes, an area which had a lot of *macoutes*, was seriously *déshoukéd* following 7 February 1986. At a dinner I attended in April 1986 at the home of the managers of an AID-funded agricultural development project in Les Cayes, a hush fell in the room when one particular group of guests entered the house. It appeared that the *entourage* included a local functionary who was too important not to be invited but who had been involved with abuses prior to 7 February. The hostess remarked to me that her kitchen window looked out on the prison and that there were times when she had had to leave the house with her children due to the screams next door.

141. Conference of Haitian Bishops, *Message á L'Occasion de la Fête de Noël* (Port-au-Prince: CHB, 1985).

142. Hugo Triest, interview with author, Lanham, MD, 28 September 1988. Much of the historical background on *Radio Soleil* was provided by Father Triest. Conyard had previously started a radio station, *Santa Maria*, in the Dominican Republic before coming to Haiti.

143. While rare, programs in Creole were not new. The first to do it was the Haitian broadcaster, Jean Dominique, who was forced into exile in 1980 along with many other broadcasters and journalists.

144. Raymond Etienne, interview with author, Hotel Montana, Port-au-Prince, 11 July 1986. Etienne recalled how careful and prudent one had to be with the Duvalier government at that time.

Ernest Preeg, interview with author, Department of State, Washington, D.C., 31 March 1988. The ambassador remembered that Father Conyard "was not prudent" and described his view as "radical." His forceful stance was obvious in meetings and reports. According to the priest, everything was wrong in terms of social justice. Wealth had to be distributed.

Hugo Triest, interview with author, Lanham, MD, 28 November 1988. Father Triest simply said that "like so many charismatic people, Conyard lacked the ability to work with others so he had to leave."

145. Hugo Triest, interview with author, Lanham, MD, 28 September 1988. As the atmosphere grew more tense in the midst of threats and power outages, "the staff drew closer together, and would gather to talk about the situation." Only one person left *Radio Soleil* out of fear.

146. Ibid.

147. Undated one page printout from *Radio Soleil* on the purpose of the station. Received in Port-au-Prince, 6 July 1986.

148. A Haitian professional characterized *Radio Soleil* as "a program to which ones maid and children would listen. It was very religious."

149. Leopold Berlanger Jr., Haitian President, International Institute of Haiti for Research and Development (IHRED), interview with author, Montana Hotel, Port-au-Prince, 5 July 1986.

150. Daudier's reputation was established with that song. He currently lives in New York and performs with bands in Brooklyn that advertise him as *L'Homme Solèy.*

151. Hugo Triest, interview with author, Lanham, MD, 28 September 1988.

152. René Poirier, interview with author, Villa Manrèse, Port-au-Prince, 12 July 1986. Another particularly controversial program, from the government standpoint, was called "Honor-Respect."

153. The economic assistance that the Church received due to its international connection cannot be overrated. If a Priest wanted to start a social or economic development project but needed funding, he could frequently turn to his order's headquarters abroad. A bishop might turn to a foreign conference of bishops for similar reasons. The protection that the Church received was equally important. When Gérard Duclerville was arrested, mail poured in from all over the world. Without the Church connection, *Radio Soleil* would certainly have been closed along with other stations that provided critical commentary.

154. The Church was not monolithic, and its hierarchy was composed of individuals with varying views. Threatened with closure, not all of them came to the defense of the station.

155. Hugo Triest, interview with author, Lanham, MD, 28 September 1988.

156. A medical doctor who knows Haiti, interview with author, Port-au-Prince, 7 July 1986.

157. Hugo Triest, interview with author, Lanham, MD, 28 September 1988.

158. Jean-Robert Estimé, interview with author, Wheaton, MD, 5 May 1988. The ambassador remembered the event differently, describing his meeting with Father Triest as "good," when he showed the priest "the dangers and injustices in the reports, he stopped transmitting them." Estimé maintained that the reports of murders in the Dominican Republic "were not correct."

159. "Le Clergé Catholique S'Elève Contre les Arrestations Arbitraires," *Haïti Demain Hebdo*, 21–27 November 1984. *Haïti Demain Hebdo* reported that by November 1984, *Radio Soleil* was isolated, but despite the "*grand terreur*," it continued to do its work.

160. The purpose of the referendum was to legalize political parties, create a post of prime minister, and bestow on Jean-Claude Duvalier the mantle of president-for-life.

See "L'Ordre de la Peur en Haïti," *Haïti-Observateur*, 16–23 August 1985. *Haïti-Observateur* called *Radio Soleil* in mid-August 1985 "the principle source of all news for a public which is eighty percent illiterate." Before the referendum, *Radio Soleil* "offered its listeners a rare experience, a political discussion. Numerous opinions were expressed, including that the referendum would be a farce to assure the perpetuation of Duvalier as president-for-life."

161. Officially, of 2,600,000 eligible voters, 2,375 voted yes and 499 no. The government wanted an impressive show of support in order to encourage more foreign investment and assistance.

162. Hugo Triest, interview with author, *Radio Soleil* Headquarters, Port-au-Prince, 14 July 1986.

163. Washington Office on Haiti, *The Government of Haiti: Noncompliance with the Criteria for United States Foreign Assistance*, Report to Congress, vol. 1 (Washington, D.C.: The Washington Office on Haiti, February 1985), 9–11.

164. "Elimination Physique de Certains Prêtres; L'Exile Pour d'Autres." *Haïti-Observateur*, 14–21 June 1985. According to this report, "A source close to the government" says that the government had decided to get rid of some "*intransigeants*" and *irréductibles*" priests in accidents, and to exile others. Its motive was self-preservation. The Church was behind the youth and a youth march had been scheduled for 21 June. The plan had to go into operation before that.

165. Included with Hugo Triest were two other members of the Congregation of the Immaculate Heart of Mary: Jean Hostens, a priest at Pointe-à-Raquette, la Gonâve, and Yvan Polleyfet, a priest at Montrouis. The government made two accusations against Hostens and reproached Polleyfet for his 24 April homily against the government, which was particularly critical of the *macoutes*. The Church observed that although a commission had been established to deal with Church-State relations, it was not convoked to deal with any of these cases.

See "Haitian Government Expels Three Priest in Wake of Referendum," (Washington, D.C.: Office on Haiti, 25 July 1985) for analysis of the connection between the government's blaming the Church for discrediting the 22 July referendum and the expulsion of the three priests. See also "Protest by the Haitian Bishops," (Port-au-Prince: Conference of Haitian Bishops, 26 July 1985), translated by the Washington Office on Haiti, and "Trois Prêtres Eminents Expulsés," *Haïti-Observateur*, 26 July-2 August 1985, for details on the television announcement. A concluding editorial comment predicts "that events are going to snowball now."

182   Chapter 4

166. Americas Watch and National Coalition for Haitian Refugees, *Haiti: Human Rights Under Hereditary Dictatorship* (New York: Americas Watch and National Coalition for Haitian Refugees, 5 October 1985), 10. "Listen Father, you are here in the country for evangelization and nothing else. Whenever you cross the line we will cut your balls off."

See "L'Ordre de la Peur en Haïti," *Haïti-Observateur,*12. The minister of state is quoted as warning Triest that "Every time you pass the limits, we'll castrate (châtrer) you."

Father Tom Quigley, meeting at Saint Charles Church, Arlington, VA., 12 July 1989. Quigley, an American priest and long-time resident of La Gonâve, was at the nunciature eating cream puffs with Hugo Triest when Lafontant broke in looking for the director of *Radio Soleil.* Since them, cream puffs have been dubbed "Lafontants."

167. Hugo Triest, interview with author, *Radio Soleil* Headquarters, Port-au-Prince, 14 July 1986.

168. Conference of Haitian Bishops, *Protestation de la Conférence Episcopale d'Haïti,* 26 July 1985.

See also "L'Ordre de la Peur en Haïti," *Haïti-Observateur,*12, for details.

169. Hugo Triest, interview with author, Lanham, MD, 28 September 1988.

170. The Youth of Jérémie, *Declaration.*

Groups of predominantly Catholic students formed in Jérémie, Les Cayes, Port-au-Prince, and other cities following the murder of the students in Gonaïves in October 1985. They called on the government to make amends for Gonaïves and correct its human rights, political, and economic policies. The groups encouraged each other to take a stand and get involved.

171. The Youth of Les Cayes, *Greeting.*

172. Hugo Triest, interview with author, *Radio Soleil* Headquarters, Port-au-Prince, 14 July 1986. Although the government had no right to close the Catholic-run station in the first place, and despite its agreement to let it reopen, it remained closed until 31 December. On the last day of December 1985, the president announced the reopening of *Radio Soleil,* the departure of four ministers of state, and the formation of a new cabinet.

Radio Soleil's closure severely restricted the flow of news. Without the station, information was sporadic and delayed. Many Haitians learned that a state of siege had taken place in ten Haitian towns on 15 December by reading about it in the French newspaper, *Le Monde.*

See *Présence de l'Église En Haïti,* 108, for a description of the events leading to the reopening of *Radio Soleil.* Following the *mémorandum* to President Duvalier, the presidents of the CHB and Bishops' Commission on Social Communication met with the ministers of religion and information. After four hours of discussion, the government authorized the station to reopen.

173. Fritz Longchamp, Director of the Washington Office on Haiti, interview with author, Washington Office on Haiti, Washington, D.C., 9 August 1989.

174. Conference of Haitian Religious, *Dossier, A Year After,* 18 November 1981.

175. Jean Sosa, telephone interview with author, Washington, D.C., 30 June 1986. Jean Sosa was an American diplomat stationed in Haiti at the time. In 1982–83, she traveled into the countryside to interview members of the clergy and obtained a large amount of documentation concerning the arrest, torture, and deportation of foreign priests. In addition, she found that while some of the priests were radical, they were not demanding that the government be overthrown, only that it make some immediate economic improvements.

See Yves Colon, "Saint Maverick's Obsession," *Miami Herald*, 25 January 1985. Gérard Jean-Juste was the first U.S. ordained Haitian priest. After the seminary, he returned to Haiti during the Jean-Claude Duvalier administration; he stayed only five months. Assigned to a remote parish, after refusing to sign an oath of allegiance to the government and beginning to oppose Duvalier's policies, he was targeted by the police and obliged to leave the country. He returned to the United States, where he founded the Haitian Refugee Center in Miami.

176. Thomas Ricks, "Defying Duvalier," *Wall Street Journal*, 9 March 1983. The increasingly feisty sermons throughout 1982 led the minister of religion to announce that this talk could lead to arrest and exile.

See Chamberlain, , "Difficult Days for Haiti's R. C. Church." Chamberlain cites "a high government source" as saying that the regime "does not intend to be goaded into a new wave of arrests before the pope's visit." However, Colonel Albert Pierre, the tough new police chief of the capital, drove a *Radio Soleil* reporter into hiding when he dared wonder on the air how the pope could come and associate with "these assassins." He is also reported to have compiled a list of thirty-five priests he wanted to deport. Chamberlain concludes that the "Duvaliers are well aware that the clergy, because they cannot be touched as readily as the rest of the population, are potentially the most serious threat to their power, short of an attempted military coup."

177. Conference of Haitian Religious, *Letter to All Members of the Religious Orders of Haiti*. The directing office acknowledged, "For a while now, the summoning of priests and friars to the Ministry of Foreign Affairs for an explanation has been occurring at an accelerated pace. Some have even been summoned personally without their Ordinary and they have received barely veiled threats." It was obvious that this was a "campaign of intimidation aimed at the Church through its often most active members." The letter concluded with "a declaration of total solidarity" with them.

See *Amnesty International Report*, 18 January 1983.

Two days later, on the 25th, the minister of religion called several of the bishops into the ministry to warn them that the government would not tolerate any more of their criticism. The mayor of Port-au-Prince added his voice, speaking out publicly against the Church and what he regarded as a bunch of radical priests.

See also Joseph, "The Church Challenges Baby Doc," 16 April 1983.

178. Ernest Preeg, interview with author, Department of State, Washington, D.C., 31 March 1988. Ambassador Preeg attributed the action to someone in the security apparatus.

Jean-Robert Estimé, interview with author, Wheaton, MD, 5 May 1988. The ambassador did not think the arrest was warranted. In his judgment, Duclerville was "not doing anything especially bad. It was just another case of Interior Minister Roger Lafontant interceding to show his strength." On the other hand, the government did not predict the outcry. Estimé characterized the response as "an over-reaction . . . it was not expected."

179. Conference of Haitian Bishops, *Declaration of the Bishops of Haiti on the Foundations of Church Intervention*. See "La Iglesia de Haití Reclama Justica," *C.R.I.E./ECCLESIA* 6 August 1983 for further discussion of the papal visit on the Haitian Church. According to these authors, two documents, this one and the *Global Plan* of the CHR "simply translate the Pope's words and the social doctrine of the Church." They observe that "these documents, with their political and social objectives, have not fallen on deaf ears." Ernest Bennett, for example, declared in *Le Petit Samedi Soir* that "los sacerdotes se refugian bajo la sotana para atacar directamente al Gobierno," the priests are hiding under their cassocks to directly attack the government.

180. Conference of Haitian Bishops, *Pastoral Letter*, 3 March 1984. See Ministry of Religion, *L'Eglise Catholique et l'Etat*, 11.

181. Conference of Haitian Religious, *Inaugural Message by Father Yvon Joseph* (Port-au-Prince: CHR, 23–26 April 1984).

182. Conference of Haitian Religious, *Global Plan of the Conference of Haitian Religious* (Port-au-Prince: CHR, April 1983). The CHR concluded that "the hour has come for us, the 1,500 Men and Women Religious of the country, gathered in our first Plenary Assembly from the 4th to the 8th of April, 1983, to go on to a new phase of our development since the creation of our organization in 1963."

183. Ibid.

184. Washington Office on Haiti, *The Government of Haiti: Noncompliance* 1: 25.

185. François Gayot, "Explanation of the Press Release of the Haitian Bishops," June1984. Priests and lay people were being subjected to threats of arrest and torture, accusations, and made to leave their parishes. According to the bishop, ministers and bishops conducted a study to find out why this was happening, and they came up with two explanations. The government had established tax rates for market vendors, but some of them were still charging higher prices; when clergy and lay people intervened, the vendors went after the clergy. In addition, some military people wanted to regain the power they had lost since the president had asked them not to beat, torture, or arrest people without warrant. Bishop Gayot concluded that the ministers intended to inform the president so these things could be stopped. Meanwhile, the bishops urged their people "to continue to work with the same courage, we are with you all the way."

186. Washington Office on Haiti, *The Government of Haiti: Noncompliance with the Criteria for United States Foreign Assistance*, Report to Congress, vol. 2 (Washington, D.C.: The Washington Office on Haiti, October 1985), 11.

187. Freeland, *Religious Elites and Political Activity in Haiti*, 24. In Freeland's view, the crackdown on the Church was a result of a government decision to counterattack more aggressively, and the attacks on organization, such as Institut Diocesain d'Education pour Adultes, the Groupe de Recherche Independent, and the Commission on Literacy, were attempts to diffuse the power of the Church.

188. Bussels, Marcel, et al., "Letter to the Bishops" from a group of Christians in Cap-Haïtien expressing solidarity with initiatives to denounce the climate of terror and insecurity in Haiti. Unpublished Church document. Cap-Haïtien: 12 November 1984.

189. Conference of Haitian Religious, *Letter to All Members of the Religious Orders of Haiti*, 14 November 1984. The CHR accused the government of withholding information on the arrests and for delays in bringing prisoners to trial. According to the CHR, the government was guilty of violating and disregarding rights guaranteed by the constitution and recognized by the social teaching of the Church. The CHR concluded that it was the mission of the Church to be with the people and to intercede when "true human values were threatened." Assuring the bishops of its solidarity, the CHR urged them to intervene.

190. "Le Clergé Catholique S'Elève Contre les Arrestations Arbitraires," *Haïti Demain Hebdo*, 21–27.

See *The Amnesty International Reports, 1975–1986*, Spanish ed. (London: Amnesty International, 1985), 165–69. On 7 December, the minister of the interior announced the discovery of a Marxist-Leninist plot against the state.

191. "Conférence Haïtienne des Religieux." *Haïti-Observateur*, 28 December 1984–4 January 1985. The CHR published a number of letters concerning government treatment of the clergy. The readers were invited to decide if it was persecution. One letter, by a Sister Jeannette Rousey to Bishop Constant, reported that the prefect, deputy

prefect, and armed VSN had begun to attend their religious functions, causing members to stay away, and even resign. People involved with the Church had stopped going out alone—even during the day, and priests no longer stayed alone at night. They avoided eating or drinking anything offered them. In their view, the situation was impossible.

192. Jean-Robert Estimé, interview with author, Wheaton, MD, 21 May 1988. Estimé explained that "these local officials would take it upon themselves to act. They did it to show support, out of an excess of zeal." The ambassador drew a distinction between the minister of the interior and himself. Lafontant "wanted to take a tougher position toward the Church and use more surveillance," while he wanted to maintain a dialogue.

193. Ibid. According to Ambassador Estimé, Robinson was not instructed to take this action.

194. Ministry of Religion, *L'Eglise Catholique et l'Etat.*

195. Pax Christi International, *Report of the Mission to Haiti*, 79.

196. Ibid., 78.

197. Ibid., 79.

198. *Présence de l'Église En Haïti, Mémorandum de la Conférence Épiscopale du 12 Décembre, au Président à vie de la Républic*, 1984, 105. The bishops mention that they wrote to the minister of religion following the wave of arrests throughout the country, but did not receive an answer. In the aftermath of a succession of Church invasions in Cap-Haïtien, Dessalines and Milot, they were writing to the president, and hoping he would personally intervene (108). On 6 May 1985, on the instruction of the president, the minister of religion answered the bishops' letter. Estimé assured them the *animateurs* held since November 1984 would be freed, in accordance with a presidential amnesty for all political prisoners.

199. Pax Christi International, *Report of the Mission to Haiti*, 79.

200. Joseph Serge Milot, permanent secretary, *Letter to Ambassador Jean-Robert Estimé* (Port-au-Prince: Conference of Haitian Bishops, 7 November 1984).

201. Vanessa Levi, "Manifestation Contre Roger Lafontant à Ville Mont-Royal," *Haïti-Observateur*, 14–21 February 1986, 26. Dr. Lafontant's political adroitness and weak ethical standards surfaced early in life. In medical school, he made money by providing the government with names of fellow students he identified as communists. François Duvalier rewarded him by making him the chief campus *macoute.*

202. Minister Lafontant used different pretexts to justify repression, one of his favorites was a communist plot. He discovered them everywhere. Following the papal visit in 1983, he blamed the flurry of excitement and independent thinking on communist agitation. In mid-November 1984, thirty people were arrested.

See "Communiqué, in the *Nouvelliste* on 7 December 1984 in which Lafontant explains that the arrests were the result of a Marxist-Lenninist plot against State security. Later, the minister uncovered "Marxist-Leninist plots" that forced the government to delay its promised democratic initiatives.

Concerning Lafontant's brutality, See Vanessa Levi, "Manifestation Contre Roger Lafontant." When Lafontant wanted to have someone arrested, beaten or killed, he turned the job over to Police Chief Albert Pierre.

See also *The Amnesty International Reports*, the *1979 Report* details the torture of *L'Information* editor Auguste. On at least two occasions, torture victims revealed that Lafontant himself had done the beating. See also Washington Office on Haiti, *The Government of Haiti: Noncompliance*, which describes Roger Lafontant's threat to Father Hugo Triest.

203. James Ferguson, *Papa Doc, Baby Doc* (Oxford: Basil Blackwell, 1987). Ferguson speaks of the trouble that AID Director McPherson and Ambassador McManaway had

with Dr. Lafontant. Firing Lafontant was a logical way to improve relations with the United States.

204. Jean-Robert Estimé, interview with author, Wheaton, MD, 19 December 1988.

205. Max-Abner Etienne, "Interview de l'Archêveque Francçois Wolff Ligondé." The event that had prompted Lafontant to call Ligondé into the ministry had been a homily that the archbishop had given at the Church of Sainte Marie on 2 February in honor of the IYY in which he discussed the problems of youth and the evils that plagued the country.

206. François Gayot, interview with author, episcopate, Cap-Haïtien, 10 July 1986. Generally, when the government had some complaint about the Church, the Churchmen in question would be summoned to see the minister of religion. Bishop Gayot recalled being summoned to the ministry fifteen times.

Hugo Triest, interview with author, Lanham, MD, 28 September 1988. In response to the intimidating reception he repeatedly received at the ministry, Treist ultimately declined to go there without being accompanied by a bishop.

207. Emile Joseph, "Attentat Manqué Contre le Père Emile Joseph le 22 avril 1985" (Port-au-Prince: 23 April 1985). Father Joseph described the incident. On the way to his room to prepare an exam, Joseph greeted and passed a soldier and a militiaman. Only the first responded. Later, when Joseph rose to take a break, the militiaman appeared, daring him to "try to walk over me." The priest stopped; and, as he invited the militiaman into his room, the man began to shoot, saying, "you don't respect me." The soldier ran up, demanding to know why the militiaman had fired. "Because he doesn't respect the local chiefs. I don't care if he is a priest. I don't have anything to do with priests." The gunman had begun to recharge his Uzi when the soldier put himself between the two of them. Other people arrived, they searched the room, interrogated the participants, and took Joseph Larose away. He was subsequently revealed to be a *macoute*.

208. Washington Office on Haiti, *The Government of Haiti: Noncompliance in the Criteria for U.S. Foreign Assistance*, vol. 2, October 1985.

209. Priests and Religious of the Archdiocese of Port-au-Prince, *Déclaration*, 14 May 1985.

Jean-Robert Estimé, interview with author, Wheaton, MD, 5 May 1988. In the opinion of Ambassador Estimé, the Church made too much of the event. "The priest over reacted and dramatized the situation." On the other hand, the incident was historically important. The ambassador called it "the first open confrontation between the government and Church."

210. "Grande Marche de la Jeunesse d'Haiti Contre Le Présidence à Vie," *Haïti-Observateur*, 14–21 June 1985. The purpose of this march was to demand recognition and respect for the political, economic, and social rights of Haitians. The organizers had sent a letter to the minister of the interior on 1 June, saying that they refused to accept a president-for-life, and demanded open elections. The organizers of the abortive march appealed to youth to "form a national chain of solidarity."

211. Jean-Robert Estimé, interview with author, Wheaton, MD, 21 May 1988. The ambassador dismissed the rallies and marches as "normal in the Year of the Youth."

212. Washington Office on Haiti, *The Government of Haiti: Noncompliance* 1: 13. This report asserted that at least sixteen people associated with the Catholic youth workers, *IDEA*, and *CARITAS* were arrested in Cavillian, Verrettes, and Petit Goâve after refusing to enroll in Jean-Claude's organization and charged with subversive activities, and that six more Church layworkers were arrested in late May under the same pretext.

See *The Amnesty International Reports*,1975–1986, 164–68. Amnesty made an appeal on the 24th on behalf of nine people associated with Catholic youth organizations detained in early April. It described how three *CARITAS* workers had been detained, beaten, them forced to walk barefoot for thirty kilometers to Port-au-Prince on 20 May. Amnesty International speculated that their crime was refusal to join the National Jean-Claude Action Committee.

213. Americas Watch and National Coalition for Haitian Refugees, *Haiti: Human Rights Under Hereditary Dictatorship*

214. Conference of Haitian Bishops, *Letter to his Excellency Jean-Claude Duvalier, President-for-Life of the Republic of Haiti,* 9 July 1985.

215. Conference of Haitian Bishops, *Pastoral Message of the Bishops of Haiti on Political Parties,* 16 July 1985.

216. It is clear in retrospect that this referendum was a mistake for the government. It was another case in which it spoke about liberalization, but offered the opposite, and the Church pointed out the disparity. *Radio Soleil* further validated itself by accurately predicting that the referendum would be rigged and that the government would falsify the results.

217. Jean-Robert Estimé, *Letter to the Conference of Haitian Bishops* Port-au-Prince: 30 July 1985.

218. Ibid., Puebla reference, 161.

219. Jean-Robert Estimé, interview with author, Wheaton, MD, 19 April 1988.

220. This metaphor of the Church as "ayatollahs" was apparently popular. Minister of the Interior Roger Lafontant used it also.

221. Conference of Haitian Bishops, "Protestation de la Conférence Episcopale d'Haïti." The bishops named the victims, described their work, explained the charges against them, and refuted them. After relating the events leading up to the expulsion of the priests, the bishops asked whether "the Church was confronting a situation of persecution," and called on everyone to observe a day of prayer and fasting on 2 August 1985. As a postscript, they informed the President that, in the future, there would be fewer *Te-Deums.*

222. See "Haitian Masses Canceled," *Washington Post,* 30 July 1985.

223. Washington Office on Haiti, *The Government of Haiti: Noncompliance* 1: 17.

224. Conference of Haitian Bishops, *Bulletin d'Information, 1985,* Année Internationale de la Jeunesse. This bulletin shows the comings and goings of people related to the Church during the year. Bishop Gayot attended the Ordinary Assembly of CELAM in Costa Rica in March. Joseph Lafontant, the rector of the Grand Séminaire, attended the Annual Meeting of USLAM (seminaries) in Bogota in November. The bulletin notes that the bishops in Haiti received dozens of letters from the Episcopal Conferences in other countries and from other organizations, particularly Amnesty International, which it concludes contributed importantly to the liberation of political prisoners.

225. Conference of Haitian Bishops, *Message on the Opening of the Session National du Pastorale Sociale,* 23–27 October 1985. The Church continued to emphasize the shortcomings of the government. When the bishops held a meeting on "Justice and Charity in Pastoral Action of the Church," 23–27 October, they said that in Haiti people did not have the right to exist or be recognized as human beings.

Haiti's human rights situation was so serious at the time that as AID Administrator Peter McPherson departed Haiti after a visit, he warned that "progress in the domain of democracy is a condition of American economic aid to all countries and that includes Haiti."

226. "Les Evêques Maintiennent Leur Demand," *Haïti-Observateur,* 16–23 August 1985. Those demands included firing the minister of the interior, Roger Lafontant, and

the minister of information, Jean-Marie Chanoine, and bringing to trial the murderers of Father de Smet. The minister of justice, Théo Achile, was sent to the Vatican to discuss matters, but he returned rebuffed.

227. "Le Vatican Demand Explications au Régime," *Haïti-Observateur,* 2 September 1985.

228. Jean-Robert Estimé, interview with author, Wheaton, MD, 21 May 1988. The ambassador maintained that the government did not order the shooting. He recalled that the president was at Jacmel when he heard the news. When he telephoned to learn more about it, "it was clear he was extremely upset." Subsequently, he sent a commission to investigate.

229. Emmanuel Constant, "Message to the Citizens of Gonaïves," 28 November 1985. Cited in *Bulletin d'Information, 1985,* Année International de la Jeunesse, Imprimerie la Phalange, 1985.

230. Bill Quigley, interview with author, Wheaton, MD, 19 July 1989. Quigley recalled the official response to the day of mourning in La Gonâve. He and two colleagues, including a Filipino nun, were arrested and brought before a military captain to explain their behavior. However, their group was larger than the captain expected. Since he could not hurt all of them, he pretended to accept the school closures and a day of mourning as a sign of their solidarity with the dead. Then he released them, pretending not to have arrested them in the first place.

231. In the wake of Gonaïves, protests spread to other cities including Cap-Haïtien, Les Cayes, Jérémie, and Petit Goâve. News about what was happening in these cities was coordinated through Church networks and subsequently reported on its radio stations.

232. Jean-Marie Chanoine, minister of the interior and national defense, "Letter Announcing Provisional Closing of *Radio Soleil,*" 5 December 1985.

233. Estimé was adamant on this point. The station acted irresponsibly. It routinely went beyond its legislated mandate, which he interpreted as to provide religious instruction.

234. The areas of contention were the treatment of Haitian cane cutters in the Dominican Republic, the economic conditions that forced them to go there, the unresolved murders of the student in Gonaïves, and the closure of *Radio Soleil.*

235. The Council of Haitian Youth, *The Root Causes of this Suffering.*

236. The government formed a civilian-military commission rather promptly to investigate the events and bring charges against those responsible for the killings. However, it took the commission until 17 December to submit a report, and when it did the contents were classified. The public, already exasperated at the delay and the demeaning government offer of two thousand dollars to the family of each slain child, was infuriated.

237. The Youth of Les Cayes, *Greeting.*

238. On 29 November, hundreds of students in Jérémie added their voices in opposition to the government.

239. Conference of Haitian Bishops, *Mémorandum de la CHB au Président de la Défense de la République* (Port-au-Prince: CHB, 18 December 1985). The bishops described the events surrounding the closure of the station, presented their objections, and made some recommendations. *Radio Soleil* had been closed on 5 December by order of the minister of state, Jean-Marie Chanoine, without consulting the CHB or the Commission Mixte. Authorities charged that the station had failed to fulfill its objectives and they would not renew its license. The bishops called on the president to intervene so the station could carry out its mission to provide evangelization, education, and news. The bishops wanted the station to be repaired, and then reopened.

240. Conference of Haitian Bishops, *Message à L'Occasion de la Fête de Noël*

241. "Jean-Claude et Michèle Allaient S'Envoler," *Haïti-Observateur*, 13–29 December 1985. The *Haïti-Observateur* described the atmosphere in the capital at this time: "Silence." The military had taken precautions against intervening against strikers and demonstrators, which necessitated calling in the *macoutes* and police under Albert Pierre. The *Haïti-Observateur* speculated that one of the demonstrators' slogans, "Vive l'Armée" may have neutralized them by getting their sympathy—a possibility which contributed to Duvalier's fears.

242. Michael Servill, "Small Stirrings of Change," *Time*, 13 January 1986. See Ferguson, *Papa Doc, Baby Doc*, 96–99.

243. "Jean-Claude et Michèle Allaient S'Envoler." According to a "highly confidential source," the *Haïti-Observateur* learned that after Gonaïves, a contingency escape plan was devised to get the Duvaliers out of the country.

244. Jean-Robert Estimé, interview with author, Wheaton, MD, 21 May 1988.

245. Ministère de l'Intérieur et de la Défense Nacionale, *Lettre du Ministère de l'Intérieur et de la Défense Nacionale à Mgr. E. Constant donnant Une Nouvelle Autorisation de Functionnement à Radio Soleil*, Port-au-Prince, 23 December 1985.

246. The government was in a defensive mode. Although it was obliged to announce the school closure to save face, it announced the same day through the interior department that the *forces de l'ordre*, supported by the VSN, had been advised to vigorously repress all illegal acts.

247. Ferguson, *Papa Doc, Baby Doc*, 105.

248. Ibid., 106.

249. Ibid., 109.

250. Kelly, "Rocks in the Sun," 85. Kelly reports that "Repression took on a new savagery during the last few weeks and several hundred people were killed before Jean-Claude fled the country."

251. François Gayot, *Message on the Occasion of the Events of 26 and 27 January 1986*, 27 January 1986. Those killed were: Adelin Pierre, 13, Claudin Ambroise, 14, and Christophe Chanel, 50.

252. U.S. foreign assistance resumed in 1973, after a ten-year interval, and continued unabated until it was cut off at the end of 1985. Concerns about Haiti's commitment to development in 1981, caused the U.S. government to demand biannual proof of cooperation in halting illegal emigration to the United States, implementation of U.S. development, food, and other economic assistance programs in Haiti, and improvement in its human rights situation.

Josh De Wind, "Economic Assistance and Democracy in Haiti" (Hunter College, paper for NYU Conference on Haiti, December 1989), 1. One week after the department of state announced it $7 million suspension of economic assistance to Haiti, Duvalier was gone. Three weeks after the CNG took office, it was reinstated.

253. There are a number of accounts of the final days of the Jean-Claude Duvalier government. Among them are: Ferguson, *Papa Doc, Baby Doc*, 112–14; Georges Salomon Révèle," *Haïti-Observateur*, 29 August-5 September 1986; and "Bad Times for Baby Doc," *Time*, 10 February 1986.

254. "Never, Never Again," *Time*, 24 February 1986, 45.

255. James Brooke, "Duvalier Flight Leaves Haitian Industry Hopeful," *New York Times*, 14 February 1986, D1, D6. Brooke reported that one week before Jean-Claude left Haiti, the palace called for all the remaining foreign exchange, leaving between $3 and $5 million dollars in exchange reserves—enough for two to three days' imports and only enough oil stocks to get through February.

256. By March 1992, the dismal score had increased to eight governments—four overtly military, one quasi-military, two quasi-democratic, one civilian caretaker, two failed elections, four coups, and at least one failed coup attempt.

257. Adams subsequently distinguished himself as an outspoken supporter of democracy in Haiti. In 1991, he and the French ambassador also demonstrated their bravery by interceding with the military to spare the life of President Jean-Bertrand Aristide during the coup.

258. Silvio Claude was a victim of the violence that occurred during the ouster of Jean-Bertrand Aristide from Haiti in October 1991. He was in Les Cayes, where a tire was put around his neck and he was burned to death.

259. Jean-Bertrand Aristide continued to attack Duvalierists, *macoutes*, and social injustice. In 1990, he was elected president of Haiti by the poor Haitians for whom he had become a champion. Within eight months, however, he was ousted in a military coup. He has subsequently tried to regain power through international intercession.

5

The Role of the Church in the Overthrow of Jean-Claude Duvalier

This chapter assesses the role of the Church in the ouster of the Haitian president, Jean-Claude Duvalier. The president was thrown out of office by urban Haitians demoralized by presidential behavior and unfulfilled promises. The Catholic Church played an important leadership role in the ouster. Numerous individuals and the CHR had key roles. Church activists led many critical events in the final six or seven months of the Jean-Claude presidency. Why did the Church, which had a history of passivity toward despotic governments suddenly become involved? In part, it was embarrassed by its past, which condoned slavery, racism, brutality, venality, and disloyalty. In part, it was inspired by a vision of a new Church envisioned by Pope John XXIII, liberation theologians, and others, that would dedicate itself to the poor. As governmental authority crumbled, the Church found itself the moral conscience of the nation.

CAUSES OF THE OUSTER OF JEAN-CLAUDE DUVALIER

Duvalier was ousted from the presidency by his countrymen after their hopes for democracy, economic development, and decency had been repeatedly frustrated. By the time Jean-Claude became president in 1971, many Haitians were aware of the disparities between life in Haiti and elsewhere. They had heard stories on the radio, received reports from returned boat people, and had descriptions from relatives working abroad. Many Haitians hoped that the country was on the verge of better times.

In its mission to serve the poor, the Church substantially increased its areas of operations during the Jean-Claude era, building clinics, hospitals, schools, day care centers, and banking facilities.[1] Its network of CEBs was particularly inspiring—producing leaders, community spirit, and economic expertise.[2]

The new president was, in a sense, a victim of heredity, the only male born into a family dynasty. The reluctant young chief of state inherited an impoverished and brutalized country, craving relief. It was his vacillations, changing policies and, especially, the dichotomy between his promises and reality that caused his downfall.[3] Jean-Claude launched his presidency by pledging to improve the economic situation of the country. He also promised to introduce democratic reforms and liberalizations. One vow he did not have to make, but was expected to keep, was to perpetuate his father's pro-black Duvalierist agenda. None of these expectations was met. The Church, international commentators, the U.S. Embassy, and various organizations and individuals kept up the pressure on Duvalier to follow through on his commitments. With time, it became clear that he would never be the instrument of change for a better Haiti.

On the twentieth anniversary of Duvalierism, Jean-Claude announced that his father had made the political revolution, and he would produce the economic revolution.[4] This heartening prospect of economic development, termed "Jeanclaudism," faded as the Haitian and foreign business communities tired of trying to do business in an atmosphere of graft, greed, and extortion, where economic mismanagement and inattention to the rural sector compounded matters, and expanded drug involvement corrupted legitimate business. Increasingly desperate Haitians attempted to leave the country, often risking their lives and packed into unseaworthy boats, after paying exorbitant sums for the privilege. The lifestyle of the rich, and particularly, the first family, contrasted sharply with the reality for most Haitians. One of Michèle's international, multidollar spending sprees took place while the country was in the midst of a major fuel crisis. By 1985, Haiti had virtually depleted its foreign exchange and, with it, the ability to pay for necessary imports. In January 1986, the United States showed its lack of confidence in the government by withholding the foreign assistance on which Haiti had become dependent. The country's bankruptcy was inevitable.

Jean-Claude promised elections, political parties, and unions. The prospect of legislative elections in 1979 was exciting and novel. But opposition candidates were not allowed to participate, and the results were rigged. This experience was repeated in the 1983 municipal elections and the 1984 and 1985 legislative elections. The referendum on political parties in July 1985 provided the *coup de grace* for illusion and hope. A vote ostensibly legalizing political parties, not only placed limitations on them but also reaffirmed Jean-Claude's presidency-for-life, authorized him to name a successor, and appoint a prime minister. Haitians were disgusted by the charade and distraught to discover that Father Hugo Triest, after accurately predicted the fraud, had been summarily thrown out of the country.

A new era in civil liberties seemed to be dawning when Jean-Claude ratified the Inter-American Convention on Human Rights in September 1977, releasing 104 prisoners as a gesture of good faith. He notified his security forces that torture would not be tolerated—judicial reform was under way. Three months later, security forces beat Reverend Luc Nerée nearly to death for publishing an article on rural *macoute* violence in *Hebdo Jeune Presse.*

Jean-Claude established an organization to monitor human rights in Haiti and declared that there were no political prisoners in the jails. Those who were lucky enough to escape from prisons told stories of mass murder, torture, and routine inhuman treatment of prisoners, who often were held without charges for prolonged periods. By the time three school children were riddled with bullets, bayoneted, and beaten in Gonaïves in November 1985, Haitians had reached the end of their patience with government instigated and condoned violence.

Collectively, several occurrences in 1985 convinced people that the Duvalier government was not going to change. These formative events were the 22 July Referendum, the 24 July expulsion of the three Belgian priests, the November 28 murders in Gonaïves, and the 4 December closure of *Radio Soleil.* People were not taken in by the subsequent conciliatory government gestures, such as the 17 December Commission of Inquiry Report on the events in Gonaïves, the 31 December reopening of *Radio Soleil* and new cabinet, the 26 January 1986 reform of the armed forces, or the dissolution of the political police.

Haitians forced the president out of office and rejected his last-minute efforts to salvage the presidency. The United States made the prospect of his continued stay less congenial in January 1985 by refusing to recertify Haiti for foreign assistance, funds on which it had grown increasingly dependent. On 31 January 1985, the military lashed out again at innocent victims, this time turning machine guns on the citizens of Léogâne for refusing to go to the wretched camps in the Dominican Republic to cut sugar.

François Duvalier had built his political career on the support of blacks, but Jean-Claude failed to appreciate his father's strategic wisdom. Jean-Claude's classmates in school were mulattos. As president, he increasingly appointed mulattos to his cabinets. As a consequence of his racial favoritism, the president lost important sources of support. The *macoutes* did not feel as beholden to him as they had to his father and began to run their own operations. Powerful rural blacks no longer felt indebted and ceased providing the president with kickbacks and information about what was happening in the countryside. Urban upper-class blacks grew disillusioned. The most spectacular proof of the president's abandonment of Duvalierism was his marriage to Michèle Bennett in 1980. His bride was a light-skinned mulatto whose first husband had tried to kill François

Duvalier and whose disreputable family was involved in the drug business and other shady dealings.

The Principal Protagonists in the Overthrow of the President

Duvalier's overthrow was due to urban opposition. It was the inhabitants of the provincial cities, especially the young people and students,[5] who held the demonstrations and marches that convinced the President he had lost popular support. The rural poor were largely uninvolved.

Jean-Claude had generated hope for the future with his inaugural promise to improve the economic situation and his subsequent pledges to promote democracy. Initially, urban residents found jobs as small assembly plants settled in Haiti, and the Caribbean Basin Initiative lured industry. However, by 1985, economic conditions had deteriorated in the wake of the AIDS scare, political instability, and governmental mismanagement. Industries were leaving, but the internal migration to the cities continued to accelerate, spurred on by untenable rural conditions.

By 1979, prospects for democracy began to dim. Without the international focus on human rights, the Haitian government began to clamp down on critical elements in the country. Again, it was urban Haitians who were most affected by government policy. They owned the businesses and the press. They were the consumers, and among them were the country's current and prospective leaders.

Although rural Haitians had ample reason to hope for a government that would address their worsening situation, experience had taught them not to expect anything beyond campaign promises from leaders. Sapped of its vigor and health by poverty, and its confidence by isolation, fear, and suspicion; the rural sector did not participate in the overthrow of President Duvalier.

On his March 1983 visit, Pope John Paul II, speaking of the need for change in Haiti, underlined the point that the poor had to take heart, or hope, again, *"il faut que les pauvres de toutes sortes reprénnent à espérer."* [6] From their absence from the events leading to the overthrow of the president, it is clear that the papal message had not reached the country's poorest. They had not become convinced that they had a stake in the system or Haiti's future.

CHURCH INVOLVEMENT IN THE OUSTER OF JEAN-CLAUDE DUVALIER

Actors

Hugo Triest, director of the Catholic radio station *Radio Soleil,* played a pivotal role. As other critical commentators disappeared, Father Triest came under increasing attack from the government, but he continued to broadcast. His programs kept the largely illiterate, disparate Haitian public up-to-date and encouraged it to analyze the significance of events.

Pope John Paul II played an essential role with his brief visit to Haiti on 9 March 1983. Addressing thousands gathered at the airport in Port-au-Prince as well as millions worldwide through the media, the pontiff condemned conditions in Haiti and called for immediate corrections. His words served to reinforce the religious momentum and resolve recently generated by the Eucharistic and Marial Conference.

Some additional Churchmen played important roles from behind the scenes. Former Papal Nuncio Luigi Conti was among them. Aware of Haiti's problems, critical of the government, and having excellent access to the pope,[7] he appears to have been instrumental in bringing John Paul II to Haiti and providing him with the text of his two statements.

In Colonial Latin America, the Church hierarchy sympathized and identified with the Crown to a greater extent than did the clergy. Few bishops favored independence until the last minute, when it was inevitable. On the other hand, the priests, who worked with the people, tended to share their perspective. In Haiti, the bishops were more conservative than the clergy. They too were more insulated from the people. Despite a disposition within the Church in recent years to become less hierarchical, the bishops' positions led them to associate with high-level government and business leaders, Vatican officials, and others who were part of the system and consequently less critical of it.

It was the priests (particularly those who had taken the vow of poverty in addition to those of chastity and celibacy), nuns, development, literacy, and media workers who were most in touch with conditions in Haiti. These were the people who had taken to heart the papal injunctions and conference messages to work with the poor and directly saw misery and injustice firsthand on a daily basis. Many of them repeatedly risked their lives on behalf of justice for the poor. Through repeated, courageous moral stands, their organization, the CHR, composed predominantly of women, played a significant role during the Jean-Claude era.

Sometimes the CHR took its case directly to the hierarchy; on other occasions, its appeals, messages, and pastoral letters simply suggested the necessity of the bishops' involvement, reminding them of their mission. In their historic 4 December 1980 *Communiqué*,[8] the CHR asked the bishops pointblank why they were not doing anything, cautioning them that "silence is betraying God, the people, the Church and our mission." CHR and CHB[9] issued a pastoral letter on 27 January 1982 objecting to the detention of lay worker Gérard Duclerville. The next Sunday, priests all over Haiti read it from their pulpits. In April 1983, the CHR released a *Global Plan* urging immediate social changes to benefit the most deprived classes. It recommended the establishment of commissions to deal with education, justice, and migration. It called for increased use of Creole and CEBs, reinforcement for *Radio Soleil* and *Bon Nouvèl*, and more involvement in national issues. There were additional arrests in November 1984. The CHR distributed a letter from all religious congregations saying that it was "in solid" with the bishops. It also sent a letter to the religious denouncing the arrests and urging them to support some intervention by the bishops.

Solidarity

As the Church began to identify with the people, Haitians came to trust and lean on the Church. Some of the Church's sense of solidarity with the people is reflected in its pronouncements. In the wake of the mass ouster of Haitian journalists in 4 December 1980, the CHR issued its powerful and moving pastoral letter that began, "When the rights of man are threatened, we must raise our voices . . . the Church cannot remain silent for her duty is to make life more human."[10] At the conclusion of the Symposium of the Eucharistic and Marial Congress held in Port-au-Prince 2-6 December 1982,[11] bishops, priests, nuns, and lay people in attendance put out a statement in Creole admitting its past mistakes and its intention to change. It spoke of plans to build a new Church, based on solidarity with the poor and the marginalized. "The Church is us, we are the Church." Following the arrest of Duclerville, the CHR and CHB issued a pastoral letter[12] demonstrating their solidarity with all victims: "Today it's Gérard and those whose names we do not know." Launching the International Year of Youth (IYY) on 6 January 1985, the bishops appealed to young people to "make something of the year," to create a better society, and to count on their support.[13] Addressing the Council of Youth in April 1985, Bishop Romélus declared, "Enough, people are in chains. It's time to take to the street, to unify. When one suffers, all do."[14]

The Church showed its identification with the people through its increasing use of Creole, the language of the vast majority of Haitians. Ultimately, most Church services and radio programs were presented in Creole, as was *Bon Nouvèl*, the Catholic monthly.

Group activities created a feeling of unity. The CEBs fostered a sense of community and empowerment. After Duclerville's abduction in December 1982 and the July 1985 deportation of the Belgian priests, the Church called on all Catholics to fast and devote the day to prayer. Some of the Church-sponsored marches had 100,000 to 200,000 participants.

Leadership

The Church made people more aware of their rights and power. Bible study demonstrated that it was possible to affect one's fate. The *Ti-légliz* gave people a sense of community and encouraged empowerment. In a country with few means of communication, the Church kept people in touch with each other. As long as it was open, *Radio Soleil* served this purpose. When the government closed it, messages traveled across the country by *teléjol*, or word of mouth, via another Church network, the CEBs, which copied and disseminated letters in their pastoral formation centers.

The Church stood-up for victims of official oppression. When Churches were invaded, priests shot, land stolen, and lay and literacy workers harassed, arrested, or disappeared, the Church spoke out during mass and on the radio, in pastoral letters, and directly to the government.

The International Year of Youth (IYY) provided the bishops with an opportunity to reach out to the nation's young people, form groups, and hold marches with a modicum of safety. On 6 January, the bishops urged the young people "to make something of the year," to improve society, and to count on their support.[15] To consolidate the message and symbolize the exodus, the Church organized youth marches that took place in almost all the parishes.[16] Tens of thousands of young people crossed the country, praying, singing, and chanting slogans such as, "Stand up young people! The future of the Haitian Church is in our hands! The most spectacular demonstration took place in the capital. On 2 February 50,000 to 60,000 people assembled in Port-au-Prince for peace, justice, participation, and democracy. Apart from the visit of the pope, it was the biggest gathering the city had ever experienced.[17]

Stands

In addition to the countless examples of individual bravery by bishops, priests, nuns, and lay workers who dared to confront authorities, there were a number of occasions when the Church as a whole, or a substantial sector of it, acted in some significant way. The end of the period of so-called liberalization in the Duvalier presidency came on 7 November 1979— and the Church was involved. The civic-minded Belgian Order of Salesians hosted the meeting at their hall. A year later, almost to the day, the government clamped down again on journalists following Grégoire Eugene's exposé in Fraternité on the government's abandonment of its citizens in Haiti and Cabo Lobos. The CHR released an official declaration that day reiterating intention of the Church to speak out to protect rights and lives.[18]

When Duclerville was arrested, the bishops and religious superiors issued a pastoral letter on 27 January 1983,[19] saying although they were looking forward to the pope's visit, the Church was living through difficult times, and they recommended that the faithful consecrate 9 February as a day of prayer and sacrifice for his liberation. *Radio Soleil* played its theme song, *Lè M'Pa We Solèy La,* nonstop. Bishop Romélus went on *Radio Soleil* to ask the faithful to boycott Carnival to let authorities know that the Church was in mourning. The director of the Petit Séminaire Collège Saint Martial also denounced the government on *Radio Soleil.* On 8 February, a battered Gérard Duclerville was released from prison and checked into a hospital. The Church had effectively forced the authorities to free him. Its concerted action engendered a sense of power and righteousness.

John Paul II came to Haiti on 9 March 1983.[20] Taking the slogan of the Eucharistic and Marial Congress, the pope told the thousands who had gathered at the airport to greet him, it is necessary that something change here, *"il faut que quelque chose change ici,"* and urged the audience to make it happen. He went on to describe the conditions in Haiti that had to change and how the changes could be effected. The solution was solidarity. It was necessary for the poor to take heart again. *"Il faut que les pauves de toute sorte se reprénnent à espérer."* The Church had a prophetic mission, inseparable from its religious mission, to take part in that change. On leaving Haiti later in the day, Pope John Paul II said he was pleased to be there for the closure of the Eucharistic Congress, which should continue and bear fruit, *"celui-ci doit se poursuivre je veux dire porter ses fruits."* In conclusion, the pope promised to stay close to Haiti and carry the people's hopes and concerns in his prayers.[21]

The Haitian bishops released their *Declaration on the Foundations of Church Involvement in Social and Political Affairs* on 11 April 1983.[22] In it, they cited papal authority, earlier Church documents, and the Universal Declaration of Human Rights, to justify Church participation in social and political matters. The Church reserved the right to speak up whenever moral values and human dignity demanded it. They ended the *Declaration* by urging the government to avoid anything contrary to human rights.

Another government crackdown occurred between May and July 1984, which led to new press censorship, food riots, and violence. *Radio Soleil* continued to cover the events, despite danger and harassment. The government reacted by closing *Radio Soleil* on 4 December 1985, "charging the media with preventing inaccurate information from harming or alarming the population."[23] The bishops sent a memo to the president on 18 December demanding that the station be reopened and its equipment returned to working order.[24]

A demonstration in Gonaïves on 26 November 1985 to commemorate the November 1980 suppression of labor leaders and journalists turned into an anti-government strike and protest two days later. Government troops stormed a rally, chased the participants into a nearby Catholic school, and shot uninvolved students. Bishop Constant of Gonaïves denounced the police action and demanded justice.[25] The Church dedicated 3 December as a National Day of Mourning, and the Papal Nuncio Luigi Conti gave the occasion his blessing and expressed his solidarity with the young.[26]

Activism

Church activism began with a commitment of solidarity with the poor, support for economic development and literacy, and led to defense of human rights, justice, and democracy. Eventually it became clear that these goals were unobtainable as long as Jean-Claude remained president. The isolated and somewhat ambiguous calls for change and liberation that began in 1983 became widespread and specific by December 1985. Ultimately, a wide spectrum in the Church, ranging from Catholic students to bishops, demanded new leadership.

The word "liberation," used in a political context, began to appear in Church documents in 1983, following the detention of Duclerville. *Radio Soleil* began to play its theme song, some of whose words were, "the flag of violence has been raised," whenever the government acted repressively. In their 30 January 1983 pastoral letter, the bishops wrote, "we pray God to liberate the country from torture and pray He will give Haitians a sense of sacrifice, engagement, responsibility and sacrifice."[27]

By 1984, a take-to-the-streets mentality was developing in association with the religious marches. A group of lay workers concluded an *Appeal* on 7 July 1984 that protested police exactions, profiteering, attacks against priests, the economic situation, and exploitation,[28] saying they were tired of the situation. The renewed June-July press repression provoked widespread criticism. The Church was infuriated by the interruption of a mass by a prefect in Cap-Haïtien in November.[29] In the subsequent 19 November street demonstrations, people called on "God's help in these dark hours." At the Cathedral in Cap-Haïtien on 24 November, one priest said, "we've crossed the line now, and must be ready die so justice can reign in the land." At a rally in Gonaïves on 28 November the crowd shouted, "down with misery and the Constitution."

The bishops told the Haitian young people in their 6 January 1985 *Message*, "We're with you. We count on you and with you . . . stand-up!"[30] Addressing 20,000 young people at the Youth Council in Jérémie on 11 April, Bishop Romélus informed them it was their mission to change things, to work for the country and the Church.[31] "We can't accept our brothers living under these conditions. The people have had enough. It's time to take to the streets. People are in chains, they aren't free, they don't have freedom of speech, we have to deliver these people. Be ready to die, brothers." The Youth of Jérémie subsequently sent a message to youth, Church leaders, and other Haitians in which they thanked the papal nuncio for the idea of the Council and expressed their appreciation to *Radio Soleil*.[32] They concluded by saying that the economic and social system in Haiti was not working and demanded reforms, including an end to government abuse.

The November 1985 killings of students in Gonaïves and the belated and insensitive official response, including the closure of Church radio stations, produced widespread outrage, pronouncements, demonstrations, and arrests. On 29 November, students in Jérémie shouted out, "long live liberty, down with the dictatorship," and demanded justice for Gonaïves, a government apology, and arrests. They would not return to school until matters were resolved. The Youth of Port-au-Prince protested the closure of *Radio Soleil*. On 13 December the Youth Les Cayes protested "the gagging of *Radio Soleil* and the criminals governing us."[33] The Council of Haitian Youth called for a battle to liberate the country: "Do not forget the three youths who died in one year. This means leaders do not respect lives of young Haitians."[34] "We have to battle to liberate the country, to dig out the foundation until the whole structure is crushed . . . all these things causing people to suffer in this country. We who are believers in Christ must create another model of society. We will fight until we obtain what we need. Where's the liberating blood of our ancestors? This is the country that had pride to throw off its masters."[35]

In their Christmas Message,[36] the bishops described the Year of Youth as "sullied" and, referring to the nation's "lack of peace, education, its institutionalized lies, and fear of liberty," concluded that "The Church can't resolve all the problems. This job calls urgently for all Haitians."[37]

Motivations

The Haitian Church was motivated by embarrassment, determination, and frustration in its relations with the Jean-Claude Duvalier government. After almost a five hundred year presence on the island, and more than a century of continuous existence in Haiti, the Church's accomplishments were overshadowed by its failures. As a result of internal and external events, it began to change in the late 1950s, evolving in the next two decades into a socially-committed institution. By the 1980s, trying to carry out its responsibility to the population, the Church found itself in an uncharacteristic position, at odds with the government.

Churchmen landed with Christopher Columbus and his fellow treasure-hunters at Môle Saint Nicholas on 6 December 1492. The Spaniards mined the gold through the exploitation of the native labor force. With rare exceptions, the Church did not protest the enslavement and decimation of the native Indians. When the Dominican order did object, it was forced to leave the island. One priest, Bartolomé de las Casas, did oppose the exploitation of the Indians, but it was his recommendation to import Africans as an alternative that led to the slave trade.

The Church presence in the French colony was equally uncritical. When the French took possession of the western part of Hispaniola, St. Domingue, as a consequence of the Treaty of Ryswick in 1697, King Louis XIII broke the tradition of freeing people in lands the French conquered,[38] demanding only that the Church make Christians of them. Slaves were to be baptized within eight days of arrival in St. Domingue. Due to the short preparation period, increasing numbers of newcomers, and lack of clerical and slave owner commitment, most converts were ill-prepared for their new religion.

Clerical acceptance of slavery is clear—many priests were themselves slave owners. The priests in St. Domingue, themselves a diverse bunch, were scorned by slaves and landowners alike,[39] both of whom wanted to be rid of them.

From independence in 1804 to 1860, there were no official ties between the Vatican and the Haitian State. That the Church was allowed to remain in Haiti was largely due to Toussaint L'Ouverture, who had had a positive formative religious experience with the Jesuits in Cap-Haïtien. Despite L'Ouverture's regard for the Church and his successors' tolerance of it, all of the early presidents sought to control the institution by limiting its power and becoming its leader.

The Vatican remained estranged from Haiti until 1860, protesting state interference in what it regarded as Church business. During this schism, the few remaining clergy in Haiti took advantage of the freedom. After thirty-six years of negotiations, the Vatican and Haiti concluded a concordat in 1860, the effect of which was to regularize relations, ultimately improve the quality of clergy in the country, and provide Catholicism with a privileged position among religions in Haiti. Among the important provisions of the concordat [40] was Article IV, which stipulated that bishops would be selected by the president with papal approval, and that the president alone would name the priests. Another was that the Church would be the religion of the majority and that laws would not be passed to its detriment.

The period from 1860 to the occupation was one of institutionalization for the Church, in which it set out to increase its clergy, build Churches and schools, make conversions, and combat Voodoo, Freemasonry, and Protestantism. Despite mass confirmations, conversions were not complete. Few boys attended Church, couples seldom sanctified their unions in Church, and those who did attend mass rarely abjured Voodoo ceremonies. Efforts to expand the priesthood and the education system fared badly. It was hard to attract priests to Haiti and keep the small number who came.

The bishop of Cap-Haïtien made annual recruiting trips to France, but some of his novices perished en route at sea; others could not endure the rigors of the tropics or the isolation.

Following the Concordat, the Church got more heavily involved in education, forcing out the Protestants whenever possible. Not only did Catholic schools proliferate, but priests began to teach in state schools, further narrowing the separation between Church and State. But the Church was unable to establish rural schools and unwilling to adapt its curriculum to Haiti. Consequently, it continued to teach only the children of the urban mulatto elite, instilling in them a French education and outlook.

In response to government instability, the United States landed an occupation force in Haiti in 1915 that stayed until 1934. During this period, the Church agonized about the growing Protestant population and the tenacious voodoo presence and grew close to the occupiers. The Church complained to the marines that they were favoring Protestantism and exhorted them to enforce already existing laws to eradicate voodoo. In 1915, the Church came close to getting the antisuperstition campaign it wanted, when other events intervened causing its postponement until the 1940s.

Pursuing a policy of private diplomacy and public support of the occupation, the Church alienated many Haitians. It produced unfortunate pastoral letters[41] that implied the military presence was necessary. It refused to join forces with the Patriotic Union, an organization dedicated to ending the invasion, by claiming a commitment to remain outside politics.

When the occupation forces left, the Church was in disrepute, but its reputation had not yet reached bottom. This occurred as the result of the antisuperstition campaign that the Church launched with the blessings of President Elie Lescot and tactical support of the National Guard. Between 1941 and 1943, Church and State sought to destroy voodoo by demolishing every shrine and holy object associated with it. At the apogee of the campaign, the Church tried to impose an anti-voodoo oath on Catholics which stated that they had renounced Voodoo completely. The violence, desecration, and audacity were excessive. Following one too many bloody incidents, people objected and the campaign ended.

The occupation and the antisuperstition campaign produced immediate and long-lasting effects. The succeeding Dumarsais Estimé and François Duvalier administrations were nationalistic, anti-Church, and pro-Voodoo. Like early Haitian presidents, each sought to control the Church and limit its power. Estimé did it principally through the encouragement of Voodoo, while Duvalier employed a number of techniques, including an attempt to co-opt the Church by appointing a priest to his cabinet, while ousting priests, bishops, a papal nuncio, and a whole religious order from the country, and altering the legal relationship between Church and State.

Duvalier accomplished administratively on 25 October 1966 what the Church had been unable or unwilling to do in a hundred years; he Haitianized the bishops, which opened the process of Haitianization of the entire Church. Despite the fact that Duvalier had mistreated churchmen and confiscated Church property, the Vatican conceded to him the right to name Haiti's bishops, with its concurrence. When Duvalier became president, only one bishop was Haitian; by 1966, all but one were.

Although Duvalier continued to brutalize the clergy and confiscate Church property, the grateful bishops did not complain. Enthused by the Haitianization of the Church and motivated by a new sense of purpose, increasing numbers of clergy and lay workers began to move to rural areas to work with the poor. Initially, most were unaware of or unaffected by the prophetic criticism of detractors, such as the Christians for Socialism and liberation theologians, who maintained that economic development was pointless in the absence of human rights. It remained for the Church to discover for itself that its efforts on behalf of the poor would require it to expand its infrastructure, communications system, and investment in the country, all of which would lead to competition and confrontation with the government.

The occupation and the antisuperstition campaign not only produced presidents committed to containment of the Church, but also led to introspection within the Church. By the 1950s, a group of Spiritan teachers from the Collège Saint Martial, having unsuccessfully urged Church reforms on their superiors, departed for France. In Paris, they joined forces with some similarly disenchanted African priests and wrote *Des Prêtres Noirs S'Interrogent,* [42] a book that defended Catholicism in black, Third World countries, but recommended ways to make it more relevant. In particular, they suggested that the Church utilize aspects of the local culture, particularly its language, music, and folklore.

Coincidentally, the Church was moving toward more substantive changes spurred on by Liberation Theology and the example of the Christian Base Communities. Liberation Theology, developed in the decades between the 1940s and 1960s, was the product of various scholars, including two Latin Americans, Peruvian Gustavo Gutiérrez and Brazilian Leonardo Boff. Contending that Jesus was a liberator who had confronted the authorities of his own time, they urged the Church to recall its nonhierarchical roots and original mission.

Christian Base Communities (CEBs), which date from the 1950s and 1960s and were perhaps a Brazilian creation designed to make up for the shortage of priests, provided liberation theologians with a demonstration model. Small groups of rural families would meet regularly to study the Bible and together devise solutions to their problems.

When Pope John XXIII announced the opening of the 1962-1965 Second Vatican Council, he introduced a new Church focus.[43] It was henceforth going to be "the Church of all the people and, in particular, the poor." The sixteen documents from Vatican II confirm this theme, justify Church involvement in social justice issues, and call for increased Bible study and use of local languages in the mass.

The Latin American Bishops' meetings (CELAM), at Medellín, Colombia in 1968, and Puebla, Mexico in 1979, reaffirmed Church commitment to the poor and to change. The Church would work for the "liberation" or "salvation" (words they decided were synonymous) of the poor and oppressed, whether victims of social systems, governments, or individuals. At Puebla, the bishops restated the legitimacy of Church involvement in both social and political spheres.

The Haitian Church's accommodation with slavery and subsequent absence of moral leadership, its lack of loyalty during the occupation, failure to thoroughly convert Haitians and minimal progress in education and literacy, its neglect of rural black Haitians and association with urban, upper-class mulattos, its abuse of privilege and power, particularly toward Voodoo through anti-Voodoo campaigns, and its vehement opposition to Protestants and Freemasons were all causes of embarrassment that created a dynamic for change from outside and within the Church. Haitianization plus international forces provided the impetus for a transformation of the Haitian Church.

Priests, nuns, and lay workers moved to rural areas to work with the poor and organize CEBs. Voodoo drums, music, and customs were incorporated into Catholic services. Protestant rituals, such as Bible reading, holding Sunday services in chapels (even in the absence of a minister), and broadcasting religious programs by radio to remote areas, were eagerly replicated. Confronted by official neglect and an increasing lack of alternative institutions, the Church took on the responsibility for providing the country with news and other services. Its expanded mission and increasing understanding of the country's problems ultimately brought the Church into conflict with the state. When members of the human rights and development community, press, political organizations, and trade unions were arrested and deported following the government repression in 28 November 1980, the Church took up the slack. Lay workers and priests intervened on behalf of dispossessed and imprisoned peasants. Bishops met with officials when *macoutes* and local authorities attacked Church workers. Participants at the December 1982 symposium in Port-au-Prince announced their intention to identify more closely with the people. Later that month, the Church went to the rescue of an imprisoned lay worker and gained his release.

Pope John Paul II came to Haiti in March 1983 and gave his blessing to this new activist Church. The following month, the Haitian bishops released a *Declaration* in which they documented their view that the Church had a legitimate right to be involved with politics and social issues. In March 1984, Archbishop Wolff Ligondé delivered a pastoral letter[44] rejecting "passivity, fear, injustice, cupidity, and a situation of sin." Later that year, in November, the CHR addressed a letter of concern to all members of the religious congregations in Haiti concerning the wave of recent arrests and the lack of official information about them, urging their colleagues to work in solidarity with the suffering people, and to protest when their rights were threatened.

By 1985, the population was taking its lead from the Church. The bishops addressed Haitian young people in January 1985, on the occasion of IYY, assuring them of their support and encouraging them to make a better society. As a result, Haitian youth formed groups, held marches and meetings and established communication with young people in other dioceses. When the bishops delivered a pastoral message on 16 July 1985 condemning the upcoming referendum "as exclusionary and biased against religion," many voters stayed home. Church sentiment began to affect public policy. A Belgian priest was murdered and three others were expelled from the country on 26 July. The bishops and youth groups denounced the abuses. On 4 October, Roger Lafontant, the minister of the interior, who had authorized the abuses, was himself fired.

Following the assassination of the students in Gonaïves in November 1985, Bishop Constant addressed a *Message to the People of Gonaïves* in which he called for justice. His appeal was echoed by youth groups throughout the country. In their *Christmas Message*, the bishops said, "with God it's the moment to say no to lies, servitude, egoism, torture, violence, injustice, and hate."[45] Shortly after Christmas, nationwide protests were launched against the regime that continued throughout January 1986. On 6 and 7 January, school and university students went on strike. On 7 January, schools were officially closed because students had vowed not to return to classes. On 13 January, Haitians held a general strike. On 26 and 27 January, there was an antigovernment demonstration at Cap-Haïtien. It was followed by demonstrations at Les Cayes and Léogâne. Several professional organizations and unions spoke out against the government and tracts calling for the overthrow of the regime were widely disseminated.

Conclusion

At the beginning of this book, we raised the question of the role of the Church in the overthrow of Jean-Claude Duvalier. The answer is leadership.

Particularly in the aftermath of Vatican II, Puebla and Medellín, the Church dedicated increased attention to the service of poor and rural Haitians, helping them establish a network of services, including CEBs, clinics, banks, and technical assistance. The effect was to raise the standard of life of those affected, promote optimism, and identify and train leaders. It also enhanced the reputation of the Church as a caring institution, in contrast to the government.

During the Jean-Claude era, the Church began to defend people who were victimized by the government, those who were unjustly arrested, deprived of their land and other possessions. As a consequence, Haitians discovered that they had the collective power to get the government to reverse itself and to affect public policy. These actions further enhanced the reputation and moral authority of the Church.

Following the arrests and exile of many of those who had heretofore provided Haitians with critical commentary, the Church took up the slack. *Radio Soleil* became the preeminent news source, but Church newspapers such as *Bon Nouvèl*, pastoral messages and letters, and Sunday sermons were also important. This commentary kept people informed about the continuing pattern of abuse, unfulfilled promises, and prospects for the future. As predictions came true, confidence in the Church increased.

When 1985 was designated the International Year of Youth by the United Nations, the Church capitalized on the happenstance to call on the nation's young people to organize and make something of the year. All over the country, young Catholics formed groups, got in touch with each other, held marches, and in so doing created solidarity and momentum for change. Given the esteem which the Church enjoyed by this time, the return of Hugo Triest and reopening of *Radio Soleil* became non-negotiable demands from an aroused public.

By Christmas 1985, the Church called on all Haitians to make change happen in Haiti. The Church urged the public not to settle for presidential concessions such as cabinet, price reductions of basic foodstuffs, and more promises of liberalizations. The people took to the streets. Within a month, Jean-Claude Duvalier was gone.

In the final chapter, we will summarize developments in the country and Church since the ouster of Jean-Claude Duvalier, and offer some predictions about the Haitian Church.

NOTES

1. Ministry of Foreign Affairs and Religion, *L'Eglise Catholique et l'Etat: Evolution des Rapports*, 1985.

See Alain Rocourt, Chairman and Superintendent General, The Methodist Church of Haiti, "The Role Played by the Churches" (Seminar for the Coordination in Development Conference, New York, 21 October 1988), 7. In discussing the "extraordinary phenomenon of masses of people developing a new consciousness and wanting to be masters of their own destiny," Rocourt says we have to inquire how this has been made possible. "The simple answer is: through the action of the Churches. . . . Thanks to the Churches, the countryside was having more and more elementary schools open; fairly well-equipped and well-staffed dispensaries or outpatient clinics have been created. Development projects in the countryside have all been under the sponsorship of the Churches."

2. Mary Evelyn Jegen, *Haiti: The Struggle Continues*, Just World Order Series (Erie, PA: Benet Press, 1987), 23.

3. Jean-Robert Estimé, interview by author, Wheaton, MD, 17 November 1989. The ambassador concluded that when Jean-Claude was confronted by challenges, he was unable to overcome the internal division in his government; "he was not a real Chief."

4. Elizabeth Abbott, *Haiti: The First Inside Account: The Duvaliers and their Legacy* (New York: McGraw-Hill, 1988), 195-96.

5. Although some of the students came from rural areas and were only residents of cities during the academic year, the overthrow of Jean-Claude Duvalier should be viewed as an urban phenomenon because people in rural Haiti did not participate.

6. Homily of His Holiness, Pope John-Paul II at the airport in Port-au-Prince, 9 March 1983.

7. Ernest H. Preeg, interview with author, State Department, Washington, D.C., 31 March 1988. The ambassador recalled that the nuncio was "outspokenly negative about the Government."

8. Conference of Haitian Religious, *Communiqué* from twenty-four heads of orders, Port-au-Prince, 4 December 1980. This was the first time the Church had officially taken a political stand, calling on the government to "reconsider the cases of deportation and imprisonment" of his critics.

John P. Hogan, "Haiti's Brief Hour of Hope," review of *The Rainy Season* by Amy Walentz, *Commonweal* 116, no. 16 (22 September 1989): 507. Hogan writes that while many credited the Church, particularly the bishops, with a large share in the overthrow of Baby Doc, "In truth, the credit for the downfall of Jean-Claude Duvalier belongs to other elements of the Church: *Radio Soleil*, *CARITAS*, *Ti-légliz*, the Conference of Religious, and *Mission Alpha*. It is these groups that heeded the 1980 warning of the CHR: 'Woe betide you and us if we do not preach the Gospel. Keeping silent today is betraying God, the people, the Church, and our mission. . . .'"

9. Conference of Haitian Bishops and Executive Board of Conference of Haitian Religious, *Pastoral Letter* (Port-au-Prince: CHR, 27 January 1983).

10. Conference of Haitian Religious, *Communiqué*, 4 December 1980.

11. Toumédia, ed., *Haïti-Pape 83* (Port-au-Prince: Imprimerie Henri Deschamps, 1983), 112-18.

12. Conference of Haitian Bishops and Executive Board of Conference of Haitian Religious, *Pastoral Letter*.

13. Conference of Haitian Bishops, *Message from the Bishops to the Young of Haiti in Honor of International Youth Year*, 6 January 1985. Text from the *Bulletin d'Information*, *1985*, Année International de la Jeunesse, Imprimerie la Phalange, 1985.

14. Willy Romélus, *Homélie de Monseigneur Romélus*, Concile des Jeunes, 11 April 1985.

15. Conference of Haitian Bishops, *Message from the Bishops to the Young of Haiti*.

16. Alfonso Chardy, "We Sparked Revolt in Haiti, Students Say," *Miami Herald*, 15 February 1986. Chardy reported that some students told him they had been responsible for the end of the Duvalier dynasty. According to them, the core group was from Gonaïves and consisted of students of one sociology professor at the Immaculate Conception School. These students formed a group called the Assembled Young Students of Gonaïves and met a number of times in late October. Then, they dispatched envoys to other cities to encourage additional students to join their struggle. Ultimately, groups were established in seven provincial cities.

The students told Chardy the sources of their inspiration were the French Revolution, foreign news broadcasts, other dissidents, and Liberation Theologists, but particularly Bishop Romélus.

Following the food riots in Gonaïves, they formed another group called *Deéshouké*, which they credited with being the first group to go to the streets on 27 November to protest poverty, lack of fuel, and the arrest of Pollux St. Jean. They met again on 23 December and decided to print anti-Duvalierist tracts, to resume demonstrating on 7 January and to boycott classes.

This is the only testimony I have encountered in which students take credit for having organized the overthrow of Duvalier. Their participation is unquestioned and their reference to a professor at Immaculate Conception is intriguing, perhaps helping to explain why the students ran there in an effort to elude the security forces.

17. Pax Christi International, *Report of the Mission of the Pax Christi International to Haiti* Erie, PA: Pax Christi International, 1986), 82-83.

18. Conference of Haitian Religious, *Communiqué*.

19. Conference of Haitian Bishops and Conference of Haitian Religious, *Pastoral Letter* prepared for reading in all churches and chapels on 30 January 1983.

20. Homily of His Holiness, Pope John-Paul II at the airport in Port-au-Prince, 9 March 1983.

21. Farewell speech by His Holiness, Pope John-Paul II at the airport in Port-au-Prince, 9 March 1983.

22. Conference of Haitian Bishops, *Declaration of the Bishops of Haiti on the Foundations of Church Intervention in Social and Political Affairs* (Port-au-Prince: CHB, 11 April 1983).

23. Jean-Marie Chanoine, Minister of the Interior and National Defense, Letter announcing the provisional closure of *Radio Soleil*, 5 December 1985.

24. Conference of Haitian Bishops, *Mémorandum de la CHB au Président de la Défense de la République* (Port-au-Prince: CHB, 18 December 1985).

25. Emmanuel Constant, "Message to the Citizens of Gonaïves," 28 November 1985. Translated by the Washington Office on Haiti, Washington D.C. on 8 November 1985.

26. Luigi Conti, *Letter to Father Jacques Mesidor, President of the Haitian Conference Religious*, Port-au-Prince, 6 December 1980.

27. Conference of Haitian Bishops, *Pastoral Letter*.

28. Pax Christi International, *Report of the Mission to Haiti*, 75.

29. Ministry of Foreign Affairs and Religion, *L'Eglise Catholique et l'Etat*.

30. Conference of Haitian Bishops, *Message from the Bishops to the Young of Haiti*.

31. Willy Romélus, *Homélie de Monseigneur Romélus*.

32. The Youth of Jérémie, *Declaration of the Youth of Jérémie* 5 December 1985.

33. The Youth of Les Cayes, *Greeting in Solidarity to the Youth of Port-au-Prince* (Les Cayes: Youth of Les Cayes, 13 December 1985).

34. The Council of Haitian Youth, *The Root Causes of this Suffering* (Port-au-Prince: Council of Haitian Youth, December 1985).

35. The Council of Haitian Youth, *The Root Causes of this Suffering*. Dedicated to Jean Robert Cius, Mackenson Michel, and Daniel Israel.

36. Conference of Haitian Bishops, *Message à L'Occasion de la Fête de Noël* (Port-au-Prince: CHB, 1985).

37. It is important to recognize the divisions within the Church and varying views on the limits to legitimate action of the Church. While the activist sectors of the Church ultimately dominated events in Haiti by the end of the Jean-Claude Duvalier presidency, the institution continued to remain aloof. Other people in the Church only became critical when the attacks were directed against the Church or those most involved with it. The Church was most united when lay workers, priest, and Church radio announcers were attacked, arrested, or abducted. On 7 November 1984, Father Joseph Serge Milot, secretary to the CHB, sent a letter to Ambassador Estimé alerting him to the arrest of three IDEA *animateurs*. He did not know why they had been arrested but asked for the minister's intercession so that none of them would be harmed. In December 1985, Bishop Gayot prepared a document that analyzed crimes against Church authorities, criticized government interference in the freedom of the Church, and concluded that these offenses violated the concordat. Some criticism appeared self-serving and bordered on the melodramatic such as when Bishop Gayot protested the interruption of a service in Cap-Haïtien, characterizing the event as "without precedent in the history of relations between the Church and State," adding that it was "all the more humiliating as it was a Protestant prefect who interrupted the service." Until the end, some Churchmen remained committed to a Jean-Claude Duvalier presidency. Bishops Gayot and Constant may actually have gone to the president a few days before his departure and asked him to stay, if Ambassador Jean-Robert Estimé's account is accurate (telephone interview with the author, Wheaton, MD, 17 November 1989). He claimed these bishops and the papal nuncio met with Jean-Claude Duvalier several days after the president let it be known he might go, and urged him to stay, as well as to fire some people, announce elections, and demonstrate his intention to create a democracy.

38. Michel S. Laguerre, *Voodoo Heritage* (Beverly Hills: Sage, 1980), 38.

39. C. L. R. James, *Black Jacobins, Toussaint L'Ouverure and the San Domingo Revolution*, 2d ed. (New York: Random House, 1963), 87. *See also* page 32.

40. Toumédia, ed., *Haïti-Pape 83*.

41. J. M. Jan, *Collecta Pour L'Historie Religieuse du Diocése du Cap-Haïtien*, vol. 3 (Port-au-Prince: Editions Henri Deschamps, 1960), 335.

42. A. Abble, et al., eds., *Des Prêtres Noirs S'Interrogent* (Paris: Editions du Cerf, 1956).

43. Harvey Cox, *Religion in the Secular City: Toward a Postmodern Theology* (New York: Simon and Schuster, 1984), 110.

44. Conference of Haitian Bishops, *Pastoral Letter*, 3 March 1984.

45. Conference of Haitian Bishops, *Message à L'Occasion de la Fête de Noël*.

6

The Post-Duvalier Church

While this book is centrally focused on the role of the Church in the overthrow of President Jean-Claude Duvalier from Haiti, this chapter provides a discussion of subsequent Church-State relations, some observations on worldwide changes in the Church, and remarks on the apparent effects of Church activism.

THE POST-DUVALIER CHURCH

Initial Political and Religious Reactions

Following the departure of Duvalier, the Church hierarchy offered little direction to a population that had come to expect it.[1] Even *Radio Soleil's* voice seemed somewhat muted. Only the CHR proposed bold plans for the future, assigning itself a significant role. There are a number of reasons why the hierarchy may have wanted to retreat, but the most likely one is pressure from the Vatican.[2]

On 7 February 1986, the day Duvalier left Haiti, the bishops issued a pastoral message[3] asking for restraint and forgiveness. In it, they urged people to behave like Christians. They should respect property and lives, resist killings, pillage, dishonoring God, or weakening the country. The next day, Archbishop François Wolff Ligondé exhorted Haitians not to turn to violence and hate. They must "pardon the outrages, forget the insults and love one another."[4] Preventing further violence and maintaining stability appeared to be the principle objectives. In the course of the next few weeks, the Church continued to urge parishioners in Sunday sermons to be patient and give the new leadership time to organize.[5] Some who wished that the Church were taking a more overtly influential role speculated that it must be working behind the scenes with the National Governing Council (CNG) to produce an election timetable.[6] Public messages from the bishops emphasized the country's needs and priorities without criticizing the government.[7]

Radio Soleil's programming seemed more or less empty, despite denials from its director, Hugo Triest,[8] who argued that although the circumstances were different, its line remained the same. Nevertheless, Father Triest did allow that Duvalier's departure had produced some confusion at the station. *Radio Soleil* had had to change some structures established for working under repressive conditions. While it was not talking much about political parties, *Radio Soleil* was putting together programs on the meaning of democracy and the Constitution.

However, the CHR did not hold back. By 26 February 1986, it announced that Duvalierism was still present in Haiti. The people had not yet taken power. All they had gotten was what they took. The CNG was letting the *macoutes* escape–there was no proof that the guilty would have to pay for their crimes. The CHR concluded that the government was incapable of new action or real changes, yet these issues had to be addressed or the country would get another Duvalier.

The CHR saw a broad and active role for itself in future events. It would accompany the people during this change and birth of democracy. It would help them organize. Paying special attention to the young and alienated, it would produce educational programs on radio and TV, instill an understanding of democracy, civics and politics. It would promote and lead social and professional organizations and unions concerning the social teaching of the Church.[9]

With the conspicuous exception of the CHR, the Church no longer played a leadership role. Young people complained that it no longer seemed to have anything to say in the mass. Detractors claimed the Church was supporting the government out of fear of the army, communists, or a U.S. invasion. Defenders maintained that the Church no longer needed to play a preeminent role because other critical institutions had returned to Haiti.[10]

Pope John Paul II told a general audience on 12 February 1986, "I endorse the words of the Bishops of Haiti [7 February message] and I send a warm greeting to the dear people of Haiti asking the Lord to guide them on a road to peace, prosperity, and national accord."[11] This brief message implies Church cooperation and seems to discourage continued political leadership. Like the U.S. government, the Vatican appeared to be afraid of revolution and Church involvement in it.

Over the course of the next four years, conservative members of the Church were rewarded and more politicized members punished. In 1989, Françcois Gayot was promoted to archbishop and Françcois Wolff Ligondé remained the archbishop of Port-au-Prince, despite widespread criticism of his conservatism and links with the Duvaliers.[12] Father Jean-Bertrand Aristide was variously chastised,[13] the CHR was largely silenced,[14] and Father Hugo Triest was removed as director of *Radio Soleil.*

Déshoukaj began with Duvalier's departure. The principal targets were *macoutes*. However, Voodoo leaders alleged that some of the victims were simply *houngans* and *mambos*, and they blamed the Church for encouraging an anti-Voodoo atmosphere. The Church denied participation in a latter-day antisuperstition campaign, but its comments indicated a lack of ecumenicalism, at the very least. For the first time in history, Voodoo leaders began to organize to protect and promote themselves.

In February, 1986 crowds were reportedly hunting down *macoutes* and killing one or two a day.[15] By April, an ethnology panel[16] documented that sixty-two Voodoo practitioners had been killed in the previous three months. In May, a mob attacked the Voodoo leader Max Beauvoir's temple, and shots were fired at him and his family.[17] Clearly, it was not only *macoutes* who were being pursued. Some Voodoo priests were reportedly paying protection fees. Joseph Eliantus, a Voodoo priest in Delmas, a suburb of Port-au-Prince, was defensive and reluctant to talk in July 1986. He denied any involvement with politics. He was only concerned with "good Voodoo, serving Erzuli." Nevertheless, some Voodoo priests were in danger, and he claimed that people who had done nothing wrong were being killed.[18]

Voodoo leaders charged that the Church was behind the violence. The Voodoo priest Herard Simons[19] charged that the *Déshoukaj* was a "well-arranged strategy" by the Catholic bishops to mobilize youth groups against Voodoo. Max Beauvoir maintained that much of the "religious aggression" stemmed from Rome. In Haiti, the worst excesses against Voodoo were occurring in the south, which Beauvoir attributed to Bishop Willy Romélus. Father Aristide had added fuel to the fire with an incendiary tract, which called for ridding Haiti of evil: the evil was Voodoo. Beauvoir alleged that an army of Catholic "vagabonds" called the *Comités de Relèvement*, formed four years before, intended to kill Voodoo leaders in the countryside.

Asked on 23 April 1986 whether the Church was behind the persecution of Voodoo, Archbishop Ligondé responded that the perpetrators were fanatics, pushed by personal vengeance; the Church had not encouraged a religious war.[20] Bishop Verrier said that the Church condemned vigilante violence.[21] Triest denied that there had been any Church-inspired *Déshoukaj* on *Radio Soleil.* The most he had heard was that some priests said they were unable to stop parishioners from going after certain Voodoo practitioners.[22]

Whether or not the Church had instigated the anti-Voodoo *Déshoukaj*, nothing was published by the Church or the Protestants to stop it.[23] Comments made it clear that the level of sympathy and understanding of Voodoo was limited. Papal Nuncio Paulo Romeo[24] described Voodoo as "a difficult religion, based on the ignorance of the people." In his opinion, there would not be space for Voodoo in the future. With literacy, it would not survive. The continuing violence was by people who opposed Voodoo supporters who were also *macoutes*. A foreign priest in Haiti with a doctorate in history denied categorically that the Church was behind the persecution of Voodoo leaders. However, he thought the Voodoo priests had a bad reputation because "they eat children and have catacombs under their houses."

In March 1986, Voodoo leaders took an unprecedented step by organizing. They set up the first organization of Voodoo priests and priestesses, *Bode Nasyional*, the National Body.[25] Within three months, *Bode Nasyional* had 6,000 members and a spokesperson, Max Beauvoir. The organization's initial plans were to start a radio station and a clinic that would do research on Voodoo medicine.

In 7 March Beauvoir sent a letter to the CNG, not only protesting crimes against Voodoo leaders and demanding retribution, but asking for representation in government and the adoption of Voodoo and Creole as the State religion and language.[26]

Despite the novel Voodoo initiatives, and hopes generated by talk of ecumenicism and tolerance, relations between the Voodoo and Catholic religions was again on a downswing.

CHURCH-STATE RELATIONS FROM NAMPHY THROUGH AVRIL

Church-State relations have varied considerably in the following four years due to differences among presidents, changed circumstances, and alterations in the Church. Relations were off to a generally amicable start following Jean-Claude's departure, with the Church hierarchy assisting the CNG by urging Haitians to be calm and patient, and the State making some concessions to the Church. Although there were assaults on people associated with the Church in the early months, they remained sporadic until Fall 1986. Conditions did not change noticeably for another year, when tensions heightened over increasing incidents of human rights abuses and the pending elections. Subsequently, relations worsened to the point that the Church lost confidence in the ability and willingness of the government to conduct fair elections or turn control over to a civilian administration. Relations were strained between Leslie Manigat and the Church before he took office, and they did not improve conspicuously thereafter. His election, inauguration, and program were all sources of concern to the Church. While Manigat maintained that improving relations with the Church was one of his goals, it clearly was not a priority.[27] During his brief return to office, General Namphy did not resort to democratic pretense. He dealt harshly with opposition, including the Church. General Avril took over the presidency with a conciliatory gesture toward the Church and the Church appeared grateful. It reined in potentially faultfinding elements and remained uncritical almost to the end.[28]

The Namphy/CNG Stewardship–7 February 1986 to 7 February 1988

Although the CHR took the government to task for inaction and incompetence in late February 1986, the bishops were considerably more restrained and supportive.[29] When Haitians complained about the composition of the CNG, they held back. When people were indignant because Albert Pierre, former police chief, was allowed to escape, they were silent. Following violence at Fort Dimanche on 26 April 1986, they cautioned everyone to be peaceful.[30] The grateful government allowed the Jesuits and Holy Ghost orders, expelled twenty years before, to return to Haiti.

Sporadic attacks against Church people that began in March intensified by September 1986, at the time the VSN was disbanded. When popular literacy monitor Charlot Jacquelin was abducted and Vladimir Jeanty was murdered, an outraged crowd of more than 100,000 gathered on 7 November 1986 in Port-au-Prince to demand justice. This demonstration was followed by a transportation strike and a police crackdown, in which authorities retaliated by firing on Church buildings and at *Radio Soleil.*[31]

Violence escalated again the following summer and reached a crescendo during the November elections that continued to the end of the Namphy government. When the CNG wrested control from the Provisional Electoral Council (CEP) on 22 June, infuriated Haitians went on strike.[32] By 29 July 1987, the pope was led to issue an appeal against violence in Haiti in which he said violence was not the solution for the grave problems afflicting the nation. His words were seconded by the bishops, who also called for peaceful resolution of problems. Even so, on 23 August four Catholic priests and their driver were badly beaten by a paramilitary group after passing an army checkpoint in Freycineau. Between August and December, there were attacks on rectories and parish offices, especially in the Artibonite. *Mission Alpha* was forced to close in late 1987 following death threats,[33] and *Radio Soleil* was bombed. On 23 September, 320 members of *Tet Ansanm*, a religious cooperative, were killed in a land dispute. On 3 October, *macoutes* broke into the home of Belgian priest, Lawrence Bonhen, shooting one person, wounding another, and handcuffing a third. The man who was wounded had earlier protested army violence.[34]

The bishops denounced the fraudulent election and violence associated with it.[35] On 2 December, Silvio Claude, the Federation of Haitian Workers, and Bishop Romélus urged the CNG to step down. As a result, efforts were made to discredit the Church—a Catholic bishop was depicted throwing ballots into the latrine, and attacks were renewed against Church-related organizations and property, including *Radio Soleil's* transmitters.[36] Attempts were undertaken on 4 December, to replace their representation on the CEP. On 7 December, the bishops issued a statement describing the mounting violence, crimes and terror, the attacks on Haiti's "little people," their homes and Churches, and the shots fired on voters and foreign journalists. The bishops concluded by expressing their "extreme disapproval of these odious acts."[37] On 21 December, they issued another statement in response to government harassment of the hierarchy and clergy, which they termed "a smear campaign against the Church." By 24 December the eight Catholic bishops announced that they would encourage people not to vote in the upcoming election. In their opinion, the conditions necessary for free elections were not present because authorities would be allowed to inspect the ballots and soldiers would be authorized to enter the polling booths.

In January, momentum grew for an election boycott. On 1 January, a number of organizations signed a document entitled the *Declaration in Support of Democracy*.[38] Its signatories, which included the Brotherhood of Committed Lay People and Christian Youth Workers, claimed that the rescheduled elections would be bogus and demanded a new, *macoute*-free provisional government. On 17 January, the Civil Society Coalition was founded to support a boycott of any election carried out by the current junta. Among its members were fifty civic and religious organizations and Catholic lay groups.[39] A "Peoples' Manifesto" that also called for a boycott was circulated. It was signed by representatives of the Catholic Church, among others. In the week before the election, more than one hundred dissenters were arrested, among them scores of Church lay workers and members of literacy brigades.[40]

Following the January elections, the bishops issued another statement. They had witnessed problems with the elections during which people involved with the Church had been apprehended, including chapel directors, school officials, and literacy workers.[41] The elections had been neither morally free, fair, or genuine. The bishops observed that a systematic campaign to denigrate the Church and those charged with animating them was continuing.

The Manigat Presidency—7 February 1988 to 20 June 1988

The conditions under which Leslie Manigat ran for president and was elected were disconcerting to all involved, including the Church, which quietly boycotted the elections. The inauguration did nothing to dispel Church concern. Apart from the papal nuncio, none of the Church hierarchy attended. Manigat had not invited them, fearing they would not come.[42] Consequently the customary *Te Deum* was not part of the ceremony.[43] For the first time ever, the inaugural blessing was given by a *houngan* instead of a Catholic priest. When Leslie Manigat received this blessing, he was wearing the insignia of the Freemasons, having accepted the title offered to all incoming Haitian presidents, of Most Serene High Protector of Freemasons.[44]

His speech appeared to be conciliatory toward the Church and, at the same time, to bait it.[45] It begged the question about his attitude toward Voodoo and his perspective on the legitimate privileges of the Church.[46]

We guarantee the churches that they will be able to flourish, thanks to equal freedom for all creeds—a freedom that everyone knows we do not intend to attack in any way—because under my government, no religion, no church, no creed will ever be persecuted. No one can doubt—since the voice emerging from my mouth is a Christian voice and the heart that is expressing itself today is a Christian heart—we want to entertain harmonious relations with the Catholic Church as well as with the other different creeds among which the living faith of our people is divided. It takes two to entertain such relations. Peace is created first and foremost in peoples' minds, and the action of the churches takes place in the domain of things spiritual.

Even though President Manigat expressed confidence that he could have cooperated with most of the bishops and that his relations with many of the religious was good to excellent,[47] the Church kept its distance from him and became increasingly alarmed by his agenda.[48]

In May, he told the papal nuncio that he was obliged to change Church-State relations—the senate was "aggressive against the Church and wanted to change the Concordat." He had "had a strong feeling from them, a nationalistic feeling, that change was needed."[49]

In a particularly resented decision, taken in order to "put the country to work," the president announced that he was going to reduce the number of religious holidays. In another unpopular arrangement, in order to give "free and equal treatment" to all the religions in Haiti, Protestants and Catholics were prohibited from outdoor Easter gatherings in 1988 and the Church was forbidden to hold a Corpus Christi procession a few months later.[50]

According to Manigat, "the Church was puzzled by the government, knowing that he was friendly but concerned that relations with him would be detrimental to it in some way."[51] At the end, it attempted to strengthen the government, but by then it was too late. The one bright spot in relations between Church and State during the Manigat months was the minimal human rights transgressions against the population or Church.[52]

Namphy Returns—20 June 1988 to 17 September 1988

General Namphy's three months in office were marked by violence as the regime sought to quiet political opposition. A distinguished lawyer and human rights advocate, Lafontant Joseph, was murdered. A Canadian priest, René Poirier, was summarily expelled from the country on 11 August, presumably for refusing to participate in a pro-Namphy gathering.

The presbytery at Fonds Verrettes was attacked, and the priests and nuns were forced to leave. In response to these actions, the bishops issued a *Declaration on the Difficult Situation Taking Place in the Country*,[53] informing Haitians that they had not been abandoned, that the bishops had heard the "cries and appeals of nuns, priests, lay people and share their suffering. Things have to change (because) no-one can live in this state of insecurity." Although the road to democracy was long and difficult, they were confident it would come.

In September, three Churches were attacked within one week. The first assault was the most vicious. Approximately twenty to thirty men, armed with guns and machetes, burst into St. Jean Bosco on Sunday, 11 September, during the 9:00 A.M. mass, killing eleven worshipers and wounding seventy in an unsuccessful attempt to reach Jean-Bertrand Aristide, who was the officiating priest. Police and soldiers saw the attack but did not intervene. By the time firefighters arrived one hour later, the Church was destroyed. The following evening on television, the perpetrators bragged that they were going to do it again. Two nights later the Chapel of the Immaculate Conception in Cité Soleil was burned and reporters chased away. Later that week, St. Gérard Church was stoned.[54]

The outcry against these attacks was international. Archbishop John May, president of the National Conference of Bishops, wrote to Bishop Gayot on 20 September concerning the "tragic events in recent days" and the shock and distress of the North American Church. All told, the Haitian Church received about fifteen hundred letters protesting the disappearance of Church literacy worker Charlot Jacquelin.[55]

The Avril Period—17 September 1988 through 10 March 1990

General Avril's relations with the Church were relatively peaceful and apparently cooperative until late 1989.[56] Perhaps Avril won some of the Church over with his initial conciliatory words and actions. On taking power, he said that he "was sickened by the recent violence against the Churches" and promised a human rights reform. In addition, he purged some military who were believed to have taken part in the attack on the St. Jean Bosco Church. The Church refrained from criticizing Haiti's second military coup. On 26 September 1988, the bishops suggested disarming the *macoutes* and recommended an economic and social recovery plan, requiring international aid and moral support from the United States that had been denied to President Manigat. The relationship between the Church and State seemed too close to some.

Following a crackdown on political critics in January 1990, the government began to unravel. On 4 March, eleven political parties and a civic organization formed the Group of Twelve—then called for Avril's resignation. On 5 March 1990, a little girl named Roseline Vaval was killed in Petit Goâve while soldiers dispersed a manifestation. Within two days, there were demonstrations in seven cities, and participants asked rhetorically where Jérémie, Cap-Haïtien, Les Cayes, Port-au-Prince, Saint Michel de l'Atalaye, and Jacmel were in order to garner additional support.[57] On 8 March, there were riots and three people were killed in Port-au-Prince in police-related incidents, but the Army high command released an official *communiqué* telling the service to avoid violence. Students stayed out of school and joined forces with political parties, the business community, and an employers' group, to urge Avril to leave office.[58] President Bush made a public statement; Haiti and Cuba were the only two countries in the region preventing the Americas from being totally democratic.[59] On Saturday, 10 March, General Avril resigned and the following Monday, flew to Florida aboard a U.S. military transport C-141 Starlifter. On 13 March 1990, Ertha Pascal Trouillot, a member of the Supreme Court of Appeals was installed as provisional president of Haiti.[60]

The Church played public and diplomatic roles in the events. In February, Aristide urged the political parties in Haiti to unify in order to make the elections work.[61] *Radio Soleil* interviewed opposition groups on the upcoming elections, asking whether they should take place, would be meaningful if held, and would require Avril's prior resignation.[62] In early March, a group of priests in Port-au-Prince encouraged Haitians to ask for a government they could trust.[63] Father Aristide urged Haitians to mobilize to remove Avril from power and the country so he could not maneuver behind the scenes.[64] Once General Avril and his entourage had departed, stories began to surface concerning the pivotal role that had been played by Father Antoine Adrien, a Catholic priest, in getting the president to leave.[65]

NEW CHURCH DIRECTIONS

Identifying a Mission

As the CNG was supposedly preparing for the November 1987 national elections, the bishops produced a document on 27 June 1986 entitled *The Fundamental Charter for the Transition to a Democratic Society*,[66] detailing their expected involvement in the transition and the limitations of their involvement. In it, they said that they intended to be of service to the national community in building "a new, reconciled and fraternal society," but the Church was not a political power and had no duty to replace the government in politics or compete with political parties. Its role was to promote and defend human rights and train followers to participate in and influence political activities. The following month, Bishop Gayot described the mission of the Church as threefold: catechistic, liturgical, and social. In recent years, he added, its social role had increased as the Church grew closer to the people, but, "it is not the political situation that determines its mission."[67]

Between 1886 and 1990, the Church became increasingly preoccupied with the political aspects of its social mission, which influenced its programs and interfaith relations. While the hierarchy was able to exert its will, to some extent, it was unable to convert or quiet all of the activist sectors, who continued to make their opinions heard. The future of the Church depends on how these issues are resolved.

On 7 March 1986, Bishop Gayot announced a crash literacy program. Delivering a message on *Radio Soleil* on 15 March concerning the needs and priorities for Haiti, the bishop put literacy at the top.[68] The future role of the Church, according to Archbishop Ligondé in April 1986, was literacy.[69]

The vehicle the Church would use to further literacy was a five-year program called *Mission Alpha*, which had actually begun in September 1955. Its goals were to furnish basic literacy training in Creole[70] to up to 3 million adults and young people, and "to provide them with an education that affirms their reasoning and analytical thinking skills, in order that they may participate more effectively in the development of communities and in building of a just, equitable, and democratic society." From inception, the program was controversial. Detractors during the Jean-Claude era accused it of being communistic. Participants were advised to stay away from it and its monitors were frequently harassed. The same things continued to happen following Jean-Claude's departure. In September 1986, literacy monitor Charlot Jacquelin and Premius Jasmin were arrested. In addition to being provocative, the program was underfunded, understaffed, and over-ambitious. However, its operations were almost certainly suspended in November 1987 by a hierarchy increasingly sensitive to the communist epithet and concerned about activism, and for whom the program's objectives had become incompatible with their scaled-back, post-Duvalier social and political agenda.

Dealing with Other Religions

Church-Voodoo relations were better during the Jean-Claude Duvalier administration than during almost any period in Haitian history. The Church and government both contributed to this.

Vatican II encouraged the incorporation of elements of indigenous religions into Catholicism. As a result, in Haiti the mass began to be said in Creole, to the accompaniment of Voodoo drums. Even conservative members of the Haitian Church hierarchy acknowledged positive contributions of Voodoo in such areas as traditional medicine.[71] Voodoo no longer challenged Catholicism's preeminent religious position in the country, as had been the case during the François Duvalier era. The State contributed unintentionally to a relaxation of tensions between the Church and Voodoo through its perceived abandonment of the black rural population and its reliance on *houngans* as informers. Government relations with Voodoo became so relaxed that Ambassador Estimé characterized Voodoo simply as being "no problem" for the government.[72]

During the Jean-Claude Duvalier presidency, the CHR and Archbishop Wolff Ligondé both suggested initiatives for closer Voodoo-Church relations. At their April 1983 Conference, the CHR proposed establishment of a Commission on Medicine and Social Affairs that would take the contributions of traditional medicine into account. In addition, the CHR proposed that the Church be more responsive to the needs of the vast majority of the population, who were, after all, adherents of Haiti's traditional religion.[73] On 3 March 1984, Archbishop Ligondé signed a pastoral letter, which spoke of the need for more dialogue between cultures, religions, and races.[74]

Although the Church was somewhat more receptive to certain Voodoo customs than others, there were indications that the tolerance did not extend to the religion itself. One bishop spoke of some intellectuals who mistakenly characterized Voodoo as a religion. According to him, religions reject lies, evil, an attachment to magic and sorcery, and have moral values and principles. Therefore, Voodoo was not a religion. "By utilizing lies and a psychosis of fear, Voodoo, as it is at present, cannot be an agent of development. To the contrary, it maintains and favors underdevelopment."[75]

Disapproval of Jean-Claude became widespread, reaching well beyond the Catholic community. Many Voodoo adherents, Protestants, and non-believers alike ultimately joined forces to oust the president. Criticism has been leveled at the Voodoo community for not taking a more active part in the ouster, but such criticism fails to take into account three factors. First, Voodoo is not organized around a central authority who recommends and coordinates activities. Second, Voodoo is the predominant religion of rural Haitians, who continue to be less educated and less attuned to political issues. They were not significant participants in the overthrow of the president. The people behind his ouster were overwhelmingly urban. Finally, to the extent that Voodoo had been favored during the François Duvalier years, and its adherents had taken advantage of the power conferred on it, there was justifiable fear of reprisal. These fears proved to be well-founded when numbers of Voodoo *houngans* and *mambos* were killed in the aftermath of Jean-Claude's departure.

Prospects for reaching a *modus vivendi* between the Church and the Voodoo religion dimmed due to events following Duvalier's departure and have not improved subsequently. The lone, and by no means loud, voice from the Church in opposition to *Déshoukaj* came from the CHR. The ecumenical emphasis of Vatican II and the CELAM meetings has been otherwise conspicuously absent.[76]

From the perspective of Max Beauvoir, the designated Voodoo spokesperson, the Duvalier period was preferable to the succeeding period because, "the Voodoo practitioners had the right to exist." In his view, the post-Duvalier persecution was due to the Church. Beauvoir cited a report aired on *Radio Nationale* on 9 July 1986 that accused a Brother Jean-Marie in northwestern Haiti of handing out machetes to parishioners to use against Voodoo followers. In a report on 16 April 1986, Estelle Beauvoir described the lynching of *mambos* and *houngans* in the north, saying that all who had lost their lives were accused of being *malfaiteurs*, evildoers, or *houngans*, and no one could furnish the slightest proof. Catholics and Protestants were intolerant everywhere.[77]

Voodoo practitioners saw themselves as victimized legally and culturally, as well as physically.[78] In order for relations to improve, they called for a retraction of the 1860 Concordat and the 1935 Anti-Voodoo Law, recognition of Voodoo sacraments, reintroduction of the black pigs used in Voodoo ceremonies, and promulgation of antiproselytism laws. They wanted to have medicine restructured, taking account of traditional medicine, and to allow *houngans* access to hospitals.

Anti-Voodoo sentiment was renewed and continued by stories of babies being abducted from hospitals for use in Voodoo ceremonies[79] and of bones from such orgies stuffed under houses. It was aggravated by concern over such things as an inaugural blessing of a president by a Voodoo priest and the registering of a Voodoo association as a corporation.[80]

Church-Protestant relations showed signs of improvement during the Jean-Claude Duvalier administration. This was obvious in the increasing number of joint organizations and committees. It was clear, particularly from the statements of the CHR and Catholic youth groups, that there was a desire, particularly from the progressive sectors of the Church, for increased cooperation and ecumenicism. However, the Protestant denominations continued to grow rapidly during this period, maintaining their distance from politics and their uncompromising policy toward Voodoo, all of which generated a sense of competitiveness and some bad feelings. Individual Protestant ministers opposed the government, and a number were victims of its repression. Ultimately, Protestant organizations added their voices in opposition to the dictatorship.[81]

Prior to 1973, ecumenical cooperation was limited to monthly prayer meetings.[82] That year, from 9–13 July, more than one hundred Protestants and Catholics met in an effort to work together to find solutions to Haiti's development problems. Methodist Minister Alain Rocourt spoke of the role that churches could play in development and of their current shortcomings.[83] Dr. Julio de Santa Ana from the Ecumenical Council of Churches reminded the audience of papal support for development and social justice.[84]

More schools and teachers were needed.[85] Catholic schools continued to be located predominantly in urban areas while Protestant schools accounted for half of the schools in rural areas.[86] The Church was accused of teaching students inappropriate subjects and instilling in them a foreign culture.[87] They needed to get away from this emphasis on French language and culture. It was suggested that it was the duty of the state to take over education. The Church should get out of it and not use it as a means of proselytizing.[88] Others argued that with such a small number of children attending school and only 1.7 percent continuing on to secondary school, Catholics and Protestants needed to cooperate on education.[89] Bishop Gayot spoke about a new, nonhierarchical Church that was concerned about the social and economic dimensions of man's life, and making a link between evangelization and development.[90] The Reverend Charles Poisset Romain spoke of a negative aspect of Catholicism and Protestantism, which they shared with the Voodoo religion. According to him, all three encouraged resignation and fatalism, and he cited religious songs to make his point.

Since 1973, ecumenical collaboration can be seen in the work of a number of organizations. Christian Service, an organization that depends on the National Council of Churches, provides aid, does development work, and collaborates with the Catholic Church.[91] There is also the Haitian Commission of Churches for Development (CHED), which dates from 1974, and the Medical Christian Commission of Haiti (CMCH), which began in 1975.[92]

Protestants and Catholics have worked together on other programs and committees.[93] In December 1985, when *Radio Soleil* made a "pilgrimage" across the country, broadcasting the problems of various parishes, Protestants joined in for the final two days and "visits" were made to their churches also. The program ended with religious services, and the next month Catholic and Protestant denominations shared religious services on *Radio Soleil.*[94]

One Protestant with a long perspective on Church-Protestant relations is Luc Garnier, the Haitian bishop of the Episcopal Church of Haiti.[95] He recalled that a long time ago there were no relations between the Catholics and Protestants, but this had changed since the Haitianizing of the Church. In his opinion, an advantage of working with the Catholics is that their "limits are known." By contrast, the Protestants have "too many leaders." Priests and nuns routinely come in to discuss problems and there are some joint projects, including a current irrigation project. He concluded that there is more "congeniality" now, recalling that the Church used to excommunicate people who attended the Episcopal Church. He was quick to point out that the Episcopal Church did not care if its members attended the Catholic Church. Walter Turnbull, the son of a prominent Baptist minister in Haiti, who lives at Mountain Maid, L'Artesian, a Baptist enclave above Port-au-Prince, also spoke of their "good working relationship" with the Catholics, observing that he served on a number of development committees with them.[96]

Communications and relations with the Protestants improved in certain ways during the Jean-Claude Duvalier era but some saw more room for improvement. After Catholic young people held a Council in Jérémie under the patronage of the bishops, they issued a message to the youth, Church leaders, and Haitians in general in which they criticized the economic, social, and religious situation in the country. Among other things, they blamed many Church leaders for their lack of dialogue and interaction with the Protestants.[97] A delegation from Pax Christi visited Haiti in January-February 1985 with the objective of understanding and supporting the role and engagement of the local Church in working for the promotion of the Haitian people. Among its recommendations were that the World Council of Churches, which is established in Haiti, set up a National Council of Churches so as to not be confused with the American denominations. In this way, they could officially start an ecumenical dialogue with the Catholic Church.[98]

The remarkable growth of Protestantism continued throughout the Jean-Claude Duvalier years so that by 1986, it is calculated that there were one million Protestants.[99] In other terms, 15 percent of the population was Protestant, the majority of whom were Baptists.[100]

The Protestants' success in making conversions has provoked envy and is responsible for some of the criticism. When Bishop Gayot wrote to Jean-Robert Estimé on 24 November to complain about the interruption of mass at the cathedral in Cap-Haïtien on 18 November 1984, he was particularly mortified because it had been a Protestant who had made this "affront to our religion."[101] Fundamentalist ministers are accused of tolerating poor political and economic situations and of encouraging resignation among their parishioners.[102] Protestants in general are accused of not understanding the structure of the society, of lacking a sense of community, of not being concerned with the rights of man, and of being latecomers to the literacy business.

The Protestants' success has also led the Catholics to adopt some of their ways. This has brought about a greater emphasis in the Church on the use of the Bible, Creole, the laity, and open air services.[103]

There is a hint of skepticism from Protestants who have been patronized and criticized by the Church. The Episcopal Church brochure says that it is not in competition with any other religion. Unlike the Catholic Church and some other Protestant churches, it believes that being a Christian does not entail living a western way of life but "accepting Christ." In an interview, Bishop Garnier criticized the Catholic Church for publicizing its new literacy campaign. In light of its recent involvement, it "should have been ashamed."[104]

In his work on Protestantism in Haiti, Charles Poisset Romain criticized Protestant denominations for their refusal to become involved in Haitian culture, society, and politics.[105] He took issue with their focus on spiritual matters and disregard for earthly events, which he argued, promoted a "ghetto mentality" and led them to defend the status quo. Dr. McClure[106] described the Protestants in "Lenor," the Haitian community in which she lived in the early 1980s as "a small but slowly growing minority there, as in Haiti as a whole. Lenor's congregations are small but enthusiastic, and uncoordinated with one another . . . the congregations as such are not active in community affairs."

It was just this lack of involvement in community affairs and politics that the government found endearing. Ambassador Estimé's description of the Protestants in Haiti verges on the rhapsodic.[107] There were never any problems with *Radio Lumière*. The advantages of the Protestants included their approach, style, and independence. With their pragmatic approach, they could achieve social projects. They were generally seen as more effective at fighting poverty and Voodoo than the Catholics. They were more morally correct and had a better reputation, or "*image*."

That the government played the Protestants off against the Catholics is clear. When problems began to emerge with the Catholics, the decision was made to improve relations with the Protestants. The Ministry established a *Commission Mixte*, "to show the Catholics that they did not enjoy a unique relationship with the state." The result was very good, according to Ambassador Estimé. Five of the seven reform denominations participated. The meetings consisted of discussions about economics, "a real information flow was established."[108]

A ministry of foreign affairs and religion document on Protestant religions in Haiti traces the evolution of Protestantism in Haiti, its legal basis, its structures, function, and social activities, and offers some suggestions for dealing with them. Dating Protestantism from 1816, during Pétion's government, it describes its early relations with the Church. "Coexistence with the Catholic Church was not without difficulty." The author quotes Jean Marie Gailloux, the Archbishop of Port-au-Prince, in his work *Collecta* about the growth and the increasing influence of the Protestants,[109] who built schools, got into various forms of employment and "*l'influence qu'ils exercerent tourna au détriment de l'Eglise*," or, whose influence was at the expense of the Church.

All constitutions in Haiti have promised religious liberty. Articles IV and XXVII of the August 1983 Constitution reconfirmed this point. Citizens had the right to profess their own religion as long as they did not trouble the public order. The Catholic Church's privileged position in 1860 was amended in the 1984 Concordat, to assure equal rights to other religions.

Unlike the Catholic Church, Protestants do not have a hierarchical structure and are not linked, nor are their operations covered by the concordat but by the ministry of foreign affairs and religion. According to Article XVI, the head of all foreign missions (a Protestant mission is a religious organization consisting of a minimum of five churches) has to be a Haitian minister. The minister of religion is the one who confers the title of minister or pastor.[110] A number of other articles assure the state total control of their functions (III, IV, V, VII, XIII). The "Report on Protestant Religions" continues, saying, "the relations between the Protestant churches and the state have evolved in a climate of security, confidence and mutual respect. They generally stay out of politics. When they complain about some injustice, it is not against the state or as a mouthpiece of the masses. They confine themselves to social works that are useful to Haiti.[111] Their importance should not be minimized, "cette force paisable et laborieuse est un atout sérieux pour le développement économique et social du pays," or "this peaceful and hardworking force is a winning card for the economic and social development of the country."[112] The "Report" concluded with the recommendation that the Protestants integrate their actions into a global development plan. A meeting was held on 16 November 1984 to organize the churches; forty attended. One outcome was the suggestion that the Ministry of Foreign Affairs and Religion provide two inspectors for each geographic department to oversee the activities of their denominations and establish a statistical information service to keep track of the activities of all of the faiths.[113]

Although the Pentecostals in Haiti have incorporated some of the country's folklore and include its drums in their services, most Protestant denominations are actively anti folklore and uncompromisingly anti-Voodoo.[114] This unyielding attitude toward Voodoo is at variance with Church thinking since Vatican II. Subsequently, the Church has emphasized the value of native religions and encouraged the incorporation of certain elements.

Protestant relations with the government were not perfect during the Jean-Claude Duvalier administration. Individual churchmen were arrested and tortured and, following the death of the students at Gonaïves, Protestant leaders issued a statement of condemnation. In Gonaïves at the end of November 1984, a Protestant preacher, Mr. Lebeni, was abducted in the middle of his sermon by the brother of the deputy. The faithful parishioners were beaten and the church was subsequently closed. The preacher had denounced the activities of "a powerful authority in town."[115] On 30 November 1984, a Protestant minister, Antoine Leroy, the pastor of Mission La Foi Apostolique and founder of the Centre d'Amour Chrétien, an adult education center in Port-au-Prince, was detained by authorities, as were many people connected to development projects. He was arrested again on 30 October this time departing for Miami.[116] Luc Garnier, bishop of the Episcopal Church in Haiti, recalled that the government was "against him," believing that he had been too close to his predecessor, whom François Duvalier had earlier thrown out of the country. During the Duvalier administration, Episcopal youth had "fought tyranny" with their Catholic contemporaries and spoke out in general terms about respect and in opposition to human rights abuses.

When the children were killed at Gonaïves, Bishop Garnier made a broadcast on *Radio Soleil.*[117] Gonaïves prompted other Protestant leaders to sign a statement condemning "injustice and oppression" and advocate a rapid end to the crisis. Consequently, *Radio Lumière* was shut down along with *Radio Soleil*, but because its staff was Haitian, no one was exiled. According to Bishop Garnier, Episcopalians generally take seriously the Bible injunction to pray for leaders and believe a government in power should be supported. These factors made it hard for Protestants to confront the government.

However, some of the most persistent critics of the administration were Protestants, such as the Baptist ministers Silvio Claude and Luc Nerée. Pastors were rounded up, beaten and had their churches invaded. Because of their philosophy of allegiance to sitting governments, their isolation, and the small size of their congregations, the Protestant community as a whole did not make its force felt before Gonaïves in November 1985. The Church was the leader that others followed.

Following Jean-Claude Duvalier's departure, relations with Protestant denominations did not progress as anticipated by Vatican II and by some sectors of the Haitian Church. Catholics and Methodists began to design a civics training program, the Christian Citizen Training Program, which they hoped would lead to a post 1987 election literacy training program. Their demonstration model was not successful, however. When other Protestant churches were invited to participate, according to the Rev. Alan Rocourt, former chairman of the Haitian Methodist Church, "they weren't interested. They still think their mission is to save people for Heaven. They aren't concerned with life on earth."[118]

Without planning to, Catholics and Protestants were finding themselves thrown together and confronting the same problems. Protestant and Catholic representatives served on the CEP, and were consequently both objects of attack. *Radio Lumière* was a firm supporter of the November 1987 elections, and, like *Radio Soleil*, had its AM transmitter blown up. Both Catholics and Protestants were prohibited from holding outdoor Easter rallies on Champs de Mars. Despite mutual interests, conservative members of the Church hierarchy continued to regard Protestants as brazen, self-serving interlopers.[119] "They don't understand the structure of society; they are not concerned about the rights of man. Some lack common sense; they have moved into the literacy business. Realizing that something was changing in January, they tried to get in on it."

President Manigat explained that he accepted the title of The Most Serene High Protector of Freemasons at his inauguration in order to show that when he spoke of religious liberty, he meant liberty for all the country's religions. While Manigat concluded that his action had been a source of concern for the Church, Freemasonry, a preoccupation of the nineteenth-century Haitian Church, has virtually ceased to be an issue.[120] Port-au-Prince has a temple and an annual festival, but little other influence.

The Future

Predicting how the Church will handle its long-term problems is complicated by the immediate difficulty in predicting the outcome of its current internal crisis, the division within its ranks. Bishops Constant and Ligondé were called to Rome in March 1986[121] and widely believed to have been told that the Church should get more involved with its pastoral work and withdraw from the political debate. Subsequently, Church conservatives, including much of the hierarchy, particularly bishops Ligondé and Gayot and the papal nuncio, Paulo Romeo, also have adopted this position. In the future, according to Gayot, the Church would be the "director of the conscience." Romeo summed it up succinctly when he said, "The Church should remain the Church."[122] Subsequently, many in the Church were frustrated by bishops who appeared to be more interested in what Rome wanted than what they believed the people wanted. In their view, a pro-democracy, anti-communist, hands-off position was unsatisfactory.

Among those opposing the conservatives in varying degrees were members of the *Ti légliz*, women religious, CHR, CARITAS, and liberation theologians.[123] Agreed on the need to improve the quality of life in Haiti and the legitimate and necessary involvement of the Church in the process, they differed on how it could be accomplished. It is the fear that their involvement will lead to participation in political parties, communism, or, in the most extreme case, revolution, which seems to most concern the conservative side of the Church.[124] The Church hierarchy took steps to defuse the activists, telling the CHR and Jean-Bertrand Aristide to keep a low profile,[125] removing Hugo Triest from *Radio Soleil* on 31 March 1989, and, according to rumors,[126] planning to dismiss several progressive seminarians.

The activist Church emerged from 7 February 1986 with a sense of empowerment. Its goals were to clean house and continue its work. Haitian priests and nuns, joined by others returning to Haiti from exile, approached Archbishop Ligondé at a meeting of Archdiocesan workers on 4 March 1986, and asked him to resign because of what they regarded as his collaboration with the Duvalier government. An unsigned letter on 7 March, apparently from a group of priests, made the same charges and demands.[127] In June 1986, Bishop Gayot was attacked in Cap-Haïtien at a Church meeting by a priest who called him a traitor to the revolution. The sentiment was echoed by anti-Gayot graffiti on city walls.[128]

According to Father Aristide, the solution was for a few activist members of the bourgeoisie and the masses of poor to form an alliance in a class struggle.[129] Not all Church activists were as sure as Aristide about how to proceed. Finding drawbacks in the capitalist and communist systems, the Youth of the Archdiocese of Port-au-Prince[130] spoke of the need for a new system for Haiti, a collaborative, cooperative system that includes God and stresses helping the peasants organize and become participatory.

THE CHURCH ELSEWHERE

By the late 1950s and early 1960s, Catholic scholars, participants at Vatican II, and the Bishops' Conferences were coming to an historic conclusion; the conservative and ancient Catholic Church needed fundamental change. In their opinion, the basic mission of the Church should be to be with and serve the world's poor. They recommended techniques and structures to handle this new commitment. Thirty years later, elements of this newly committed Church can be detected worldwide.

Vatican II endorsed the idea of creating an indigenous clergy. The idea bore fruit and the results are apparent in Haiti and many other countries. The African Church, seen by many as a symbol of colonialism, with its white prelates, status, and privilege, began to indigenize in the early 1960s. Black priests, African music, masses in local languages, and incorporation of tribal rituals have made the Church more meaningful for many. The Church in the Philippines also began in the 1960s to replace its foreign, elite hierarchy with Filipinos who were generally more concerned than their foreign predecessors had been in the needs of their countrymen.

Concern about the ever increasing number of baptized but non practicing Catholics, many living in remote areas without benefit of a priest but perhaps with access to a minister, challenged the Church. It needed to devise new strategies for staying in touch with its flock, and the introduction of Catholic radio stations, pastoral letters, and CEBs have all helped unify and hold together the rural Church.

Emulating the Brazilian and Colombian Churches, many other countries began to use the radio to teach and spread the gospel. The Haitian Church station, *Radio Soleil,* broadcast a wide-ranging variety of programs. With its network of transmitters, the Church made daring use of the radio to circumvent press censorship. *Radio Soleil* was the only station that dared to report the indictment of Colonel Jean-Paul Claude to the Haitians in 1988. In the Philippines, *Radio Ventus,* operated by the archdiocese in Manila, kept Filipinos in touch with events, despite the danger, and it was the only station to report the murder of Benigno Aquino in 1983.

Pastoral letters have been used by the hierarchy as a means of communication and mobilization. The Filipino bishops used pastoral letters to urge their parishioners to vote in 1984. Bishops in South Africa[131] used this medium to inform their parishioners in 1988 that it was duty of Church to oppose injustice. They tried to fortify Catholics with their pledge that if secular groups opposed to apartheid were banned, religious leaders would come fill in the gaps.

CEBs, begun in Latin America in response to the shortage of priests, have become a worldwide phenomenon. Not only have the CEBs proved to be an effective way of bringing religion to rural areas, they have allowed groups to solve problems they would not have been able to handle as individuals.

Encouraged by Vatican II, ecumenicism has made some progress, but it is suffering somewhat due to current Vatican reservations. In Haiti, ecumenical efforts are taking place, despite continued differences of opinion about the earthly role of religion and bad feelings resulting from competitiveness.[132] In Czechoslovakia, Protestants and Catholics have been sharing services in churches and in private homes.[133]

The Effects of Activism

Being in closer contact with the people it serves has made the Church increasingly aware of and sympathetic to their problems. It has led the Church to support the people in their travails. A side effect of this commitment has been that the Church has gained new respect from its parishioners. In some countries, the Church is the strongest independent institution and the mouthpiece for the people. This was the case in Haiti. In

Poland as well, the Church has become a unifying, nonpartisan defender of society, a popular institution with the power to extract concessions from the government.[134] In the Philippines during the Marcos era, the credibility of the Church caused it to become the voice of people.[135] In Paraguay, the Church was the only institution strong enough to criticize the Stroessner regime–and absorb the blows.

Wherever they have been outspoken activists the clergy and Church have become targets of retaliation. Priests, nuns, and lay workers have been murdered, exiled, and arrested. Churches have been attacked and burned and Church offices raided. In Haiti and Paraguay, thugs have stormed into the Churches during masses, attempting to kill or beat up the officiating priest or congregation, or interrupt the service to deliver their own message.[136]

The activist Church has attracted membership and clergy. One hundred thousand people participated in a pilgrimage in Czechoslovakia in 1985. The Czech hierarchy has increased and there are new female orders. The experience in Haiti was similar.

It appears that a widespread religious revival in under way, which extends beyond Catholicism. Dissatisfaction with government immorality and neglect has led many to turn to their religions for leadership. Egyptians are increasingly relying on Islamic institutions to meet the need for high quality, efficiently run services, including clinics, schools, and banks. Dr. Issan al-Irian, an Islamic fundamentalist and now a member of the Egyptian parliament, predicts that "in twenty or thirty years, all people of the world will turn back to God.[137] This is not only related to Egypt. The systems that govern the world today are going to be discredited. People must find another system. Religion is the alternative."

Working with the poor has had a consciousness-raising effect, causing many in the Church to become activists or leftists. This evolution has been a source of concern to Rome.

Archbishop Romero of El Salvador went through a personal conversion of sorts as the result of his own experience with the poor. It led him to proclaim that the Church would be the voice of the voiceless. The Chilean prelate, Cardinal Etchegaray, dared to declare that Church had the mission to defend human rights everywhere, even in Chile. In the Philippines, Cardinal Jaime Sin denounced official abuses of all kinds.

In a number of countries which house oppressive regimes, the Church or sectors of it became activists. Archbishop Sin in the Philippines, moved from a position of critical collaboration with the regime to one short of open support for Ms. Aquino. The Czechoslovakian Church took a main line role in an attempt to force the state to provide greater religious freedom.[138]

Repressive governments and inequitable social structures have caused some of the Church to move left, join guerrilla forces, and advocate revolution, as Camillo Torres Restrepo did in Colombia in the 1960s. Corruption and human rights abuses led some Filipino clergy and nuns to support the communists and others, such as Conrado Balweg, a rebel priest and NPA commander, to play an important role in the insurgent operation.

On the other hand, the Filipino Church co-opted the radical left, to some extent, through the establishment of CEBs. In Haiti, the Church also helped the poor improve their economic lot and, at the same time, reinforce their religious commitment. The question remains how far the CEBs can go, given uncooperative governments and entrenched economic systems, toward righting profound inequalities. Some Churchmen, including the current Haitian president, Jean-Bertrand Aristide, have maintained that a revolution will be required.

As a consequence of increased Church activism, the legitimate role of the Church in politics has become an important and controversial question. Many involved with the Church have come to believe that the institution has a legitimate role as a monitor of human rights, and they are comfortable with this degree of political involvement. Although increasing numbers of Church people would probably agree with two priests in the Philippines who accompanied their parishioners on a prayer march against army atrocities because "the Church has to provide more than the solace of religion and charity, it has to actively resist the system of bondage," their language and active participation would make many uncomfortable.[139] There are few Ernesto Cardinals or Camillo Torres Restrepos because most Church people still do not believe that the Church has a legitimate role to play in governments, political parties, or guerrilla groups. Church people have a tendency to attempt to create a psychic distance between themselves and politics by saying they are not "meddling in politics."[140]

In light of its increased political activity, Church-State relations may need re-examination. Concordats devised to protect the Church from dictatorships in Europe and from pressure from communist countries after World War II, may be out-of-date. The concordat covering Haiti calls for a harmony and cooperation that neither side has been able or willing to achieve. Churches may want to have more independence, and governments may want Churches to be more accountable. Former Haitian Minister of Religion Jean-Robert Estimé strongly believed that if the Church was going to act like a political party, then it had to be ready to be treated like one.[141]

The experience of activist Churches needs continued study. In the early 1960s, there were demands that the Church be more relevant in Africa. After getting a black priesthood, indigenous music, and customs incorporated in religious ceremonies in a number of countries, some of the newly Africanized Churches began to take an active role in politics. They ultimately discovered that they were unable to compete with other revolutionary forces. For one thing, the Churches were unwilling to resort to their methods. In places where revolutionaries came to power, rather than being grateful to the Church, they clamped down on it, seeing it as a threat. In Guinea, the government threw the Archbishop out of the country and removed Catholics from pivotal positions, such as the unions and radio. There was a big crackdown and persecution of the Church as well in the French Congo. A country in which the Church and State have maintained good relations was the Ivory Coast, where the Church has stayed largely non-political.[142]

The activist Church has accomplished a great deal by encouraging the poor, protecting the oppressed, and participating in the ouster of dictators. It has drawn the line at subsequently contributing to the construction of new democratic governments, shyly maintaining that this is the work of the people. In countries with little or no democratic experience, this attitude may be too modest. Hanging back was a disaster in Haiti. Even in the Philippines, where a liberal, democratic government did take over, the Church perhaps could have offered more advice. Some priests are now reporting that there has been no improvement for the poor under Aquino, that she has not been able to act against the interests of her powerful supporters and institute land reform. The CEBs are once again being called communist fronts.[143]

Cardinal Joseph Ratzinger, prefect of the Vatican's Congregation for the Doctrine of Faith, probably echoed the sentiments of the pontiff when he said on 1 November 1984 that the Church has been "collapsing" in the twenty years since Vatican II.[144] The Vatican has been doing its best to stop the cataclysm. Liberation theologians Boff and Gutiérrez were reprimanded at the Vatican. Ernesto Cardinal, the Nicaraguan minister of agriculture, was ordered not to celebrate mass because he held a government post. A number of conservative appointments have been made, particularly to countries where there had been an activist clergy and hierarchy, such as Brazil and Colombia. Issues that immediately concern women, including abortion and birth control, have been dismissed. The Church leadership in Poland, no doubt responding to Vatican conservatism, has launched a legislative initiative to repeal Poland's liberal abortion law and replace it with a prohibition that would mandate jail terms for women who have had them and doctors who perform them. Despite the desperate economic situation in Haiti, the Church has yet to endorse a nationwide family planning program.[145]

Summary

Initially, the Haitian Church seemed to lose interest, with only the CHR protesting the continued presence of Duvalierism in Haiti and pledging to continue to play an active role, accompanying the people in their quest for democracy. Moreover, following Duvalier's departure, a number of Voodoo leaders were *déshoukéd*, and the question of Church complicity was raised. The Church seemed to be reverting to its old ways.

Church-State relations between 1986 and 1990 were varied. The good relations between the Church and Namphy soured by Fall 1987 over human rights and elections. Relations between the Church and Leslie Manigat were poor from the start, due to the circumstances of the election, the inauguration, and a program which seemed to prejudice the Church. Relations were bad throughout Namphy's short second presidency. Relations improved with Avril and were generally conciliatory through 1989. It is obvious that the Church, or its hierarchy at any rate, has had second thoughts about the political aspects of the social mission of the Church.

The Church has undergone some remarkable changes elsewhere. As in Haiti, the tendency has been toward indigenization of the clergy and services, and adoption of some new tools to make up for a lack of clergy, such as the media, lay workers, and CEBs. As a consequence of its new mission, the Church has gained respect, converts, and new clergy. Through its identification with the poor, it has become more socially and politically involved and critical of governments that perpetrate the status quo, and repressive governments increasingly regard the Church as a major enemy. However, the appropriate role of the Church in social and political matters is not unambiguous. While it was all right for the Church to lead Haitians and Filipinos out of dictatorships, the Vatican has been unwilling to have it participate in the establishment of democracy.

NOTES

1. John P. Hogan, "Haiti's Brief Hour of Hope," review of *The Rainy Season* by Amy Walentz, *Commonweal* 116, no. 16 (22 September 1989): 507. Hogan, a former director of Catholic Relief in Haiti, credits the Church with being the principal institution in Haiti from the late-1970s until roughly mid-1987, giving impetus to peasant organization and development, literacy training, human rights, and support for the 1987 Constitution. After that, there was change. "Institutional self-interest, the period of *déshoukaj*, and the events of 1987, however appeared to burst the institutional seams. Their [the bishops'] responses were few and diluted with ambiguity. Even Bishop Romelus remained silent."

2. Following the pope's appeal to the Haitian Church on the morning of 9 March 1983, he addressed the opening of CELAM. At that meeting, he warned against clerical involvement in ideology or politics. Apparently this later message is the one that the pope conveyed to the bishops following 7 February 1986.

3. Conference of Haitian Bishops, *Message Pastoral des Evêques d'Haïti* (Port-au-Prince: CHB, 7 February 1986).

4. Joseph B. Treaster, "Stop the Killing, Church in Haiti Asks," *New York Times,* 10 February 1986, A4.

5. Marlise Simons, "Haiti's New Era is Unfolding Slowly," *New York Times*, 24 February 1986, A3.

6. Léopold Berlanger Jr., president and general director, IHRED, interview with author, Montana Hotel, Port-au-Prince, 5 July 1986.

An opposing explanation was given by a businessperson in Pétionville, who had been critical of the Church throughout the Duvalier era. In her opinion the Church did not have any solutions to the country's problems. *Radio Soleil* had baited people, encouraging them to riot, but to no avail.

7. *Message de la Conférence Episcopale d'Haïti, Priorités et Changements: Haïti Liberée*, 15 April 1986 (delivered over *Radio Soleil* on 15 March 1986). This message stressed the need for agricultural reform; jobs; economic political and, social decentralization; and foreign assistance. It also called for removal of former Duvalierists from the government, respect for human rights, and an analysis of the new laws concerning the constitution and political parties prior to their publication.

8. Hugo Triest, interview with author, *Radio Soleil* Headquarters, Port-au-Prince, 14 July 1986.

9. Conference of Haitian Religious, *Document d'Information et de Réflexion Produit à l'Intention des Religieux Par le Bureau de la CHR* (Port-au-Prince: CHR, 27 February 1986).

10. Henri Tinco, "L'Eglise Haïtienne Débordée Par les Revendications," *Le Nouvelliste*, 11 April 1986 (reprinted from *Le Monde*, 9 April 1986).

11. Papal announcement to a general audience on 12 February 1986 at the Vatican.

12. It is possible that the red scare which affected Church thinking following Jean-Claude Duvalier's departure has led to undue protection for a very conservative element in the Church. In July 1989, Father Sicot, an old *macoute* friend of the Duvaliers who openly favored Jean-Claude's return, was found to be storing gasoline and guns at his home in Kenscoff. To date, the bishops have not said anything about him.

13. Despite efforts to quiet Aristide by removing him from his Church, his order, and summoning him to Rome to explain himself, clearly he has not been silenced. See "Priest Calls for Arrest of 'Murderers' by 29 March," Port-au-Prince *Radio Antilles Internationales* in French, 1230 GMT, 26 March 1990, FBIS-LAT-90–060, 28 March 1990, 30.

14. Bill Quigley, interview with author, Wheaton, MD, 19 July 1989. Quigley, an American priest who has lived on the island of La Gonâve since 1974, described the CHR as having lost its vigor, or, as he put it, its "umph." He, along with a number of other priests, did not attend its May meeting.

15. Simons, "Haiti's New Era is Unfolding Slowly."

16. Julia Preston, "Voodoo Adherents Attacked in Haiti," *Washington Post*, 17 May 1986.

17. Max Beauvoir, *houngan* and agronomist, interview with author, at his residence and *humfort, Le Péristyle* de Mariani, Port-au-Prince, 13 July 1986.

When I drove up to the *houngan's Péristyle* on 12 July by appointment, the road was blocked by a locked gate. After giving my name to an armed guard and waiting while he communicated with someone by walkie-talkie, I was allowed to continue into the compound. I parked, looked around and waited again until a servant appeared, inquiring my business. I should wait there. After a few minutes she reappeared and took me inside. Max Beauvior was in his study but he apologized, saying we would have to postpone our appointment until the next day; he was going to have to leave unexpectedly. With that, he and his family rushed into his car. At that moment, Beauvoir noticed that one of my tires was flat. I should follow him to a service station. So saying, he shot out of the driveway and onto the road with me in pursuit. Several miles later, he swerved into a gas station, jumped out of his car to be greeted warmly by an attendant. He asked the man to put air in my tire and told me where to get a new tire in Port-au-Prince. I should call tomorrow to see if he was still in the country, and off he sped. I was astonished to find him alive, well, and home the next day, quietly ensconced in his study and ready for a lengthy interview.

18. Joseph Eliantus, *Houngan* (deceased), interview with author, Delmas, Haiti, 9 July 1986.

19. Preston, "Voodoo Adherents Attacked in Haiti."

20. Max-Abner Etienne, "Interview de l'Archêveque François Wolff Ligondé," *Jeune Haïti*, 23 April 1986.

21. Preston, "Voodoo Adherents Attacked in Haiti." However, Verrier added that Catholics cannot accept mixture with Voodoo.

22. Bill Quigley, interview with author, Wheaton, MD, 12 July 1989. According to Quigley, the *déshoukaj* was simply "street justice." Nothing was organized against the Voodoo priests.

23. Dominique Levanti, reporter *Agence France Presse*, interview with author, *Agence France Presse* headquarters, Port-au-Prince, 7 July 1986.

24. Paulo Romeo, interview with author, the nunciature, Port-au-Prince, 11 July 1986.

25. Max Beauvoir, interview with author, Le Péristyle de Mariani, Port-au-Prince, 13 July 1986.

26. Ibid.

27. Leslie Manigat, interview with author, Woodrow Wilson Center, Washington, D.C., 9 December 1988.

28. This is not to say that the entire Church was passive in the between 1986-1990; far from it. Some individuals were quite active.

See Hogan, "Haiti's Brief Hour of Hope." On page 505 Hogan wrote, "The opposition [in post-Duvalier Haiti] usually functioned under a broad protective umbrella of Catholic church organizations."

29. Conference of Haitian Religious, *Document d'Information et de Réflexion Produit à L'Intention des Religieux Par le Bureau de la CHR*, 27 February 1986. In this document the CHR detailed a number of problems confronting Haiti, criticized the government for its performance, and concluded that is was incapable of resolving them.

30. Conference Episcopal d'Haïti, *Message Pastorale de la Conférence Episcopale d'Haïti au Peuple de Dieu*, 1 May 1986.

31. Nina Shea and Leslie Hunter, *The Current Status of Human Rights in Haiti* (Puebla Institute, 24 March 1988), 19.

32. Clara Germani, "Haitian from all Walks of Life Say Military Government Must Go," *Christian Science Monitor*, 9 July 1987. The striking Haitians were demanding a new caretaker government to include a human rights official, a supreme court justice, and Catholic and Protestant representative. Hugo Triest gave them his advice, "If you leave these people [the old Duvalierists] in, they are never going to allow a real election."

33. Yvon Joseph, "Impact of the Political Situation on Community-Based Development Work of the Catholic Church." Seminar for the Coordination in Development Conference, New York, 21 October 1988, 2–5. Joseph presented the chronology of events leading to the downfall of *Mission Alpha* and put considerable blame on the bishops. In an answer to charges in August 1987 that it was a communist organization, the Bishops' Conference issued a pastoral letter entitled, *Some Answers on Ti-Légliz and Eglise Popular*. The way the theme was presented gave the impression that *Misyon Alpha*, the *Ti-Légliz*, and the movement for *L'Eglise Popular* were being infiltrated.

34. Shea and Hunter, *The Current Status of Human Rights in Haiti*, 48.

35. Joseph, "Impact of the Political Situation," 3. According to Joseph, the government accused the Church of being responsible for the [election] disaster. Subsequently, "Over the national radio and television network a huge campaign was mounted against the Church."

36. Nina Shea and Leslie Hunter, *Haiti's Reign of Terror: Report on Chronic Religious Repression and Other Human Rights Abuse* (Washington, D.C.: Puebla Institute, September 1988).

37. Episcopal Conference of Haiti, *Statement on Crisis*, 7 December 1987.

38. Other signatories included the Haitian Federation of Protestant Schools, the Haitian League of Human Rights, CATH, and some other unions. They demanded that the government abide by the 1987 Constitution and reinstate the CEP. The signatories concluded by reminding the military that it worked for the country.

39. It included all three trade unions, six major human rights groups, peasant and student organizations, and the Group of Democratic Agreement.

40. Ian Simpson, "Haiti," United Press International Report (Port-au-Prince: UPI, 15 January 1988). Others arrested included peasant leaders, *Radios Haïti Inter* and *Métropole* employees, and numerous political activists.

41. *Catholic Bishops Conference Statement on January 17 Elections*, Cable to Secretary of State, 26 March 1987.

42. Leslie Manigat, interview with author, Woodrow Wilson Center, Washington, D.C., 9 December 1988. According to the president, one of the bishops did ask for an invitation, then did not attend.

43. Ibid. According to president Manigat, some priests wanted to have a *Te Deum* elsewhere later in the day, but he did not want it held on the side. The president explained that the previous government had not asked for this ceremony, so he did not want to request one. However, Manigat said, had he been sure the Church would have done it, he would have risked asking for it.

44. Ibid. President Manigat explained that by accepting this title and wearing their decoration, he was trying to make the point that there would be religious liberty in Haiti for everyone. in his view, "we have many sources of mysticism in Haiti—the Carismatics, Rosecutions, Freemasons, Voodoo, etc. What is needed is a convergence of mysticism, an ecumenicalism of mysticism."

45. Ibid. President Manigat was aware that these comments were interpreted as giving Voodoo status and he believed that the papal nuncio was concerned. Someone informed him after the inauguration that the nuncio had told him that Manigat would promote Voodoo.

It is likely that Manigat anticipated the impact of his actions and words and, at least initially, enjoyed the anxiety they provoked. The concern of some Catholic institutions and individuals did not dim.

In September 1988, the Puebla Institute, a lay Roman Catholic human rights group, wrote in *Haiti's Reign of Terror* that "the Voodoo promotion campaign seemed part of a larger effort to diminish the importance and influence of the Catholic Church. It was also undoubtedly employed to develop a grass roots constituency for an illegitimate government which came to power without popular support" (61). In the end, President Manigat needed the Church, but it was alienated.

46. FBIS-LAT-88–028, Port-au-Prince, 11 February 1988, 6. Marc Bazin, who was in the audience and interviewed by FBIS afterward, took exception, as others did, to Manigat's apparent view that the Church should limit itself to matters of the spirit. In his opinion, "the Church had a role of capital importance to guide and enlighten, to work for the liberation of Haitians, to be involved with social and pastoral matters."

47. Leslie Manigat, interview with author, Woodrow Wilson Center, Washington, D.C., 9 December 1988. The president said he had met with some of the bishops, excluding Gayot. His contact with Ligondé and Constant were good. He thought he would be able to cooperate with Laroche, Angenor, and Gayot. He assessed his relations with Kébreaux as "normal" and with Romélus as "mixed."

Manigat provided an example of how the Church tried to keep its distance from him. The Vatican presented the name of a new bishop to the CNG, which brought the matter to him. Manigat indicated that the choice would be fine with him and, on becoming president, he approved the appointment as promised. However, when the time came for the official ceremony, the new bishop tried to avoid it so as not to be seen swearing allegiance to the Haitian Constitution—although it was obligatory.

48. "President-Elect Manigat's Government Program," Cable to the secretary of state from the American Embassy, Port-au-Prince, 4 February 1988.

Summary of the April 1987 eighty-six page RDNP electoral platform entitled "Changing Life to Ensure Better Tomorrows for All." In a section devoted to education the author write that "the indicators are bad: high illiteracy rate, mediocre access, and high dropout rate, over reliance on private and church schools, irrelevant methods and curriculum, overcrowded classes, inadequate testing, aloof teacher-pupil relation, poor financing, a tiny and lousy university" (5). Since the Church has been historically heavily involved with education, in Haiti, this was a particularly unpleasant progress report.

49. Leslie Manigat, interview with author, Woodrow Wilson Center, Washington, D.C., 9 December 1988. President Manigat said that he was aware of a file concerning plans to amend the concordat begun by the previous government, but that he never saw it.

50. An unintended side effect of this presidential decision was to create interfaith solidarity.

See Shea and Hunter, *Haiti's Reign of Terror*. On 12 May 1988, *Radio Soleil*, in an editorial broadcast, pointed out that Catholics and Protestant had both been prohibited form celebrating their Easter rally on the Champs de Mars.

51. Leslie Manigat, interview with author, Woodrow Wilson Center, Washington, D.C., 9 December 1988. According to the president, the papal nuncio launched a call for Church unity, reconciliation and support for the government at Sacre Coeur on 12 June. Afterward, he began the *Cantique Domine*, which recognizes the president and asks that prayers be said for him.

52. Press censorship might have been an issue had the government endured. in February, news organizations were invited via *communiqué* from the High Command not to reprint unsubstantiated allegations about Jean-Claude Paul's drug dealings. When Paul was indicted, only *Radio Soleil* printed his name.

53. Conference of Haitian Bishops, *Déclaration des Evêques d'Haïti Sur La Situation Defficile que Traverse le Pays* (Port-au-Prince: CHB, undated [after 4 August 1988]).

54. *Haiti Insight* 1, no. 1 (May 1989), published by the National Coalition for Haitian Refugees. Namphy told reporters during an interview on the Dominican television show, "*Uno Mas Uno*," on 13 April 1989, that he held "the Catholic Church responsible for the dozens of deaths during the 29 November 1987 elections."

55. Kyle Richmond, "Picking Up the Pieces," *The Times*, August-September 1987, 9. Jacquelin was from the slums of Port-au-Prince. He was a literacy teacher with *Misyen Alpha*, a church organization that was currently providing basic education to 90,000 Haitiains. The goal of the organization was to make 3 million Haitiains literate within 5 years. Harrassment of the organization was common. It was accused of being a communist trend. When Jacquelin was abducted and disappeared, the assumption was that he was murdered.

56. The human rights abuses in late 1989 appear to have revived the critical faculties of the bishops. See Conference of Haitian Bishops, *Declaration de la Conférence Épiscopale d'Haïti au Peuple Haïtien* (Port-au-Prince: CHB, 7 November 1989). See also Conference of Haitian Bishops, *Declaration of the Haitian Bishops Conference* (Port-au-Prince: CHB, 26 January 1990).

57. "Anti-Avril Demonstration in Gonaïves 6 March," Port-au-Prince, *Radio Soleil* Network in Creole, 1980 GMT, 6 March 1990, 13–14.

58. "Two More Reportedly Killed in Port-au-Prince," Port-au-Prince, *Agence France Presse* in Spanish, 0226 GMT, 8 March 1990, 13.

59. Ibid., 4.

Following the coup in 1991, which threw Jean-Bertrand Aristide out of power, President Bush has attempted to force the military to relinquish control through the imposition of a trade embargo.

60. Hérold Jean-François, "Ertha Pascal Trouillot: Sans Serment ni Canon une Femme pour le Changement," *Balance* (21–27 March 1990): 2. Jean-François reviews the political history of the past four years. Despite his evident enthusiasm for the provisional president, he recognizes that she could have problems controlling the Army and opposition forces, and gaining popular and international support.

Trouillot fulfilled her mandate, but not easily. Before turning the presidency over to Jean-Bertrand Aristide, who was elected to that office in December 1990, former interior minister, Roger Lafontant, tried to oust her in a coup. In office, Aristide refused to let her leave the country until his administration could investigate whether she had used government funds illegally.

61. "Father Aristide Calls for General Consensus, Port-au-Prince *Radio Métropole* in Creole, 0950 GMT, 16 February 1990, FBIS-LAT-90–034, 20 February 1990, 15.

62. "Soleil Continues to poll Parties on Elections," Port-au-Prince *Radio Soleil* Network in Creole, 1000 GMT, 16 February 1990, FBIS-LAT-90–034, 20 February 1990, 15.

63. "Fires, Protests Reported," Port-au-Prince, *Radio Antilles Internationales* in Creole, 1230 GMT, 9 March 1990, FBIS-LAT-90–048, 12 March 1990, 5.

64. "Aristide: Avril 'Not Willing to Leave Country," Port-au-Prince, *Radio Antilles Internationales* in French, 1830 GMT, 10 March 1990, FBIS-LAT-90–048, 12 March 1990.

65. Lee Hockstader, "U.S. Envoy Spoke with Avril of Nixon's Final Days Before He Resigned," *Washington Post*, 11 March 1990. Hockstader identifies Father Adrien as the leader of the recently organized Group of Twelve, who threatened a general strike if Avril refused to leave the country.

See "Haïti à L'Heure de L'Opposition," *Balance* (21–27 March 1990): 5. Father Adrien was described as the "charismatique" and a generally unknown figure (despite an activist past) who "played a fundamental role in the process leading to the downfall of Avril."

See also "Interview Père Antoine Adrien, L'Architecte de la Transition Actuelle," *Haïti en Marche* (21–27 April 1990): 1. Father Adrien identifies the events which led to the downfall of Avril: the tortured prisoners paraded on TV; *Onè Respé's* successful telegram to the president of Taiwan urging him to withhold assistance to the Avril government; and the arrest and mistreatment of members of *Onè Respé*. Adrien describes how consensus for the departure, choice of president, type of government, and transition were achieved.

66. Conference of Haitian Bishops, *Chare Fondamental Pour le Passage à Une Société Démocratique Selon La Donctrine et L'Expérience de l'Eglise* (Port-au-Prince: CHB, 27 June 1986).

67. Francçois Gayot, interview with author, Episcopate, Cap-Haïtien, 10 July 1986.

68. Conféence Haïtienne des Evêques, *Message de la Conférence Episcopale d'Haïti*, reprinted in *Haïti Libérée* (15 April 1986). Originally delivered on 15 March 1986 by *Radio Soleil.*

69. Etienne, "Interview de l'Archeêveque François Wolff Ligondé."

70. *"Mission Alpha:* What We Do," Port-au-Prince, 1987. In a writing sample from this flyer, a participant in the program describes her plight and calls on others to join her in overcoming the shared problems of other poor Haitians, as she practices writing. "I am thirty-seven years old. Imakila Santil. I am a woman. I have been in the Center for six months. Being sick is not sweet. Food is very expensive. We don't have water for our needs. We are hungry . Let's get rid of sickness."

71. Toumédia, ed., *Haïti-Pape 83* (Port-au-Prince: Imprimerie Henri Deschamps, 1983), 9, 10.

72. Jean-Robert Estimé, interview with author, Wheaton, MD, 29 March 1988.

73. Conference of Haitian Religious, *Global Plan of the Conference of Haitian Religious* (Port-au-Prince, CHR, 1983). The Conference agreed to adopt a new pastoral attitude toward Voodoo and *plaçage,* the informal marital arrangement of many rural Haitians.

74. Conference of Haitian Bishops, *Pastoral Letter,* 3 March 1984.

75. Member of the Haitian Church hierarchy, interview with author, United States, 1988.

76. Conference of Haitian Religious, *Document d'Information et de Réflexion,* 10. In a section entitled "Traps and Temptations," the CHR comments on the *déshoukaj,* saying the Duvaliers had developed a perversion and corruption of Voodoo, as they tried to do with other cults and religions. however, they wondered whether the perpetrators of this *déhoukaj* were distinguishing between crimes, corruption, *macoutism,* and religion and if this brutal operation did not risk the destruction of rural life.

77. Estelle Beauvoir and Comité Déshoukaj, "Lynching of *Mambos* and *Houngans* in the North," 16 April 1986.

The Beauvoirs chronicled post-Duvalier anti-Voodoo behavior. In a document entitled "Some Declarations Heard on *Radio Lumière*" (the Protestant Radio Station) on 16 March 1986, they heard one minister say, "we have to pursue it [Voodoo] until it is *déhoukéd* for good." A second person added, "there are too many *houngans* in Haiti." A third person described Voodoo as "the national curse." In order to be cured, Voodoo and magic would have to be *déhoukéd.*

78. Max Beauvoir "Réunion des *Mambos* et *Houngans* d'Haïti," 16 January 1986. Probably intended for publication in a Haitian newspaper.

79. Elizabeth Abbott, *Haiti: The First Inside Account: The Duvaliers and their Legacy* (New York: McGraw-Hill, 1988), 323. Elizabeth Abbott writes that the Duvaliers and Bennetts held a last-minute, Voodoo ceremony at the palace in order "to settle their accounts and guarantee that whoever succeeded them would find the presidential throne uncomfortable indeed. That night at the palace the lights burned late; [they had] summoned Ernes Simon, one of the *houngans* traditionally called to the palace, Michèle ordered a *cérémonie* to curse the presidential bed so the next person occupying it would die a horrible death there." The ritual required two unbaptized babies, stolen from the General Hospital, because there wasn't time to get them from the usual sources. After the incantations and prayers, and the sacrifice offered and accepted, all that remained was for "the secret burial [of] the dead infants reeking and sticky with blood and rum and pocked with morsels of chopped herbs."

80. Shea and Hunter, *Haiti's Reign of Terror,* 60.

81. Jean-Robert Estimé, interview with author, Wheaton, MD, 17 November 1989. Ambassador Estimé maintained that Silvio Claude had acted as head of his political party rather than as a pastor. In his view, "the Catholic Church had been much more politically active against Jean-Claude from 1982 to 1986 than had the Protestants, who only came in at the end of January, 1986."

82. Castel Haiti, *La Participation Chrétienne Au Développement En Haïti: Rapport Du Séminaire Sur La participation Chrétienne Au Développement En Haïti* (Port-au-Prince: Castel Haïti, 9–13 July 1973), 9.

83. Ibid., 12–15.

84. Ibid., 34–36.

85. Ibid., 57. The same problems that historically confronted Haiti continued to exits. Pierre Dorismond from the Haitian ministry of education reported that while there were increasing numbers of Catholic schools, and more students attending state schools, over eighty-two percent of Haitian children did not attend any school.

86. Haiti, *La Participation Chrétienne*, 63–64. Rosny Desroches, a Methodist minister and director of the New Bird School remarked on the predominance of Catholic schools in urban areas in 1971. One hundred and sixty of the two hundred urban primary schools were Catholic, whereas about half the students in rural areas were attending Protestant schools.

87. Some of these issues have been addressed since 1973. Bill Quigley, interview with the author, Lanham, MD, 19 July 1989. Quigley reported that he found the education system had been "Africanized" by the time he arrived in 1974, but the next step, which he termed "Haitianizing," remained to be done.

88. Haiti, *La Participation Chrétienne*, 67.

89. Ibid., 70–71.

90. Ibid., 85.

91. Pax Christi International, *Report of the Mission of the Pax Christi International to Haiti* Erie, PA.: Pax Christi International, 1986), 110.

92. Charles Poisset Romain, *Le Protestantisme dans la Société Haïtienne* (Port-au-Prince: Imprimerie Henri Deschamps, 1986).

93. A priest who has lived in Haiti for many years said he works with Protestants all the time and serves with them on various road and water committees

94. René Poirier, interview with author, Villa Manrèse, Port-au-Prince, 12 July 1986.

95. Luc Garnier, interview with author, bishopric, Pétionville, 14 July 1986.

96. Walter Turnbull, telephone interview with author, Kenscoff, Haiti, 7 July 1986.

97. Pax Christi International, *Report of the Mission to Haiti*, 88.

98. Ibid., 112.

99. Dominique Levanti, journalist for the *Agence France Presse*, interview with author, *Agence France Presse* headquarters, Port-au-Prince, 7 July 1986.

100. David Nicholls, "Haiti: The Rise and Fall of Duvalierism," *Third World Quarterly* 8, no. 4 (October 1986): 1239.

Rod Prince, *Haiti: Family Business* (London: Latin America Bureau Limited, 1985). Prince calculated that there were about fifty largely U.S.-financed evangelical denominations each with between thirty and three thousand members in Port-au-Prince.

101. Conference of Haitian Bishops, *Open Letter to the Heads of the Three Branches of the Government* (Port-au-Prince: CHB, 24 November 1984).

102. Bill Quigley speaking at a meeting at St. Charles Church, Arlington, Va. on 12 July 1989. Father Quigley said the Protestants, particularly the evangelicals, misguide people, telling them they will be rewarded in heaven. Consequently, they do not try to improve their economic situation on earth.

103. Bill Quigley, St. Charles Church. Father Quigley described the organization of his parish in La Gonâve and its reliance on lay workers. Twelve chapels offered services three times each Sunday. "Committed lay workers" preached very good homilies, "ten times better than his," and willingly visited the sick. His best chapels were run by women, both of whom were teachers. He concluded that he would not know what to do without these lay workers.

104. Luc Garnier, interview with author, bishopric, Pétionville, Haiti, 7 July 1986.

105. Romain, *Le Protestantisme dans la Société Haïtienne*, 312.

106. Marian McClure, "The Catholic Church and Rural Social Change: Priests, Peasant Organizations, and Politics in Haiti" (PhD. diss., Harvard University, November 1985), 223–24.

107. Jean-Robert Estimé, interview with author, Wheaton, MD, 19 April 1988.

108. Ibid. In an earlier interview on 19 March 1988, the ambassador had pointed to the *Commission Mixte* as one more example of the failure of the Church and state to come to "meaningful conclusions." Apparently the Commission was only successful as it related to relations between the Protestant denominations and the state.

109. J. M. Jan, *Collecta Pour L'Historie Religieuse du Diocése du Cap-Haïtien*, vol. 2 (Port-au-Prince: Editions Henri Deschamps, 1960), 165–66.

110. Ministry of Foreign Affairs and Religion, "Les Eglises Protestantes ou Cultes Reformes," Article 6, 13 December 1985, 3.

111. Ibid.

112. Ibid., 6.

113. Ibid.

114. Romain, *Le Protestantisme dans la Société Haïtienne*, 312, 171–73. Romain reported that in some churches members would go to the home of former Voodoo adherents and destroy all of the sacred memorabilia, or they would go to the home of former Catholics and break all of the images, and candles to show that a rupture had occurred. Romain remarked on the divisive impact on families of this sort of conversion.

115. Pax Christi International, *Report of the Mission to Haiti*, 79, 80.

116. *The Amnesty International Reports 1975 through 1986*, (London: Amnesty International, 1985). AIR 1985, Ambassador Jean-Robert Estimé, 165–69.

117. Luc Garnier, interview with author, Bishopric, Pétionville, Haiti, 14 July 1986.

118. Richmond, "Picking Up the Pieces," *The Times*, August-September 1987.

119. Member of the Church hierarchy, interview with author, Port-au-Prince 11 July 1986.

120. Leslie Manigat, interview with author, Woodrow Wilson Center, Washington, D.C., 9 December 1988. Leslie Manigat's interest in Freemasonry was political as well as persona. in the 1970s, he had been initiated into the Grand Lodge in France, a mystical branch of masonry.

121. Marlise Simons, "Haitian Prelate is Under Attack," *New York Times*, 3 April 1986.

122. Paul Romeo, interview with author, nunciature, Port-au-Prince, 11 July 1986. The nuncio continued, saying that while it was logical for the Church to work for democracy, it should not prepare financial plans for the country. This should be the work of the people.

123. See *Declaration of a Group of Priests Regarding the Radio Soleil Affair*, Haiti 6 July 1989 (translated by the Washington Office on Haiti 31 July 1989). The authors of the *Declaration* said the bishops were always calling for dialogue but were not doing it. "As the position of the Bishops' Conference gets more rigid every day, we have decided

to make this declaration. . . ." The substance was that they opposed the bishops' unexplained decision to fire the nine members of *Radio Soleil* and "pray to God to permit *Radio Soleil* to take up its work again in service to the poor, as the voice of the voiceless in our country."

124. A Haitian bishop recently said he was no longer going to use the term *Ti-légliz* because it implied that there is more than one Church in Haiti.

125. By 1986, the bishops were trying to get Father Aristide to leave the country and go to Canada, but he refused to leave or even moderate his sermons.

Radio Nationale. FBIS-LAT-88–028, "Leslie Manigat Delivers Inaugural Address," Port-au-Prince, 7 February 1988, 12. Following President Manigat's inauguration, Aristide told reporters "the committed Church is ready to fight Mr. Manigat's diabolical government." He thought Haitians should go on the streets armed, not empty-handed because Leslie Manigat was going to make a dictatorship, and that this view was shared by a large number of priests.

In September 1988, Father Aristide was in Church when it was stormed. Aristide's parishioners defended him but a number of them were killed or injured. Nevertheless, he was not giving up, "God is with us. The cleaning up has just begun."

Bill Quigley, interview with author, Lanham, MD, 19 July 1989. Quigley explained that on 8 November 1989, Aristide was removed from his Church, expelled from his order, and scheduled for a hearing at the Vatican. His plight elicited support in Haiti (graffiti on walls in Port-au-Prince proclaimed, "Aristide or no Church"), and from abroad. Forty-eight Latin American priests soon offered him their support.

126. Bill Quigley, interview with author, Lanham, MD, 19 July 1989. Quigley reported that a number of seminarians had been dismissed in the past couple of years.

127. Simons, "Haitian Prelate is Under Attack."

128. While these attacks were undoubtedly personally embarrassing, they were not obviously effective—the Vatican does not have a history of responding to that kind of pressure. The criticism clearly did not hurt Gayot, who was subsequently promoted to archbishop and appears to be priming himself to become a cardinal. Two adjunct bishops have been appointed to work with Ligondé but he has not been replaced.

129. Kyle Richmond, "Haiti's Aristide: Hunger, Injustice, Slavery, Capitalism Have No Religion," *Inter-America Press*, 12 November 1987.

130. Youth of the Archdiocese of Port-au-Prince. *Message of the Youth of the Archdiocese of Port-au-Prince*, 25–27 July 1986.

131. William Claiborne, "Catholic Clerics Vow Battle South African State," *Washington Post*, 12 March 1988, 18.

132. The Vatican Secretariat for Promoting Christian Unity (SPUC) successfully completed an initial round of dialogues in 1982. In light of its progress, a second round of negotiations was undertaken to see whether Roman Catholicism and Anglicanism could recognize each other's priest and bishops, thus ending four and a half centuries of separation between two major wings of Christianity. however, the appointment of a female Episcopal bishop in Massachusetts in February 1988, with others scheduled in Canada and New Zealand, derailed negotiations because the Church maintains that bishops, like Christ's disciples, should be male.

133. William Echikson, "A Czech Who's Shaking the System," *Christian Science Monitor*, 22 August 1988.

134. Jackson Diehl, "Solidarity-Church Ties Seen Fraying," *Washington Post*, 16 May 1989, A-14.

135. U.S. Congress, Senate, Select Committee on Intelligence, *The Philippines: A Situation Report*, Washington, D.C.: GPO, 1 November 1985, 13.

136. Clara Germani, "Pope Visits Latin American as Church Faces Tougher Times," *Christian Science Monitor*, 9 May 1988.

137. Robin Wright, "Quiet Revolution: Islamic Movement's New Phase," *Christian Science Monitor*, 6 November 1987, 19.

138. Echikson, "A Czech Who's Shaking the System," 28.

139. Kristin Helmore, "Priest Helped Philippine Poor Resist System of Virtual Serfdom," *Christian Science Monitor*, 21 March 1988, 12–13.

140. William Claiborne, "Catholic Clerics Vow Battle South African State." In a pastoral letter, six South African bishops said the Church had the duty to oppose injustice but did not want to be construed as "meddling in politics. However, if any government violated basic human rights then it was the duty of the Church to point this out and plead for redress."

141. Jean-Robert Estimé, interview with author, Wheaton, MD, 29 March 1988.

142. Helmore, "Priest Helped Philippine Poor," 12–13.

143. Ibid.

144. Peter Hebblethwaite, *In the Vatican* (Bethesda, MD: Adler and Adler, 1986), 89.

145. Conference of Latin American Religious Superiors, *Message to the Conference of Haitian Religious*, Port-au-Prince, 20 October 1983, 4. The Major Superiors, who assembled the Conference of Latin American Superiors, "deplored" the fact that *Global Plan*, which reflected a new model of religious life recommended by the pope, did not get more publicity. They took exception to the 1983 Constitution that "gives privileges to the state at the expense of the nation." They lamented a number of events and circumstances which have made the situation of the people worse, such as the loss of their pigs. But despite these concerns for the welfare of Haitians, they also criticized the pharmaceutical companies and their "chemical products, which are used in the most crude manner to sterilize people and control our birth rate. This creates serious problems for our Christian conscience while we try to teach responsible parenthood."

7

Plus Ça Change

This book has investigated the history of Haiti and the presence of the Catholic Church to understand the role of the Church during the Jean-Claude Duvalier era. An epilogue seems appropriate in light of recent events. In 1990, when the first, unambiguously democratic, Haitian elections were held since the ouster of Jean-Claude Duvalier, the winner was Jean-Bertrand Aristide, a Catholic priest. This chapter comments on his brief presidency and its political and economic consequences.

THE JEAN-BERTRAND ARISTIDE PRESIDENCY

The transfer of power from caretaker chief of State, Supreme Court Justice Ertha Pascal Trouillot, to an elected president on 7 February 1991 was unexpected and unprecedented. The winner was after all, not only a civilian, but a controversial, outspoken, activist Catholic priest. Few observers expected Jean-Bertrand Aristide to be allowed to take office, or, if that occurred, to last long in office. The predictions proved right.

Elections

The elections on 16 December 1990 were unusually smooth and honest. The considerable pre-election press coverage and the presence of international observer teams from the United Nations and the Organization of American States, and an independent team headed by former U.S. President Jimmy Carter, contributed to the success.

The leading candidates were Marc Bazin and Jean-Bertrand Aristide. Bazin was a senior World Bank official who had lived in the United States for a number of years and was consequently referred to as the "American" candidate. This *soubriquet*, together with his absence from Haiti during much of the Jean-Claude era, contributed to his defeat.

245

In contrast, the other candidate, Jean-Bertrand Aristide, had not only been in Haiti calling for Duvalier's departure, but subsequently spearheaded efforts to eliminate residual traces of Duvalierism.

As we have seen, after the ouster of Duvalier, conservative forces in the Church both inside and outside the country led the institution to retreat from its activist role. Consequently, the irrepressible Aristide, with his flamboyant manner and insistence on a new social order, became a special source of irritation. On the other hand, many Haitians came to adore him. On election day, the 37 year old "Titid," or Little Aristide, as he was affectionately called by supporters, garnered more than 60 percent of the vote.

If much of the Church was unhappy about the election outcome, it was not alone. The nation's wealthy elite, military, non-sectarians, and Voodoo supporters were also distressed. They viewed Aristide as a threat to their continued well-being.

The forces arrayed against Aristide were so substantial that many people concluded that an Aristide presidency was unlikely. Even though anti-Americanism had been one of Aristide's historic themes, once the outspoken priest had been elected, high-level U.S. officials, including Bernard W. Aronson, assistant secretary of state for inter-American affairs in the Bush presidency, pledged that the United States would respect the outcome. The Haitian military did not.

The Expulsion

On the morning of 30 September 1991, President Aristide, accompanied by the French Ambassador, was stopped in his car on the way to the palace by soldiers. Later that day, he was forced to leave the country.[1]

His expulsion was accompanied by widespread military violence. Anti-Aristide soldiers rampaged in Port-au-Prince, invading neighborhoods to kill his supporters. This violence was not restricted to the capital. In Les Cayes, one of its victims was Silvio Claude, the ardent anti-Duvalierist and perennial Protestant presidential candidate. He died after a tire had been placed around his neck and set on fire, in a gruesome procedure referred to as "necklacing."

On 3 October, the military held a news conference to introduce the new *Junta* and explain its rationale for destabilizing the Aristide presidency. The triumvirate led by General Raoul Cedras, the head of the *Junta*, Colonel Alix Silva, his deputy, and Colonel Henri Robert Marc Charles, a former military attaché in Washington, justified their intervention on the basis of what they termed Aristide's "flagrant abuses of power." The most serious: he had undermined the Constitution. These men did not mention that Aristide had also retired the army high command and was training a private security force. Neither did they mention dissatisfaction among the enlisted men with the Aristide administration.

The military undoubtedly had the support of others the president had challenged, among them the Duvalierists and *macoutes*. Aristide had authorized a commission to investigate their post-1986 crimes and had even brought some of them to trial. In addition, he appeared to be encouraging Haitians to hunt them down with his praise of necklacing. "What a beautiful tool . . . [it] smells good, everywhere you go you want to breathe it."[2]

Although the Church was not an active participant in the overthrow of the president, it is unlikely to have shed many tears at the departure of its increasingly hostile Brother. On one occasion, after Archbishop François Wolff Ligondé had been critical of his administration, Aristide appeared to encourage his followers to retaliate against the Church. Soon afterwards, the Cathedral and the prelate's residence were set on fire.

Aristide had alarmed Haitians concerned with honest government. In one instance, he appeared to have intimidated the court into imposing a life sentence on Roger Lafontant in punishment for his coup attempt against Trouillot—although the Constitution does not provide for life sentences. Aristide's cabinet appointments were another issue. His appointments went to friends whose backgrounds were inauspicious. In particular, his prime minister was an old friend and former baker. In another disconcerting move, Aristide used presidential funds to support a personal charity. Finally, Aristide attempted to intimidate wealthy Haitians with threats that he planned to redistribute their wealth.

Foreign Response

Foreign reaction to the ouster of Aristide was swift and negative. The Organization of American States (OAS) immediately convened its Permanent Council to condemn the action. An ad hoc meeting of foreign ministers from the region approved a resolution in "support of the democratic government of Haiti." They additionally recommended diplomatic and economic measures to facilitate his return and isolate the usurpers. They appointed a commission to share their decisions with the *Junta*. After a 2 October emergency meeting of the foreign ministers and Aristide, the Organization of American States voted unanimously to impose a trade embargo on Haiti.

The United States followed suit. The same day, economic and military aid to Haiti were suspended.[3] Five hundred marines at Guantánamo stood by to evacuate Americans from Haiti, if necessary. On 4 October, President Bush met with President Aristide, reportedly making his determination to see the military coup reversed, if possibly without force and preferably through O.A.S. auspices. The following day, the European Community froze its $148 million dollar aid package to Haiti and on 9 October, France and Canada did likewise. For its part, the U.N. Security Council issued a statement of moral support for Aristide's return, stopping short of a formal resolution, due to opposition from the nonaligned nations, which are traditionally opposed to involvement in other states' internal affairs.

On 4 October, OAS envoys flew to Haiti to warn the coup leaders that they were facing a diplomatic and economic quarantine if they did not restore Aristide to the presidency. They were turned away, and the mayor of Port-au-Prince, Evans Paul, who had been waiting to receive them at the airport, was abducted and beaten. A subsequent delegation a month later was equally unsuccessful.

After that, the OAS rejected a proposal to send five hundred civilians to Haiti to help restore constitutional rule. However, on 8 October, it voted unanimously to urge OAS member countries to freeze Haitian Government assets and to impose a trade embargo.[4]

THE CURRENT SITUATION

Military Entrenchment

Meanwhile, in Haiti, the Junta was consolidating its position. On 8 October, the military installed Joseph Nerette, a Duvalierist Supreme Court justice, as president. After numerous attempts, on 14 October, it succeeded in assembling a quorum in the legislature and a vote in which half of the deputies present finally approved Jean Jacques Honorat as prime minister.

Meanwhile, the Junta released negative statements for foreign consumption about Aristide, especially that he had encouraged necklacing, and, on 8 November, they announced that Aristide and his former prime minister would face arrest should they attempt a return.

Domestically, the regime continued the crackdown on those critical of its rule. The French Ambassador, Jean-Rafael Dufour, was nearly expelled after calling Jean-Jacques Honorat a "*crétin*" and the army a "bunch of cowards."[5] In December, the Junta celebrated the anniversary of Aristide's election with additional violence against his supporters. Amnesty International calculated that fifteen hundred Haitians had been killed in the intervening year and its report cited allegations of massacres, political arrests, torture, disappearances, attacks on grassroots labor, community and Church organizations, and the rebirth of a repressive network of regional political bosses. One intended victim was the long-time Communist, presidential candidate René Théodore, who was holding a political meeting when police attacked and beat a dozen politicians, himself included, and killed his bodyguard.[6]

Foreign Reassessment

Enthusiasm for Aristide's return to Haiti diminished as unflattering publicity emerged concerning his presidential conduct. As a result, Aristide was obliged to make concessions to governments and institutions in return for their continued support. One was to select a new prime minister. On 12 December, he suggested Victor Benoît, but on 23 December, he agreed to accept an old adversary, René Théodore, in deference to the wishes of Parliament and the United States. By late February, the principal obstacle to Aristide's return was the military.

As time passed and hope faded for Aristide's speedy return, some exiles began to call for an invasion by Haitian refugees or other Latin Americans. In Haiti, the declining political and economic situation caused an unprecedented number of desperate people to try to get out.

Embargo

The international community carried out its threat. On 8 October, the OAS imposed a trade embargo on Haiti, and, by the end of the month, additional countries and international donor organizations cut off trade and assistance. The United States and France suspended aid, and Japan and Canada threatened to do the same. The United States Agency for International Development (USAID), the Peace Corps, and The World Health Organization (WHO) cut their programs, many of which had provided vital help in education, sanitation, and environmental areas. The United States trade embargo, imposed on 29 October, was particularly important because of the scale of the two countries' economic relationship. Sixty-five per-cent of Haiti's imports are from the United States and 85 per-cent of its exports go there.

By late November, the impact of the embargo was quantifiable: it had put 65,000 people out of work, caused fuel and food shortages, and paralyzed public services. By December, electricity had to be rationed, limiting public transportation and even curtailing surgical procedures.

Relief groups, such as CARE, tried to organize food distribution programs to feed increasing numbers of desperate people. In November and January, two illegal deliveries of diesel oil to Haiti provided a short-term injection of fuel for power plants that had been forced to reduce operation to a few hours a day.

With no respite in view, increasing numbers of Haitians sought to leave the country. Some attempted to reach the Dominican Republic by land over the rugged mountains that divide the two countries, but this prospect dimmed after 6 February, when the Dominican president, Dr. Joaquin

Balaguer, announced his support for the Haitian Junta, and his opposition to the influx of Haitians. Most Haitians, however, attempted to get to the United States, mainly by sea and usually in little fishing boats not constructed to carry so many so far.

Refugees

In 1981, a law was passed to deal with the predominantly Haitian boat people found at sea en route to the United States. According to its statutes, the boats would be intercepted by the Coast Guard, the passengers interviewed, sometimes held while their cases were pending, then repatriated if they were economic migrants, or allowed to remain in the United States if they were political migrants.

This law has drawn criticism for a number of reasons. Holding centers are reported to be inadequate and even dangerous. Selection is said to favor Cubans over Haitians, suggesting racial discrimination. Interviews are described as cursory and confusing to already frightened, uneducated, Creole speakers. Distinction between economic and political refugees is said to be decided in an arbitrary and simplistic way.

The exodus of Haitians increased to the extent that, by the winter of 1992, their numbers were reminiscent of the 1980s, a decade of intense Duvalier repression.[7] Each new symptom of repression and jolt to the economy would cause additional Haitians to try to leave the country. A wave of Haitians attempted to flee after the military announced it would hold presidential elections, establish an unpaid rural constabulary, and prohibit negotiations between Parliament and the OAS for Aristide's return.

Those people who attempted to leave consisted of Aristide supporters, who feared for their lives under the military, and those who feared for their economic future. In many cases, the groups overlapped.

Interdiction guidelines for field officers require Immigration and Naturalization Service (INS) officers to be "keenly attuned during any interdiction program to any evidence which may reflect an individual's well-founded fear of prosecution."[8] This is a significant responsibility; since the migrants have no legal right to an attorney, the decision may mean the difference between life and death. Those persons who are returned to Haiti must go through immigration, be fingerprinted, and are consequently at the mercy of the government they sought to leave. Reports abound of reprisals against returnees, and in one case, against an entire town, where one hundred and twenty houses were burned down.

Reports about bad camp conditions are also common . Detainees at centers in Puerto Rico, Texas, Louisiana, and Guantánamo have spoken of mistreatment, including sexual exploitation, beatings, and solitary confinement.[9] Seventy-three Haitians who volunteered to return to Haiti from a camp in Venezuela later recounted how they had been arrested, interrogated, and robbed by the police before being allowed to leave the country.[10]

On 28 October 1991, the American Embassy in Port-au-Prince reported "credible reports of indiscriminate killings, political harassment, illegal searches and looting of private homes and radio stations, arrests without warrants, and the detention of persons without charges, and the mistreatment of persons in custody of Haiti's *de facto* authorities." For a short time thereafter, the U. S. government relaxed its repatriation policy. However, when more Haitians began to leave the country, the United States abruptly resumed repatriation and within twenty-four hours had returned 538 Haitians, giving each fifteen dollars, bus money, and food aid.[11] The exodus continued anyway. Three weeks after the coup, 2,819 Haitians had left the country, crowded onto 43 boats, in a fourfold increase over the past six months.[12]

After its initial hesitation, the Bush administration continued to assert that the Haitians were economic migrants, fleeing poverty, rather than political repression, and to insist on their repatriation. Distinguishing between economic and political migrants has been more troublesome for many individuals, organizations,[13] and institutions.

Fifteen hundred people rallied on 13 December in Washington, D.C. to protest the repatriation policy. The protesters, led by Jesse Jackson, Rep. Charles Rangel, and the director of the American Jewish Committee, Gary Rubin, argued that returning of Haitians is not only racist but contradictory, in light of United States policy toward repatriation of the Vietnamese from Hong Kong. Members of Congress have sponsored legislation on behalf of the boat people. Rep. Romano Mazzoli (D-Ky) introduced a bill to bar repatriation of refugees temporarily and give them a protective status in United States.[14] The *Washington Post* editorialized on 30 December that U.S. refugee policy was out-of-date. Rules pertaining to refugees were made during the Cold War to deal with people escaping communist countries. In the post cold war world, people have continued to flee violence—civil wars, lawlessness, and tyranny—and, in these cases, should not be repatriated until legal governments were re-established and the level of violence reduced.[15]

Some efforts have been made to change policy. On 19 October 1991, C. Clyde Atkins, a U. S. District Court judge in Miami, issued a restraining order to prevent the deportation of Haitian refugees, pending a hearing because, in his estimation, repatriated Haitians faced persecution. When his order was overruled on 17 December by a three-court panel, the judge issued a second restraining order to give the Haitians the opportunity to appeal. Requests were made to the Supreme Court in January and February 1992 to consider the case, but the Court declined, saying that the administration had not found specific proof to justify claims that new evidence indicated that repatriated Haitians were fleeing again due to abuse.

Conclusion

The Haitian situation as of this writing is bleak. The military Junta entrenched while international support for Aristide's return has become less intense. Grassroots support continues, but it is calculated that more than 1,500 of Aristide's partisans have been killed so far and that 15,000 Haitians have tried to leave the country, many perishing in the attempt.

The already fragile Haitian economy worsened further since the coup and now faces collapse as a consequence of the OAS trade embargo. Many of the Haitians who lost their employment are risking their lives to leave the country. Those who escape drowning are likely to be picked up by U. S. Coast Guard boats, interviewed, and found to be economic migrants, then returned to Haiti, perhaps after detention at a holding center. In February, the U. S. government was repatriating 2.000 Haitians a week, some of whom would try again.[16]

In summary, the conduct of the presidential election in December 1990 and its winner were both unusual, but the outcome was familiar. Without powerful support from some combination of forces within the Church, elite, and military, the victor was doomed. Popular support for Father Aristide by Haiti's poor majority was inadequate to the forces arrayed against the new president.

Aristide contributed to his own downfall. He became a hero to some and a villain to others as a result of his support for social justice, the poor, a new social order, and liberation theology. However, he frightened even erstwhile supporters with some of his methods for dealing with opponents that included *déshoukaj*, necklacing, and forced redistribution of wealth

Support for democracy and democratic institutions in the region caused the OAS to impose a trade embargo against Haiti to force the military to return the elected president to power. However, the ethical justification for this action is debatable, given the extreme poverty of most Haitians.

History has gone full circle. Haiti is once again an isolated, pariah state, where the military runs the country, and the elites manipulate the military for the benefit of a small percentage of the population. Rulers prosper at the expense of the masses, who are kept subservient through violence and intimidation until they become desperate enough to risk everything to leave.

The Church has also reverted to the past, silent in the face of a military coup, political repression, and economic misery. There are few brave, committed Church people among the hierarchy or clergy taking the side of the people against their oppressors.

Plus ça change, plus c'est la même chose. This old adage that the more things change, the more they stay the same applies once again to Haiti.

NOTES

1. Ironically, only four days previously, Aristide had addressed the United Nations, where he had boasted that "democracy [in Haiti] has won out for good; the roots are growing stronger and stronger."

2. Robert Glass, "Reformer President Alarmed Haitians by Backing Violence," *New York Times*, 8 October 1991.

3. This amounted to approximately $86 million dollars. In addition, it froze Haitian assets in the United States.

4. Sixty-five thousand Haitians reportedly lost their jobs due to the embargo.

5. Lee Hockstader, "Haiti Orders the Expulsion of Outspoken French Ambassador, *Washington Post*, 16 November 1991.

6. *Haiti Insight* 1, no. 7 (25 January 1991).

7. Lee Hockstader, "Even with Nowhere to Go, Haitians are Taking to the Sea," *International Herald Tribune*, 22 November 1991. In the first three weeks after the coup, 2,819 Haitians fled their country. By the end of January, four months after the coup, the number had increased to 10,000.

8. John Lancaster, "Judge Again Blocks Return of Haitians," *Washington Post*, 21 December 1991.

9. "Outrage Over Abuse of Refugees at Krome, *Haiti Insight* 2, no. 1 (May 1990): page 1.

10. United Nations Human Rights Commission, 3 December 1991.

11. By February 1992, the federal government had spent $24 million intercepting, housing, and returning Haitians following the coup. One critic of the program concluded that it would be better to pay potential refugees $1,500 not to get on boats in Haiti.

12. "Giving Haitians the Rush," *International Herald Tribune*, 22 November 1991.

13. "Court Intervenes for Haitians," *International Herald Tribune*, 20 November 1991. Sylvana Foa, a spokeswoman for the U.N. High Commission for Refugees, said her agency was "concerned about Haitians because they were fleeing political and individual violence following the overthrow of a democratically elected government."

14. Hockstader, "Even with Nowhere to Go, Haitians are Taking to the Sea, and "135. Haitians Said to Drown Off East Cuba," *Washington Post*, 22 November 1991.

15. "Who's a Genuine Refugee?" *Washington Post*, 30 December 1991.

16. Al Kamen, "White House Urges all Factions to Adhere to Haitian Agreement, " *Washington Post*, 25 February 1992.

Appendix A: Glossary of Terms

CEB. Basic Christian Communities (CEB) are composed of small numbers of Catholic families who have banded together for religious, political, and social reasons.

CELAM. The Conference of Latin American Bishops. The CELAM meeting at Medellïn, Colombia, in 1968 and the subsequent meeting at Puebla, Mexico, in 1978 were particularly important.

CEP. The Provisional Electoral Council (CEP) was created in May 1987 to draft a constitution for Haiti.

CHB. The Conference of Haitian Bishops (CHB) is an organization consisting of all the nation's bishops.

Church. I refer to the "Catholic Church" on occasion as the "Church." Other denominations are identified separately.

CHR. The Conference of Haitian Religious (CHR) is the organization of the nation's priests, nuns, and lay workers.

CNG. The National Governing Council (CNG) was the name given to the interim government that ruled Haiti from the departure of Jean-Claude Duvalier on 7 February 1986 until Leslie Manigat became president on 7 February 1988.

Déshoukaj. This Creole term means "to uproot" and was widely used, following the departure of Jean-Claude Duvalier, to mean getting rid of what was bad. The term was applied to Duvalierists, *macoutes, houngans,* and *mambos.*

Houngan and *Mambo.* These are the words for Voodoo priests and priestesses, respectively.

Maroons. Maroons is the term applied to the escaped slaves.

255

Papa Doc. François Duvalier was sometimes referred to as "Papa Doc." "Papa" is a term of respect meaning "father," but it also has a connotation for Voodoo adherents. "Papa Legba" is an important spirit in the Voodoo lexicon.

The Religious. The Religious is a term that refers to men and women in the Catholic Church who have taken the vow of poverty as well as chastity and obedience, and are members of a Congregation.

Ti-légliz. Literally, "Little Churches" in Creole, the term refers to Haiti's Basic Christian Communities.

Tontons Macoutes or *Macoutes.* The security police force established by François Duvalier in 1959. The term means "Uncle Knapsack" and refers to scary figures from a Haitian legend who are said to come out at night to carry off naughty children.

Voodoo. There is no standard orthography for the name of Haiti's popular religion. I will use this spelling because it is the most common form.

VSN. The Volontaires de la Sécurité Nationale or Volunteers for National Security were a security force established from the macoutes by François Duvalier in 1962.

Appendix B: Chronology of Important Dates

1492, 6 December. Columbus landed at Môle St. Nicholas, Haiti.

1492-1697. Spain colonized Hispaniola.

1697, Treaty of Ryswich. Spain ceded the western part of Hispaniola to France following the War of the Grand Alliance.

1791, August. Beginning of the slave insurrection in St. Domingue.

1804, 1 January. Haiti became independent.

1804-1806. Jean-Jacques Dessalines presidency.

1807-1818. Alexandre Pétion presidency in the south.

1807-1820. Henry Christophe presidency in the north.

1815-1820. First protestants arrived in Haiti.

1818-1843. Jean-Pierre Boyer presidency.

1847-1859. Faustin Soulouque presidency.

1860, 25 September. Concordat restored relations between the Vatican and Haiti.

1859-1867. Nicholas Geffrard presidency.

1867-1869. Silvain Salnave presidency.

1879-1885. Lysius Salomon presidency.

1889-1896. Florvil Hyppolite presidency.

1915-1934. U.S. Marine occupation of Haiti.

1941-1943. Antisuperstitious campaign.

1940s-1960s. Liberation theology developed.

1946-1950. Dumarsais Estimé presidency.

1950-1956. Paul Magloire presidency.

1957-1971. François Duvalier presidency.

1958-1963. Pope John XXIII.

1962-1965. Vatican II.

1963-1978. Pope Paul VI.

1966, 25 October. Revision of the concordat.

1968. CELAM meeting at Medellín, Colombia.

April 1971-7 February 1986. Jean-Claude Duvalier presidency.

1978-present. Pope John Paul II.

1978, April 30. The inauguration of *Radio Soleil.*

1979. CELAM meeting at Puebla, Mexico.

8 December 1981-9 March 1982. Eucharistic and Marial Conference in Haiti.

1982, 2 December. Arrest of Gérard Duclerville. Released 9 February 1983.

1982, 2-6 December. Church symposium.

1983, 9 March. Pope John Paul II visited Haiti.

1984, May. Father Hugo Triest became the director of *Radio Soleil,* a position he held through March 1989.

1984, 8 August. Agreement modifying the concordat.

1985. The United Nations designated it as International Youth Year.

1985, 26 July. Ouster of Father Triest and two other Belgian priests.

1985, 26-28 November. Events in Gonaïves led to death of three school children.

1985, 5 December. *Radio Soleil* closed. Reopened 31 December.

1986, January. The United States withheld recertification for foreign assistance.

1986, 7 February. Jean-Claude Duvalier left Haiti.

1986-8 February-7 February 1988. General Henri Namphy headed the National Council of Governments (CNG).

1987, 29 November. The presidential elections.

1988, 17 January. The rescheduled presidential elections.

1988, 7 February-20 June 1988. Leslie Manigat presidency.

1988, 20 June-17 September 1988. General Henri Namphy regime.

1988, 17 September-10 March 1990. General Prosper Avril regime.

1990, 13 March-present. Ertha Pascal Trouillot provisional presidency.

Bibliography

The data for this book were compiled from both primary and secondary sources. Two trips to Haiti were undertaken. Contact was established during those visits with numerous Haitian, American, French, Belgian, and Canadian religious and political leaders, journalists, and development specialists. In Washington, communication was made with members of the U.S. and Haitian diplomatic corps, and members of Congress and their staffs who are involved in Haiti. In addition, relations were initiated with members of the Haïtian exile community who remain in Miami, New York and Washington, and with others who have returned to Haiti.

The Library of Congress, Howard University and the Prince George's Library system were used, as was the U.S. Government. The Freedom of Information Act documents were important sources of information.

It would have been extremely useful to have had access to Vatican documents. Unfortunately, they are closely held. Apart from some correspondence between the Holy See and the Government of Haiti prior to the papal visit in March 1983, this book relied on other sources. It remains consequently for a future scholar to uncover that material.

BOOKS

Abble, A., J.C. Bajeux, J. Bala, G. Bissainth, et al. *Des Prêtres Noirs S'Interrogent.* Paris: Editions du Cerf, 1956.

Abbott, Elizabeth. *Haïti, The First Inside Account: The Duvaliers and Their Legacy.* New York: McGraw-Hill, 1988.

Adams, R.N., et al. (publisher). *Social Change in Latin America Today.* New York, 1960.

Anonymous. *My Odyssey: A French Creole's Journal.* Only eye-witness account of the revolution of 1791, translated and edited by Althea de Puech Parham. Baton Rouge: Louisiana State University Press, 1959.

Anonymous. *Spéciale Opération "Déchouké."* Chicago: Cohen & Haley, undated [after 7 February 1986].

Assmann, Hugo. *A Theology for a Nomad Church.* Maryknoll, New York: Orbis Press, 1976.

Bajeux, Jean-Claude. "Mentalité Noire et Mentalité Biblique," in *Des Prêtres Noirs S'Interrogent*. Paris: Editions du Cerf, 1956.

Baskett, J. *History of the Island of St. Domingo from its First Discovery by Columbus to the Present Period*. Westport, CT: Negro University Press, 1971.

Berryman, Phillip. "What Happened at Puebla," in *Churches and Politics in Latin America*, ed. Daniel Levine. London and Beverly Hills: Sage Publication, 1979.

Binnendejk, Hans, ed. *Authoritarian Regimes in Transition*. Washington, D.C.: Center for the Study of Foreign Affairs, Foreign Service Institute, U.S. Department of State, 1987.

Bissainte, Gérard. "Catholicisme et Indiginisme Religieux," in *Des Prêtres Noirs S'Interrogent*. Paris: Editions du Cerf, 1956.

Bonhomme, Colbert. *Révolution et Contre-Révolution en Haïti de 1946 à 1957*. Port-au-Prince: Imprimerie de l'Etat, 1957.

Boff, Leonardo. *Church: Charism and Power, Liberation Theology and the Institutional Church*. New York: Crossroad, 1985.

_____. *Ecclesiogenesis*. New York: Orbis, 1986.

_____. *Jesus Christ, Liberator*. New York: Orbis, 1978.

Breathett, George, ed. *The Catholic Church in Haiti (1704–1785): Selected Letters, Memoires and Documents*. Salisbury, NC: Documentation Publications, 1982.

Brinkerhoff, Derrick W., and Jean-Claude Garcia-Zamor. *Politics, Projects and Peasants: Institutional Development in Haiti*. New York: Praeger, 1986.

Brinton, Crane. *The Anatomy of Revolution*. New York: Prentice Hall, 1938, 1952.

Cabon, Le R. Père Adolphe. *Notes sur l'Histoire Religieuse d'Haïti, de la Révolution au Concordat (1789–1860)*. Port-au-Prince: Petit Séminaire Collège St Martial, 1933.

Castel Haïti. *La Participation Chrétienne Au Développement En Haïti: Rapport Du Séminaire Sur La Participation Chrétienne Au Développement En Haïti*. Port-au-Prince: Castel Haïti, July 1973.

Cave, Hugh B. *The Cross on the Drum*. Garden City, NY: Doubleday, 1959.

Chidester, David. *Patterns of Power: Religion and Politics in American Culture*. New Jersey: Prentice-Hall, 1988.

Comblin, Joseph. *The Church and the National Security State*. New York: Orbis, 1979.

Cornevin, Robert. *Que Sais-je? Haïti*. Paris: Presses Universitaires de France, 1982.

Corvington, Georges. *Port-au-Prince au Cours des Ans: La Capitale d'Haïti Sous L'Occupation 1915–1922*. Port-au-Prince: Henri Deschamps, 1984.

_____. *Port-au-Prince au Cours des Ans: La Capitale d'Haïti Sous L'Occupation 1922–1934*. Port-au-Prince: Henri Deschamps, 1984.

Courlander, Harold, and Remy Bastien. *Religion and Politics in Haïti*. Washington, D.C.: Institute for Cross-Cultural Research, 1966.

Cox, Harvey. *Religion in the Secular City: Towards Post Modern Theology*. New York: Simon and Schuster, 1984.

Craige, John H. *Cannibal Cousins*. New York: Minton Balch, 1934.

Dash, J. Michael. *Literature and Ideology in Haiti, 1915–1961*. Ottowa, New Jersey: Barnes and Noble, 1981.

Davis, H.P. *Black Democracy, The Story of Haiti*. New York: Dodge Publishing Company, 1963.

Davis, Wade. *The Serpent and the Rainbow*. New York: Simon and Schuster, 1985.

Diederich, Bernard, and Al Burt. *Papa Doc: The Truth About Haiti Today*. New York: McGraw-Hill, 1969.

Druneau, Mooney, and L. Gabriel, eds. *The Catholic Church and Religions in Latin America*. Monograph Series Number 18. Montreal: Center for Developing Area Studies, McGill University, 1985.

Du Bois, Victor D. *Churches and States: The Religious Institution and Modernization.* New York: American University Field Staff, 1967.

Duvalier, François. *Mémoires d'un Leader du Tiers Monde.* Paris: Hachette, 1969.

_____. *Oeuvres Essentielles,* vol.1 Paris: Hachette, 1966.

_____. *Oeuvres Essentielles,* vol. 2 Paris: Hachette, 1966.

_____. *Oeuvres Essentielles,* vol. 3 Paris: Hachette, 1967.

_____. *Oeuvres Essentielles,* vol. 4 Paris: Hachette, 1967.

Eugène, Grégoire. *Le Miracle Haïtien Est Possible.* Port-au-Prince: Ateliers Fardin, 22 July 1985.

Ferguson, James. *Papa Doc, Baby Doc.* Oxford: Basil Blackwell, 1987.

Foster, Charles R. and Albert Valdman, eds. *Haiti Today and Tomorrow.* Lanham, MD: University Press of America, 1984.

Fouchard, Jean. *Les Marrons de la Liberté.* Paris: Editions de l'Ecole, 1972.

Freire, Paulo. *Pedagogy of the Oppressed.* New York: Seabury, 1970.

Gayot, Gérard. *Clergé Indigène.* 2d ed., 1956. Copyright Montréal: Comité de Clergé Indigène, Canada, 1955.

Gilfeather, Katherine Anne. "Women Religious, and the Poor, and the Institutional Church in Chile," in *Churches and Politics in Latin America,* ed. Daniel Levine. London and Beverly Hills: Sage Publications, 1979.

Girod, François. *La Vie Quoditienne de la Société Créole.* Paris: Hachette, 1972.

Greene, Graham. *The Comedians.* New York: Viking Press, 1966.

Gutiérrez, Gustavo. *A Theology of Liberation, History, Politics and Salvation.* Maryknoll, NY: Orbis Books, 1973.

Harrison, John. "Preface," in *Churches and Politics in Latin America,* ed. Daniel Levine. London and Beverly Hills: Sage Publications, 1979.

Hebblethwaite, Peter. *In the Vatican.* Bethesda, MD: Adler and Adler, 1986.

Heinl, Robert Debs, Jr. and Nancy Gordon Heinl. *Written in Blood: The Story of the Haitian People, 1492–1971.* Boston: Houghton, Mifflin, 1978.

Herring, Hubert. *A History of Latin America from the Beginnings to the Present.* 3d ed. New York: Knopf, 1972.

Honorat, Jean-Jacques. *Enqûete Sûr le Développement.* Port-au-Prince: Imprimerie Centrale, 1974.

Hopkins, Jack W., ed. *Latin America: Perspectives on a Region.* New York and London: Holmes and Meier, 1987.

Huxley, Francis. *The Invisibles: Voodoo Gods in Haiti.* New York: McGraw-Hill, 1966.

James, C.L.R. *The Black Jacobins: Toussaint L'Ouverture and the San Domingo Revolution.* 2d ed. New York: Random House, 1963.

Jan, Jean Marie. *Collecta Pour L'Histoire Religieuse du Diocèse du Cap-Haïtien,* vol. 2. Port-au-Prince: Editions Henri Deschamps, undated [1960].

_____. *Collecta Pour l'Histoire du Diocèse du Cap-Haïtien, 1886–1953,* vol. 3. Port-au-Prince: Editions Henri Deschamps, 1958.

Keohane, Robert, and Joseph Nye, eds. *Transnational Relations and World Politics.* Cambridge: Harvard University Press, 1970.

Laguerre, Michel S. *Voodoo Heritage.* Beverly Hills: Sage Publications, 1980.

Lawless, Robert. *Bibliography on Haiti.* Gainesville: University of Florida, Center for Latin American Studies, June 1985.

Lemoine, Maurice. *Bitter Sugar.* London: Zed Press, 1985.

Levine, Daniel, ed. *Churches and Politics in Latin America.* London and Beverly Hills: Sage Publications, 1979.

Leyburn, James. *The Haitian People.* New Haven and London: Yale University Press, 1966.

Lundahl, Mats. *Peasants and Poverty: A Study of Haiti.* London: Croom Helm, 1979.

Maguire, Robert. *Bottom-Up Development in Haiti.* 2d ed. Rosslyn,VA: Inter-American Foundation, April 1981.

Manigat, Leslie F. *Haiti of the Sixties, Object of International Concern.* Washington, D.C.: Washington Center of Policy Research, 1964.

Mebga, Meinrad. "Christianisme et Négritude," in *Des Prêtres Noirs S'Interrogent.* Paris: Editions du Cerb, 1956.

Mecham, J. Lloyd. *Church and State in Latin America.* 2d ed., Chapel Hill: The University of North Carolina Press, 1966.

Métraux, Alfred. *Haiti: Black Peasants and Their Religion.* London: George Harrup, 1960.

_____. *Le Vaudou Haïtien.* Paris: Gallimard, 1958.

Moreau de Saint-Méry, Méderic-Louis-Elle. *A Civilization that Perished.* Originally published by the author in two volumes in Philadelphia in 1797–1798. Translated, abridged and edited by Ivor D. Spencer. Lanham, MD: University Press of America, 1985.

Morse, Richard M., ed. *Haiti's Future: Views of Twelve Haitian Leaders* Washington, D.C.: The Wilson Center Press, 1988.

Mutchler, David. *The Church as a Political Factor in Latin America with Particular Reference to Colombia and Chile.* Cambridge: Cambridge University Press, 1979.

Needler, Martin C., ed. *Political Systems in Latin America.* 2d ed. New York: Van Nostrand Reinhold, 1970.

Nicholls, David. *From Dessalines to Duvalier: Race, Colour and National Independence in Haïti.* Cambridge: Cambridge University Press, 1979.

_____. *Haiti in Caribbean Context.* New York: St. Martin's Press, 1985.

Pacquin, Lyonel. *The Haitians, Class and Color Politics.* New York: Multi-type, 1983.

Preeg, Ernest H. *Haiti and the Caribbean Basin Initiative: A Time of Change and Opportunity, monograph 1985–1.* Miami: Institute of Inter-Studies, Graduate School of International Studies, University of Miami, 1985.

Pressoir, Catts. *Le Protestantisme Haïtien,* 2 vols. Port-au-Prince: Imprimerie de la Societé Biblique et des Livres Religieux d'Haïti, 1945–1946.

Price-Mars, Jean. *Ainsi Parla L'Oncle: Essais d'Ethnographie,* Port-au-Prince, 1928.

Prince, Rod. *Haiti: Family Business.* London: Latin America Bureau Limited, 1985.

Richard, Pablo. *Death of Christendoms: Birth of the Church, Historical Analysis and Theological Interpretation of the Church in Latin America.* Originally published in Spanish, 1978. Maryknoll, NY: Orbis, 1987.

Rodman, Selden. *Haiti: The Black Republic: The Complete Story and Guide.* New York: Devin-Adair, 1984.

Romain, Charles Poisset. *Le Protestantisme dans la Société Haïtienne.* Port-au-Prince: Henri Deschamps, 1986.

Rotberg, Robert I., and Christopher K. Clague. *Haiti: The Politics of Squalor.* Boston: Houghton Mifflin, 1971.

Seabrook, W.B. *The Magic Island.* New York: Harcourt, Brace and Co., 1929.

Silvert, Kalman H. ed. *Churches and States: The Religious Institution and Modernization.* New York: American Universities Field Staff, Inc., 1967.

Sobrino, Jon. *Christology at the Crossroads.* New York: Orbis, 1978.

Solages, F. *A La Recherche d'Une Pastorale Haïtienne.* Port-au-Prince: Imprimerie de l'Etat, 1967.

Tata, Robert J. *Haiti, Land of Poverty.* Washington, D.C.: University Press of America, 1982.

Trouillot, Michel-Rolph. *Haiti, State Against Nation: The Origins and Legacy of Duvalierism.* New York: Monthly Review Press, 1990.

Vallier, I. *Catholicism, Social Control and Modernization in Latin America.* New York: Prentice Hall, 1970.

Verdieu, E., and P. Onia. "Sacerdoce et Négritude," in *Des Prêtres Noirs S'Interrogent.* Paris: Editions du Cerf, 1956.

Walker, James. "Foreign Assistance," *In Haiti today and Tomorrow,* ed. Charles Foster and Albert Valdman (Lanham, MD: University Press of America, 1984.)

Weil, Thomas, Jan Black, Howard Blustein, Kathryn Johnston, David McMorris, Frederick Musnson. *Area Handbook for Haiti.* Washington, D.C.: The American University, 1973.

Weinstein, Brian and Aaron Segal. *Political Failures, Cultural Successes.* Praeger Special Studies, copublished with Hoover Institute Press. Stanford: Praeger, 1984.

Wilde, Alexander. "Ten Years of Change in the Church: What Happened at Puebla," in *Churches and Politics in Latin America,* ed. Daniel Levine. London and Beverly Hills: Sage Publications, 1979.

Wimpffen, Francis Alexander Stanislaus, Baron de. *A Voyage to Saint Domingo in the Years 1788, 1789 and 1790.* London: Cadell, 1817.

World Bank. *Haïti: Public Expenditure Review.* Country Study. Washington, D.C.: The World Bank, 1987.

World Book v. 20. Chicago: World Book Childcraft International, 1979. s.v."Vatican Council," by Mark J. Hurley.

JOURNAL, MAGAZINE, AND NEWSPAPER ARTICLES

Antonin, Arnold. "Haitian Church Standing Up to Duvalier." *Latinoamericano Press,* Lima, Peru, 15, no. 9 (17 March 1983).

Bajeux, Jean-Claude. "The Little Game of January 17th." *Caribbean Review* 16 (Winter 1988): 11.

Balance. "Haïti à L'Heure de L'Opposition." 21–27 March 1990.

Beauvoir, Max, Port-au-Prince, "Lettre Ouverte au Second Conseil Nacional de Gouvernement." From the archives of Max Beauvoir. Probably intended for the government and publication in a Haïtian newspaper. Undated.

_____. "Letter to the National Council of Governments (CNG)." From the archives of Max Beauvoir. Probably intended for the government and publication in a Haitian newspaper. 7 March 1986.

_____. "Lynchings of *Mambos* and *Houngans.*" From the archives of Max Beauvoir. Probably intended for the government and publication in a Haitian newspaper. 16 April 1986.

_____. "Open Letter to the People of Haiti." From the archives of Max Beauvoir. Probably intended for the government and publication in a Haitian newspaper. 17 February 1986.

_____. "Open Letter to the Second National Council of Governments." From the archives of Max Beauvoir. Probably intended for the government and publication in a Haitian newspaper. 7 February 1986.

_____. "Reportage heard on *Radio Nationale.*" From the archives of Max Beauvoir. Probably intended for the government and publication in a Haitian newspaper. 9 July 1986.

_____. "Reportage/Situation Voodoo Dans le Sud." From the archives of Max Beauvoir. Probably intended for the government and publication in a Haïtian newspaper. Undated.

_____. "Reunion of *Mambos* and *Houngans* of Haiti." From the archives of Max Beauvoir. Probably intended for the government and publication in a Haitian newspaper. 16 January 1986.

_____. "Some of the Declarations Heard on *Radio Lumière*." From the archives of Max Beauvoir. Probably intended for the government and publication in a Haitian newspaper. 16 March 1986.

_____. "Some of the Declarations Heard on *Radio Métropole*." From the archives of Max Beauvoir. Probably intended for the government and publication in a Haïtian newspaper. 22 March to 9 July 1986.

_____. "Visite avec Commandant de la Zone." From the archives of Max Beauvoir. Probably intended for the government and publication in a Haitian newspaper. Undated.

Bernardin, Renaud. "Measuring the Change in Haiti From One Duvalier to Another." *International Perspectives* (November-December 1978): 37–40.

Billington, Joy Leger. "'Avocat' Speaks for Troubled Haiti." *Washington Star,* 12 July 1981.

Binder, David. "Haitians Gain Influential Following in America." *New York Times,* 23 September 1987.

Boston Globe. "Church Officials in Haïti Decry Alleged Persecution." 30 July 1985: 4.

Boswell, T.D. "The New Haitian Diaspora." *Caribbean Review* 11 (1982): 18–21.

Brooke, James. "Duvalier Flight Leaves Haitian Industry Hopeful." *New York Times,* 14 February 1986.

Buddingh, Hans. "Haitian Catholic Church Cited as Potent Force for Change." Religious News Service, *The Catholic Transcript,* 31 August 1984.

Business Haiti. "Congressional Statement" concerning the Caribbean Basin Initiative 2, no. 2 (July-September 1982).

Catholic Transcript. "Modified Protocol Signed by Vatican and Haiti." 17 August 1984.

Central Latinoamericana de Trabajadores. "Increases Repression Against Union in Haiti." News Release. Caracas, Venezuela, 17 December 1980.

Chamberlain, Greg. "Difficult Days for Haiti's R.C. Church." *Caribbean Contact,* March 1983.

Chardy, Alfonso. "We Sparked Revolt in Haiti, Students Say." *Miami Herald,* 15 February 1986.

Charney, Marc D. "Despite Foreign Support, Haiti almost Broke Again." *Miami Herald,* 24 March 1981.

Claiborne, William. "Catholic Clerics Vow to Battle South African State." *Washington Post,* 12 March 1988, A 18.

Clitandre, Pierre. "Robinson S'en Prend Aux Evêques." *Haïti Demain Hebdo.* Cap-Haïtien: 18 November 1984.

Cobb, Charles, Jr. "Haiti Against All Odds." *National Geographic,* November1986: 645–71.

Cody, Edward. "Duvalier's Flight Ends Family Rule But Not Haitian Turbulence." *Washington Post,* 8 February 1986.

_____. "Haitian Conflict Imperils United States Aid: Protests Against Duvalier Escalate. *Washington Post,* 22 December 1985.

_____. "Pontiff, in Haiti, Pleads For Social Justice, Rights." *Washington Post,* 10 March 1983.

Colon, Yves. "Saint Maverick's Obsession." *Miami Herald*, 25 January 1985.

Conhair, J.L. "The Haitian Chief of Section." *American Anthropology* 57 (1957): 620.

Cooney, Shirley A. "United States Congressman Walter Fauntroy Proposes Strategy to Isolate Haitian Military." Haïti-Observateur, July 1988.

Copley, Gregory. "Haiti Plans for Greater Regional Role." *Defense and Foreign Affairs* 12 (December 1984): 21–35.

Cornell, George. "Church Played Crucial Role in Regime's Fall." *Miami Herald*, 23 March 1986.

Council on Hemispheric Affairs. *Cozying Up to Baby Doc.* Washington, D.C.: Council on Hemispheric Affairs, 12 July 1981.

_____. *Haitian Refugees Flee Harsh Political Situation.* Washington, D.C.: Council on Hemispheric Affairs, 4 May 1980.

_____. *Human Rights Report, 1979–1980.* Washington, D.C.: Council on Hemispheric Affairs, 1980.

Crahan, Margaret E. *Religion and Revolution: Cuba and Nicaragua.* Washington, D.C.: Woodrow Wilson Center, August 1986.

_____. *The State and the Individual in Latin America.* Washington, D.C.: Woodstock Theological Center at Georgetown University, 1979.

Crassweller, Robert D. "Darkness in Haiti." *Foreign Affairs* 2 (January 1971): 315–29.

C.R.I.E./ E.C.C.L.E.S.I.A. "La Iglesia de Haiti Reclama Justicia." 3 August 1983.

Cristianos por el Socialismo. "Haiti: la Iglesia es el Estado." *Primer Encuentro Latinamericano de Cristianos por el Socialismo.* Havana: Ediciones Camilo Torres, 1973.

Danner, Mark. "A Reporter at Large: Beyond the Mountains-I." *New Yorker*, 27 November 1989.

_____. "A Reporter at Large: Beyond the Mountains-II." *New Yorker*, 4 December 1989.

_____. "A Reporter at Large: Beyond the Mountains-III." *New Yorker*, 11 December 1989.

Davison, Phil. "World Turns Blind Eye As Haiti Gets Civilian Government." *Reuters*, 7 February 1988.

Defense and Foreign Affairs. "The Church in the Developing World: The Experience of Haiti." August-September 1986

De la France, Jean-Claude. "Haitian Minister's Mission Survives Prison." *Miami News*, 24 March 1986, 10A.

Denis, Lorimer. "La Religion Populaire." *Bulletin du Bureau d'Ethnologie*, Port-au-Prince, (March 1938): 1–57.

Denis, Lorimar, and F. Duvalier. "La Civilisation Haïtienne: Notre Mentalité est-elle Africaine ou Gallo-Latine?" *Revue Anthropologique*, 10–12 (1936): 353–73.

_____. "L'Evolution Stadiale du Vodou." *Bulletin du Bureau d'Ethnologie* 12 (1944): 9–32.

De Toledano, Ralph. "What's Next for Haiti?" *Washington Times*, 24 February 1986, 3

Devillers, Carole. "Of Spirits and Saints." *National Geographic* (March 1985): 395.

Diederich, Bernard. "A Poor King Without a Crown: A Review of the Haitian Press During the Manigat Months." *Caribbean Review* 16, no. 2 (Winter 1988).

Diehl, Jackson. "Solidarity-Church Ties Seen Fraying." *Washington Post*, 16 May 1989.

Duvalier, Jean-Claude. "Je Paye Pour Papa Doc." *Paris Match*, 12 February 1988.

_____. Letter to the pope before the papal visit concerning revision of the concordat. 23 November 1982.

Duvalier, Jean-Claude and Michèle Duvalier. *Paris Match*, 9 March 1988.

Ebert, Allan. "Porkbarreling Pigs in Haiti." *Multinational Monitor* 6, no. 18 (December 1985): 14.

Echikson, William. "A Czech Who's Shaking the System." *Christian Science Monitor*, 22 August 1988.

Economist. "Pastor Among Wolves."12 March 1983.

Etienne, Max-Abner. "Interview de l'Archêveque François Wolff Ligondé." *Jeune Haïti*, 23 April 1986.

Eugène, Grégoire. "Pourquoi, Leader du Parti Social Chrétien d'Haïti, Je Supporte le Conseil National de Gouvernement?" *Fraternité*, 15 February 1986.

_____. "Si J'Etais Tenté Par le Communisme." *Fraternité*, 21 June 1986.

_____. "Stratégie Communiste." *Fraternité*, 21 June 1986, 17.

_____. "Tonton Macoute et Milicien dans le Contexte Démocratique." *Fraternité*, 21 June 1986, 14.

_____. "Un Exemple du Cynisme d'Ernest Bennett." *Fraternité*, 15 February 1986.

Ezioba, Matthias O. "Voodoo: A Guide to the Bewildered." *Swiss Review of World Affairs*, 34 (August 1984): 12–18.

Fernandez, Irene Garzon. "CELAM Inicia Asamblea en Haïti." Puerto Principe, Haïti, 9 March 1983.

Fowler, Carolyn. "The Emergence of the Independent Press in Haiti." *The Black Collegian*, (April-May 1981): 149–51.

Garnier, Luc. *A History of the Episcopal Church of Haiti (Église Épiscopale d"Haïti)* Port-au-Prince: Episcopal Church of Haïti, [undated].

Germani, Clara. "Despite Clash, Image of Haiti's Junta Improves." *Christian Science Monitor*, 2 May 1986.

_____."Haitian Opposition Struggles to Harness Momentum for Change." *Christian Science Monitor*, 8 December 1987.

_____."Latest Coup Draws Cheers From Ordinary Haitians." *Christian Science Monitor*, 23 September 1988.

_____."Pope Visits Latin America as Church Faces Tougher Times." *Christian Science Monitor*, 9 May 1988.

_____."Putting the Squeeze on Haiti." *Christian Science Monitor*, 5 July 1988.

Girault, Christian A. "The Haitian Diaspora: A Prescription for Decency." *Caribbean Review* 16, no. 2. (Winter 1988).

_____."Giving Haitians the Rush." *International Herald Tribune* 22 November 1991.

Glass, Pierre Yves. "Candidate Blasts Duvalierists." *Times of the Americas*, 4 November 1987.

_____."Coalition Joins Politicians in Boycott Junta Run Elections." *Associated Press*, Port-au-Prince: 5 January 1988.

_____."Dozens of Candidates Crowd Haitian Presidential Election." *Times of the Americas*, 21 October 1987.

_____."Leading Candidate Vows to Steer Haiti Back to Democracy." *Christian Science Monitor*, 26 October 1897.

_____."Political Violence Continues in Haiti." *Washington Post*, 5 November 1987.

Glass, Robert. "Reformer President Alarmed Haitians by Backing Violence." *New York Times*, 8 October 1991.Glickman, Paul. "Haiti's Presidential Campaign Clouded by Violence." *Christian Science Monitor*, 15 October 1987.

Goodell, Grace. "Conservatism and Foreign Aid." *Policy Review* (Winter 1981–1982): 111–31.

Graunke, Kathy. "Gesture in Face of Haiti's Poverty." *National Catholic Reporter*, 22 January 1982.

Gugliotta, Guy. "Florida Money Keeps Parts of Haiti Alive." *Miami Herald*, 28 June 1981.

Gutiérrez, Gustavo. "Notes for a Theology of Liberation." *Jesuit Journal of Theological Studies*, 31, no. 2 (June 1970).

Gwertzman, Bernard. "Haiti Certified for More United States Aid Despite Rights Issue." *New York Times*, 5 February 1984.

Haïti Demain Hebdo. "Église et Gouvernement: La Lourde Haine de Lafontant." 19–25 December 1985.

———. "Le Clergé Catholique S'Elève Contre les Arrestations Arbitraires." 21–27 November 1984.

Haiti Insight, National Coalition for Haitian Refugees, Interview on the Dominican television show, *Uno Mas Uno* 1, no. 7 (25 January 1991).

———. "Outrage Over Abuse of Refugees at Krome," 2, no.1, (May 1990): 1.

———. United Nations Human Rights Commission findings, 3 December 1991. 1, no. 7, (25 January 1991).

Haïti Libre. "Message de la Conférence Épiscopale d'Haïti: Priorités et Changements." 15 April 1986.

———. "Message of the Conference of Haitian Bishops." 15 April 1986.

Haïti en Marche. "Interview Père Antoine Adrien, L'Architecte de la Transition Actuelle," 21–27 April 1990.

Haiti Times. "Duvalier Ready to Spill Beans." 1 June 1986.

———. "Finance Minister Delatour Speaks Out On the Economic Situation." 1 June 1986

———. "Haiti Discussed at the White House." 1 July 1986.

Haïti-Observateur. "Conférence Haïtienne des Religieux." 28 December 1984 - 4 January 1985.

———. "Conflit Persistant Entre L'Église Catholique et Régime Haïtien," 6–13 July 1984.

———. "Congressmen Call for End of Military Aid." 7–14 August 1987.

———. "Elimination Physique de Certaines Prêtres; L'Exile Pour d'Autres." 14–21 June 1985.

———. "The Haitian Government is on a Collision Course with the Catholic Church Following a Sacrilegious Act Against a Priest in the Cathedral of Cap-Haitien." 17 November 1984.

———. "Jean-Claude et Michèle Allaient S'Envoler," 13–29 December 1985.

———. "La Grande Marche de la Jeunesse d'Haïti Contre Le Présidence à. Vie." 14–21 June 1985.

———. "L'Episcopat, Le Clergé et Leur Rôle National." 28 December 1984 - 4 January 1985.

———. "Les Evêques Maintiennent Leur Demand." 16–23 August 1985.

———. "Le Vatican Demande Explications au Régime." 2 September 1985.

———. "L'Ordre de la Peur en Haïti." 16–23 August 1985, 12.

———. "Mgr. Constant Explique le Massacre des 62 Houngans." 23–30 May 1986, 18.

———. "Mgr. Willy Romélus Tells Congregation to Sever All Relations with the Government." 19 July 1985, 12.

———. "Trois Prêtres Eminents Expulsés."26 July - 2 August 1985.

———. "Une Loi Sur la Presse Inacceptable." August - September 1986.

———. "Un Prêtre Haïtien Appelle les Jeunes à 'La Guérilla.'" 22–29 November 1989.

———. "The Youth of Haiti as the Vanguard." 6–13 December 1985, 14.

Hardy, Yves. "Valses-Hésitation en Haiti." *Le Monde*, 22–24 April 1980.

Harrison, Lawrence E. "We Don't Cause Latin America's Troubles—Latin Culture Does." *Washington Post*, 29 June 1986, C1.

Healy, James K. Letter to the Most Rev. Edward McCarthy, a bishop in Miami. (undated but approximately August 1983).

_____. Open letter concerning events in Haiti. Washington, D.C.: Washington Office on Haiti, 10 December 1985.

Heine, Jorge. "Transition to Nowhere: How Haiti's Democratic Transition Might Have Worked." *Caribbean Review* 6, no. 2 (Winter 1988).

Heinl, Robert Debs Jr. "Haiti: A Case Study in Freedom." *New Republic*, 16 May 1964.

Helmore, Kristen. "Priest Helped Philippine Poor Resist System of Virtual Serfdom." *Christian Science Monitor*, 21 March 1988, 12.

Henry, F. "Caribbean Migration to Canada." *Caribbean Review* 11 (1982): 38–41.

Hertelou, Lucienne. "Eclaircissements de Mme. Vve. Dumarsais Estimé." *Le Matin*, 7 March 1986.

Hill, Kent. "The Philippine Church," Letter to the Editor. *Washington Post*, 7 November 1986.

Hockstader, Lee. "Even with Nowhere to Go, Haitians are Taking to the Sea," *International Herald Tribune*, 22 November 1991.

_____."Haiti Orders the Expulsion of Outspoken French Ambassador," *Washington Post*, 16 November 1991.

_____. "U.S. Envoy Spoke with Avril of Nixon's Final Days Before He Resigned," *Washington Post*, 11 March 1990

_____. "135 Haitians Said to Drown Off East Cuba," *Washington Post*, 22 November 1991.

Hogan, John P. "Haiti's Brief Hour of Hope." Review of *The Rainy Season*, by Amy Wilentz. *Commonweal*, 22 September 1989.

Honorat, J.J. *Haiti, The Turning Point.* Talk prepared for the Woodrow Wilson Center. New York: Institute of Haitian Studies, 20 February 1986.

Hooper, Michael. "Haiti's Despair." *New York Times*, 27 August 1985, A 23.

Hooper, Michael and Aryeh Neier. Letter to Secretary of State Shultz. *The Courrier*, 26 November 1984.

Horblitt, Stephen A. Letter to Ambassador C. McManaway. 7 January 1986.

_____. *Memorandum to Congressman Fauntroy.* 19 January 1986.

_____. *Preliminary Assessment of the Haitian Armed Forces.* Memorandum to Congressman Fauntroy. 3 May 1988.

_____. *Report on Mission to Haiti and Recommendations for Future Action.* Memorandum to Congressman Fauntroy. 1 January 1986.

Howe, Russell Warren. "Son of Papa Doc Brings Halting Progress to Haiti." *Washington Times*, 17 October 1984.

IGLESIAS. *Cristianos Haitianos Denuncian á Duvalier Ante el CELAM*, February 1983.

Impact. "Père Aristide: Déchouké ?" 21 May 1986.

International Herald Tribune, "Court Intervenes for Haitians." 20 November, 1991.

Jacobson, Roberta Steinfeld. "Liberation Theology as a Revolutionary Ideology in Latin America." *Fletcher Forum* (Summer 1986): 317–36.

Jean-François, Hérold. "Ertha Pascal Trouillot: Sans Serment ni Canon une Femme pour le Changement." *Balance*, 21–27 March 1990, 2

Jones, Bonita. "Leaders Hopeful of Change After Pope's Visit to Haiti." *Miami Times*, 17 March 1983.

Joseph, Raymond Alcide. "The Church Challenges Baby Doc." *Nation*, 16 April 1983, 463, 481–82.

_____ . "Haitian Religious and Business Leaders Stop Pampering Baby Doc." *Wall Street Journal,* 7 February 1986.

Kalke, David J. "The Pope's Agenda in Central America." *Guardian,* 2 March 1983.

Kamen, Al. "White House Urges all Factions to Adhere to Haitian Agreement." *Washington Post,* 25 February 1992

Kihss, Peter. Interview with Barbot. *New York Times,* 22 January 1959.

_____ . Interview with Colonel Robert Debs Heinl. *New York Times,* 22 July 1969.

Kohan, John. "Things Must Change Here." *Time,* (21 March 1983): 38.

Kramer, Jane. "Letter from the Elysian Fields." *New Yorker,* 2 March 1987.

Lafontant, Dr. Roger. "Communiqué." *Nouvelliste,* 7 December 1984.

Laguerre, Michel S. "The Place of Voodoo in the Social Structure of Haiti." *Caribbean Quarterly* 19, no. 2 (1973).

Lajoie, Jacques. *Letter to the Commissioner and Prefect of Cap-Haitien.* Cap Haïtien, 2 July 1984.

Lancaster, John. "Judge Again Blocks Return of Haitians." *Washington Post,* 21 December 1991.

Latin American Update. "Haiti: The Monkey's Tail Lives On." March/April 1986.

Lawless, Robert. "Creole Speaks, Creole Understands." *The World and I Washington Times,* February 1988.

Le Matin. "Michèle Duvalier Est Responsable du Renversement de Son Mari, Selon Roger Lafontant." 14 March 1986.

Le Monde, "Cache-Misère en Haïti." Editorial. 25, July 1985.

_____ . "Mounting Tensions Between Christian Churches and the Duvalier Government." 2 March 1983. Translation by the Haitian Refugee Project, Washington, D.C.

Levi, Vanessa. "Manifestation Contre Roger Lafontant à. Ville Mont-Royal." *Haïti-Observateur,* 14–21 February 1986, 26.

Long, William R. "Duvalier's Cronies Boldly Returning to Haitian Life." *Los Angeles Times,* 9 November 1986, 1.

Manigat, Leslie F. "After the Fall." *Caribbean Review* 16, no. 2 (Winter 1988): ???.

Marshall, Rick. "The Church in the Developing World: The Experience of Haiti." *Developing World Report, Defense and Foreign Affairs,* August-September 1986.

May, Archbishop John L. Letter to Archbishop Gayot. Washington, D.C.: National Conference of Catholic Bishops, 20 September 1988.

McAlmon, George. "So Callous a Nation." *Dissent* 31 (Spring 1984): 233–36.

McCarthy, Colman. "A Sign of Promise." *Washington Post,* 30 September 1984.

McCarthy, Tim. "Haitian Church: Hope in a Nation Careening Toward Chaos." *National Catholic Reporter,* 22 January 1988.

Métraux, Alfred. "Le Vaudou et le Christiantisme." *Les Temps Modernes,* Port-au-Prince, 136 (June1957), 1983–84.

Miami Herald. "Black Leaders Meet With Pope," 25 February 1982.

_____ . "Haiti Says Dissidents Misinformed Pontiff." 12 March 1983.

_____ . "Pope Decries Haiti 'Misery' and 'Fear,' Demands Change." 10 March 1983.

_____ . "Quit Assailing Regime Haiti Warns Bishops." 26 November 1982.

_____ . "Vatican Backs Right of Armed Struggle to End Long Tyranny," 5 April 1986

Michel, Father Jean. "Dimension Politique du Fait Religieux en Haïti." *Nouvel Optique,* September 1972, 13.

Miller, Edgar. "Hope Springs in Haiti." *Catholic Standard,* 12 April 1984.

Miner-Ebert, Allan. "Church's Attacks Compound Duvalier's Woes." *Guardian,* 1 June 1983.

Montalbano, William D. "John Paul Rebukes Haiti for Injustice, Inequality." *Miami Herald,* 10 March 1983.
Moody, John. "Bad Times for Baby Doc." *Time,* 10 February 1986.
Mouvement des Paysans de Papaye, Hinche. *Jezi Nan Sevis Pep La,* Hinche [undated].
Nation. "Haitian Elections: The Regime Selects an Opposition," 14 January 1984.
Nicholls, David. "Haiti: The Rise and Fall of Duvalierism." *Third World Quarterly* 8, no. 4 (October, 1986): 1239.
_____. "Politics and Religion in Haiti." *Canadian Journal of Political Science* (September 1970): 400–14.
New York Times. "Gunmen in Haiti Kill Three in Attack on a Church." 12 September 1988, A3.
_____. "In Haiti, Once Again, Murder in the Night." 8 August 1988.
_____. "In Haiti, Some Dissidents Breathe a Little Easier." 16 July 1985.
_____. "Stop the Killing, Church in Haiti Asks." 10 February 1986.
_____. "Three Rights Groups Bid United States Act to Curb Haiti." 2 December 1984.
Norton, Michael. "Three Killed, Scores Hurt in Haiti as Gunmen Attack Church Service." *Washington Post,* 12 September 1988.
Nouveau Monde. "Fondation Michèle B. Duvalier." 2 October 1981.
Nouvelliste. "Déclaration de la Conférence Épiscopale d'Haïti," 25 May 1986.
Oviedo, Alvarado, and Stepan Mamonto. "Theology of Liberation: A New Heresy?" *World Marxist Review* 24, no. 3 (March 1986).
Paley, William. "Haiti's Dynastic Despotism: From Father to Son to..." *Caribbean Review* (Fall 1985).
_____. "Power Shift Imperils Haiti's Frail Stability." *Guardian,* 13 January 1982.
Patterson, Carolyn Bennett. "Haiti: Beyond Mountains, More Mountains." *National Geographic,* (January 1976).
Payne, Karen. "Pope Has 'Great Interest' in Haitians." *Miami News Reporter,* 25 February 1982.
Peerman, Dean. "Haiti: Democracy Derailed." *Christian Century,* 16 December 1987.
Persily, Mark. Untitled paper by an intern at the Washington Office on Haiti on the Church in Haiti, summer 1988.
Petit Samedi Soir. "A Quand Une Révision de la Loi Sur les Églises Protestantes en Haïti?" [undated].
_____. "A Quoi Sert le Protestantisme?" [undated].
_____. "Dossier des Églises Evangéliques en Haïti." [undated].
_____. "La Fraternité Aziloise." Magloire Seide. [undated].
_____. "Le Pasteur André J. Louis Contre le Radicalisme Religieux." 30 June 1985.
_____. "Les Églises Protestantes et la Société Haïtienne: Le Puzzle." [undated].
Piedra, Alberto M. "Some Observations on Liberation Theology." World Affairs, (Winter 1985–86): 151–58.
Preeg, Ernest H. *Haiti and the Caribbean Basin Initiative: A Time of Change and Opportunity.* Miami: Institute of Inter-American Studies, Graduate School of International Studies, University of Miami, 1985.
Pressoir, Catts. "Historique de l''Enseignement en Haïti." *Revue de la Société d'Histoire et de Géographie d'Haïti* 4 (January 1935): 33–57.
Preston, Julia. "Voodoo Adherents Attacked in Haiti." *Washington Post,* 17 May 1986.
Price, Mars Jean. "Lettre Ouverte à Dr. R. Piquion: Le Préjugé de Couleur, est-il la Question Sociale?" Port-au-Prince: 1967.
Rawls, Wendell, Jr. "Baby Doc's Haitian Terror." *New York Times Magazine,* 14 May 1978.

Regional Center for Ecumenical Information. Joint Letter Concerning Haitian Refugees. A joint letter concerning Haitian refugees by Haitian and Dominican Bishops. Yosemite, Mexico: Regional Center for Ecumenical Information, 9 May 1985.

Richmond, Kyle. "Church in Haiti: Picking up the Pieces." *Times*, 16, no. 8 (August-September 1987).

_____. "Haiti's Aristide: 'Hunger, Injustice, Slavery, Capitalism Have No Religion.'" *Inter-America Press*, 12 November 1987.

Ricks, Thomas. "Defying Duvalier: The Pope Visits Haiti Just as Church There is Challenging Regime." *Wall Street Journal*, 9 March 1983, 1.

_____. "Haitian Priests Spurred Protests But Say They Can't Solve Crisis." *Wall Street Journal*, 5 February 1986, 32.

Rodriguez, Ramon A. *Caribbean Contact* 12, no. 12 (May 1985).

Rotberg, Robert I. "What's Needed to Bring Change in Haiti." *Christian Science Monitor*, 24 October 1988.

Ryan, Hewson A. "Haiti: Two Centuries of Well-Intentioned United States Involvement." *Christian Science Monitor*, 14 February 1986.

Salomon, George. "Georges Salomon Révèle." Review of *Dernier Chapître*, by Georges Salomon. *Haïti-Observateur*, 29 August - 5 September 1986.

Sawyer, Jon. "The Church is Catalyst of the Haitian Revolution." *St. Louis Post Dispatch*, 14 February 1986, 1, 8.

Schoenbrun, David. "Democracy Is Alive and Kicking." *Parade Magazine*, 14 December 1986.

Segal, Aaron. "Haiti: What is to be Done?— a Commentary." *Times of the Americas*, 24 February 1988.

Segundo, Juan Luis. "Capitalism and Socialism: The Theological Crux." *The Mystical and Political Dimension of the Christian Faith*, New York: Herder and Herder, 1974.

Servill, Michael. "Small Stirrings of Change." *Time*, 13 January 1986.

Sewell, Dan. "Pope Says 'Things Must Change' in Haiti." *Miami News*, 10 March 1983.

Shaplen, Robert. "A Reporter at Large: From Marcos to Aquino-1." *New Yorker*, 25 August 1986.

_____. "A Reporter at Large: From Marcos to Aquino-II." *New Yorker*, 2 September 1986.

Sigmund, Paul E. *Liberation Theology: An Historical Evaluation*. Washington, D.C.: Woodrow Wilson International Center for Scholars. Undated [after1986].

Simons, Marlise. "Haitian Prelate is Under Attack." *New York Times*, 3 April 1986.

_____. "Haitians Bemoan 'the Pope's Purge of Main Street.'" *New York Times*, 9 April 1983.

_____. "Latin American Bishops See Protestant Peril." *New York Times*, 16 March 1983, A11.

_____. "Pope in Haiti Assails Inequality, Hunger and Fear." *New York Times*, 10 March 1983, A8.

_____. "Power of Voodoo Preached by Sorbonne Scientist." *New York Times*, 15 December 1983, A2.

_____. "Shake-Up in Haiti: Ousting the Old Guard." *New York Times*, 23 March 1988.

Simpson, George Eaton. "The Belief System of Haitian Vodun." *American Anthropologist* 47 (1945).

Simpson, Ian. "Haiti." UPI, 15 January 1988.

Smith, Brian H. "Religion and Social Change: Classical Theories and New Formulations in the Context of Recent Developments in Latin America." *Latin American Research Review* 10 (Summer 1975): 3–34.

Smolowe, Jill. "A New Start, A Ray of Hope." *Time*, 26 March 1990.

Souffrant, C. "Catholicisme et Négritude à l'"Heure du Black Power." *Présence Africaine*, 1951.

Steiff, William. "Haitian Exodus." *Multinational Monitor* 6, no. 18 (December 1985): 10.

_____. Haitian Hell: A Government Gone Awry." *Multinational Monitor* 6, no. 18 (December 1985).

Stone, N. "The Many Tragedies of Haiti." *The Times Literary Supplement*, 15 February 1980.

Streit, Clarence K. "Haiti: Intervention in Operation." *Foreign Affairs* 6 (1928): 615–32.

Stumbo, Bella. "Millionaires and Misery." *Los Angeles Times*, 15 December 1985, 1: 6–7.

_____. 16 December 1985, 1: 16–17.

_____. 17 December 1985, 1: 18–19.

Sunshine, Catherine A. "A Radicalized Church Undermined Duvalier's State." *Guardian*, 5 March 1986.

_____. "The United States and Haiti: Democracy's Image." *Christianity and Crisis*, 7 March 1988.

Swedish, Margaret. "The Witness of Oscar Romero." *Central America Report*, February 1988, 1.

Time. "Never, Never Again." 24 February 1986.

_____."Small Stirrings of Change." 13 January 1986.

Times of the Americas. "Government Council Overhauls Electoral Board: New Haitian Elections Set." 16 December 1987.

_____. "Tonton Macoute Terror." 18 November 1987.

Tinco, Henri. "L'Église Haïtienne Débordée Par les Revendications." *Nouvelliste*, 11 April 1986, reprinted from *Le Monde* 9 April 1986.

Tomlinson, Alan. "Bitterness Rises as Haitians Wait Impatiently for Change." *Christian Science Monitor*, 9 December 1986, 18.

Toumédia, ed. *Haïti-Pape 83*. Port-au-Prince: Imprimerie Henri Deschamps, 1983.

Treaster, Joseph B. "As All Haiti Watches, First Duvalier Aid Is Tried." *New York Times*, 9 May 1986.

_____."Stop the Killing, Church in Haiti Asks." *New York Times*, 24 February 1986.

_____. "Without Suspense, Haitians Vote Today on President-For-Life." *New York Times*, 22 January 1985.

Trouillot, Michel-Rolph. *Nation, State, and Society in Haiti, 1804–1984*. Washington, D.C.: The Woodrow Wilson International Center for Scholars, 1985.

United Nations Human Rights Commission, 3 December 1991.

U.S. Catholic Conference. *Basic Christian Communities*. Washington, D.C.: U.S. Catholic Conference, 1976.

Vallier, Ivan. "Church 'Development' in Latin America: A Five Country Comparison." *Journal of Developing Areas* 1 (July 1967): 461–76.

Volman, Dennis. "Haiti Catholics Debate Role." *Christian Science Monitor*, 11 February 1986.

Voltaire, Yves. "Haïti: Terre d'Espérance." *Orient*, March-April 1986.

Wall Street Journal. "Defying Duvalier: The Pope Visits Haiti Just as Church there is Challenging Regime," 8 March 1983.

Washington Office on Haiti. Haitian Government Expels Three Priests in Wake of Referendum." News Release, Washington, D.C., 25 July 1985.
Washington Post. "Haitian Masses Canceled." 30 July 1985.
_____. "Haiti's Misery: Economy Remains Stagnant, Hostage to Political Unrest." 22 December 1986.
_____. "Pastoral Letter. Excerpts: The Poor Have a Special Claim to Our Concern," 12 November 1984.
_____. "Regime, Media at Odds in Haiti." 10 July 1987.
_____. "Second Catholic Radio Closes in Haiti." 8 December 1985.
_____. "United States Warns Haiti Not to Change Vote Plan." 10 July 1987, A20.
_____. "Who's a Genuine Refugee?" 30 December 1991.
Wayne, E.A. "United States Takes Firm Line on Haiti." *Christian Science Monitor,* 7 August 1987.
Wright, Robin. "Quiet Revolution: Islamic Movement's New Phase." *Christian Science Monitor,* 6 November 1987.
Wylie, Jeanie. "Religion in Haiti: Conquering Souls, Pursuing Justice." *Christianity and Crisis,* 11 July 1983.

REPORTS

Americas Watch and National Coalition for Haïtian Refugees. *Duvalierism Since Duvalier.* New York: Americas Watch and National Coalition for Haïtian Refugees, October 1986.
_____. *Haiti: Human Rights Under Hereditary Dictatorship.* New York: Americas Watch and National Coalition for Haïtian Refugees, October 1985.
Amnesty International. *The Amnesty International Reports* 1975 through 1986. London: Amnesty International.
_____. *Haiti: Amnesty International Briefing.* London: Amnesty International, March 1985
_____. *Urgent Action Letters,* 1977 - February 1985. London: Amnesty International.
Bélizaire, Joseph. "Rapport Sur Un Cas D'Injustice Survenu à Plaisance les 6, 7, 8, 9 juin 1984." Report by a townsperson of an altercation between members of the public and local law officials. Unpublished, photocopied document.
Bouchey, L. Francis, Roger Fontaine, David C. Jordan, General Gordon Sumner, and Lewis Tambs (The Committee of Santa Fe). "A New Inter-American Policy for the Eighties." Washington, D.C., The Council for Inter-American Security, May 1980.
Bourdeau, Michel. Comité Catholique Contre la Faim et Pour le Développement, *Trip Report to Haiti,* Paris, France. 22 June - 6 July 1984.
Central Latinoamericana de Trabajadores. "Increases in Repression Against Union in Haiti." News Release, Caracas, Venezuela, 17 December 1980.
Comite Haïtiano-Venezolano de Defensa de los Derechos Humanos. *La Iglesia En Haïti.* no. 5. Caracas, Venezuela, 1983.
Congressional Research Service. *Haiti: Bibliography in Brief, 1978–1986.* Washington, D.C.: Library of Congress, February 1986.
Fernandez, Irene Garzon. "Report on Pope in Haiti and Superintendent Statement." Translation of this UPI report by the Haitian Refugee Project, 14 March 1983.

Fouchard, Eric. "The Haitian Church and Dictatorship." *CIF Reports*, 5, no. 8 (16 April 1966). Translated from the Mexican daily *Novedades*, 20 February 1966, Mexico, D.F.

Freeland, Gregory K. *Religious Elites and Political Activity in Haiti*. University of California, Santa Barbara. Prepared for delivery at the 1985 Annual Meeting of the Western Political Science Association, Las Vegas, 28–30 March 1985.

"Haitian Government Expels Three Priests in Wake of Referendum." News Release, Washington Office on Haiti, Washington, D.C., 25 July 1985.

Haitian League for Human Rights. *Statement*. On the events of Gonaïves. Port-au-Prince: 28 November 1985.

Haitian Refugee Project. "Haitian Catholic Leaders Step into Human Rights Void on Eve of Mass Bahamian Deportations." Washington, D.C.: Haitian Refugee Project, 13 January 1981.

_____. "Haitian Clergy Protests Imprisonment of Catholic Lay Worker on Eve of Pope's Visit." Washington, D.C.: Haitian Refugee Project, 8 February 1983.

Hooper, Michael and Aryeh Neier. *A Democracy Through Terror, Chronology of Recent Events in Haiti and the United States Response*. New York: National Coalition of Haitian Refugees and Americas Watch, January 1988.

Horblitt, Stephen A. *Report on Mission to Haiti and Recommendations for Future Action*. Memo to Congressman Fauntroy. 1 January 1986.

Jegen, Mary Evelyn. *Haïti, The Struggle Continues*. Just World Order Series. Erie, PA: Pax Christi, 1987.

Jegen, Mary Evelyn, Thomas Gumbleton, Fritz Longchamp, and Beverly Bell. "Haiti, a Country in Crisis." Video recorded at the National Press Club by Pax Christi, Erie, PA, 12 December 1985.

Organization of American States. *Violations of Human Rights in Haiti: A Report of the Lawyers Committee for International Human Rights to the Organization of American States*. Washington, D.C.: Organization of American States, November, 1980.

Pax Christi International. *Report of the Mission of Pax Christi International to Haiti*. Erie, PA: Pax Christi International, 1986.

Puebla Institute. *Haiti's Reign of Terror: Report on Chronic Religious Repression and Other Human Rights Abuse*. Washington, D.C.: Puebla Institute, September 1988.

Rocourt, Pasteur Alain. *Pour Une Participation Effective de la Paysannerie Haïtienne à L'Administration Politique Nationale*. Undated (after February 1986)

Shea, Nina and Leslie Hunter. *The Current Status of Human Rights in Haiti*. Puebla Institute, 24 March 1988.

Storrs, Larry K. and Mark P. Sullivan. *Haiti: United States Foreign Assistance Facts*. Washington, D.C.: Library of Congress, Congressional Research Service, 22 March 1988.

Taft-Morales, Maureen. *Haiti: Political Developments and United States Policy Concerns*. Washington, D.C.: Library of Congress, Congressional Research Service, 11 October 1988.

Washington Office on Haiti. *The Government of Haiti: Noncompliance with the Criteria for United States Foreign Assistance*. Report to Congress. Washington, D.C.: The Washington Office on Haiti, vol.1 February 1985; vol. 2, October 1985.

_____. *Report to Congress*. vol.1 Washington D.C.: Washington Office on Haiti, February 1985.

Wilson Center. "Democracy in Haiti." *Wilson Center Reports*, September 29–30 conference. Washington, D.C.: Wilson Center, November 1986.

OFFICIAL DOCUMENTS: THE GOVERNMENT OF HAITI

Anonymous. Cable to Ministry of Foreign Affairs and Religion reporting and commenting on "Le Manifeste de Jérémie," (homily of Mgr. Willy Romélus). Undated [on or after 11 April 1985].

Civil Tribunal of Gonaïves. "Minutes from the Cabinet d'Instruction of the Civil Tribunal of Gonaïves." 28 November 1985.

Estimé, Jean-Robert, Minister of Foreign Affairs and Religion. *Letter to the Conference of Haitian Bishops*. Port-au-Prince: 30 July 1985.

_____. *Letter to Father Yvon Joseph*. Port-au-Prince: 21 December 1984.

_____. *Letter to Jean Claude Duvalier, President-for-Life of Haiti*. Port-au-Prince: 8 March 1983.

_____. *Letters to Papal Nuncio Luigi Conti*. Port-au-Prince: 23 February 1983 and 8 March 1983.

Haiti: Ministry of Foreign Affairs and Religion. *Concordat Entre le Saint-Siège et la République d'Haïti*. 28 March 1860.

_____. *Law Regulating the Organization and Functioning of the Political Parties in Haiti*, 9 June 1985.

_____. *L'Église Catholique et l'Etat: Evolution des Rapports*, 1985.

_____. *Les Églises Protestantes ou Cultes Reformes*. 13 December 1985.

_____. *Letter from Jean-Marie Chanoine, Minister of the Interior and National Defense, Announcing Provisional Closing of Radio Soleil*, 5 December 1985.

_____.*Lettre du Ministère de L'Intérieur et de la Défense Nationale à Mgr. E. Constant donnant Une Nouvelle Autorisation de Functionnement à Radio Soleil*, Port-au-Prince, 23 December 1985.

_____.Mémorandum: "Actualisation Du Concordat," November 1985.

_____. *The Penal Code, Annex Articles 162–168*. Rules Concerning the Conduct of the Ministry of Religion. Undated.

_____. *Talking paper concerning Church-State relations*, April 1985.

Institute Haïtien Statistique. *Guide Economique de la République d'Haïti*. Mimeograph. Port-au-Prince: Institute Haïtien Statistique, 1977.

Jacques, Raoul. *Minutes (excerpts) of the Cabinet d'Instruction of the Civil Tribunal of Gonaïves, 29 November 1986*. Gonaïves: Republic of Haiti, 28 November 1985.

Religion et Société. *Le Manifeste de Jérémie*. Undated [after 14 April 1985].

OFFICIAL DOCUMENTS: THE HAITIAN CHURCH

Bussels, Marcel, et al. "Letter to the Bishops from a group of Christians in Cap-Haïtien expressing solidarity with initiatives to denounce the climate of terror and insecurity in Haiti," Unpublished Church document: Cap-Haïtien, 12 November 1984.

Catholic Church of Haiti. *Annuaire de l'Église Catholique (Missions Catholiques), Vol. 1*. Port-au-Prince: Catholic Church of Haiti, 1986.

Clercs de Saint-Viateur d'Haïti. *Déclaration des Clercs de Saint-Viateur d'Haïti Au Sujet de L'Expulsion du Père René Poirier*. Port-au-Prince: Clercs de Saint-Viateur d'Haïti, 13 August 1988.

Commission Justice et Paix de L'Archdiocèse de Port-au-Prince. *Carte en Solidarité des Prêtres de l'Archdiocèse*. Port-au-Prince: Commission Justice et Paix de L'Archdiocèse de Port-au-Prince, 14 May 1985.

_____. *Déclaration*. Port-au-Prince: Commission Justice et Paix de L'Archdiocèse de Port-au-Prince, 25 April 1985.

_____. *Lettre de la Commission Justice et Paix d'Haïti à. la Conférence Épiscopal d'Haïti sur le Congrès Eucharistique et Marial de Port-au-Prince.* Commission Justice et Paix de L'Archdiocèse de Port-au-Prince, 9 December 1981.

Conference of Haitian Bishops. *Bulletin d'Information 1985. Année Internationale de la Jeunesse.* Port-au-Prince: Imprimerie la Phalange, 1985.

_____. *Charte Fondamentale de l'Église Catholique Sur la Promotion Humaine.* Port-au-Prince: CHB, 8 December 1983.

_____. *Charte Fondamentale Pour le Passage à Une Société Démocratique Selon La Doctrine et L'Expérience de l'Église.* Port-au-Prince: CHB, 27 June 1986.

_____. *Communiqué* Port-au-Prince: CHB, 13 November 1984.

_____. *Déclaration de la Conférence Épiscopale d'Haïti au Peuple Haïtien.* Port-au-Prince: CHB, 7 November 1989.

_____. *Déclaration des Evêques d'Haïti Sur La Situation Difficile Que Traverse le Pays.* Port-au-Prince: CHB, undated [after 5 August 1988].

_____. *Declaration of the Bishops of Haiti on the Foundations of Church Intervention in Social and Political Affairs.* Port-au-Prince: CHB, 11 April 1983.

_____. *Declaration of the Haitian Bishops' Conference.* Port-au-Prince: CHB, 26 January 1990.

_____. *Démocratie en Haïti Principes et Applications.* Port-au-Prince: CHB, Imprimerie La Phalange, 1986.

_____. *Joint Letter* signed by bishops and heads of Religious Orders urging prayers in Churches on 9 February 1983 for the release of Gérard Duclerville. Port-au-Prince: CHB, 27 January 1983.

_____. *Letter to His Excellency, Jean-Claude Duvalier and Accompanying Memorandum to the President-for-Life of the Republic.* Port-au-Prince: CHB, 12 December 1984.

_____. *Letter to his Excellency Jean-Claude Duvalier, President-for-Life of the Republic of Haiti.* Port-au-Prince: CHB, 9 July 1985.

_____. *Letter to Jean-Robert Estimé, Minister of Foreign Affairs and Religion.* Port-au-Prince: CHB, 12 November 1984.

_____. *Letter to Jean-Robert Estimé, Secretary of Foreign Relations and Religion on the Occasion of the Arrest of Three Leaders from IDEA.* Port-au-Prince: CHB, 7 November 1984.

_____. *Mémorandum de la CHB au Président de la République.* Port-au-Prince: CHB, 18 December 1985.

_____. *Message from the Bishops to the Young of Haiti in Honor of International Youth Year.* Port-au-Prince: CHB, 6 January 1985.

_____. *Message au Peuple de Dieu à. la Clôture de la Session Nationale de Pastorale Sociale.* Port-au-Prince: CHB, 25–27 October 1985.

_____. *Message on the Opening of the National Session of Pastorale Sociale.* Port-au-Prince: CHB, 23–27 October 1985.

_____. *Message à L'Occasion de la Fête de Noël.* Port-au-Prince: CHB, 1985.

_____. *Message Pastoral en la Fête de Notre-Dame du Mont-Carmel.* Port-au-Prince: CHB, 16 July 1985.

_____. *Message Pastoral Au Peuple de Dieu.* Port-au-Prince: CHB, 1 May 1986.

_____. *Message Pastoral.* Port-au-Prince: CHB, 7 March 1986.

_____. *Message Pastoral.* Port-au-Prince: CHB, 7 February 1986.

_____. *Message to the People on the Closure of the National Session of the Pastoral Session.* Port-au-Prince: CHB, 23–27 October 1985.

_____. *Official Statement of the Religious Conference of Haiti.* Port-au-Prince: CHB, 4 December 1980.

_____. *Open Letter to the Heads of the Three Branches of the Government.* Port-au-Prince: CHB, 24 November 1984.

_____. *Pastoral Letter.* Port-au-Prince: CHB 27 January 1983.

_____. *Pastoral Letter.* Port-au-Prince: CHB, 3 March 1984.

_____. *Pastoral Letter.* "Haitian Unity." Port-au-Prince: CHB, 30–31 December 1987.

_____. *Pastoral Message of the Bishops of Haiti on Political Parties.* Port-au-Prince: CHB, 16 July 1986.

_____. *Protestation de la Conférence Épiscopale d'Haïti.* Port-au-Prince: CHB, 26 July 1985.

Conference of Haitian Bishops and Conference of Haitian Religious. *Pastoral Letter.* Port-au-Prince: CHB, 30 January 1983.

Conference of Haitian Bishops and Executive Board of Conference of Haïtian Religious. *A Pastoral Letter.* Port-au-Prince: CHB, 27 January 1983.

Conference of Haitian Religious. *A Nos Chers Pères et Frères en Jesus-Christ, Les Evêques d'Haïti.* Port-au-Prince: CHR, 4 December 1980.

_____. *Communiqué* from the Conference of Haitian Religious. Port-au-Prince: CHR, 4 December 1980.

_____. *Document d'Information et de Réflexion Produit à L'Intention des Religieux Par le Bureau de la CHR.* Port-au-Prince: CHR, 27 February 1986.

_____. *Dossier, "A Year After."* Port-au-Prince: CHR, 18 November 1981.

_____. *Global Plan of the Conference of Haitian Religious.* Port-au-Prince: CHR, Translation in Washington, D.C.: Haitian Refugee Project, April 1983.

_____. *Inaugural Message by Father Yvon Joseph at the Second General Assembly of the Conference of Haitian Religious.* Port-au-Prince: CHR, 23–26 April 1984.

_____. *Letter To All Members of the Religious Orders of Haiti.* Port-au-Prince: CHR, 14 November 1984.

_____. *Letter To All Members of the Religious Orders of Haiti.* Port-au-Prince: CHR, 23 November 1982.

_____. *Letter To Our Dear Fathers and Brothers in Christ the Bishops of Haiti.* Port-au-Prince: CHR, 4 December 1980.

_____. *Official Statement of the Religious Conference in Haiti.* (Personally signed by each of twenty-four different heads of orders of men and women Religious). CHR, 4 December 1980.

Conference of Latin American Religious Superiors. *Message to the Conference of Haitian Religious.* Port-au-Prince, October 20, 1983.

Constant, Emmanuel Mgr. *Message to the Citizens of Gonaïves.* Concerning the murdered children in Gonaïves. Cited in *Bulletin d'Information 1985. Année Internationale de la Jeunesse.* Port-au-Prince: Imprimerie la Phalange, 1985.Conti, Luigi. *Letter to Father Jacques Mesidor, president of the Haitian Conference of Religious.* Apostolic Nunciature in Haiti, no. 1140. Port-au-Prince: Papal Nuncio to Haiti, 6 December 1980.

_____. *Letter to Minister of Religion, Jean-Robert Estimé.* Port-au-Prince: Papal Nuncio to Haiti, 23 February 1983.

Council of Haitian Youth. *Jean Robert Cius, Mackenson Michel, Daniel Israel.* Port-au-Prince: Council of Haitian Youth, December 1985.

_____. *The Root Causes of this Suffering.* Port-au-Prince: Council of Haitian Youth, December 1985.

"Declaration of a Group of Priests Regarding the *Radio Soleil* Affair." Haiti, 6 July 1989. Translated by the Washington Office on Haiti from French to English on 31 July 1989.

Desroches, Rosny and François Wolff Ligondé. *Homélie du Pasteur Rosny Desroches de l'Église Méthodiste and Homélie de Monseigneur François Wolff Ligonde, Achevêque de Port-au-Prince.* Semaine de Prière pour l'Unité des Chrétiens 19 January 1986. Port-au-Prince: Imprimerie La Phalange, 26 January 1986.

Diocesan Institute for Adult Education. Letter to Jean-Robert Estimé concerning the arrest of three *animateurs* from IDEA. Port-au-Prince: Diocesan Institute for Adult Education, 7 November 1984.

Diocese of Gonaïves. *Some Thoughts on the Times in Which We Are Living—.* Letter from TKL Outreach Group to each TKL Fraternity in the Diocese. Gonaïves: Diocese of Gonaïves, May 1986.

Fabian, Father Rosemond. *Report on Celebration of November 18, 1984.* Cap-Haïtien: Paroisse de la Cathédrale, 18 November 1984.

Fathers of Sainte Croix. *Letter to Jean-Robert Estimé.* Port-au-Prince: Fathers of Sainte Croix, 10 December 1984.

Gayot, François. *Address to Bishops' Conference.* Port-au-Prince: 12 December 1984.

_____. *Approches de la Culture Religieuse Haïtienne: Première Partie.* Mimeo. Port-au-Prince: 1969.

_____. *Commentaires sûr le Communiqué des Evêques d'Haïti.* Port-au-Prince, undated.

_____. *Declaration Following the Grave Offense Against the Ecclesiastical Authorities and the Liberty of the the Church Committed in the Cathedral of Cap-Haïtien, Sunday 18 November 1984 and Parochial Church of Milot.* Port-au-Prince, 8 December 1984.

_____. *Explanation of the Press Release of the Haitian Bishops.* Cap-Haïtien, June 1984.

_____. *Message de Monseigneur François Gayot, SMM, Evêque du Cap-Haïtien à L'Occasion des Evénements des 26 et 27 janvier 1986.* Port-au-Prince, undated.

Group of Religious from Hinche. *Letter to the Board of the Conference of Haitian Religious.* Hinche: 10 January 1985.

Holy Cross Fathers. *Letter to Jean-Robert Estimé, Minister of Foreign Affairs and Religion.* Cap-Haïtien, 10 December 1984.

Joseph, Father Emile. "Attentat Manqué Contre le Père Emile Joseph le 22 avril 1985." Port-au-Prince, 23 April 1985.

Ligondé, François Wolff. *Letter to Révérend Père Pétion Laroche, Recteur du Grand Séminaire, Haut de Turgeau.* Port-au-Prince: CEH, 6 May 1981.

Milot, Father Joseph Serge. *Letter to Jean-Robert Estimé.* Port-au-Prince: CHB, 7 November 1984.

Mission Alpha. "What We Do." Port-au-Prince: Mission Alpha, undated.

Présence de l'Église En Haïti: Messages et Documents de l'Épiscopat, 1980–1988. Paris: Éditions SOS, 1988.

Priests and Religious of the Archdiocese of Port-au-Prince. *Declaration.* Port-au-Prince: Priests and Religious of the Archdiocese of Port-au-Prince, undated [ca. April-May 1985].

Romeo, Papal Nuncio Paulo. *Letter to Jean-Robert Estimé.* 23 February 1983.

Romélus, Willy. Address on *Radio Soleil.* Jérémie, 16 February 1984.

_____. *Homélie de Monseigneur Romélus, Concile des Jeunes,* 11 April 1985.

Youth of Archdiocese of Port-au-Prince. *Message of the Youth of Archdiocese of Port-au-Prince at the Occasion of the Meeting in the Salesian Fathers' House at Thorland.* Port-au-Prince: Youth of Archdiocese of Port-au-Prince, 25–27 July 1986. Youth of Les

Cayes. *Greetings in Solidarity to the Youth of Port-au-Prince.* Les Cayes: Youth of Les Cayes, 13 December 1985. Youth of Jérémie. *Declaration of the Youth of Jérémie.* Jérémie: Youth of Jérémie, 5 December 1985.

OFFICIAL DOCUMENTS: THE U.S. GOVERNMENT

Fauntroy, Walter, E. "Congressman Fauntroy Declines to Visit Haiti." News Release, 14 December 1988.

———. "Congressmen Walter E. Fauntroy and Crockett call for Murderers of Yves Volel to be Brought to Justice in Haiti." News Release, 14 October 1987.

———. "Fauntroy Angered and Disturbed Over Attacks on Provisional Electoral Commission in Haiti." News Release, 5 November 1987.

———. "Fauntroy Says Caricom Abandons Haiti and Democracy." News Release, 7 January 1988.

———. "Fauntroy Supports Increased Economic Assistance to Haiti." News Release, 5 March 1987.

———. "Members of Congress Ask the President to Reject Haiti Vote." News Release, 15 January 1988.

———. *Memorandum to his Excellency Pio Laghi, Apostolic Pro Nuncio* 18 February 1986.

———. "Testimony before Subcommittee on Western Hemisphere Affairs. 18 November 1987.

———. "United States Congressional Task Force on Haiti Demands Safety and Freedom for Déjoie." News Release, 21 January 1988.

Fauntroy, Walter. Letter to Ambassador Clayton McManaway, 7 January 1986.

Fauntroy, Walter and Bob Graham. Statement on Arrival Port-au-Prince, 30 October 1987.

Fauntroy, Walter and Thirty-Seven Other Members of Congress. *Statement of Concern,* 7 August 1987.

Foreign Broadcast Information Service Daily Report. "Anti-Avril Demonstration in Gonaïves 6 March." Port-au-Prince, *Radio Soleil.* Network in Creole, 1980 GMT, 6 March 1990, FBIS-LAT 90–045, 7 March 1990, 13–14.

———. "Anti-election Petitions Cause Arrests." Network in Creole on 3 February 1988. FBIS LAT 88–028, 11 February 1988, 2–12.

———. "Aristide: Avril 'Not Willing to Leave Country.'" Port-au-Prince, Radio Antilles Internationales in French 1830 GMT, 10 March 90, FBIS-LAT-90–048, 12 March 1990.

———. "Avril appointed a Cabinet. Gourgue: Speech 'Shocking.'" Port-au-Prince, Radio Métropole. Broadcast in French 1700 GMT 10 February 1988, 10.

———. "Avril Appointed a Cabinet. 'Leslie Manigat Delivers Inaugural Address.'" Port-au-Prince, Radio Nationale in French 1605 GMT, 7 February 1988.

———. "Bazin: Wants Deeds Not Words." Port-au-Prince, Radio Métropole Broadcast in Creole 1700 GMT 9 February 1988, 8.

———. "Father Aristide Calls for General Consensus," Port-au-Prince Radio Métropole in Creole, 0950 GMT, 16 February 1990, FBIS-LAT-90–035, 21 February 1990.

———. "Fires, Protests Reported." Port-au-Prince, Radio Antilles Internationales in Creole 1230 GMT 9 March 1990, FBIS-LAT-90–048, 12 March 1990, 5.

_____."Government Newspaper Criticizes Pope, Clergy." AFP in Spanish 2002. GMT 11 March 1983, 12.

_____. "MDN: Speech Shows 'Contempt.'" Port-au-Prince, Radio Métropole Broadcast in French 1700 GMT 9 February 1988, 9.

_____. "Opposition Comments." Port-au-Prince, Radio Métropole in French, 1700 GMT 9 February 1988, 7.

_____. "Priest Calls for Arrest of 'Murderers' by 29 March," Port-au-Prince, Radio Antilles Internationales in French, 1230 GMT, 26 March 1990, FBIS-LAT-90–060, 28 March 1990, 30.

_____. "Priest States Readiness to Combat Government." Port-au-Prince, Radio Métropole in French, 1700 GMT 9 February 1988, 12.

_____. "Soleil Continues to Poll Parties on Elections." Port-au-Prince, Radio Soleil Network in Creole, 1000 GMT, 15 February 1990, FBIS-LAT-90–034, 20 February 1990, 15.

_____. "Two More Reportedly Killed in Port-au-Prince." Port-au-Prince, AFP in Spanish, 0226 GMT, 8 March 1990, FBIS-LAT-90–047, 9 March 1990, 13.

_____. "United States Ambassador Adams Acclaimed by Crowd," Port-au-Prince, Radio Nationale in Creole, 1400 GMT, 14 March 1990, FBIS-LAT-90–051, 15 March 1990.

Gershman, Carl. "Haiti: Institution Building in a Transitional Democracy." National Endowment for Democracy, undated.

_____. "Trip to Haiti, 29 June-2 July 1986." National Endowment for Democracy, 3 July 1986.

Lite, Jeffrey. *Haiti Today: The Challenge for United States Information Service.* Washington, D.C.: U.S. Information Agency, 13 March 1986.

U.S. Agency for International Development, Port-au-Prince. *Country Development Strategy Fiscal Years 1983–1987.* Port-au-Prince: January 1981.

U.S. Congress. House Committee on Foreign Affairs, Subcommittee on Human Rights and International Organizations. *Human Rights in Haiti.* Hearing before the Subcommittee on Human Rights and International Organizations 99th Congress, 1st sess.,17 April 1985.

U.S. Congress, House. House Report to the Honorable Walter E. Fauntroy. *Detention Policies Affecting Haitian Nationals.* U.S. General Accounting Office, 16 June 1983.

_____. *U.S. Assistance to Haiti: Progress Made, Challenges Remain.* U.S. General Accounting Office, 12 June 1985.

U.S. Congress, Senate. Select Committee on Intelligence. *The Philippines: A Situation Report.* Washington, D.C.: GPO, 1 November 1985.

U.S. Department of State, Agency for International Development, *Economic Assistance to Haiti.* Position Paper for the U.N. General Assembly, 40th Session, 31 October 1985.

U.S. Department of State, Bureau of Public Affairs. "Background Notes, Haiti." Washington, D.C.: GPO, 1984.

U.S. Department of State. Telegram from the U.S. Embassy in Port-au-Prince to the Department of State, 4 February 1988.

_____. "Changing Life to Ensure Better Tomorrows." Telegram from the U.S. Embassy in Port-au-Prince to the Department of State, 1 August 1980.

_____. "Duvalier Assets." Cable from the Secretary of State to the American Embassy in Paris. Secret. State 53977, 21 February 1986.

_____. "Duvalier Departure From Haiti." Press Guidance Cable to all Diplomatic Posts in American Republics. Limited Official Use State 39152, 7 February 1986.

_____. "Follow up Trip to Pastel Region." Memorandum of Conversation, Andrew Parker, 21 June 1983.

_____. "List of Duvalier's Presumed Accomplices." Cable to American Embassy Port-au-Prince. Unclass State 222726, 16 July 1986.

_____. "Memorandum of Conversation." (regarding emigration from a returnee officer), 13 and 15 October 1983.

_____. "Palace Official Warns Embassy of Threats to Regime." Cable to American Embassies in Grenada and Port of Spain. Secret. State 007554, 9 June 1986.

_____. "Statement by NDI Observer Delegation." Cable to American Embassy, Port-au-Prince, 9 December 1987.

U.S. Department of State, American Embassy Brasilia. "Government of Haiti Orders Preventive Arrest of Former Haitian Police Chief." Cable to Secretary of State. Unclass Brasilia 03358, 31 March 1986.

U. S. Department of State, American Embassy Paris. "Duvalier Update." Cable to Secretary of State. Confidential. Paris 27215, 12 June 1986.

U.S. Department of State, American Embassy Port-au-Prince. "Asylum Request by Former Minister Theodore Achille." Cable to Secretary of State. Secret. Port-au-Prince 0917, 6 February 1986.

_____. "Ousted Dictator to Move to Cannes." AP, Grasse, France, 29 May 1986.

_____. "Auguste Douyon". Biographic file, 23 October 1973.

_____. "Cambrone Visiting Economic Section U.S. Embassy in Haiti." Memorandum of Conversation, 20 January 1983.

_____. "Catholic Bishops Conference Statement on January 17 Elections." Cable to Secretary of State, 26 March 1987.

_____. "CNG Announces Measures to Respond to Popular Demand." Cable to Secretary of State. Confidential. Port-au-Prince 01434, 28 February 1986.

_____. "Confiscation of Duvalier Assets." Cable to Secretary of State, 16 February 1986.

_____. "Duvalier Family." Memorandum of Conversation. 24 May 1976.

_____. "Duvalier Family Problems—Quarrel over Chocolate Factory." Cable to Secretary of State. Confidential. Port-au-Prince 4171, 31 December 1985.

_____. "Duvalier's Last Days." Cable to Secretary of State, 19 February 1986.

_____. "Ex Defense and Interior Minister Lafontant Leaves Haiti." Cable to Secretary of State. Confidential. Port-au-Prince 6746, 7 October 1985.

_____. Follow-Up on Charles Bushnell Conversation." Cable to Secretary of State. Confidential. Port-au-Prince 3647, 1 August 1986.

_____. "Follow-Up Trip to Pestell Region." Memorandum to the File from Andrew Parker, Returnee Officer, 21 June 1983.

_____. "Government of Haiti to Pursue Criminals from Former Regime." Cable to Secretary of State, Unclass Port-au-Prince 04546, 1 July 1986.

_____. "GOH Confiscation of Duvalier Assets. Cable to Secretary of State, Secret. Port-au-Prince 1316, 24 February 1986.

_____. "Guy Noel, Medical Doctor and Former Presidential Advisor." Biographic file, 9 August 1983.

_____. "Haiti-Church." Associated Press, Port-au-Prince. 24 December 1987.

_____. "Haiti-Church." Associated Press, Port-au-Prince. 23 January 1988.

_____. "Meeting with Secretary of Finance Frantz Merceron." Cable to Deputy Assistant Secretary of State Michel. Secret. Port-au-Prince 0926, 12 February 1984.

_____. "Memorandum of conversation regarding emigration from a returnee officer," 13 and 15 October 1983.

_____. "Memorandum to the Ambassador concerning a conversation regarding illegal imports from Barry Eurnett, Chief DDE." Undated.

_____. "Memorandum to the Files regarding Duvalier's assets from John W. Vincent." Undated.

_____. "Narcotics: The Haitian Ambassador to Geneva Recalled." Cable to Secretary of State. Confidential. Port-au-Prince, 4 April 1985.

_____. "The Palace and the Cocaine Trade. Memorandum of Conversation." 18 December 1985.

_____. "Position Papers for United Nations General Assembly, 40th Session." Cable to Secretary of State from AID. 31 October 1985.

_____. "President-Elect Manigat's Government Program." Cable to Secretary of State. 4 February 1988

_____. "President Namphy's Policy Speech." Cable to Secretary of State. Unclass. Port-au-Prince 1731, 25 February 1986.

_____. "The Reemergence of Luckner Cambrone." Cable to Secretary of State. Secret. Port-au-Prince 4522, 8 August 1984.

_____. "Refugee Business and Corrupt Personal Secretary to Jean-Claude Duvalier." Cable to Secretary of State, 1 August 1980.

_____. "Régie du Tabac." Memorandum of Conversation between Frazier Meade, Deputy Chief of Mission, and Guy Noel, 26 February 1977.

_____. "Speech by Ambassador McKinley on Democracy in Haiti." (5 March 1987), 26 March 1987.

_____. "Text of Bishops' Conference Letter to the Public." Cable to Secretary of State. 12 August 1987.

_____. "Text of Bishops' Statement on Crisis." Cable to Secretary of State. 7 December 1987.

_____. "Theodore Achille." Biographic file, 22 January 1980.

_____. "Trends in Illegal Haitian Migration." Cable to Secretary of State EO 12356, 23 June 1983.

_____. "U.S. Aid to Haiti." Cable to Secretary of State, 13 February1985.

_____. "Visit by AIFELD and International Trade Union Representatives." Cable to Secretary of State. Confidential. Port-au-Prince 1425, 13 March 1985.

_____. U.S. Information Agency. "Elections in Haiti." Cable to Secretary of State Unclass. Port-au-Prince 05719, 15 August 1986

_____. U.S. Information Agency. "Manigat's Foreign Policy Program." Cable to Secretary of State. Unclass. Port-au-Prince 00704, 3 February 1988.

_____. U.S. Information Agency. "Speech by Ambassador McKinley on Democracy in Haiti." Cable to Secretary of State. Unclass. Port-au-Prince 01360, 6 March 1987.

_____. U.S. Information Agency. "President-Elect Manigat's Government Program." Cable to Secretary of State. Unclass. Port-au-Prince 00766, 4 February 1988.

U.S. Department of State, U.S. Information Service. *Institutional Analysis.* Port-au-Prince: U.S. Information Service, 1985.

U.S. General Accounting Office. *Detention Policies Affecting Haitian Nationals.* AO/GGD-83–68. Gaithersburg, MD: U.S. General Accounting Office, 16 June 1983.

_____. *U.S. Assistance to Haiti: Progress Made, Challenges Remain.* Report to the Hon. Walter Fauntroy, House of Representatives. GAO/USAID-85–86. Gaithersburg, MD: U.S. General Accounting Office, 12 June 1985.

OFFICIAL DOCUMENTS: THE VATICAN

John Paul II, Pope. "Farewell Address" at the Airport. Port-au-Prince: 9 March 1983.

_____. *Homily at the Airport during the Eucharistic Celebrations Closing the Festivities of the Eucharistic and Marial Congress in Haiti,* 9 March 1983

_____. *Pope's Haiti Mass Homily.* N.C. News Translation from French to English of the Pope's Vatican text. Port-au-Prince: 14 March 1983.

Second Vatican Council. "Declaration on Religious Freedom." *Dignitates Humane.* Documents of the Second Vatican Council. Rome: Vatican, 1965.

_____. *Decree on the Bishop' Pastoral Office in the Church.* Rome: Vatican, 1965.

_____. Pastoral Constitution on the Church in the Modern World." *Gaudiem et Spes.* Encyclical Rome: Vatican, 1965.

Spiritan News. "Return to Haiti." Rome: Congregazione Dello Spirito Santo-Clivo di Cinna 62,"May-July 1986, 195.

ACADEMIC PAPERS

Brown, O.C. "Haitian Vodu in Relation to Negritude and Christianity: A Study in Acculturation and Applied Anthropology." Ph.D. diss., Indiana University, Bloomington, 1972.

De Wind, Josh. Economic Assistance and Democracy in Haiti. Hunter College. Paper no. 19, Conference, New York University Conference on Haiti, December 1989.

Kelly, James Timothy. "Rocks in the Sun: The Roman Catholic Church in Haitian Political Development." Senior honors thesis. Harvard University, March 1988.

McClure, Marian. "The Catholic Church and Rural Social Change: Priests, Peasant Organizations, and Politics in Haiti." Ph.D. diss., Harvard University, November 1985.

Wilson, C. Larman, "Military Rule and the Hopes for Democracy in Haiti: The Limits of U.S. Foreign Policy." Paper presented at the Latin American Studies Association Meeting, Miami, 4–6 December 1989.

Wood, Fred D., III. "The Scourged Christ of Haiti: Politics, Economics, and the Church in the Island Republic." A Project-Thesis for the Doctor of Ministry Degree, Wesley Theological Seminary, March 1985.

SEMINARS

Evans, Dr Ernest. "The Changing Role of the Catholic Church in Latin America." George Washington University, 21 March 1988.

Hogan, Dr. John. "Social Change and Development in Haiti." Johns Hopkins University, SAIS, 31 January 1990.

Joseph, Father Yvon. "Impact of the Political Situation on Community-Based Development Work of the Catholic Church." Seminar for the Coordination in Development Conference, New York, 21 October 1988, 2–5.

Maguire, Dr. Robert. Speech on Haitian development with the Congressional Staff Forum on Food and International Development at the Dirksen Senate Office Building, 21 March 1986.

_____. Seminar Notes, Coordination in Development Conference, New York, 21 October 1988, 3.

Monte, Father. "A Franciscan Priest's Views on Changes in the Catholic Church" at St Camilus Church in Silver Spring, Maryland, 20 October 1986.

Rocourt, Alain. Chairman and Superintendent General, The Methodist Church of Haiti, "The Role Played by the Churches," seminar for the Coordination in Development Conference, New York, 21 October 1988, 7.

Sigmund, Dr. Paul and Dr. Brady B. Tyson. "Liberation Theology: Its Origins and Evolution."The Woodrow Wilson Center, Washington, D.C., November 1986.

INTERVIEWS

Bardon, Jane, international economist at the Department of the Treasury. Telephone interview 8 April 1987, Washington, D.C.

Bazin, Marc, (Haitian) international economist, Minister of Finance briefly in the Jean-Claude Duvalier administration and Haitian presidential candidate in 1987. Interview on 9 July 1986 at his campaign headquarters in Port-au-Prince, Haiti.

Beauvoir, Max, (Haitian) Voodoo leader and agronomist. Interviews on 12 and 13 July 1986 at Le Péristyle de Mariani in Port-au-Prince, Haiti.

Berlanger, Léopold, Jr., (Haitian) Director General of the Haitian International Institute for Research and Development. Interview on 5 July 1986 at the Montana Hotel in Port-au-Prince, Haiti.

Désinor, Clovis, (Haitian) Minister in various governments of François Duvalier. Interview on 14 July 1986 at his residence in Port-au-Prince, Haiti.

Desmangles, Leslie, (Haitian) professor in the Department of Religion at Trinity College in Hartford, CT. Telephone Interview on 18 April 1988.

Eliantus, Joseph, (Haitian) Voodoo priest (now deceased). Interview on 9 July 1986 at his hounfort and residence in Port-au-Prince, Haiti.

Estimé, Jean-Robert, (Haitian) former Ambassador designate to the O.A.S. Minister of Foreign Relations and Religion, 1982–1985. Interviews between March 1988 and November 1989 at our respective residences in Wheaton and Lanham, MD.

Etienne, Raymond, (Haitian) Deputy Director of ADIH. Interview on 11 July 1986 at the Montana Hotel in Port-au-Prince, Haiti.

Eugène, Grégoire, (Haitian) president, Social Christian Party in Haiti and presidential candidate in 1987. Interview on 11 July 1986 at his campaign headquarters in Port-au-Prince, Haiti.

Father Byas and Bishop Gayot. Washington, D.C.: Washington Office on Haiti, undated.

Fazel, Hassan, (Haitian) international economist at the World Bank. Telephone interview on 8 April 1988 in Washington, D.C.

Fauntroy, Walter, Congressman, District of Columbia and chairman of the Congressional Black Caucus. Interview on 10 May 1988 at his Rayburn House of Representatives Office Building in Washington, D.C.

Frank, Henry, (Haitian) sociologist and anthropologist. Telephone interview on 6 May 1988 in Washington, D.C.

Garnier, Luc, (Haitian) Bishop, Episcopal of Haiti. Interview on 14 July 1986 at his bishopric in Pétionville, Haiti.

Gayot, François, (Haitian) Archbishop from Cap-Haïtien. Interview on 10 July 1988 at his bishopric in Cap-Haïtien.

Gourge, Gérard, (Haitian) human rights activist, school director, former member CNG, and presidential candidate in 1987. Interviews on 7 ,8, and 9 July 1986 at the Montana Hotel and his school in Port-au-Prince, Haiti.

Horblitt, Stephen, Legislative Assistant to Congressman Walter Fauntroy. Interviews on 26 March and 6 April 1988 at the Rayburn House of Representatives Office Building in Washington, D.C.

Honorat, Jean-Jacques, (Haitian) agronomist, economist and human rights activist. Interview on 7 July 1986 at his office in Port-au-Prince, Haiti.

Inda, Caridad, (Mexican) scholar specializing in liberation theology. Interview on 15 March 1988 at her residence in Washington, D.C.

Jones, B. William, Ambassador to Haiti from 1977 to 1980. Interview on 27 April 1988 at the State Department in Washington, D.C.

Joseph, Raymond, (Haitian) publisher of *Haïti-Observateur*. Telephone interview on 19 April 1988 in New York.

Joseph, Yves Germain, (Haitian) counselor to the Minister of Finance in the Jean-Claude Duvalier government and independent journalist. Interview on 7 July 1986 at the Montana Hotel in Port-au-Prince, Haiti.

Levanti, Dominique, (French) journalist for the Agence France Presse. Interview on 7 July 1986 at the Agence France Presse headquarters in Port-au-Prince, Haiti.

Longchamp, Fritz, (Haitian) Director of the Washington Office on Haiti. Interview on 14 April 1988 at the Washington Office on Haiti headquarters in Washington, D.C.

Maguire, Robert, Inter-American Foundation representative for Haiti. Interview on 11 March 1988, in Lanham, MD.

Manigat, Leslie, (Haitian) former President of Haiti. Interviews on 9 and 16 September and 9 December 1988 at respective residences in Bethesda and Lanham, MD, and at the Woodrow Wilson Center in Washington, D.C.

Manigat, Max, (Haitian) professor of Caribbean and Haitian Studies at the City University of New York. Telephone interview on 13 March 1987.

McAlister, Robert, Haitian desk officer at AID. Telephone interview on 8 April 1988 in Washington, D.C.

McManaway, Clayton, Ambassador to Haiti from 1984–1987. Interview on 31 March 1988 at the State Department in Washington, D.C.

Paen, Leslie, (Haitian) economist at the World Bank. Interview on 19 April 1988 at the World Bank in Washington, D.C.

Poirier, René, Canadian priest in Haiti. Interview on 12 July 1986 at Villa Manrése, Port-au-Prince.

Preeg, Ernest H., Ambassador to Haiti from 1981 to 1983. Interview on 31 March 1988 at the State Department in Washington, D.C.

Quigley, Thomas, U.S. Conference of Bishops. Telephone interview on 3 March 1988 in Washington, D.C.

Romeo, Paulo, (Italian) His Excellency, the Papal Nuncio to Haiti since 1983. Interview on 11 July 1986 at the nunciature in Port-au-Prince, Haiti.

Segal, Aaron, professor and coauthor of *Haiti: Political Failures, Cultural Successes*. Telephone interview on 15 January 1988 in El Paso, TX.

Sosa, Jean, American foreign service officer who headed the Political Section at the United States Embassy in Haiti. Phone interview on 30 June 1986 in Washington, D.C.

Triest, Hugo, (Belgian) Scheut Father and director of *Radio Soleil*, the Catholic Radio Station in Haiti. Interview on 14 July 1986 at the station headquarters in Port-au-Prince and on 28 September 1988 in Lanham, MD.

Turnbull, Wally, (U.S. resident in Haiti) involved with development and brother of Walter Turnbull, leader of the Baptist Mission, Mountain Maid/L'Artisane. Telephone interview in Port-au-Prince on 7 July 1986.

Wenski, Thomas, priest at the Pierre Toussaint Haitian Catholic Center in Miami, FL, who works with Haitian refugees. Telephone interview on 29 June 1988 in Miami.

Werleigh, Claudette, (Haitian) former director of *CARITAS*, Minister of Social Affairs in the Trouillot Government. Interview on 11 May 1988 at the Washington Office on Haiti in Washington, D.C.

Index

A